Shojo Beat

Tail of the Moon

7

Story & Art by
Rinko Ueda

Tail of the Moon

Volume 7

C
O
N
T
E
N
T
S

Story Thus Far...

It is the Era of the Warring States. Usagi is a failure as a ninja, but she is a skilled herbalist. She is working hard to qualify as a ninja so she can be the bride of Hattori Hanzo (aka "Shimo no Hanzo")!

Usagi is captured by Hikaru and taken to Kouga. Goemon comes to save her, but Hikaru forces him to drink an asphyxiation potion and attacks him! On top of being in bad shape because of the potion, Goemon is now critically wounded.

Later, Hikaru sets fire to the village and attacks village leader Kanbutsu, creating havoc everywhere. Surprisingly, Goemon tries to protect Hikaru. As it turns out, Goemon was once Hikaru's only childhood friend. Because Goemon unintentionally broke a promise he made to Hikaru, Hikaru has not been able to believe in anyone since then...

The incident at Kouga was settled, and Usagi returns to Iga to practice her ninjutsu. Suddenly, her great-grandfather appears and tells Hanzo the engagement is cancelled?!

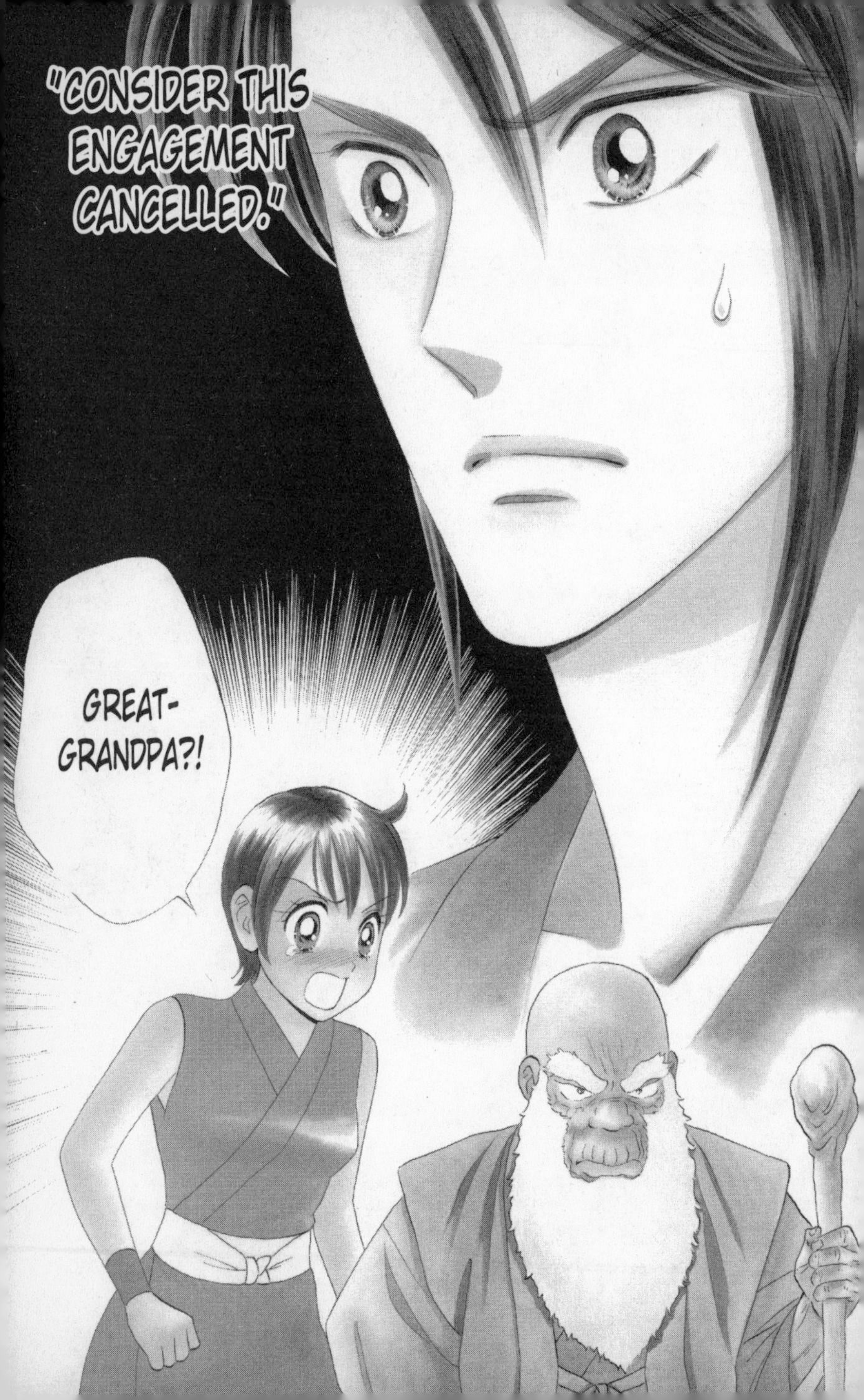
"CONSIDER THIS ENGAGEMENT CANCELLED."
GREAT-GRANDPA?!

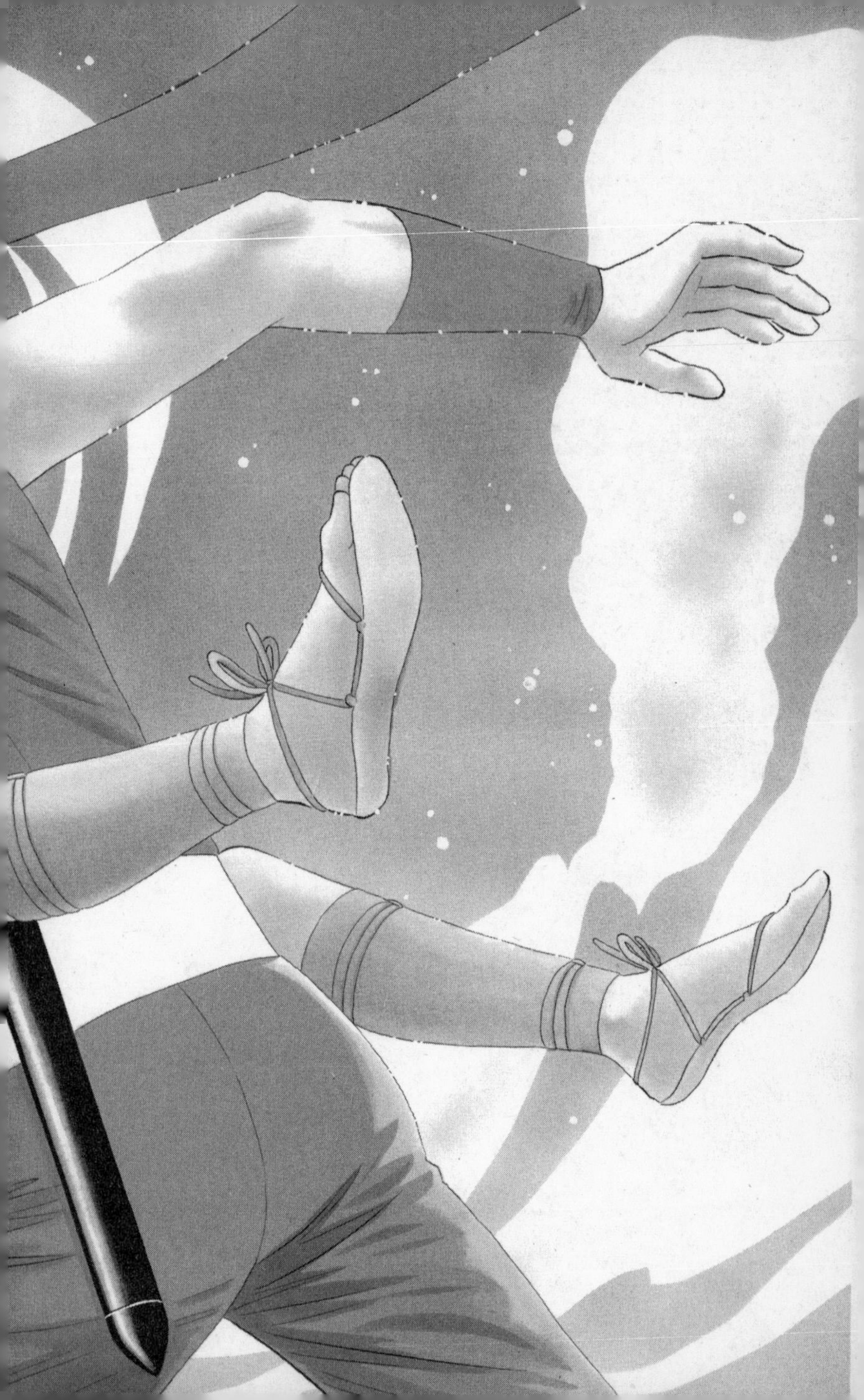

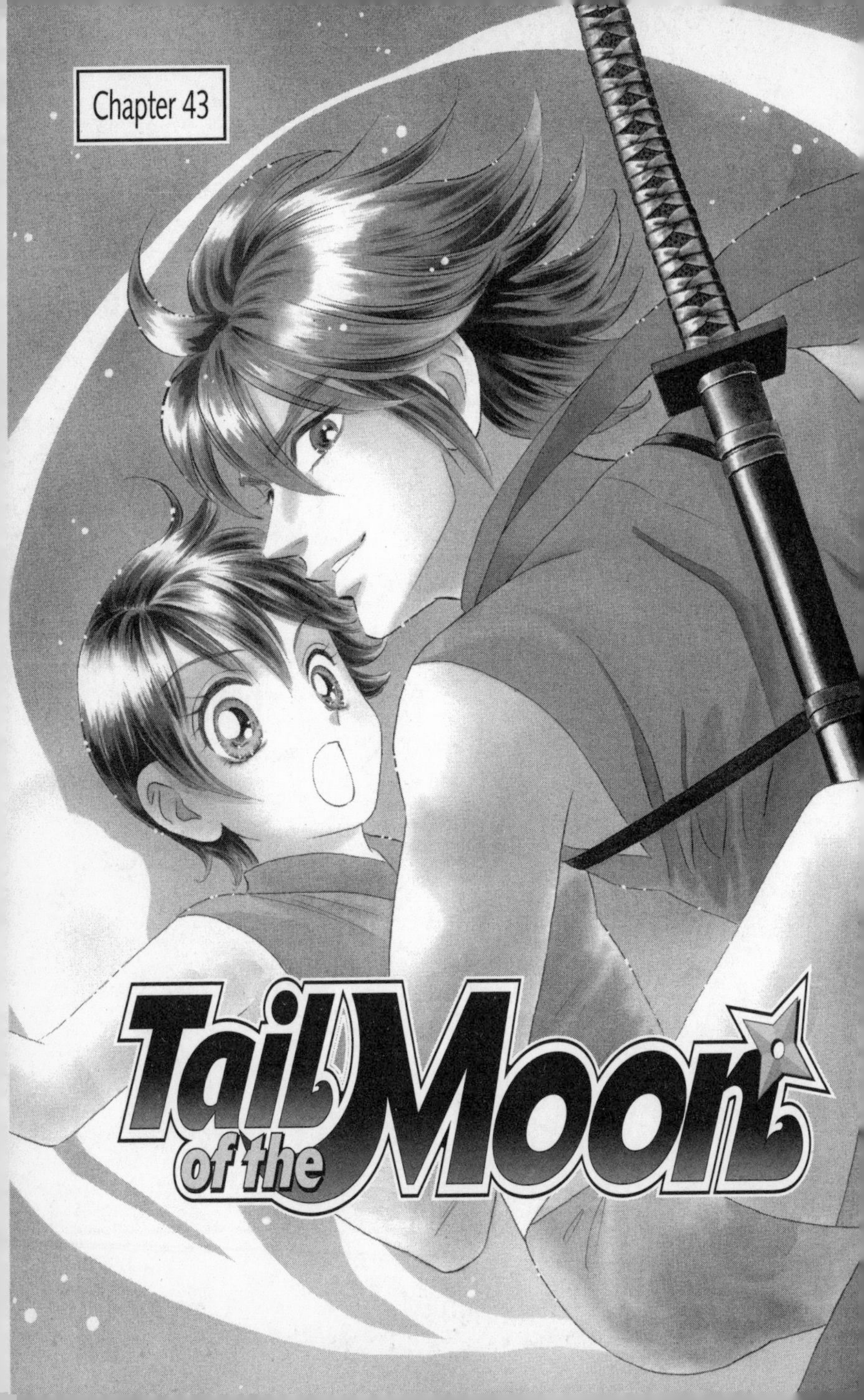
Chapter 43
Tail of the Moon

TAIL OF THE MOON EXTRA: TODAY'S MISSION

"I WANT TO SEE USAGI DO SYNCHRONIZED SWIMMING."

-TANII, SAITAMA PREFECTURE

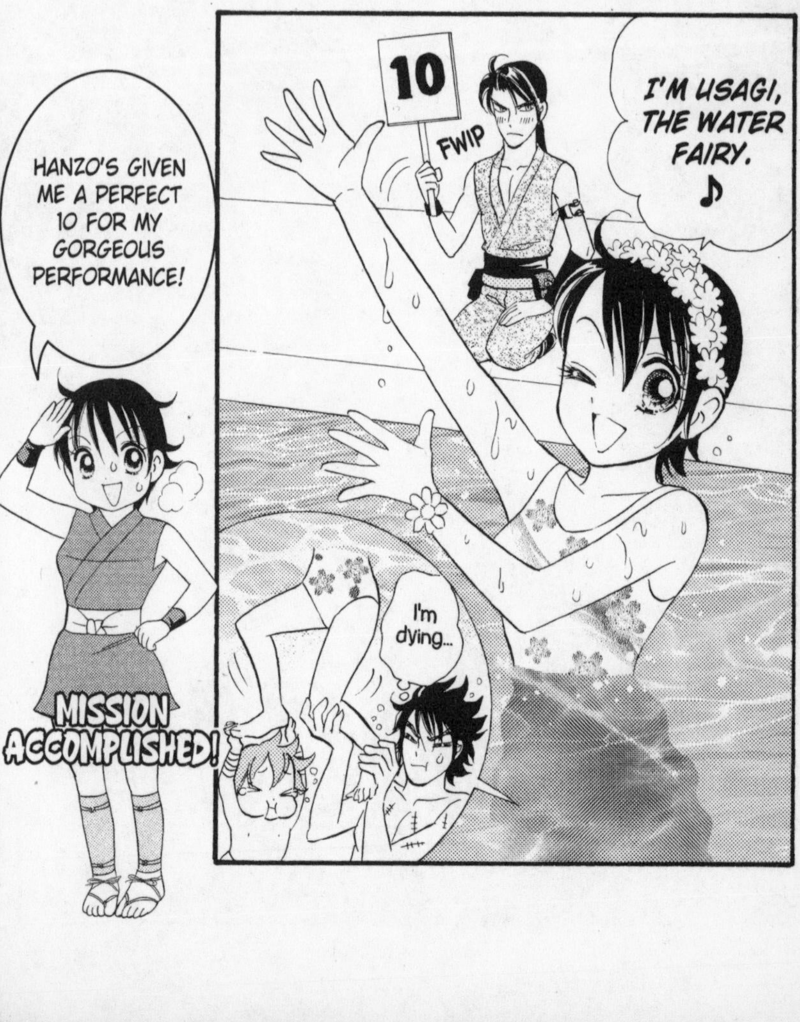
I'M USAGI, THE WATER FAIRY. ♪
10
FWIP
I'm dying...
HANZO'S GIVEN ME A PERFECT 10 FOR MY GORGEOUS PERFORMANCE!
MISSION ACCOMPLISHED!

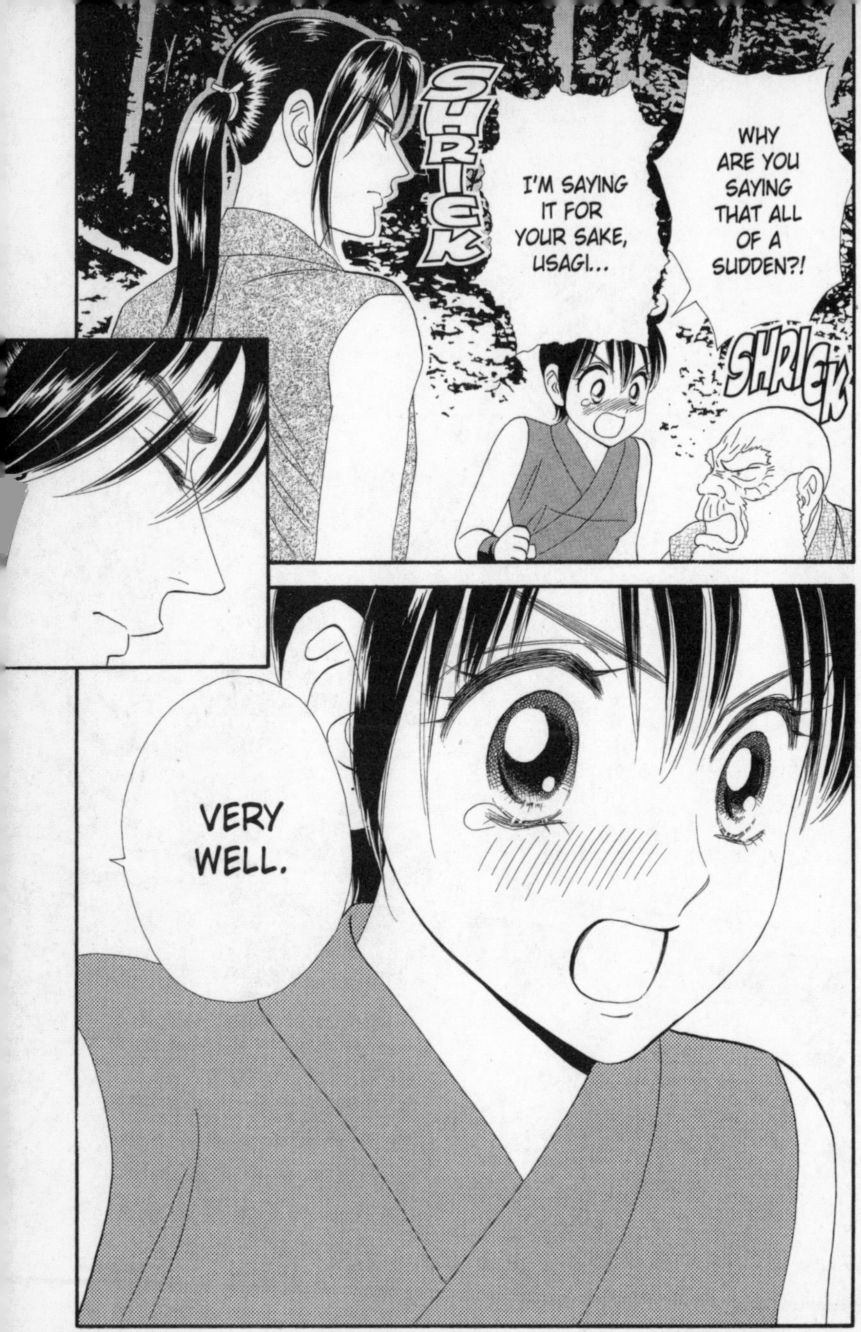
WHY ARE YOU SAYING THAT ALL OF A SUDDEN?!
SHRICK
I'M SAYING IT FOR YOUR SAKE, USAGI...
SHRICK
VERY WELL.

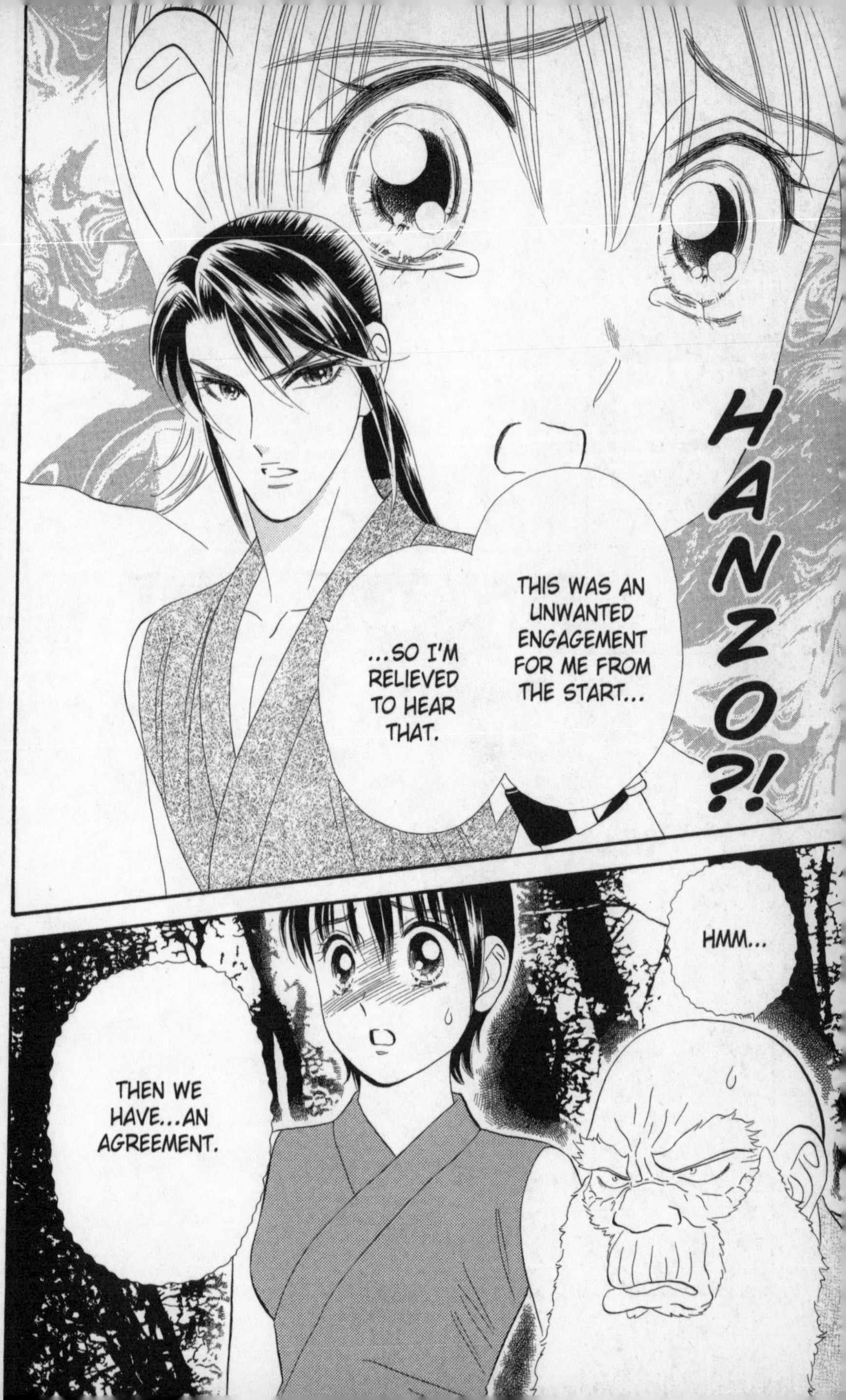
HANZO?!
THIS WAS AN UNWANTED ENGAGEMENT FOR ME FROM THE START...
...SO I'M RELIEVED TO HEAR THAT.
HMM...
THEN WE HAVE...AN AGREEMENT.

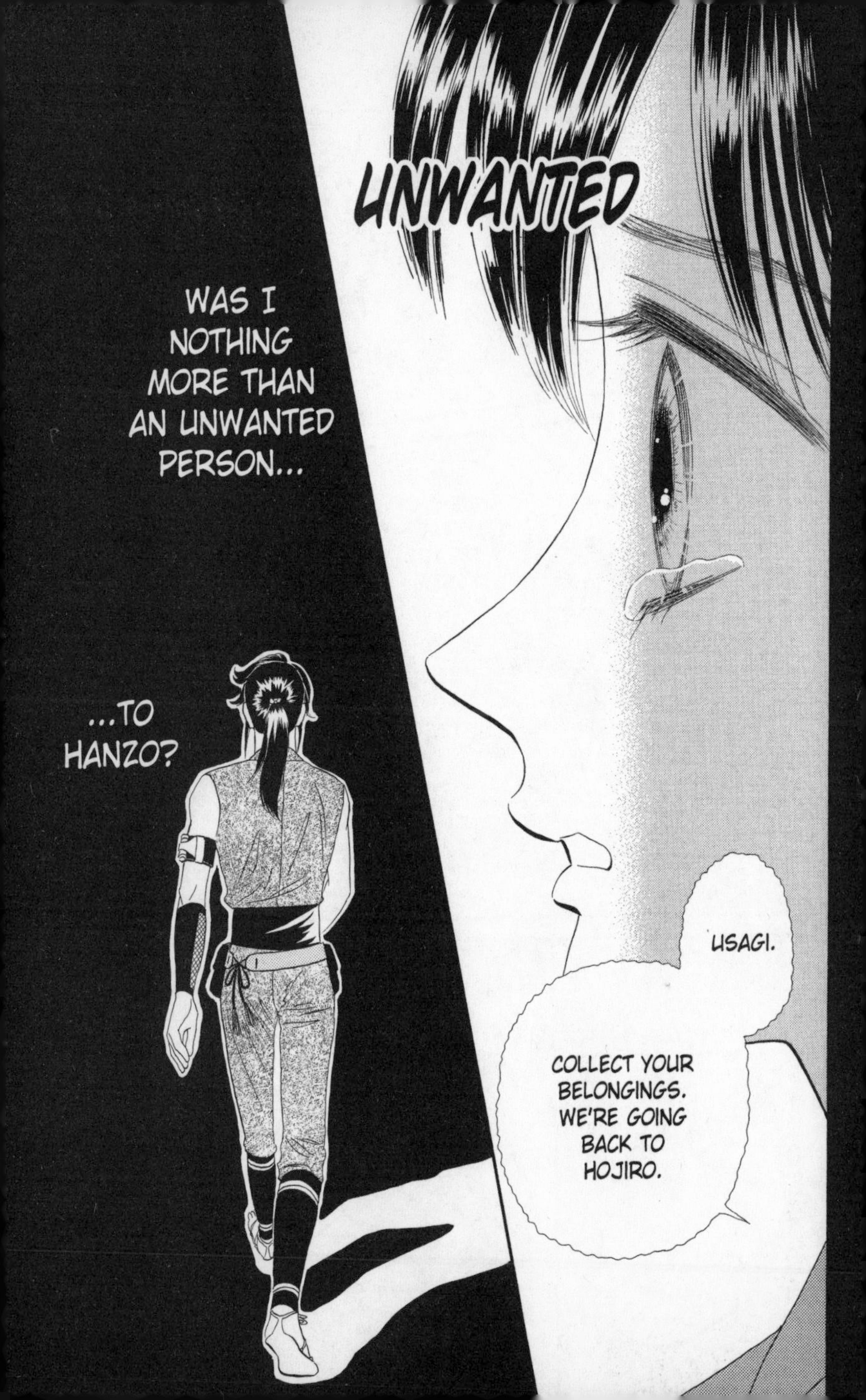
UNWANTED
WAS I NOTHING MORE THAN AN UNWANTED PERSON...
...TO HANZO?
USAGI.
COLLECT YOUR BELONGINGS. WE'RE GOING BACK TO HOJIRO.

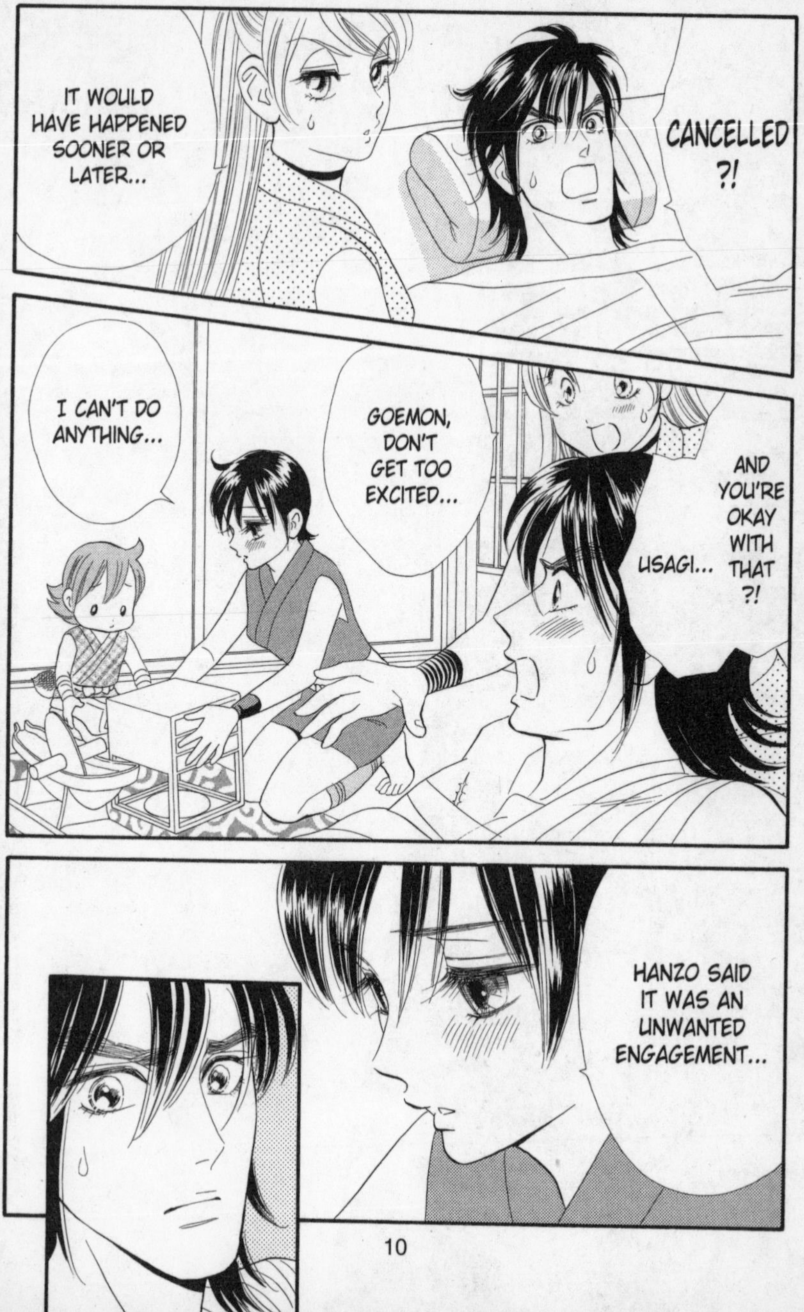

CANCELLED ?!
IT WOULD HAVE HAPPENED SOONER OR LATER...
AND YOU'RE OKAY WITH THAT ?!
USAGI...
GOEMON, DON'T GET TOO EXCITED...
I CAN'T DO ANYTHING...
HANZO SAID IT WAS AN UNWANTED ENGAGEMENT...

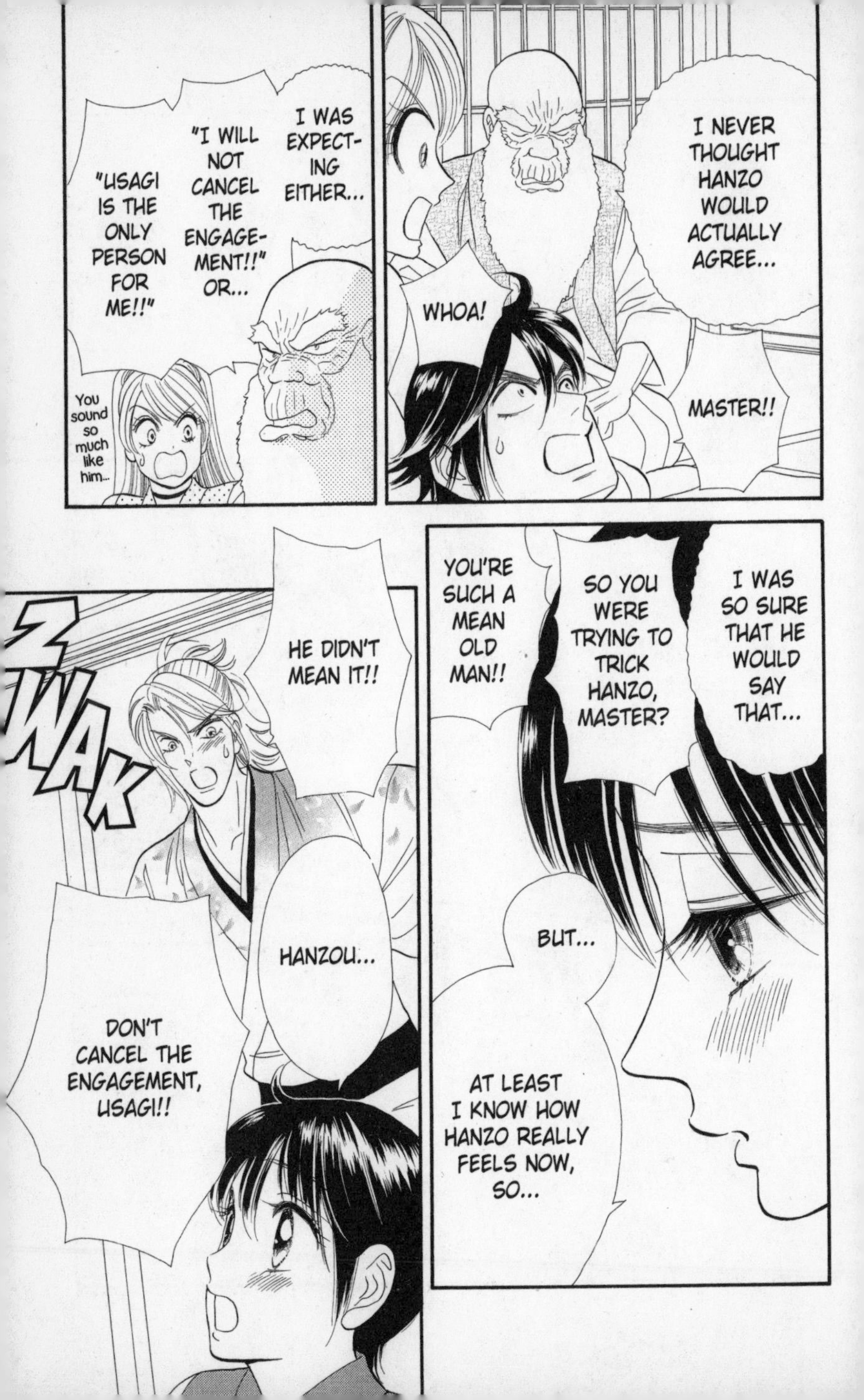
I NEVER THOUGHT HANZO WOULD ACTUALLY AGREE...
WHOA!
MASTER!!
I WAS EXPECTING EITHER...
"I WILL NOT CANCEL THE ENGAGEMENT!!" OR...
"USAGI IS THE ONLY PERSON FOR ME!!"
You sound so much like him...
I WAS SO SURE THAT HE WOULD SAY THAT...
SO YOU WERE TRYING TO TRICK HANZO, MASTER?
YOU'RE SUCH A MEAN OLD MAN!!
BUT...
AT LEAST I KNOW HOW HANZO REALLY FEELS NOW, SO...
HE DIDN'T MEAN IT!!
ZWAK
HANZOU...
DON'T CANCEL THE ENGAGEMENT, USAGI!!

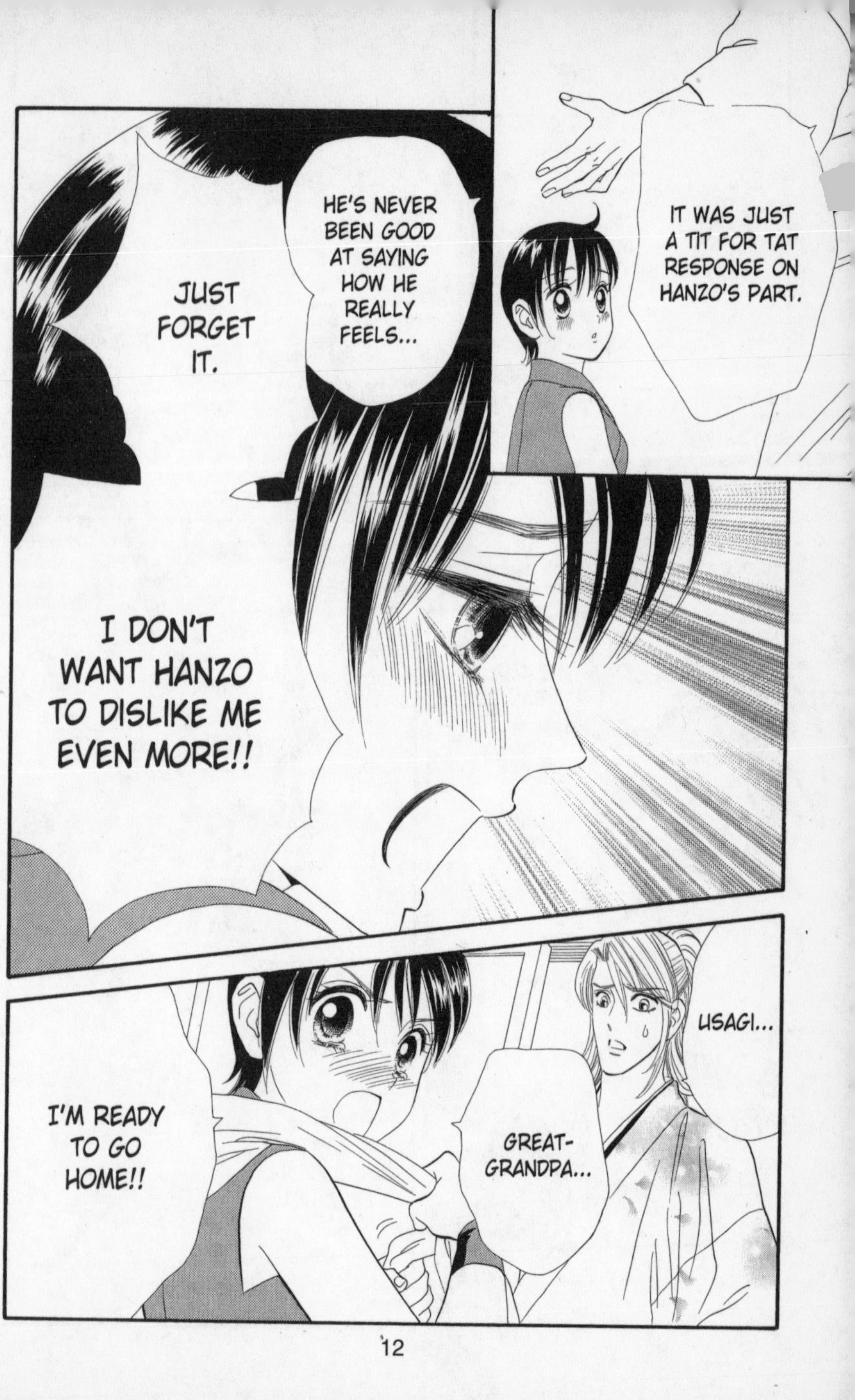
IT WAS JUST A TIT FOR TAT RESPONSE ON HANZO'S PART.
HE'S NEVER BEEN GOOD AT SAYING HOW HE REALLY FEELS...
JUST FORGET IT.
I DON'T WANT HANZO TO DISLIKE ME EVEN MORE!!
USAGI...
GREAT-GRANDPA...
I'M READY TO GO HOME!!

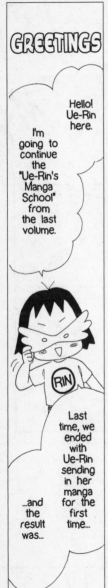

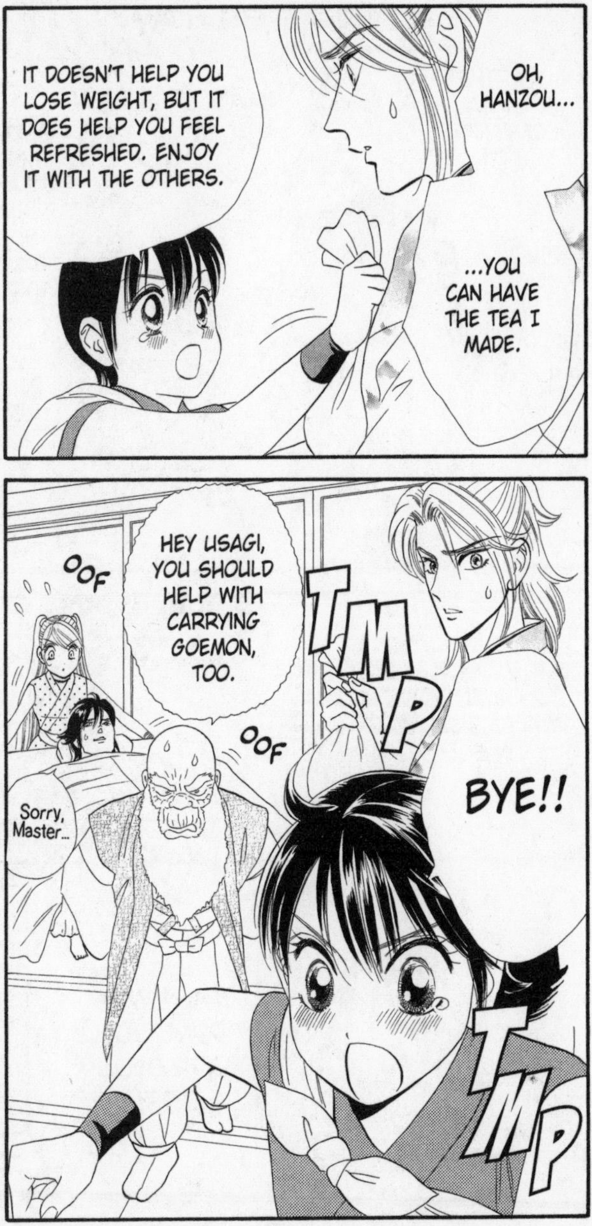
OH, HANZOU...
...YOU CAN HAVE THE TEA I MADE.
IT DOESN'T HELP YOU LOSE WEIGHT, BUT IT DOES HELP YOU FEEL REFRESHED. ENJOY IT WITH THE OTHERS.
TMP
BYE!!
HEY USAGI, YOU SHOULD HELP WITH CARRYING GOEMON, TOO.
OOF
OOF
Sorry, Master...
TMP

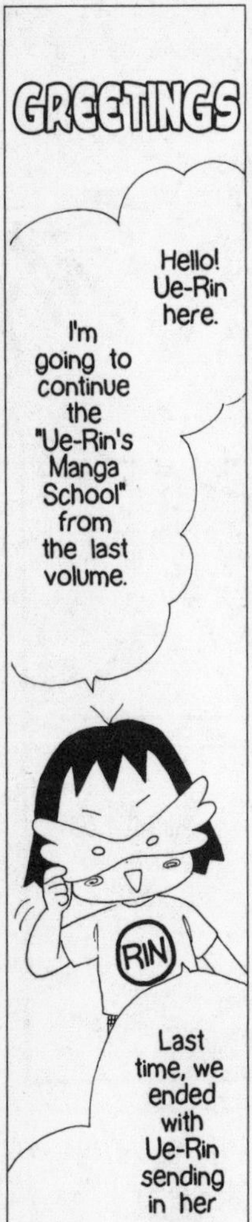
GREETINGS
Hello! Ue-Rin here.
I'm going to continue the "Ue-Rin's Manga School" from the last volume.
RIN
Last time, we ended with Ue-Rin sending in her manga for the first time...
...and the result was...

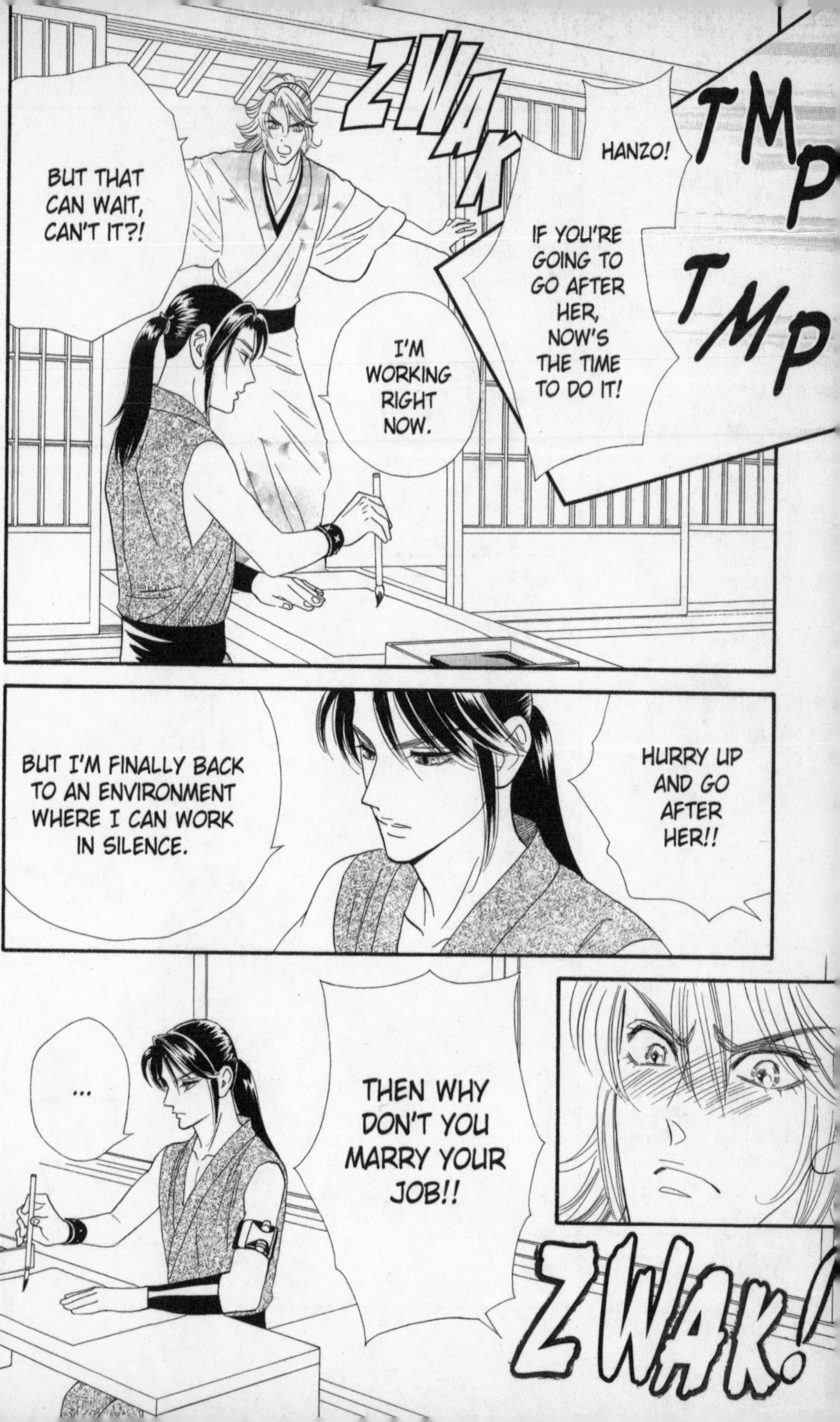
TMP TMP
HANZO!
IF YOU'RE GOING TO GO AFTER HER, NOW'S THE TIME TO DO IT!
ZWAK
I'M WORKING RIGHT NOW.
BUT THAT CAN WAIT, CAN'T IT?!
HURRY UP AND GO AFTER HER!!
BUT I'M FINALLY BACK TO AN ENVIRONMENT WHERE I CAN WORK IN SILENCE.
ZWAK!
THEN WHY DON'T YOU MARRY YOUR JOB!!
...

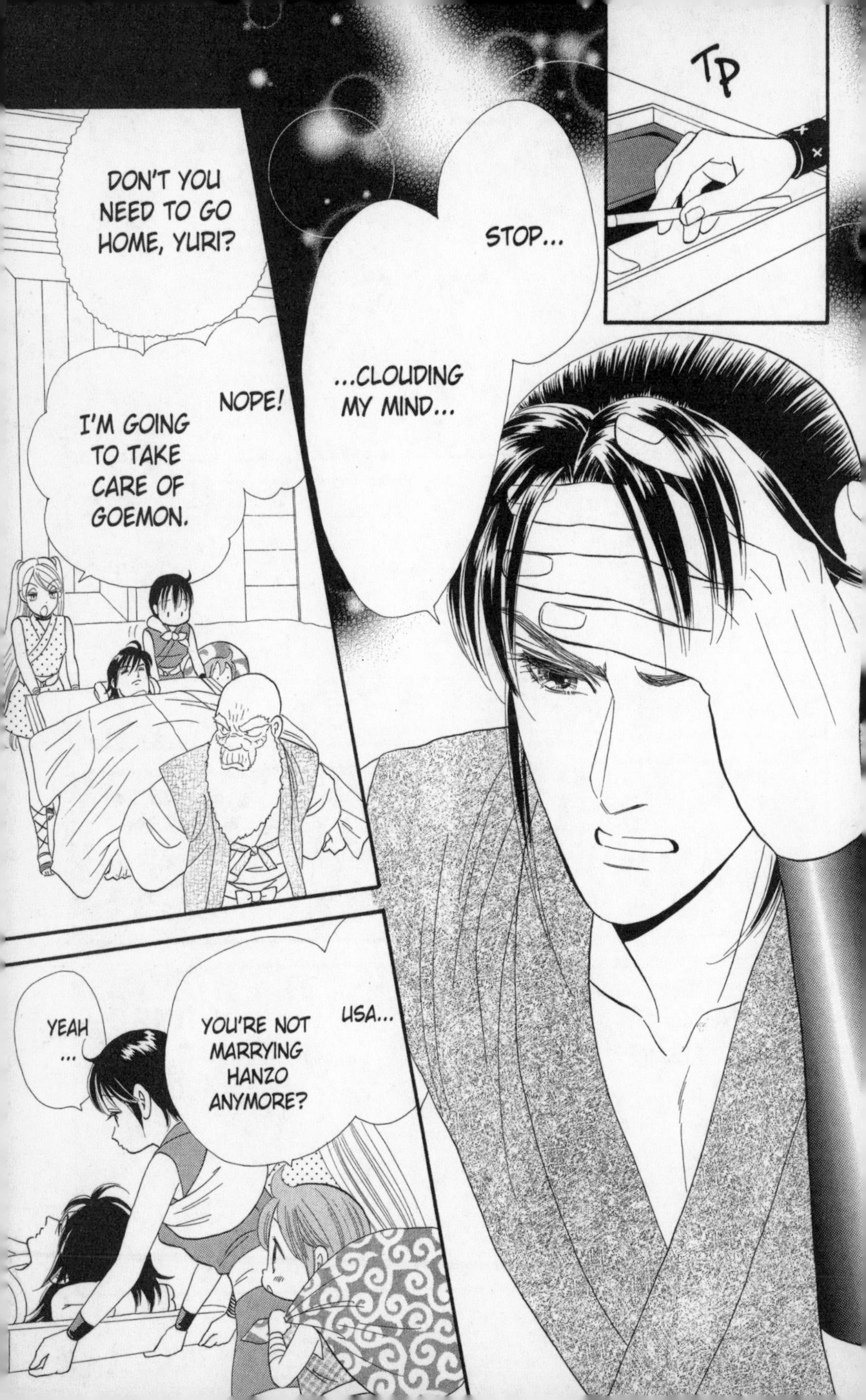
TP
STOP...
...CLOUDING MY MIND...
DON'T YOU NEED TO GO HOME, YURI?
NOPE!
I'M GOING TO TAKE CARE OF GOEMON.
USA...
YOU'RE NOT MARRYING HANZO ANYMORE?
YEAH ...

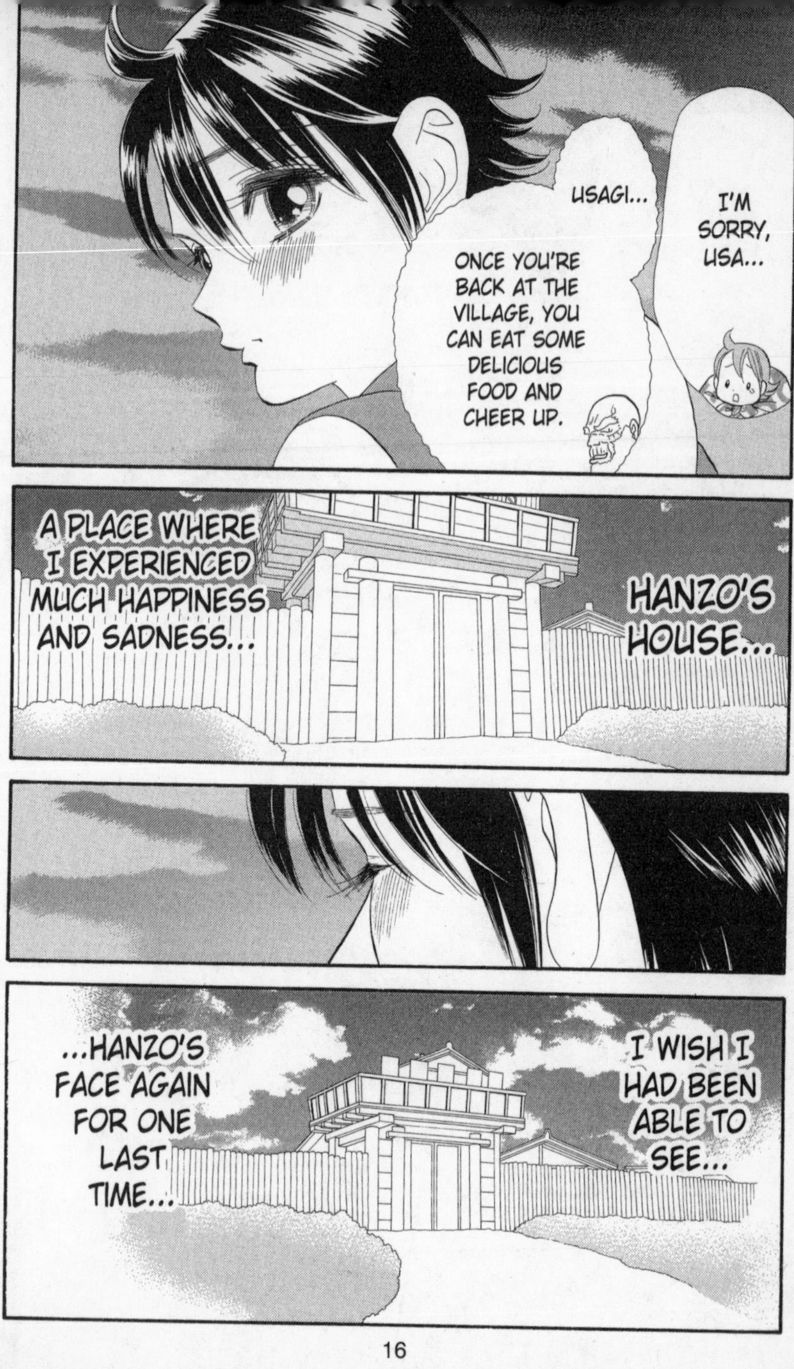
I'M SORRY, USA...
USAGI...
ONCE YOU'RE BACK AT THE VILLAGE, YOU CAN EAT SOME DELICIOUS FOOD AND CHEER UP.
HANZO'S HOUSE...
A PLACE WHERE I EXPERIENCED MUCH HAPPINESS AND SADNESS...
I WISH I HAD BEEN ABLE TO SEE...
...HANZO'S FACE AGAIN FOR ONE LAST TIME...

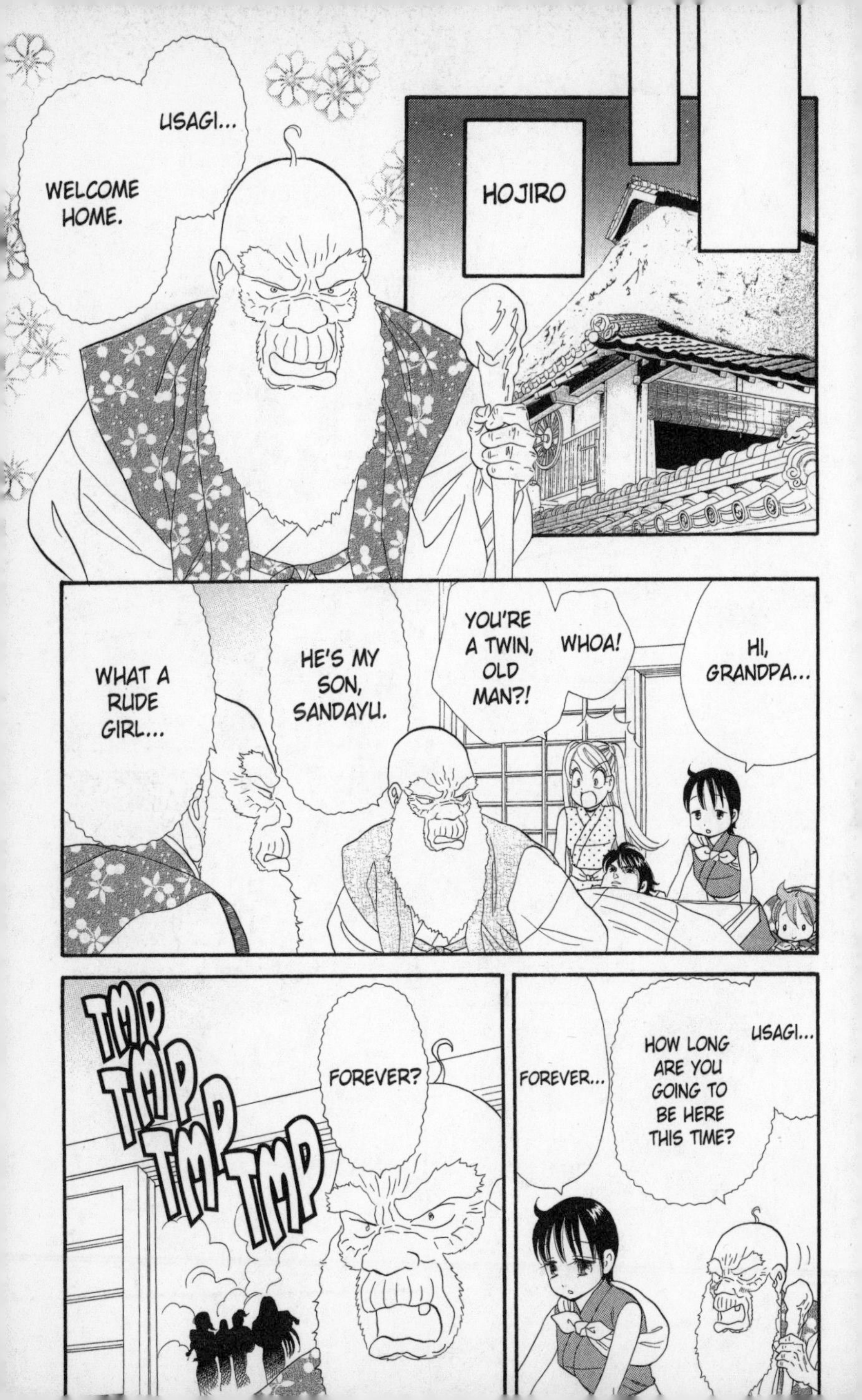
HOJIRO
USAGI...
WELCOME HOME.
HI, GRANDPA...
WHOA!
YOU'RE A TWIN, OLD MAN?!
HE'S MY SON, SANDAYU.
WHAT A RUDE GIRL...
USAGI...
HOW LONG ARE YOU GOING TO BE HERE THIS TIME?
FOREVER...
FOREVER?
TMP TMP TMP TMP

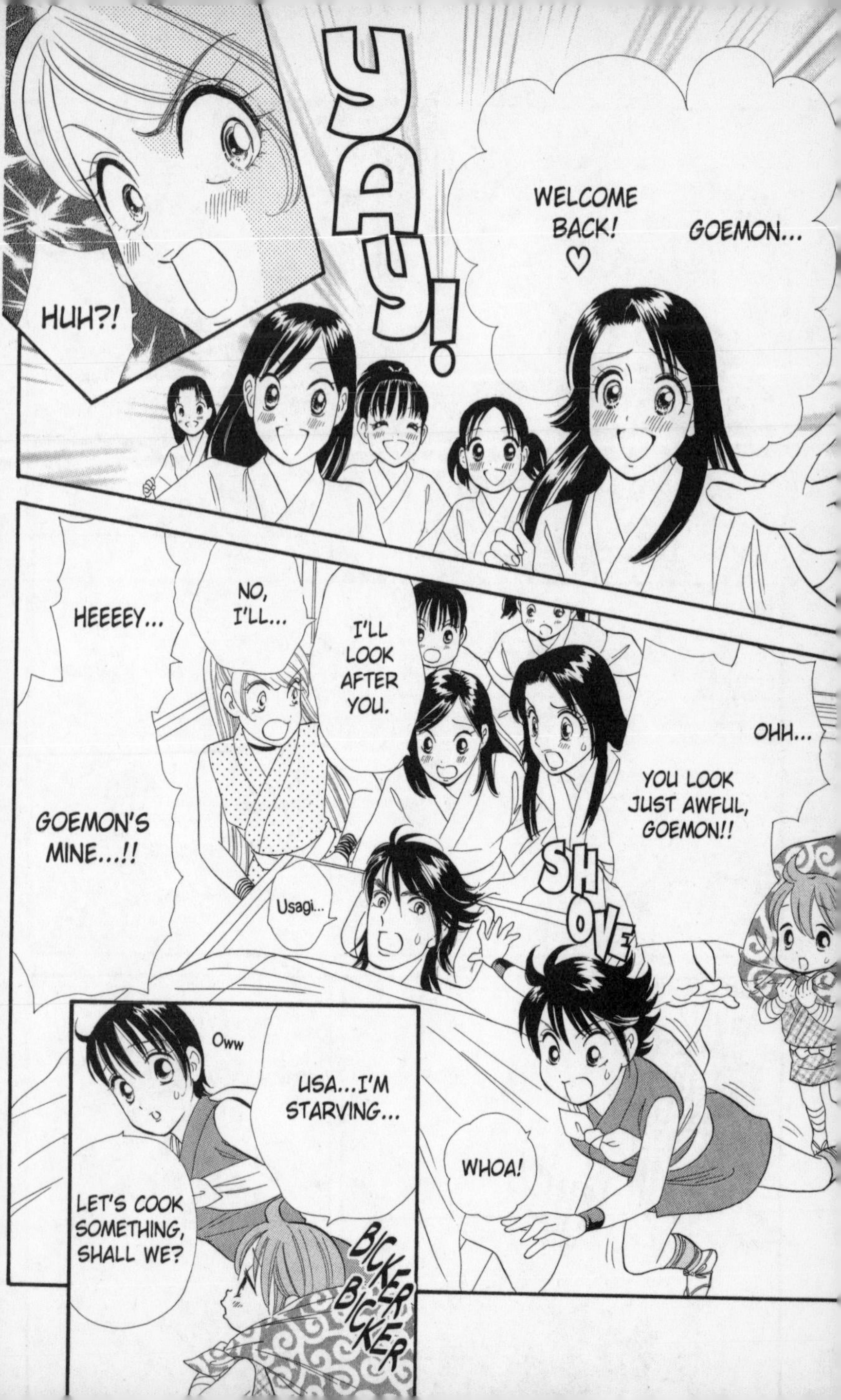
GOEMON...
WELCOME BACK! ♡
YAY!
HUH?!
OHH...
YOU LOOK JUST AWFUL, GOEMON!!
I'LL LOOK AFTER YOU.
NO, I'LL...
HEEEEY...
GOEMON'S MINE...!!
SHOVE
Usagi...
WHOA!
USA...I'M STARVING...
Oww
LET'S COOK SOMETHING, SHALL WE?
BICKER BICKER

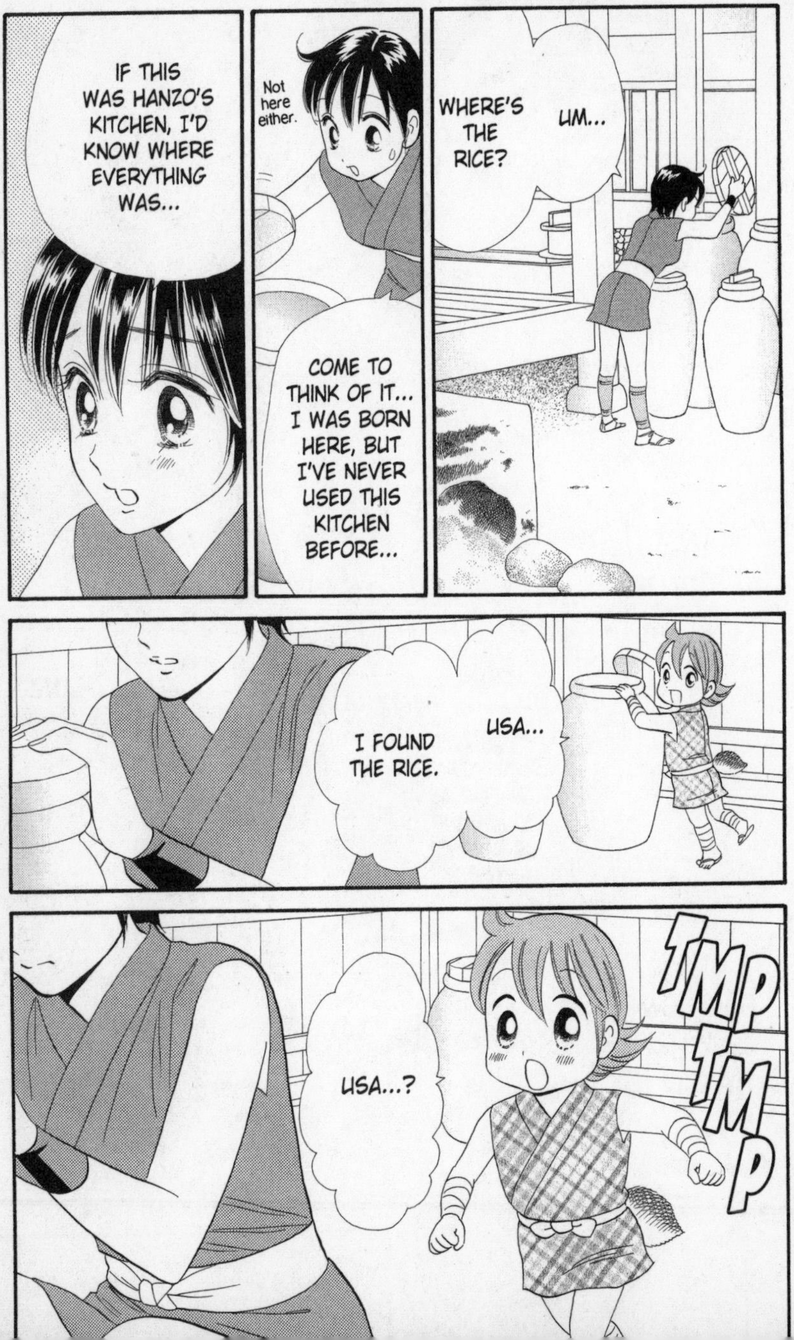
UM...
WHERE'S THE RICE?
Not here either.
COME TO THINK OF IT... I WAS BORN HERE, BUT I'VE NEVER USED THIS KITCHEN BEFORE...
IF THIS WAS HANZO'S KITCHEN, I'D KNOW WHERE EVERYTHING WAS...
USA...
I FOUND THE RICE.
TMP TMP
USA...?

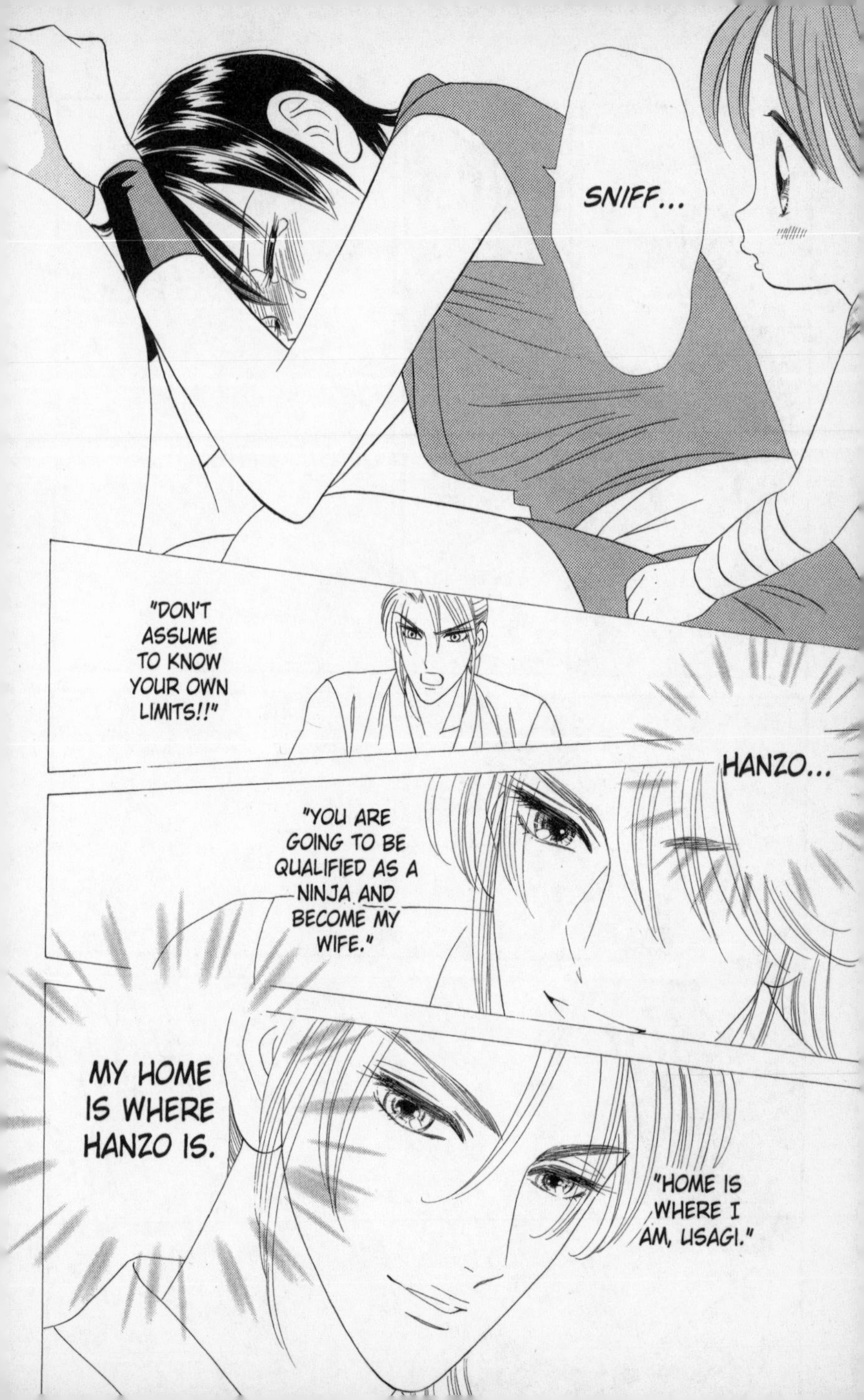
SNIFF...
"DON'T ASSUME TO KNOW YOUR OWN LIMITS!!"
HANZO...
"YOU ARE GOING TO BE QUALIFIED AS A NINJA AND BECOME MY WIFE."
"HOME IS WHERE I AM, USAGI."
MY HOME IS WHERE HANZO IS.

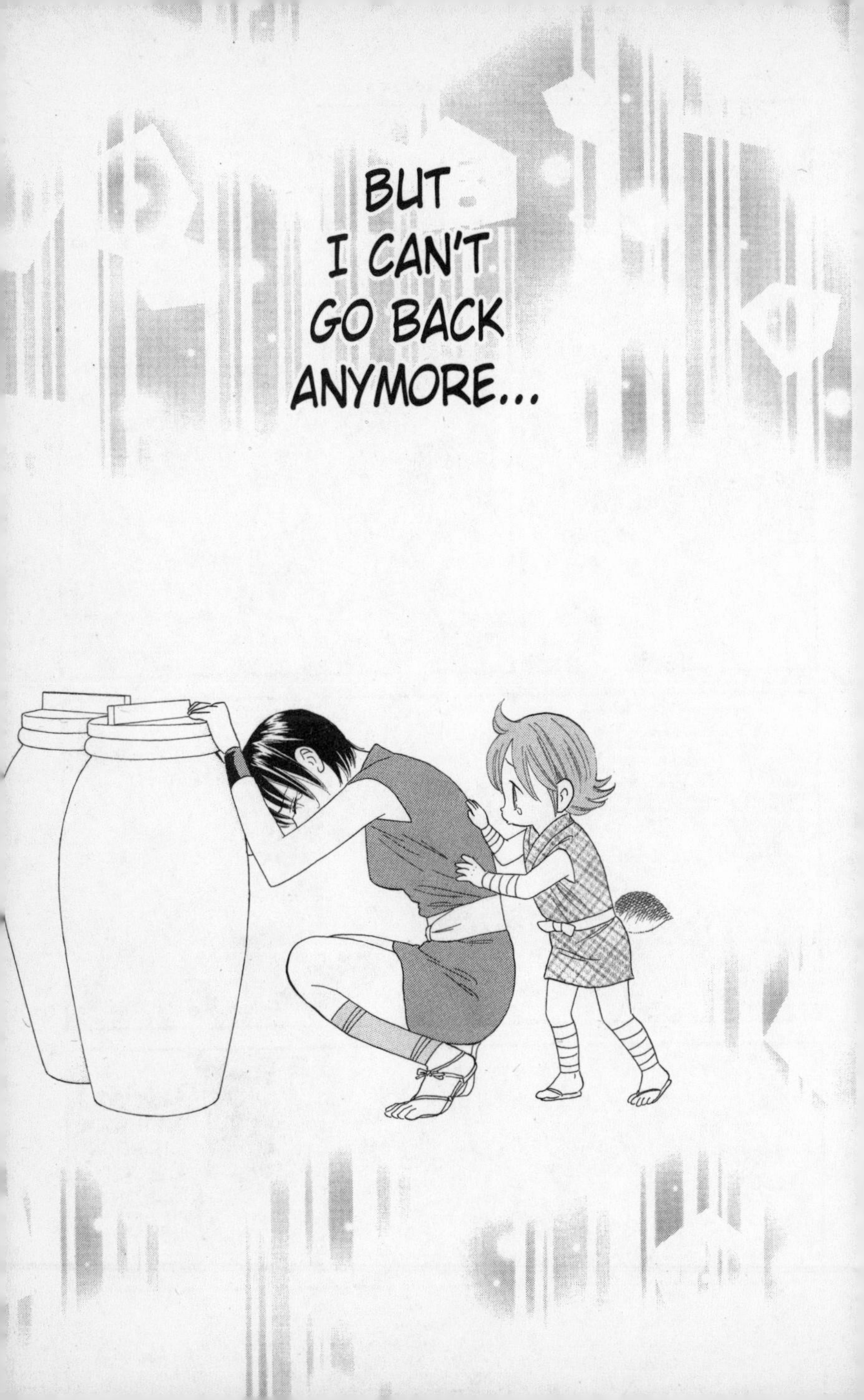
BUT I CAN'T GO BACK ANYMORE...

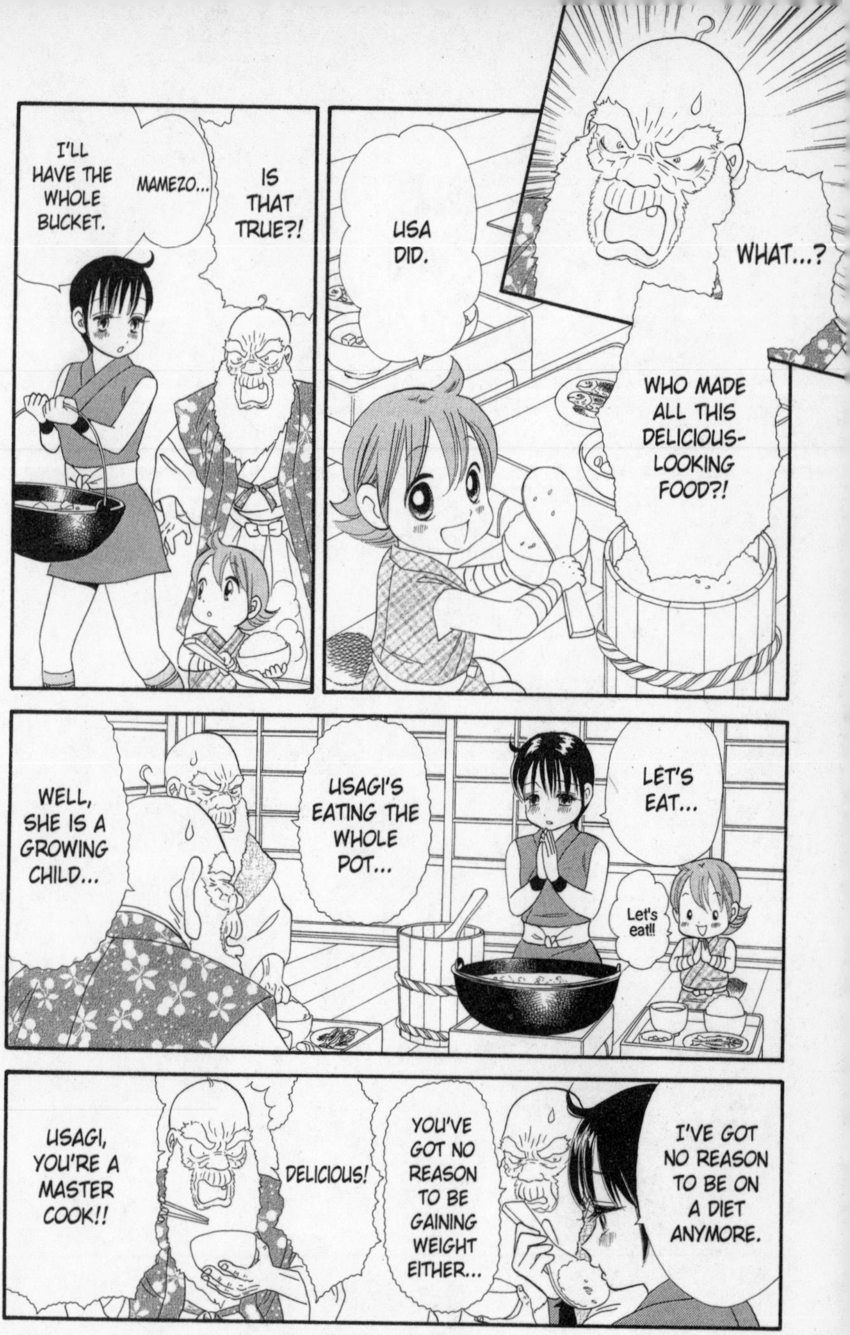
WHAT...?
WHO MADE ALL THIS DELICIOUS-LOOKING FOOD?!
USA DID.
IS THAT TRUE?!
MAMEZO...
I'LL HAVE THE WHOLE BUCKET.
LET'S EAT...
Let's eat!!
USAGI'S EATING THE WHOLE POT...
WELL, SHE IS A GROWING CHILD...
I'VE GOT NO REASON TO BE ON A DIET ANYMORE.
YOU'VE GOT NO REASON TO BE GAINING WEIGHT EITHER...
DELICIOUS!
USAGI, YOU'RE A MASTER COOK!!

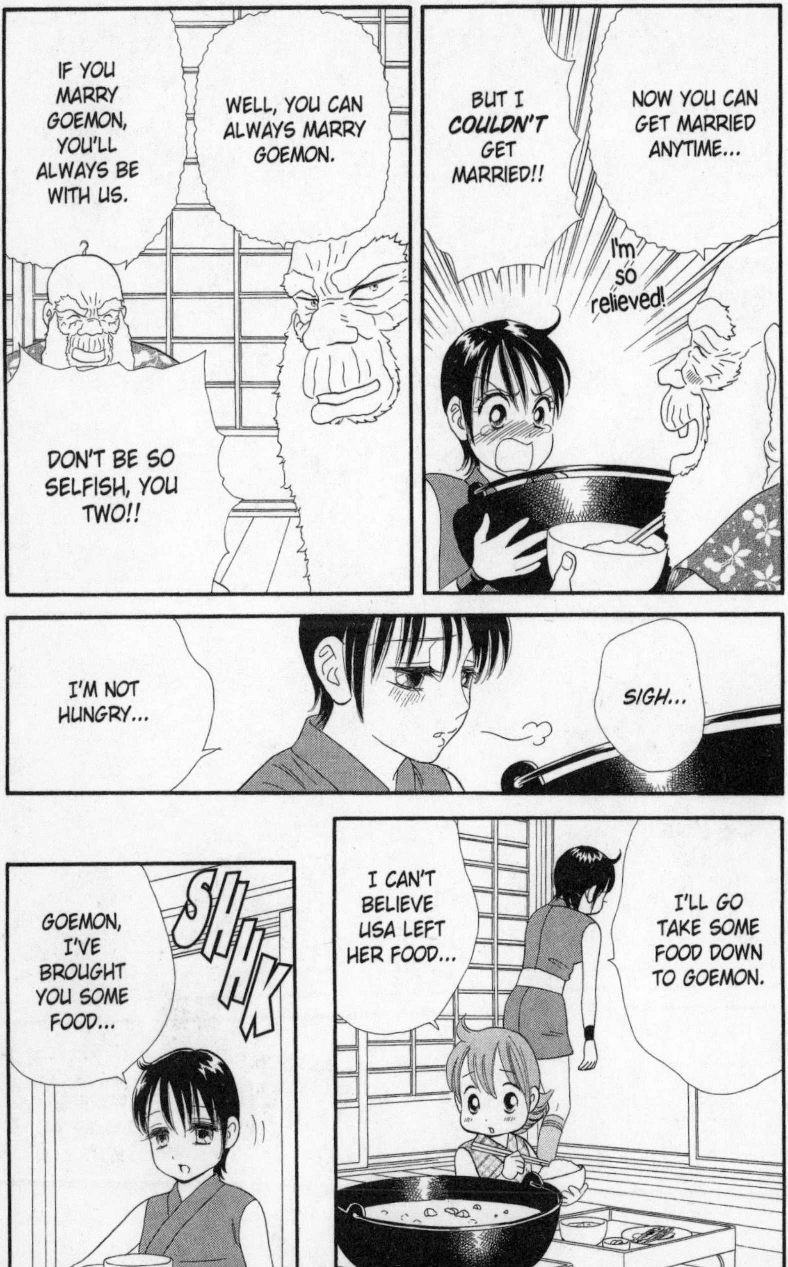
NOW YOU CAN GET MARRIED ANYTIME...
BUT I COULDN'T GET MARRIED!!
I'm so relieved!
WELL, YOU CAN ALWAYS MARRY GOEMON.
IF YOU MARRY GOEMON, YOU'LL ALWAYS BE WITH US.
DON'T BE SO SELFISH, YOU TWO!!
SIGH...
I'M NOT HUNGRY...
I'LL GO TAKE SOME FOOD DOWN TO GOEMON.
I CAN'T BELIEVE USA LEFT HER FOOD...
SHHK
GOEMON, I'VE BROUGHT YOU SOME FOOD...

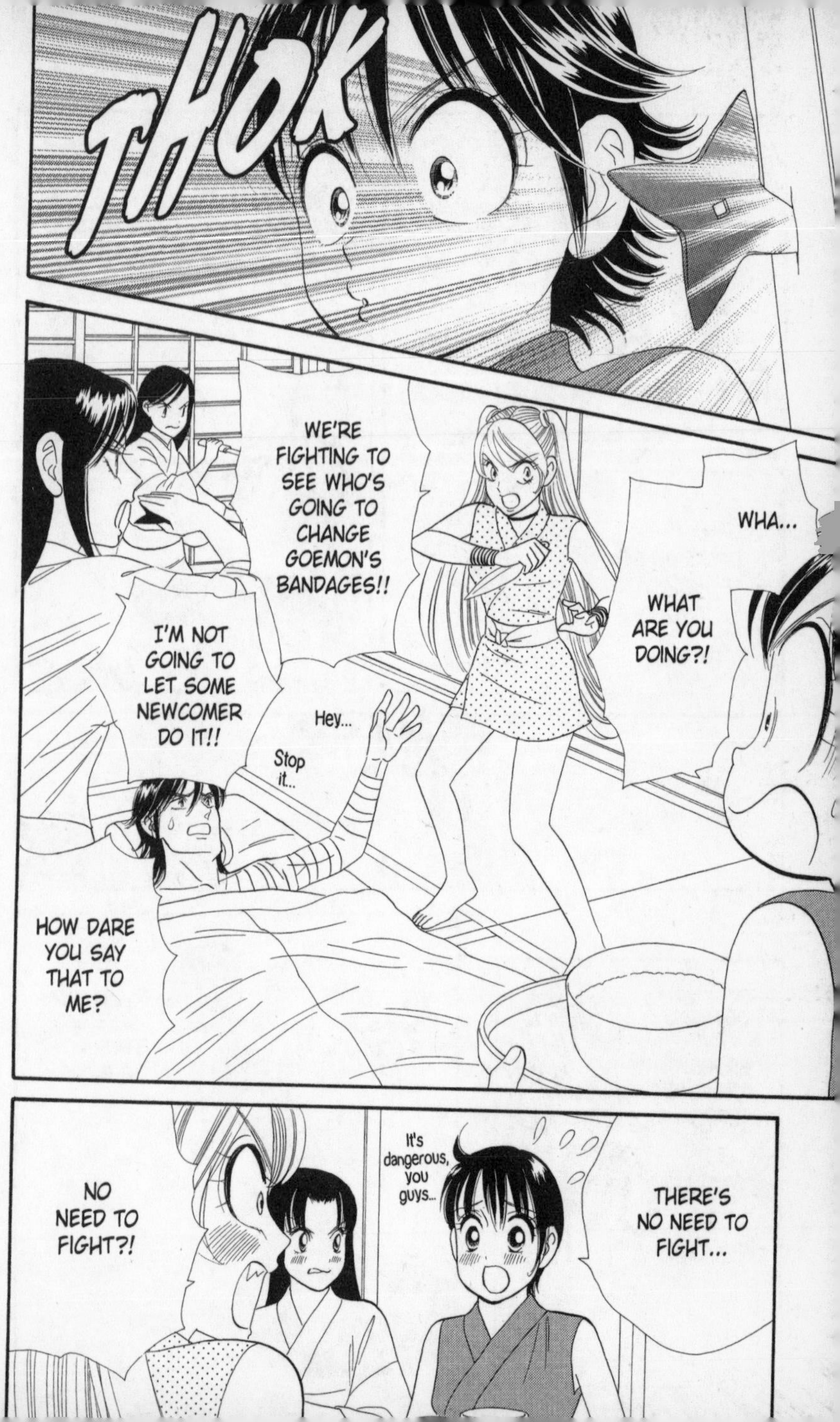
THOK
WHA...
WHAT ARE YOU DOING?!
WE'RE FIGHTING TO SEE WHO'S GOING TO CHANGE GOEMON'S BANDAGES!!
Hey...
Stop it...
I'M NOT GOING TO LET SOME NEWCOMER DO IT!!
HOW DARE YOU SAY THAT TO ME?
THERE'S NO NEED TO FIGHT...
It's dangerous, you guys...
NO NEED TO FIGHT?!

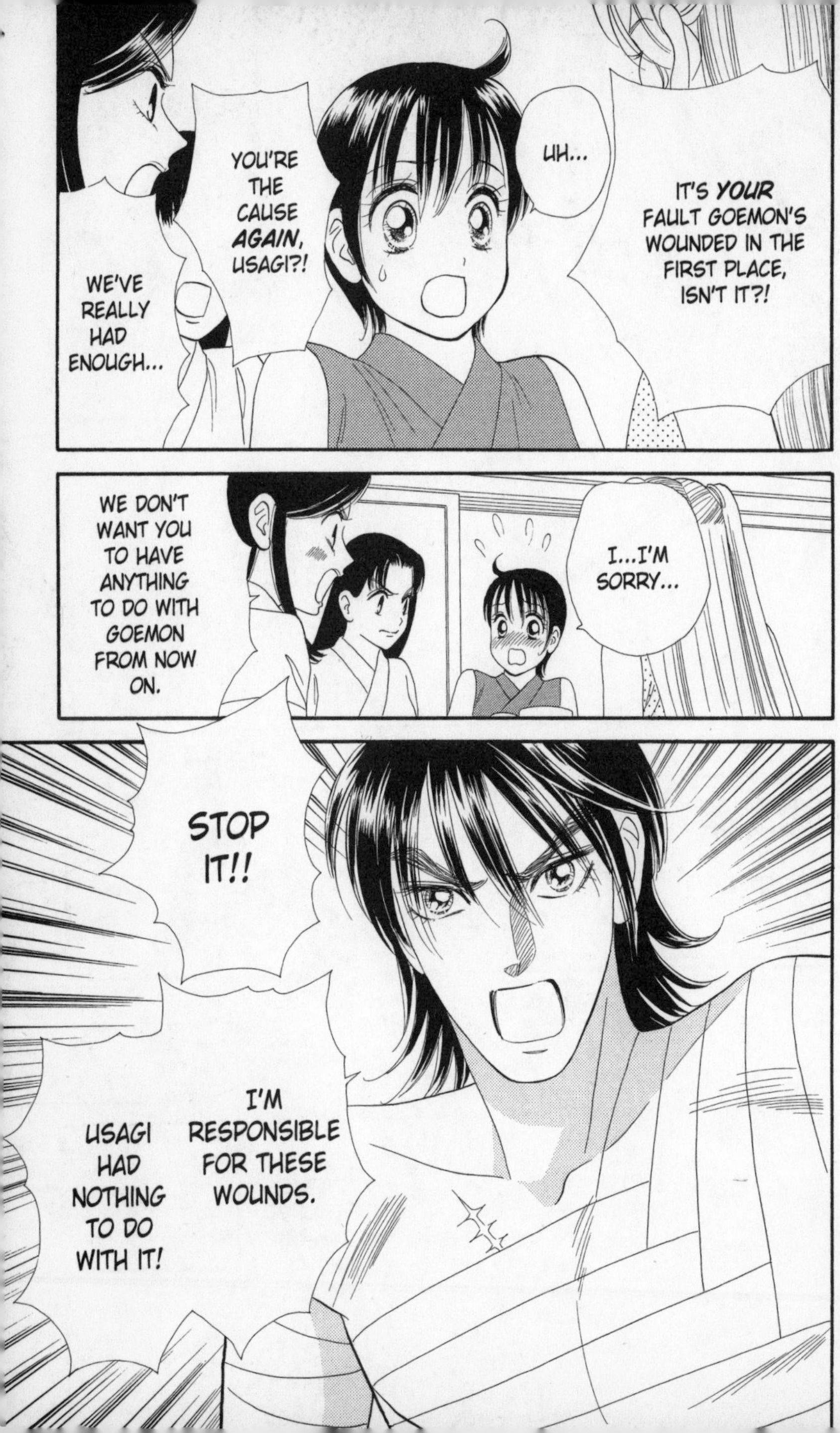
IT'S *YOUR* FAULT GOEMON'S WOUNDED IN THE FIRST PLACE, ISN'T IT?!
UH...
YOU'RE THE CAUSE *AGAIN*, USAGI?!
WE'VE REALLY HAD ENOUGH...
I...I'M SORRY...
WE DON'T WANT YOU TO HAVE ANYTHING TO DO WITH GOEMON FROM NOW ON.
STOP IT!!
I'M RESPONSIBLE FOR THESE WOUNDS.
USAGI HAD NOTHING TO DO WITH IT!

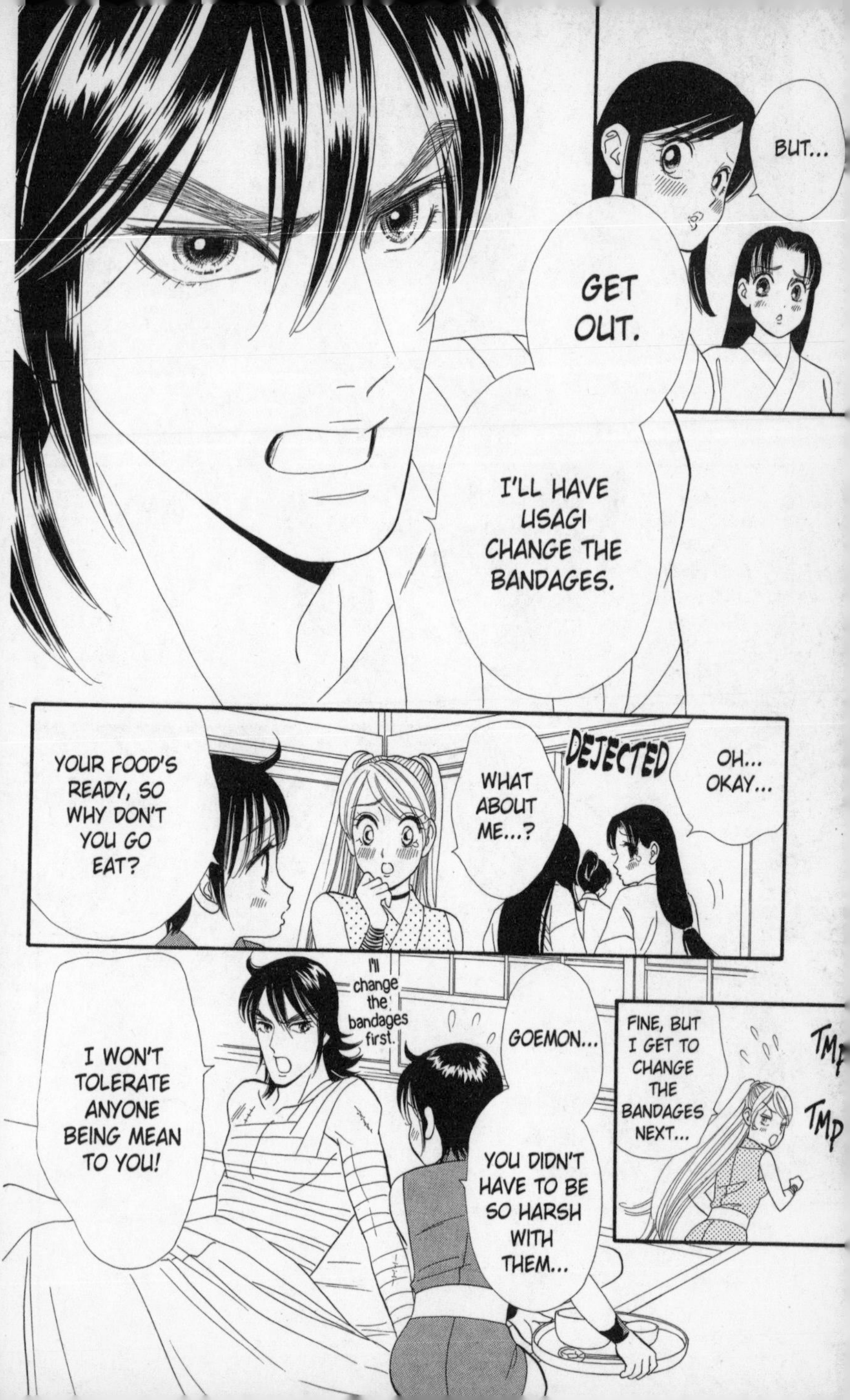
BUT...
GET OUT.
I'LL HAVE USAGI CHANGE THE BANDAGES.
OH... OKAY...
DEJECTED
WHAT ABOUT ME...?
YOUR FOOD'S READY, SO WHY DON'T YOU GO EAT?
FINE, BUT I GET TO CHANGE THE BANDAGES NEXT...
TMP
TMP
GOEMON...
I'll change the bandages first.
YOU DIDN'T HAVE TO BE SO HARSH WITH THEM...
I WON'T TOLERATE ANYONE BEING MEAN TO YOU!

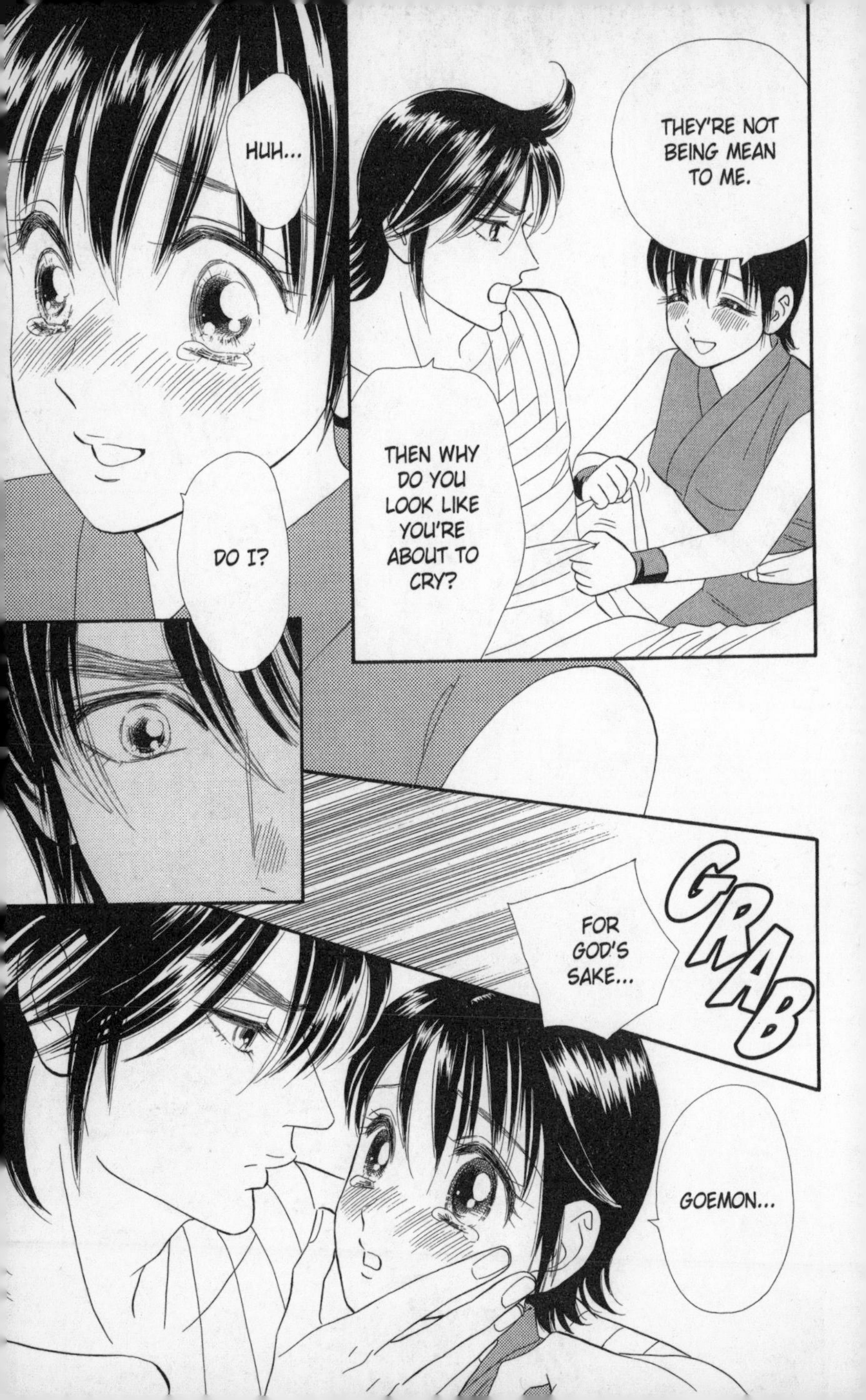
THEY'RE NOT BEING MEAN TO ME.
THEN WHY DO YOU LOOK LIKE YOU'RE ABOUT TO CRY?
HUH...
DO I?
GRAB
FOR GOD'S SAKE...
GOEMON...

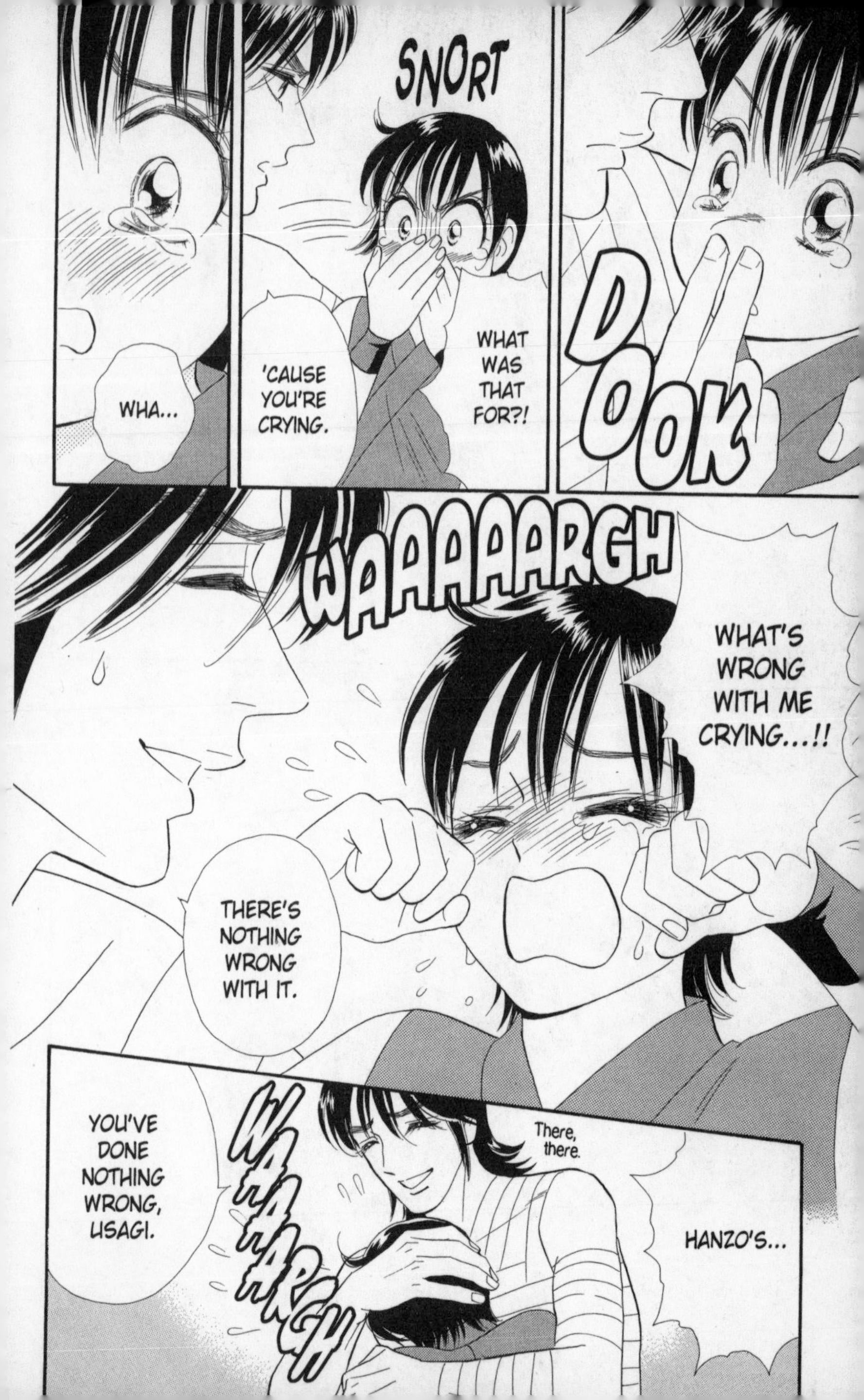
DOOK
SNORT
WHAT WAS THAT FOR?!
'CAUSE YOU'RE CRYING.
WHA...
WAAAAARGH
WHAT'S WRONG WITH ME CRYING...!!
THERE'S NOTHING WRONG WITH IT.
HANZO'S...
There, there.
WAAARGH
YOU'VE DONE NOTHING WRONG, USAGI.

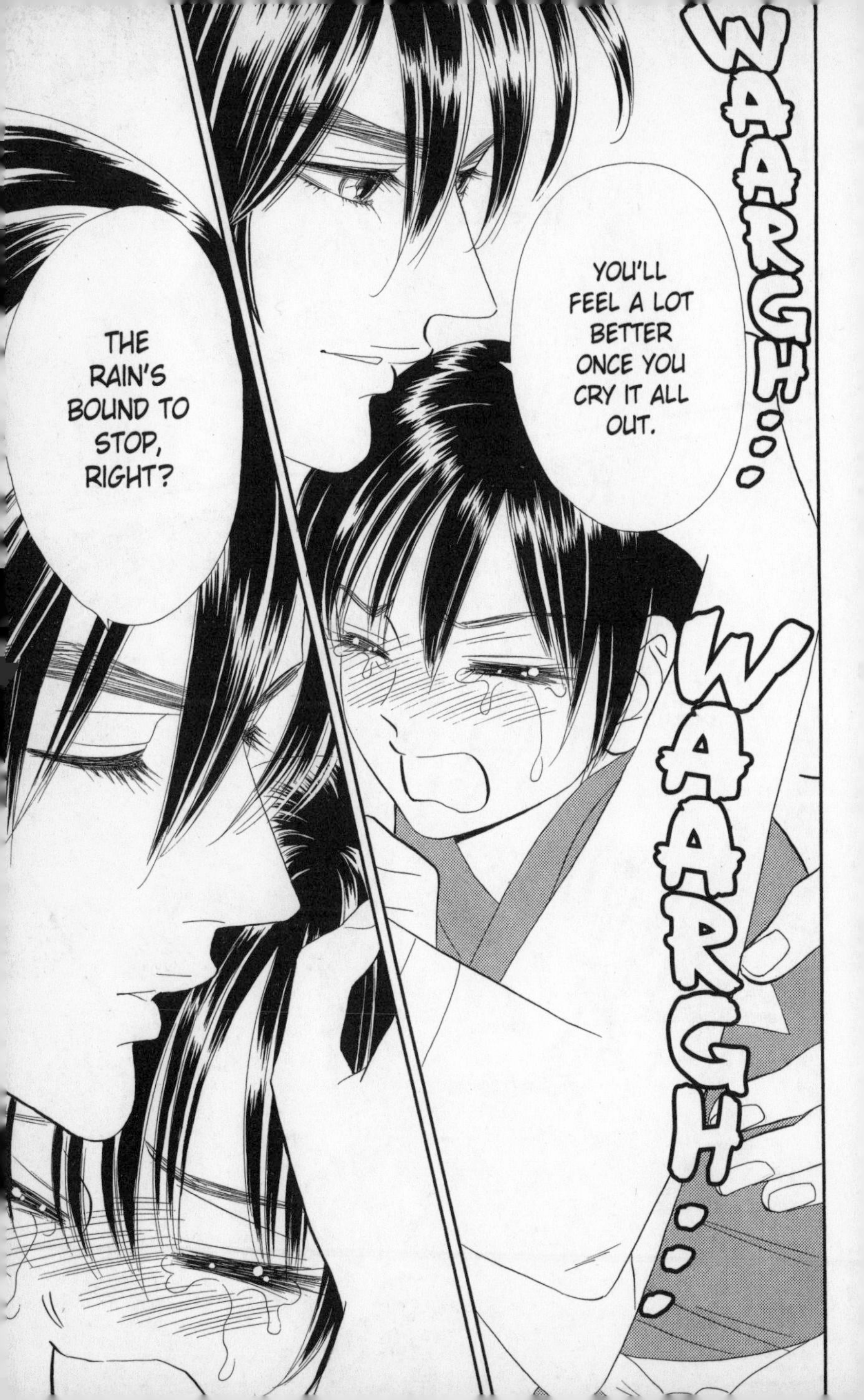WAARGH...
YOU'LL FEEL A LOT BETTER ONCE YOU CRY IT ALL OUT.
THE RAIN'S BOUND TO STOP, RIGHT?
WAARGH...

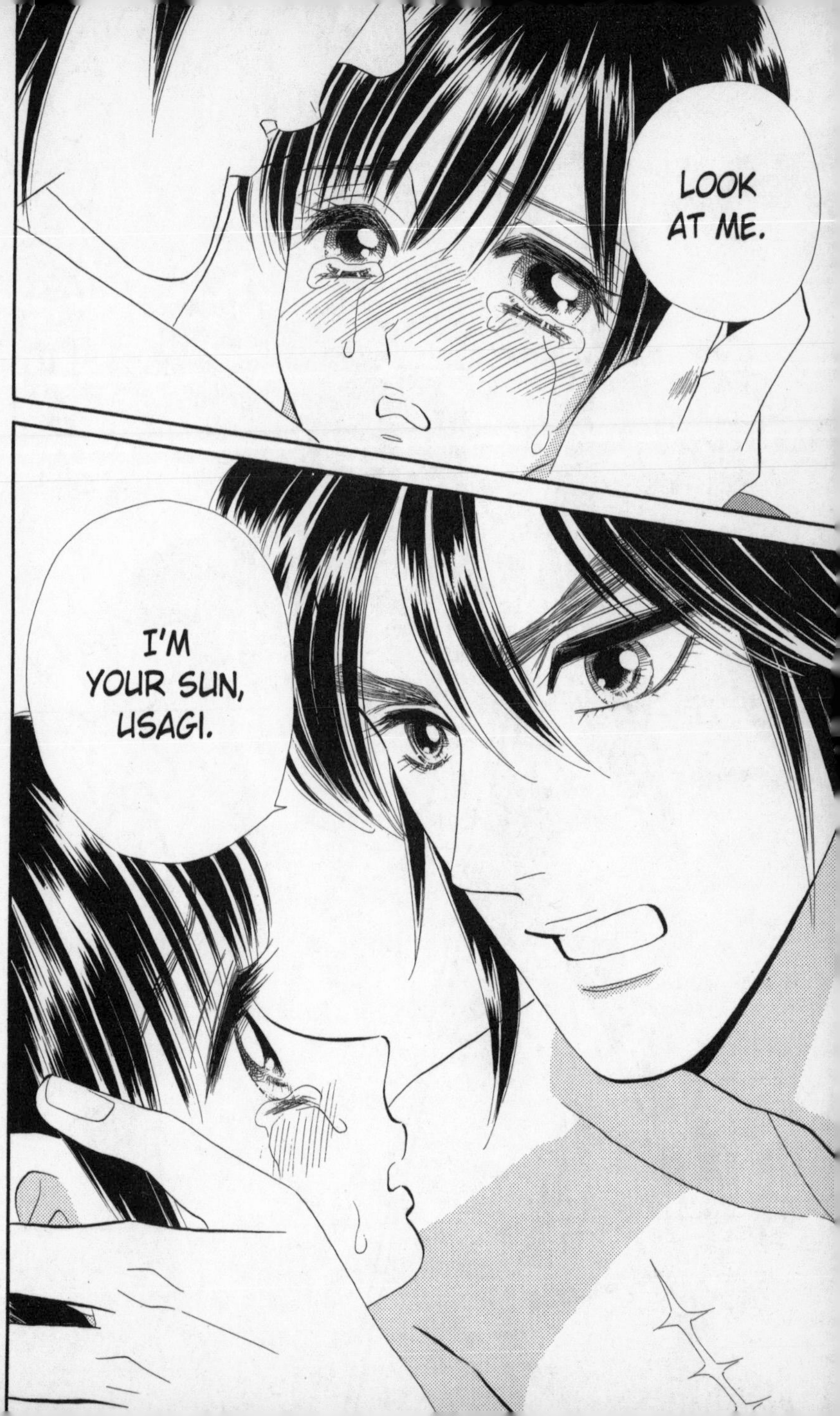
LOOK AT ME.
I'M YOUR SUN, USAGI.

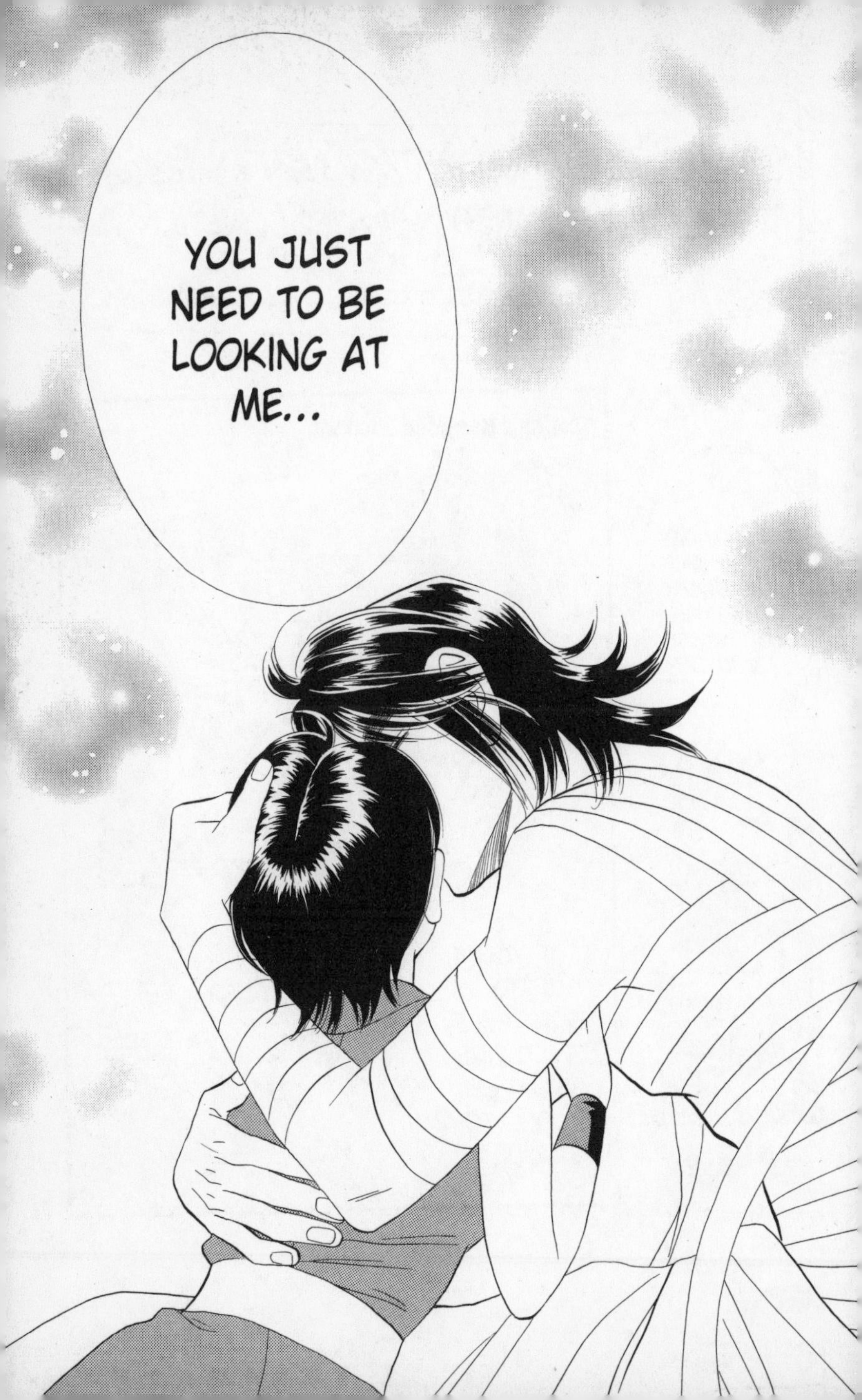
YOU JUST NEED TO BE LOOKING AT ME...

TAIL OF THE MOON EXTRA: TODAY'S MISSION

"I WANT TO SEE HANZO IN 'WINTER SONATA.'♡"

-SUZUZOU, FUKUSHIMA PREFECTURE

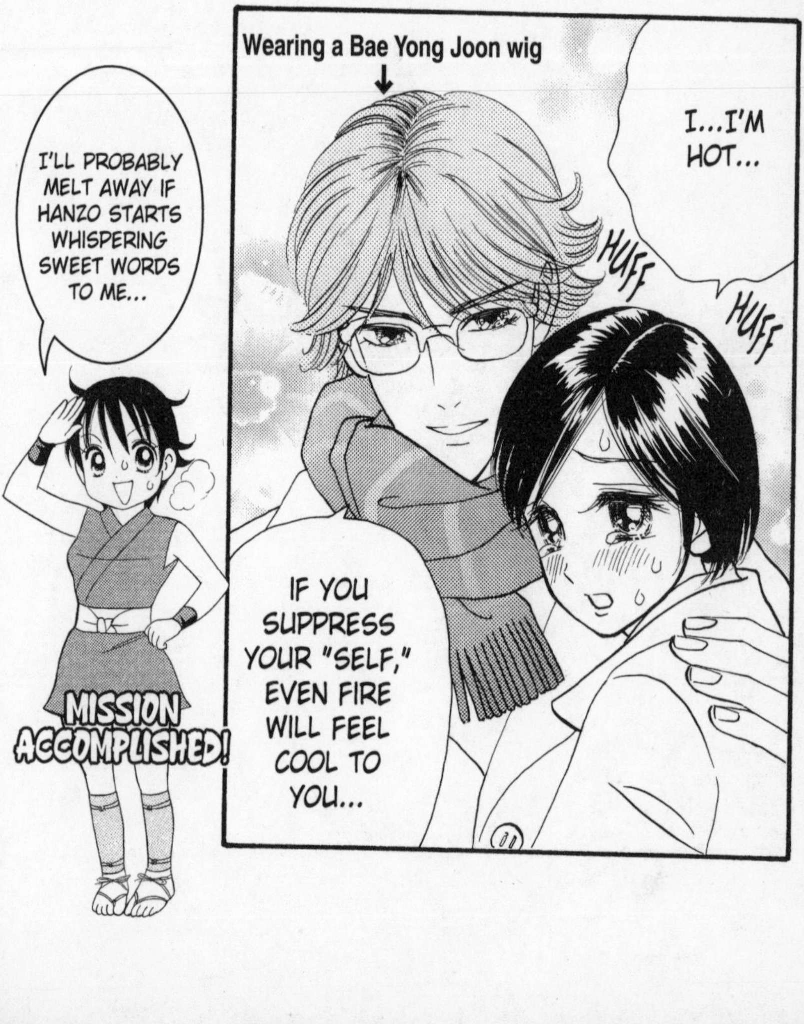
Wearing a Bae Yong Joon wig
I...I'M HOT...
HUFF
HUFF
IF YOU SUPPRESS YOUR "SELF," EVEN FIRE WILL FEEL COOL TO YOU...
I'LL PROBABLY MELT AWAY IF HANZO STARTS WHISPERING SWEET WORDS TO ME...
MISSION ACCOMPLISHED!

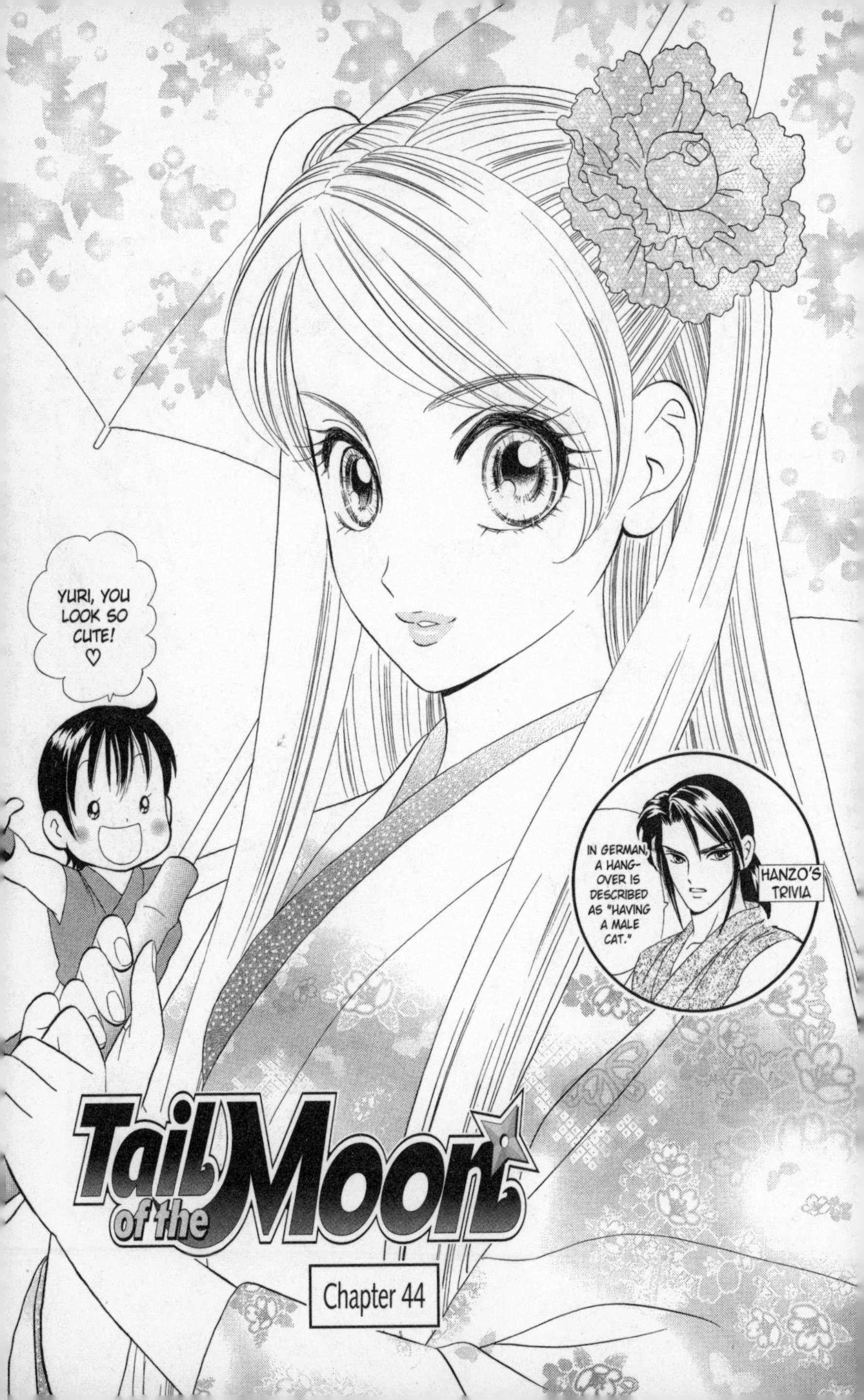

HANZO'S TRIVIA
IN GERMAN, A HANG-OVER IS DESCRIBED AS "HAVING A MALE CAT."
YURI, YOU LOOK SO CUTE! ♡
Tail of the Moon
Chapter 44

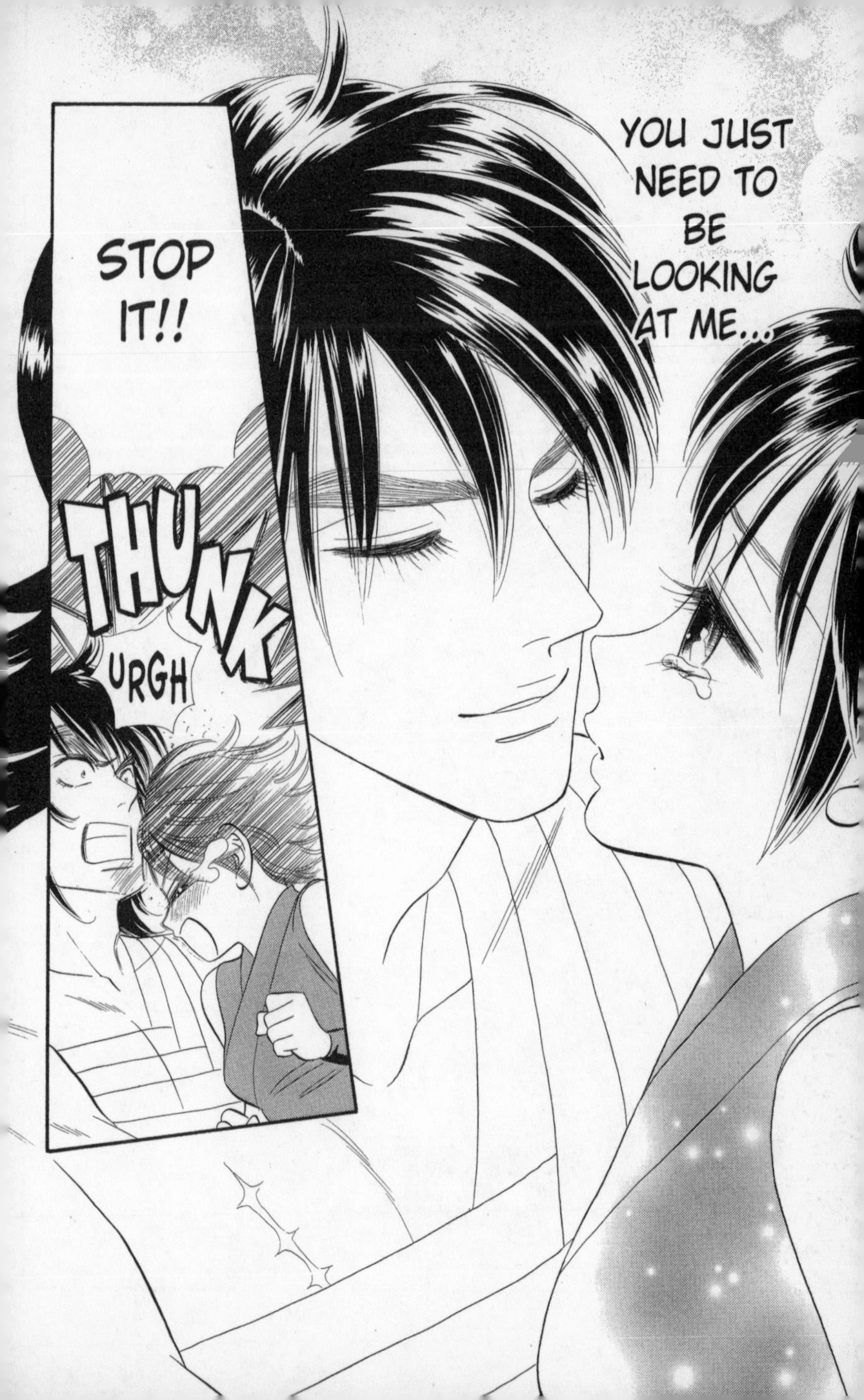
YOU JUST NEED TO BE LOOKING AT ME...
STOP IT!!
THUNK
URGH

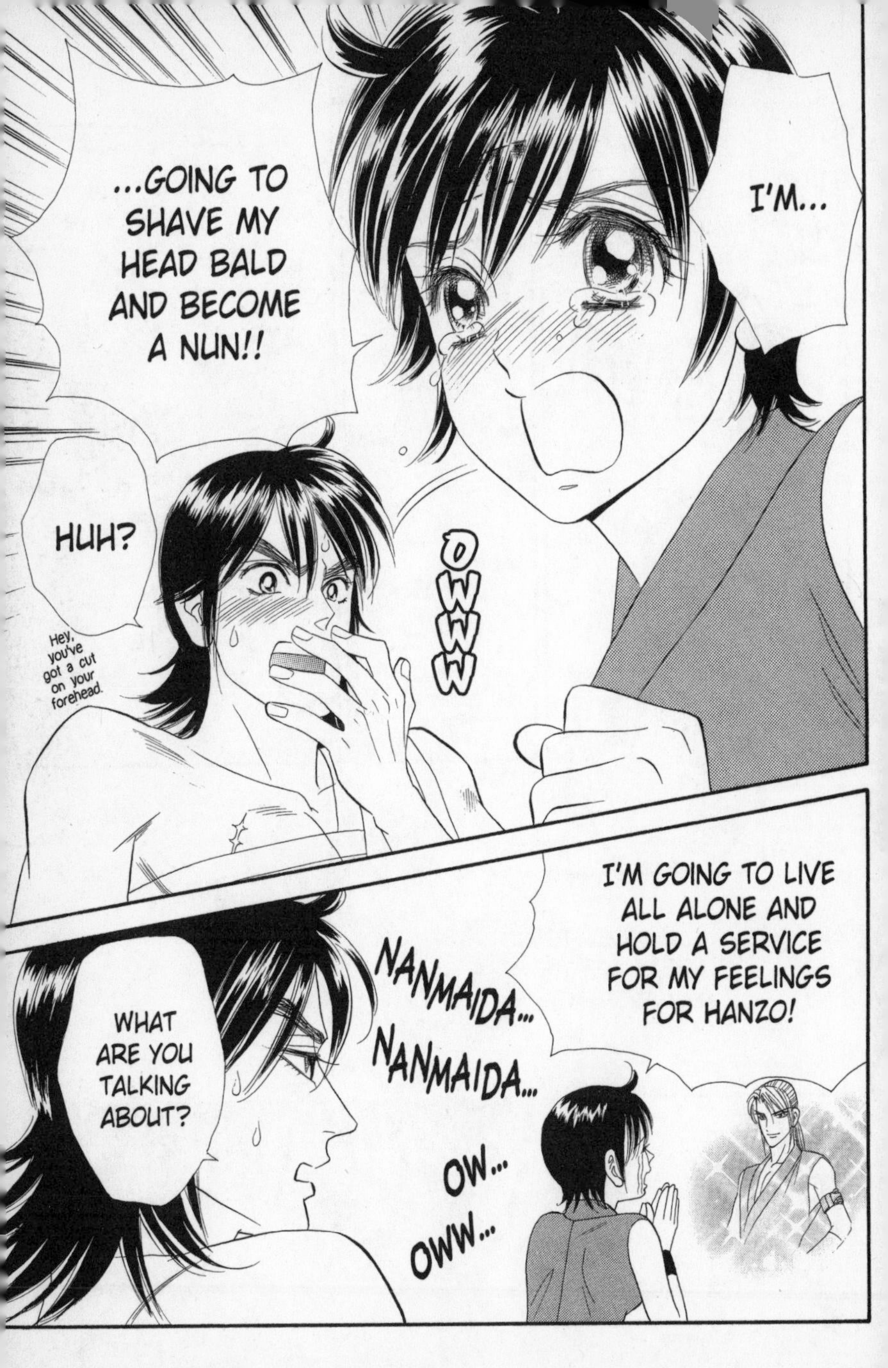
I'M...
...GOING TO SHAVE MY HEAD BALD AND BECOME A NUN!!
OWWWW
HUH?
Hey, you've got a cut on your forehead.
I'M GOING TO LIVE ALL ALONE AND HOLD A SERVICE FOR MY FEELINGS FOR HANZO!
NANMAIDA... NANMAIDA...
OW... OWW...
WHAT ARE YOU TALKING ABOUT?

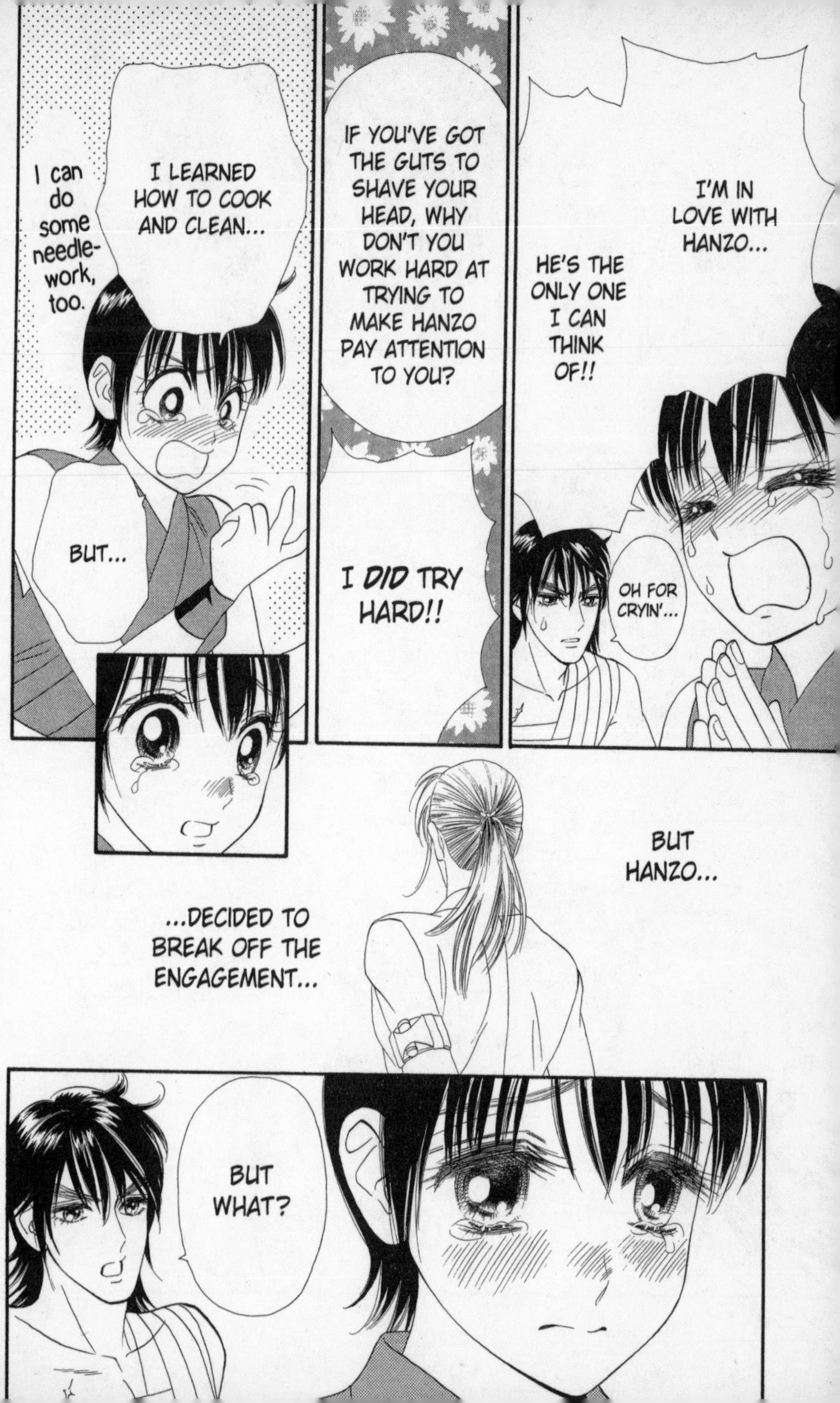
I'M IN LOVE WITH HANZO...
HE'S THE ONLY ONE I CAN THINK OF!!
OH FOR CRYIN'...
IF YOU'VE GOT THE GUTS TO SHAVE YOUR HEAD, WHY DON'T YOU WORK HARD AT TRYING TO MAKE HANZO PAY ATTENTION TO YOU?
I *DID* TRY HARD!!
I LEARNED HOW TO COOK AND CLEAN...
I can do some needle-work, too.
BUT...
BUT HANZO...
...DECIDED TO BREAK OFF THE ENGAGEMENT...
BUT WHAT?

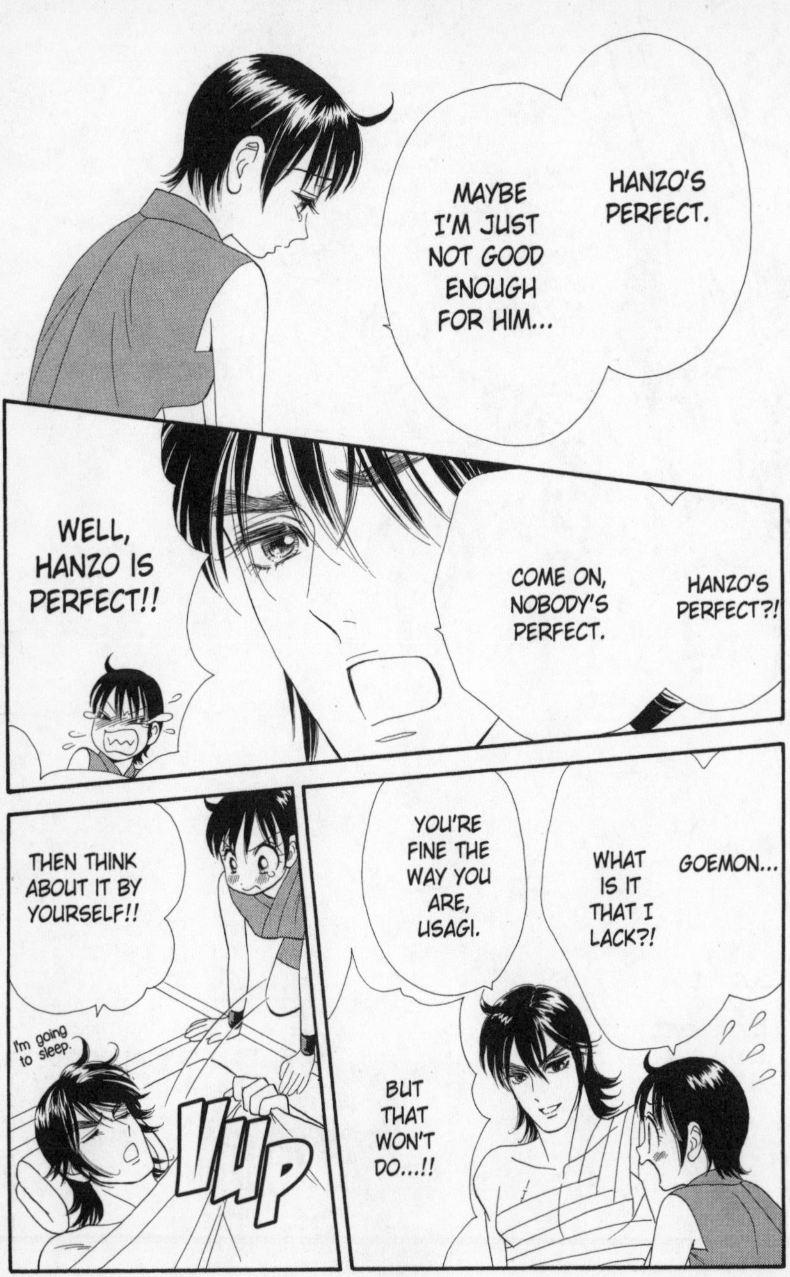
HANZO'S PERFECT.
MAYBE I'M JUST NOT GOOD ENOUGH FOR HIM...
HANZO'S PERFECT?!
COME ON, NOBODY'S PERFECT.
WELL, HANZO IS PERFECT!!
GOEMON...
WHAT IS IT THAT I LACK?!
YOU'RE FINE THE WAY YOU ARE, USAGI.
BUT THAT WON'T DO...!!
THEN THINK ABOUT IT BY YOURSELF!!
I'm going to sleep.
VUP

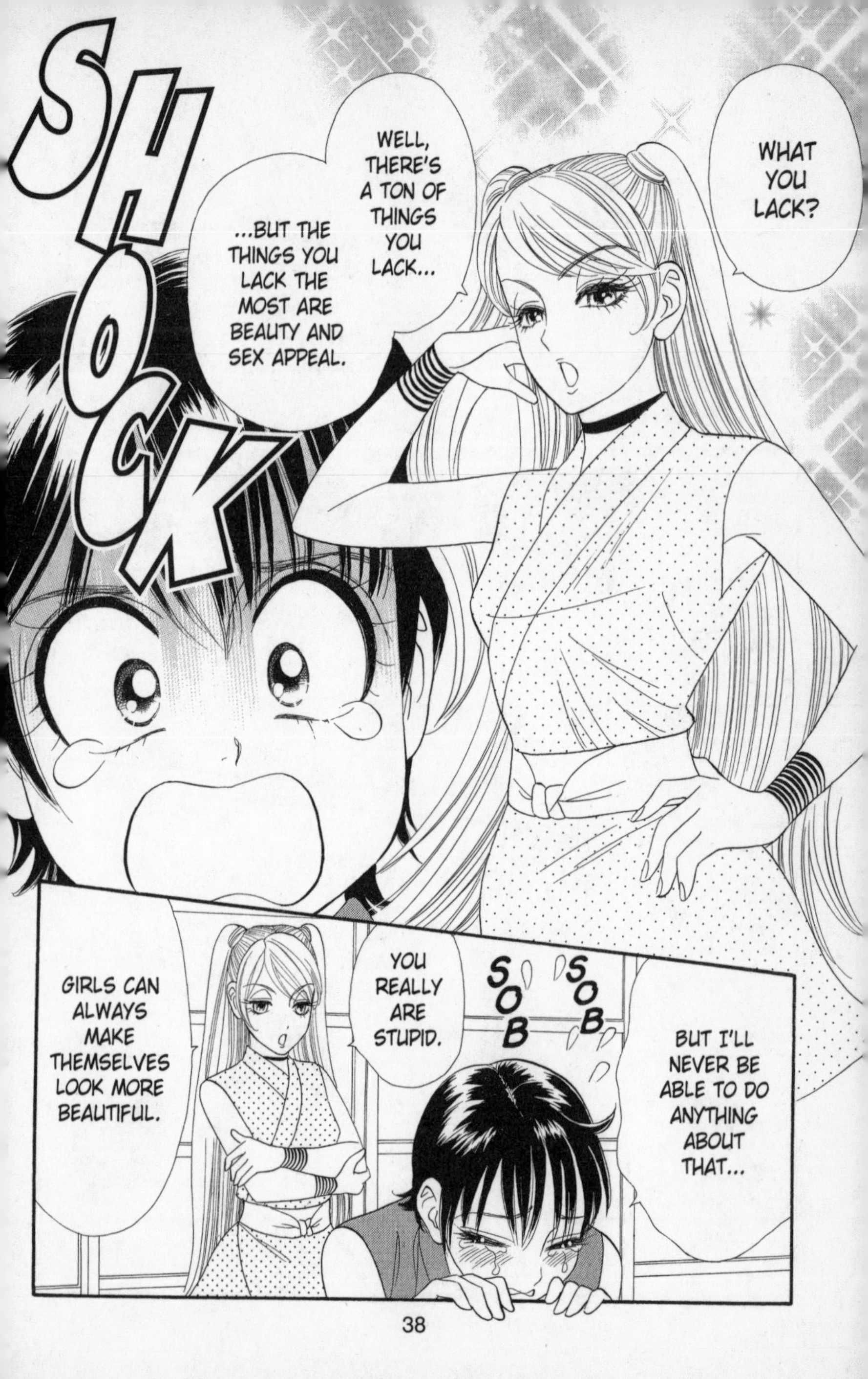
WHAT YOU LACK?
WELL, THERE'S A TON OF THINGS YOU LACK...
...BUT THE THINGS YOU LACK THE MOST ARE BEAUTY AND SEX APPEAL.
SHOCK
BUT I'LL NEVER BE ABLE TO DO ANYTHING ABOUT THAT...
SOB SOB
YOU REALLY ARE STUPID.
GIRLS CAN ALWAYS MAKE THEMSELVES LOOK MORE BEAUTIFUL.

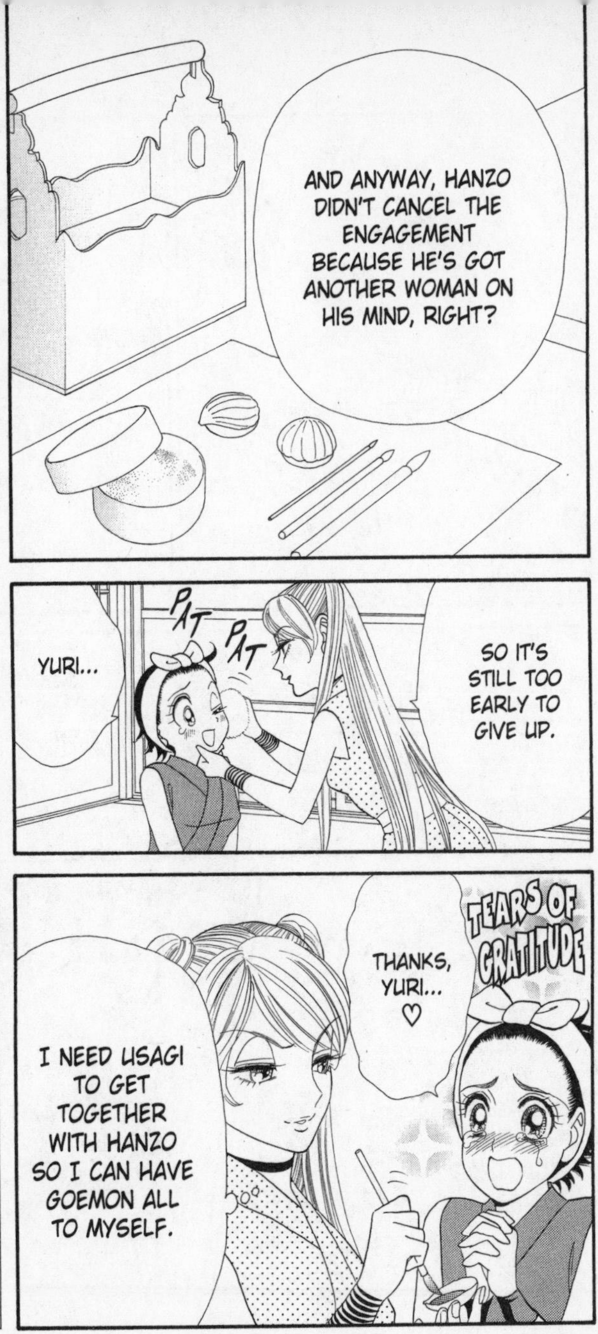
AND ANYWAY, HANZO DIDN'T CANCEL THE ENGAGEMENT BECAUSE HE'S GOT ANOTHER WOMAN ON HIS MIND, RIGHT?
SO IT'S STILL TOO EARLY TO GIVE UP.
PAT
PAT
YURI...
TEARS OF GRATITUDE
THANKS, YURI... ♡
I NEED USAGI TO GET TOGETHER WITH HANZO SO I CAN HAVE GOEMON ALL TO MYSELF.

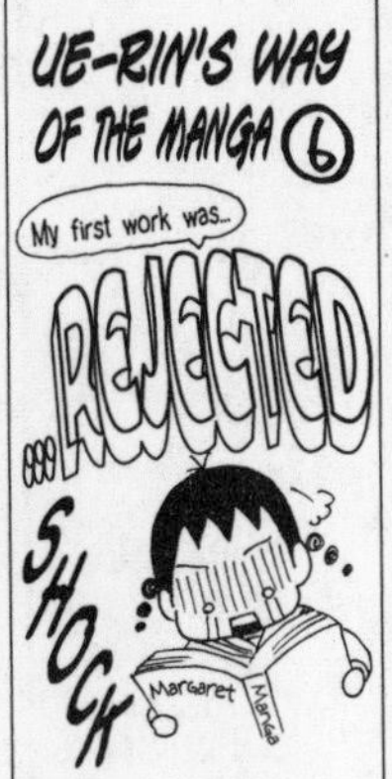
UE-RIN'S WAY OF THE MANGA 6
My first work was...
...REJECTED
SHOCK
Margaret
Manga

The reality hit Ue-Rin right in the face... Ue-Rin was forced to realize her lack of skills...

I wasn't sad, but I was frustrated.

However, the "Manga School" I sent my work to was a special edition where a brief comment and an image from the work of all the people who applied were printed in the magazine. So even though my work was rejected, I was really happy to see a small image of it in print.

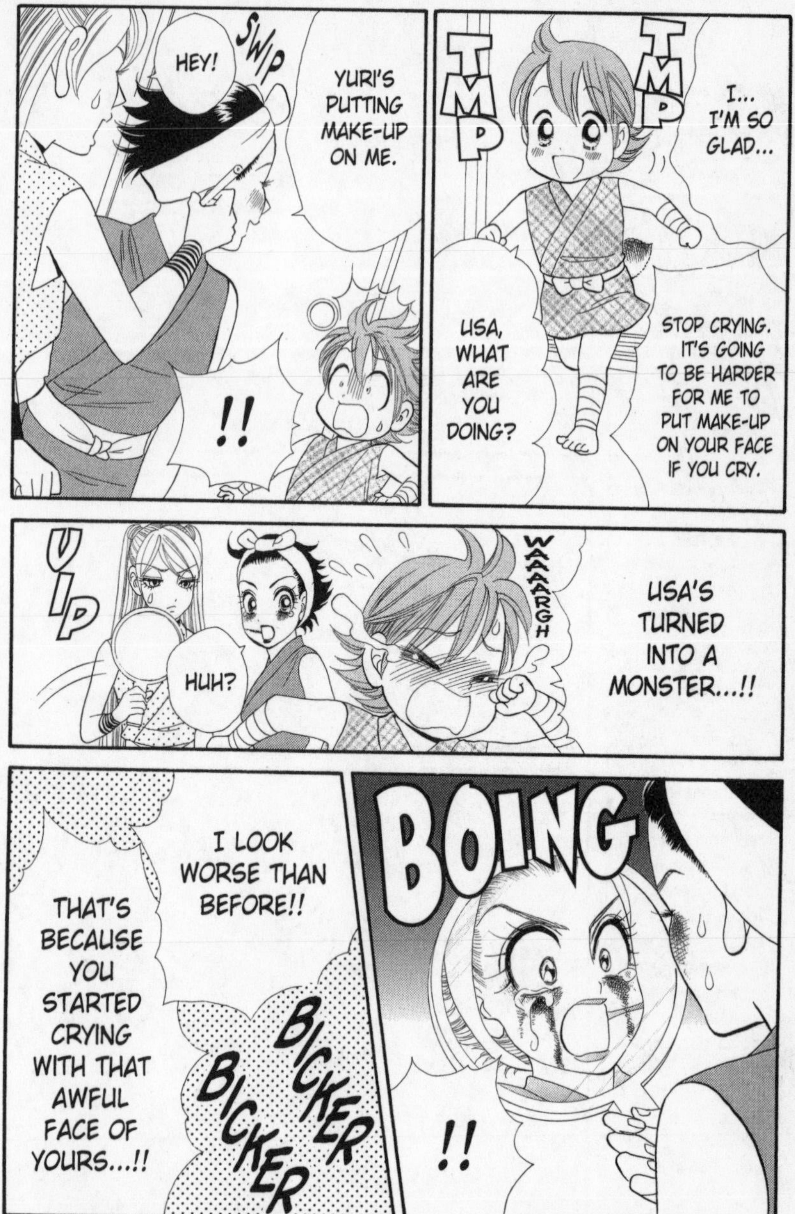
I... I'M SO GLAD...
TMP TMP
STOP CRYING. IT'S GOING TO BE HARDER FOR ME TO PUT MAKE-UP ON YOUR FACE IF YOU CRY.
USA, WHAT ARE YOU DOING?
YURI'S PUTTING MAKE-UP ON ME.
SWIP
HEY!
!!
USA'S TURNED INTO A MONSTER...!!
WAAAARGH
HUH?
VIP
BOING
!!
I LOOK WORSE THAN BEFORE!!
BICKER BICKER
THAT'S BECAUSE YOU STARTED CRYING WITH THAT AWFUL FACE OF YOURS...!!

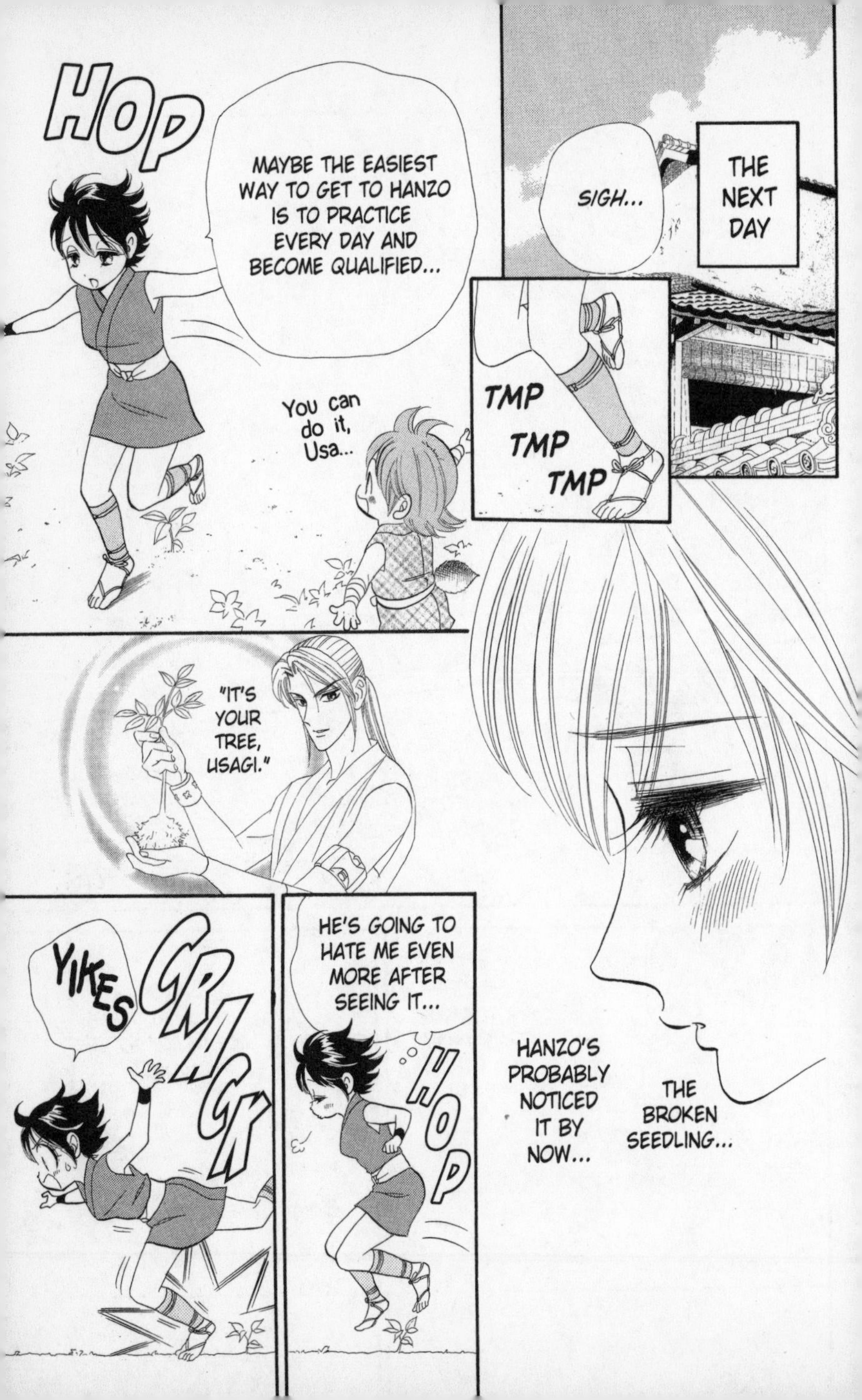

THE NEXT DAY
SIGH...
TMP TMP TMP
THE BROKEN SEEDLING...
HANZO'S PROBABLY NOTICED IT BY NOW...
HOP
MAYBE THE EASIEST WAY TO GET TO HANZO IS TO PRACTICE EVERY DAY AND BECOME QUALIFIED...
You can do it, Usa...
"IT'S YOUR TREE, USAGI."
HE'S GOING TO HATE ME EVEN MORE AFTER SEEING IT...
HOP
CRACK
YIKES

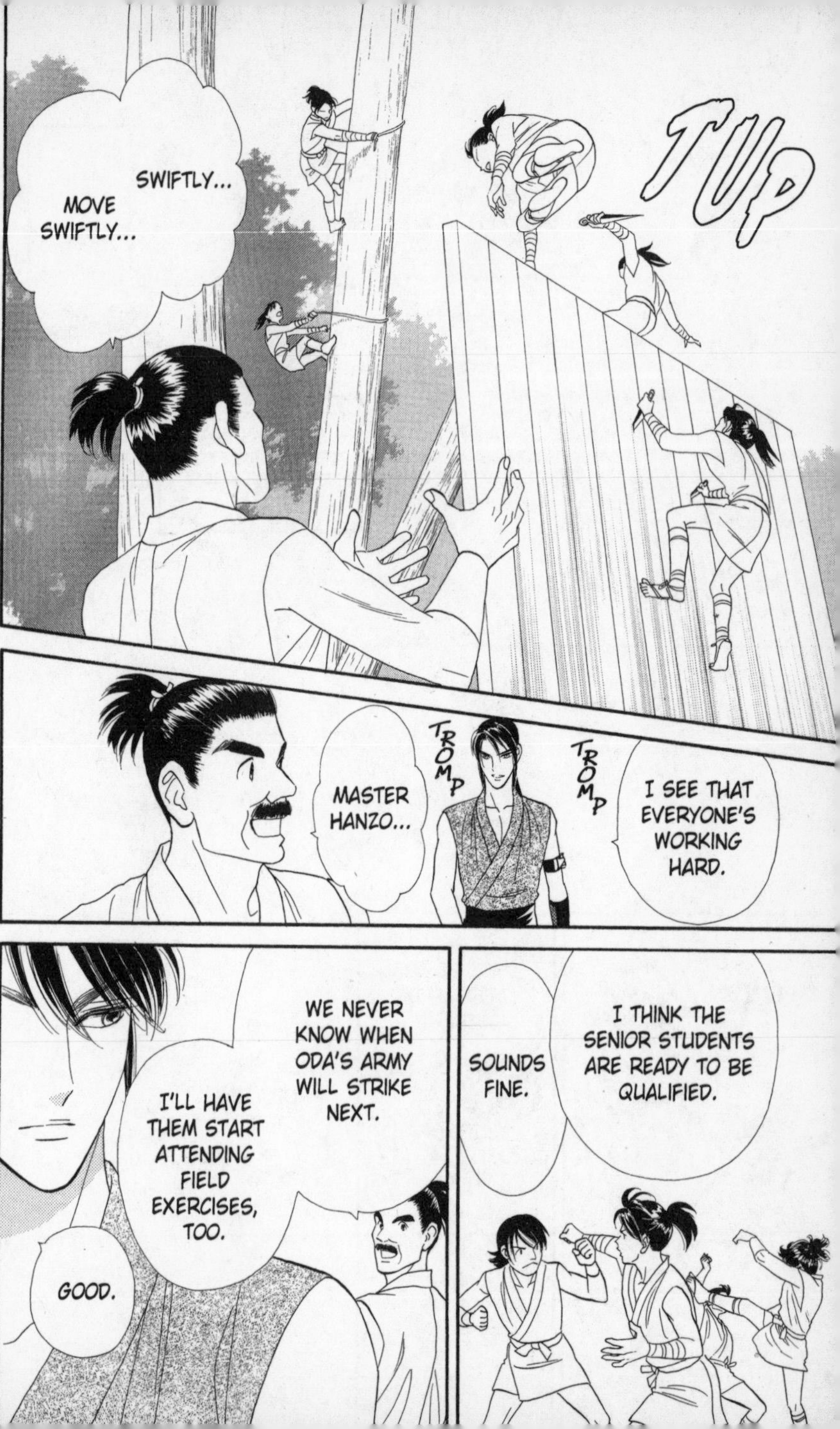
TUP
SWIFTLY...
MOVE SWIFTLY...
TROMP TROMP
I SEE THAT EVERYONE'S WORKING HARD.
MASTER HANZO...
I THINK THE SENIOR STUDENTS ARE READY TO BE QUALIFIED.
SOUNDS FINE.
WE NEVER KNOW WHEN ODA'S ARMY WILL STRIKE NEXT.
I'LL HAVE THEM START ATTENDING FIELD EXERCISES, TOO.
GOOD.

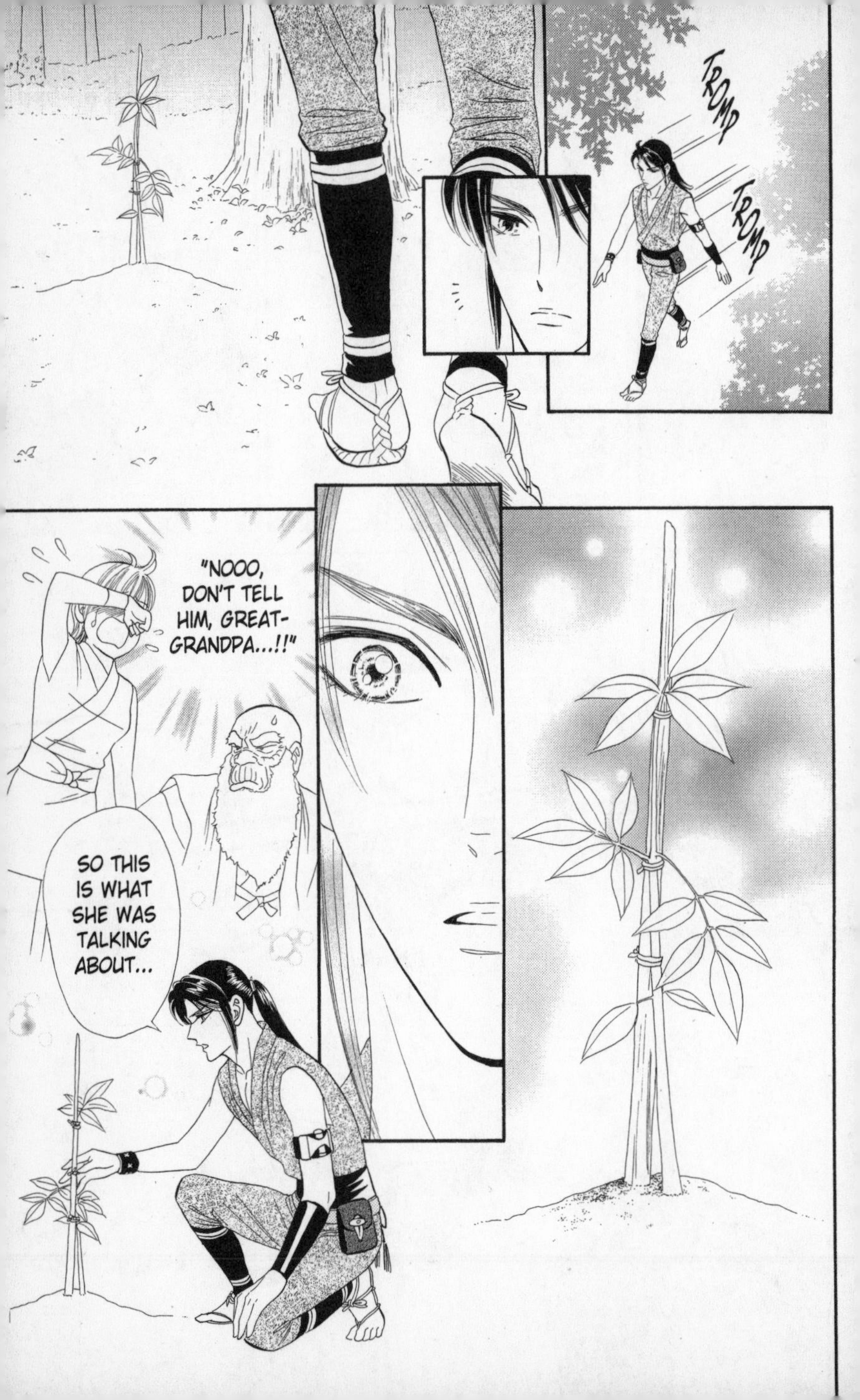
TROMP
TROMP
"NOOO, DON'T TELL HIM, GREAT-GRANDPA...!!"
SO THIS IS WHAT SHE WAS TALKING ABOUT...

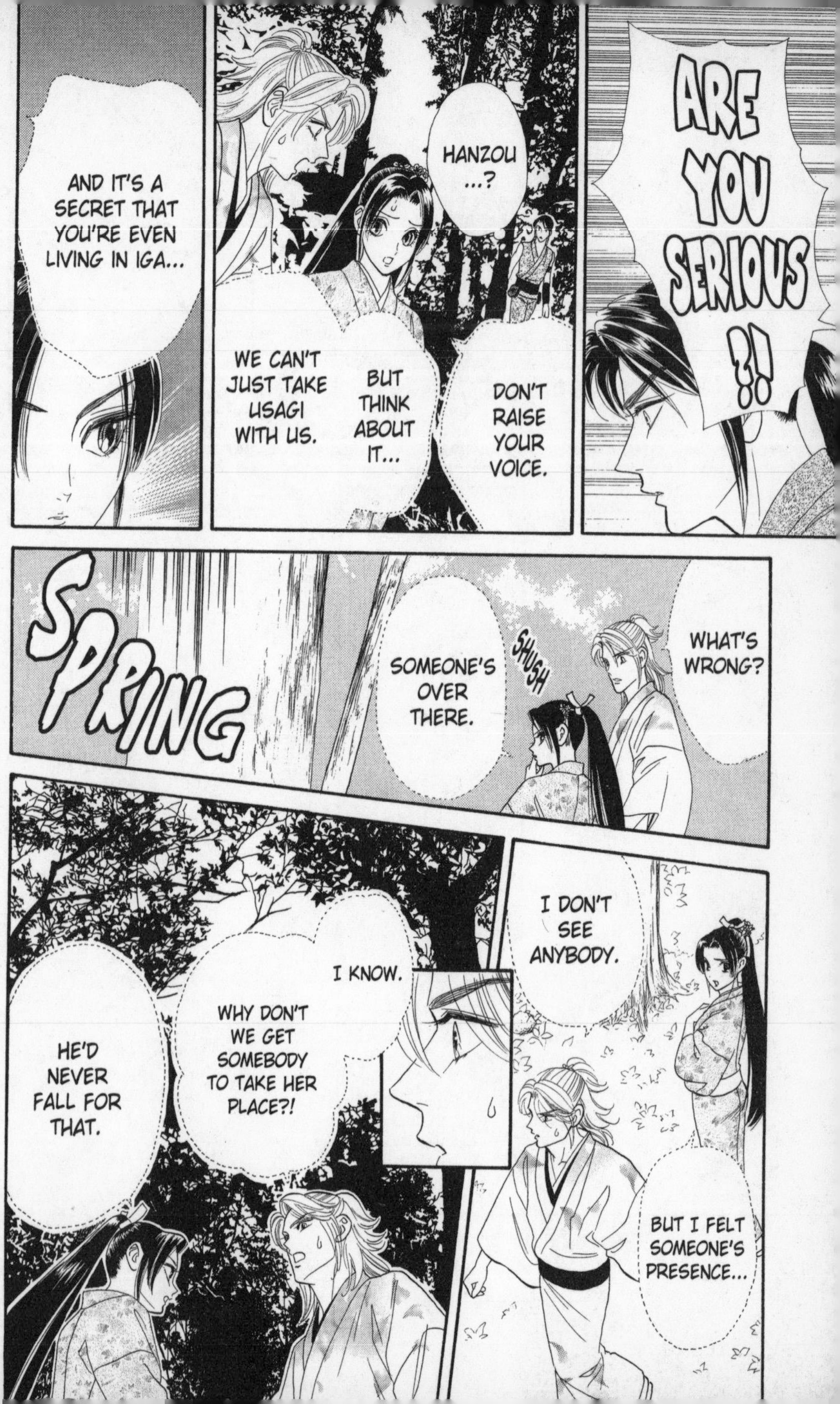
ARE YOU SERIOUS ?!
HANZOU ...?
DON'T RAISE YOUR VOICE.
BUT THINK ABOUT IT...
WE CAN'T JUST TAKE USAGI WITH US.
AND IT'S A SECRET THAT YOU'RE EVEN LIVING IN IGA...
WHAT'S WRONG?
SHUSH
SOMEONE'S OVER THERE.
SPRING
I DON'T SEE ANYBODY.
BUT I FELT SOMEONE'S PRESENCE...
I KNOW.
WHY DON'T WE GET SOMEBODY TO TAKE HER PLACE?!
HE'D NEVER FALL FOR THAT.

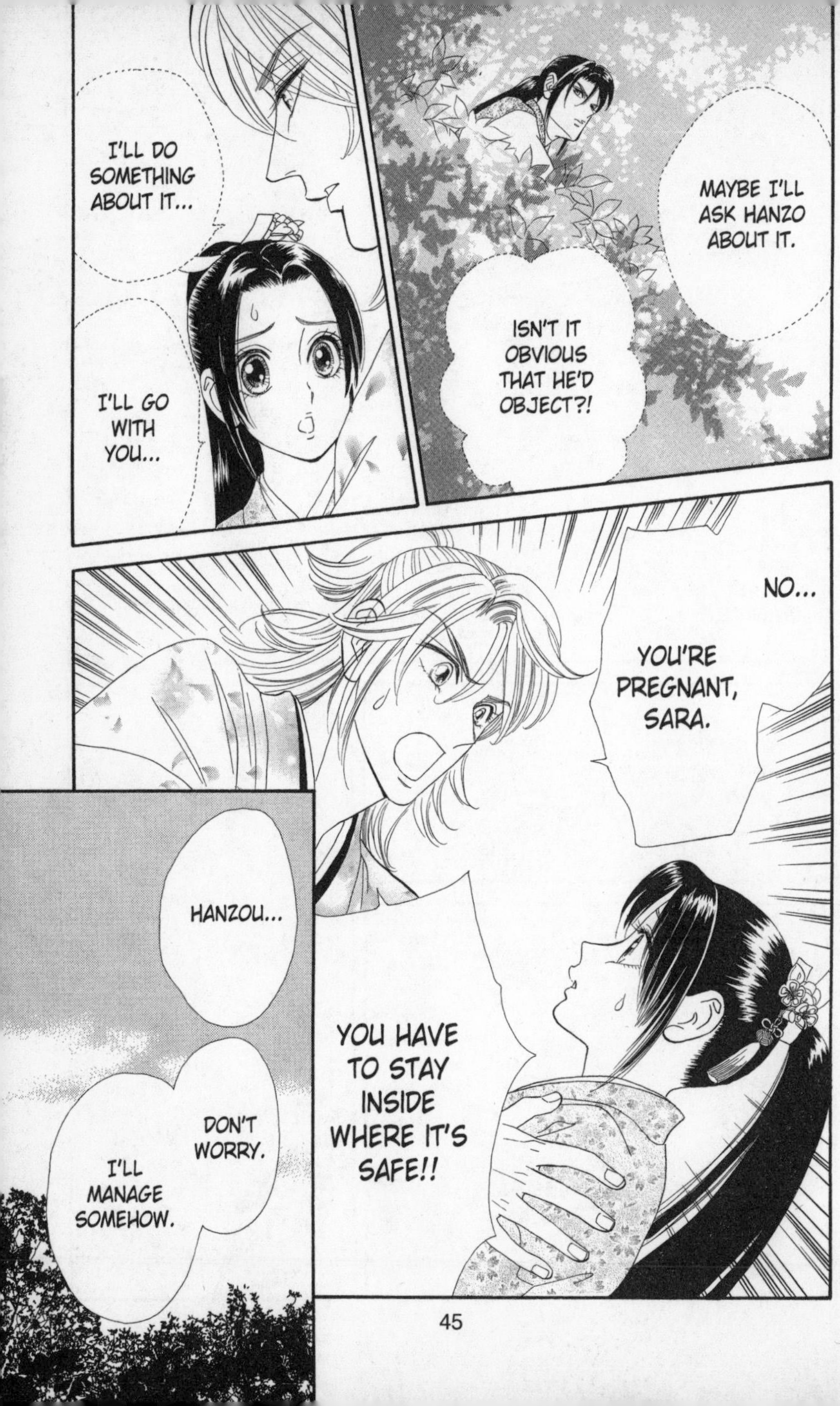
MAYBE I'LL ASK HANZO ABOUT IT.
ISN'T IT OBVIOUS THAT HE'D OBJECT?!
I'LL DO SOMETHING ABOUT IT...
I'LL GO WITH YOU...
NO...
YOU'RE PREGNANT, SARA.
YOU HAVE TO STAY INSIDE WHERE IT'S SAFE!!
HANZOU...
DON'T WORRY.
I'LL MANAGE SOMEHOW.

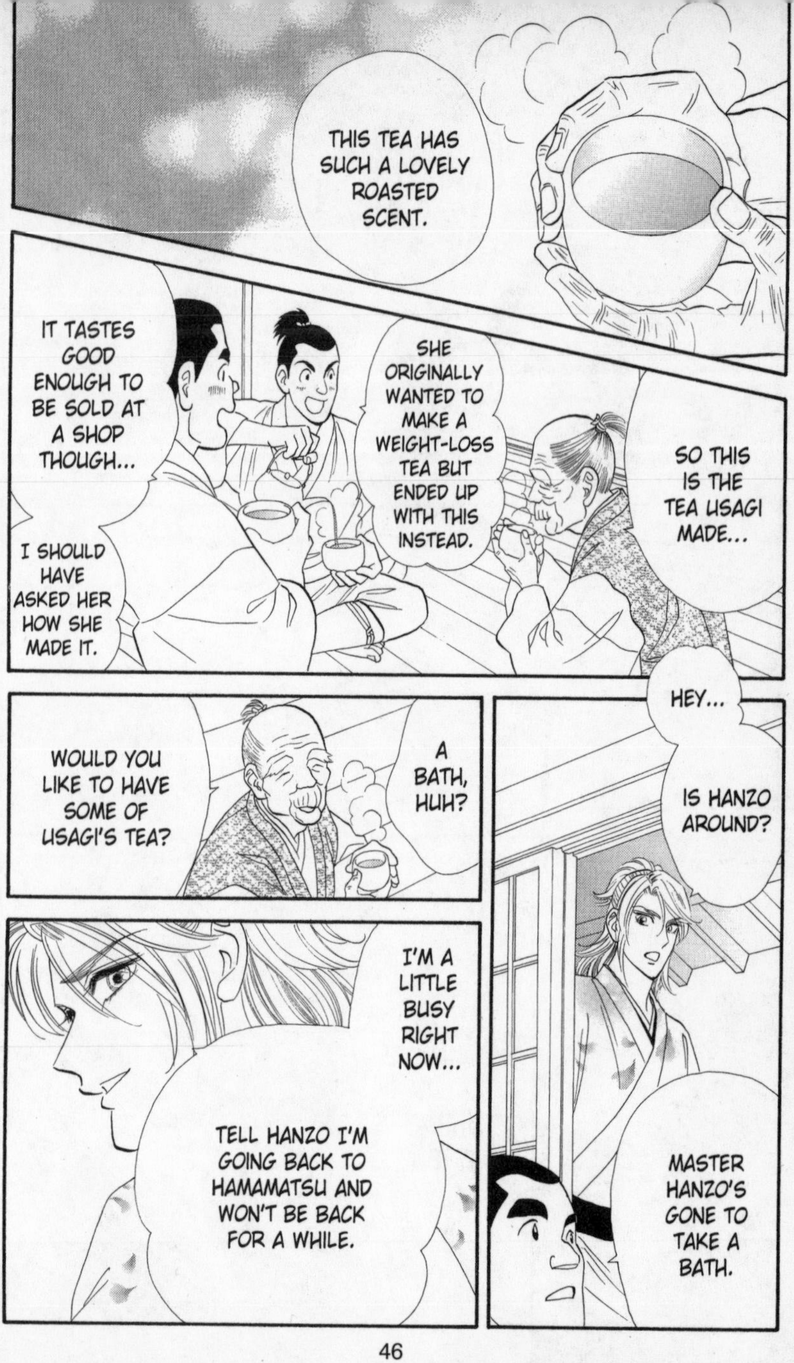
THIS TEA HAS SUCH A LOVELY ROASTED SCENT.
SO THIS IS THE TEA USAGI MADE...
SHE ORIGINALLY WANTED TO MAKE A WEIGHT-LOSS TEA BUT ENDED UP WITH THIS INSTEAD.
IT TASTES GOOD ENOUGH TO BE SOLD AT A SHOP THOUGH...
I SHOULD HAVE ASKED HER HOW SHE MADE IT.
HEY...
IS HANZO AROUND?
MASTER HANZO'S GONE TO TAKE A BATH.
A BATH, HUH?
WOULD YOU LIKE TO HAVE SOME OF USAGI'S TEA?
I'M A LITTLE BUSY RIGHT NOW...
TELL HANZO I'M GOING BACK TO HAMAMATSU AND WON'T BE BACK FOR A WHILE.

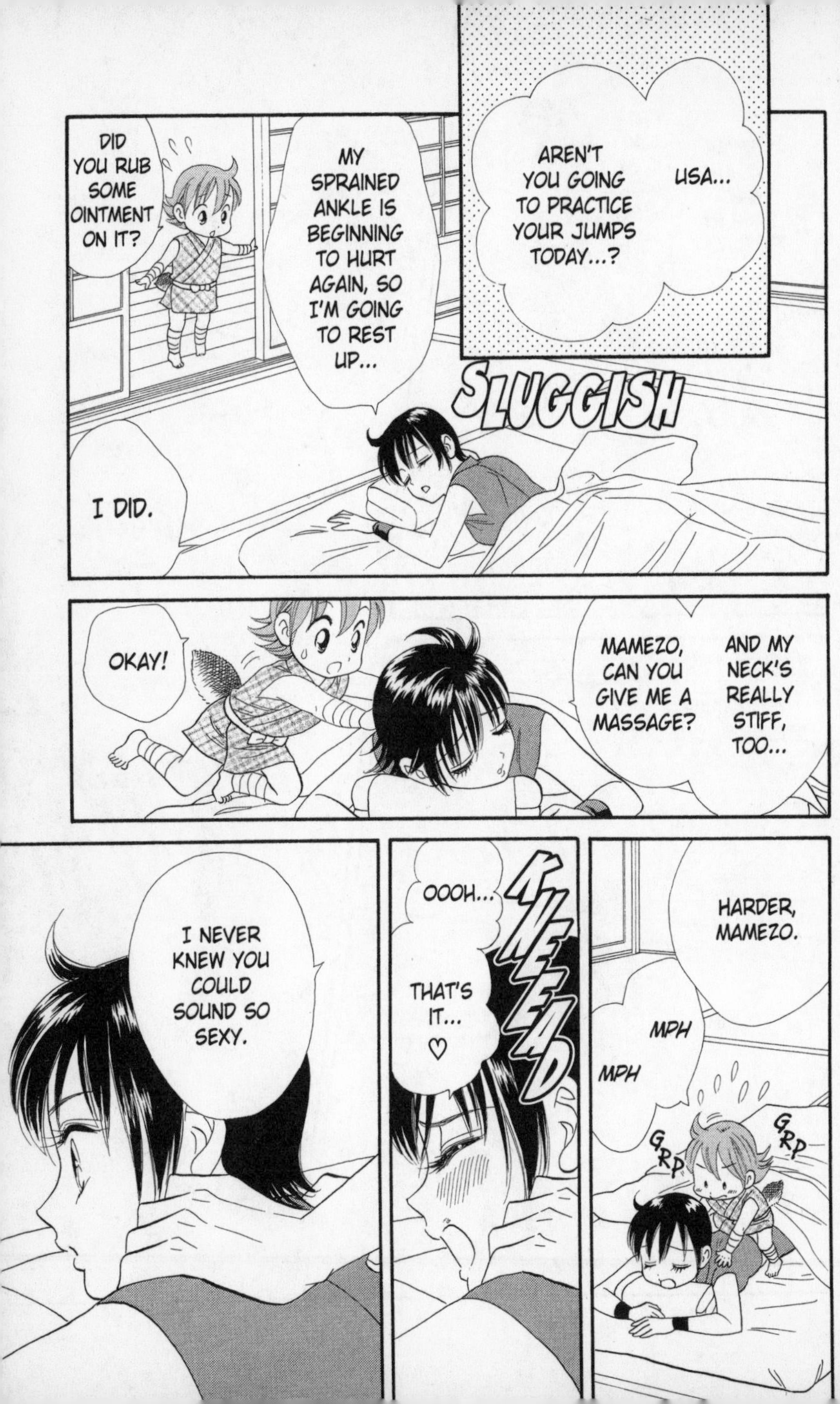
USA...
AREN'T YOU GOING TO PRACTICE YOUR JUMPS TODAY...?
MY SPRAINED ANKLE IS BEGINNING TO HURT AGAIN, SO I'M GOING TO REST UP...
SLUGGISH
DID YOU RUB SOME OINTMENT ON IT?
I DID.
AND MY NECK'S REALLY STIFF, TOO...
MAMEZO, CAN YOU GIVE ME A MASSAGE?
OKAY!
HARDER, MAMEZO.
MPH
MPH
GRP
GRP
KNEEAD
OOOH...
THAT'S IT... ♡
I NEVER KNEW YOU COULD SOUND SO SEXY.

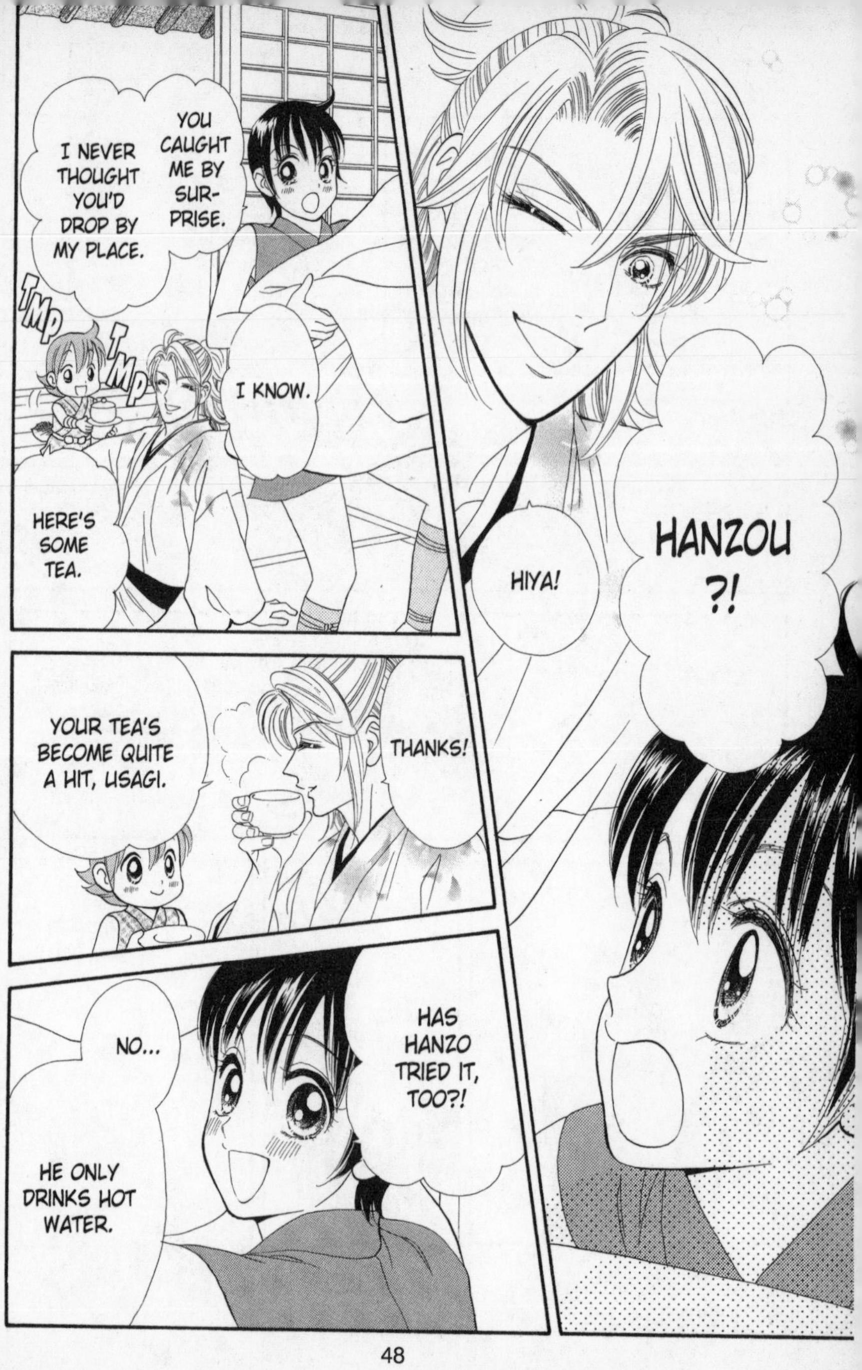
HANZOU ?!
HIYA!
YOU CAUGHT ME BY SUR-PRISE.
I NEVER THOUGHT YOU'D DROP BY MY PLACE.
I KNOW.
TMP
TMP
HERE'S SOME TEA.
YOUR TEA'S BECOME QUITE A HIT, USAGI.
THANKS!
HAS HANZO TRIED IT, TOO?!
NO...
HE ONLY DRINKS HOT WATER.

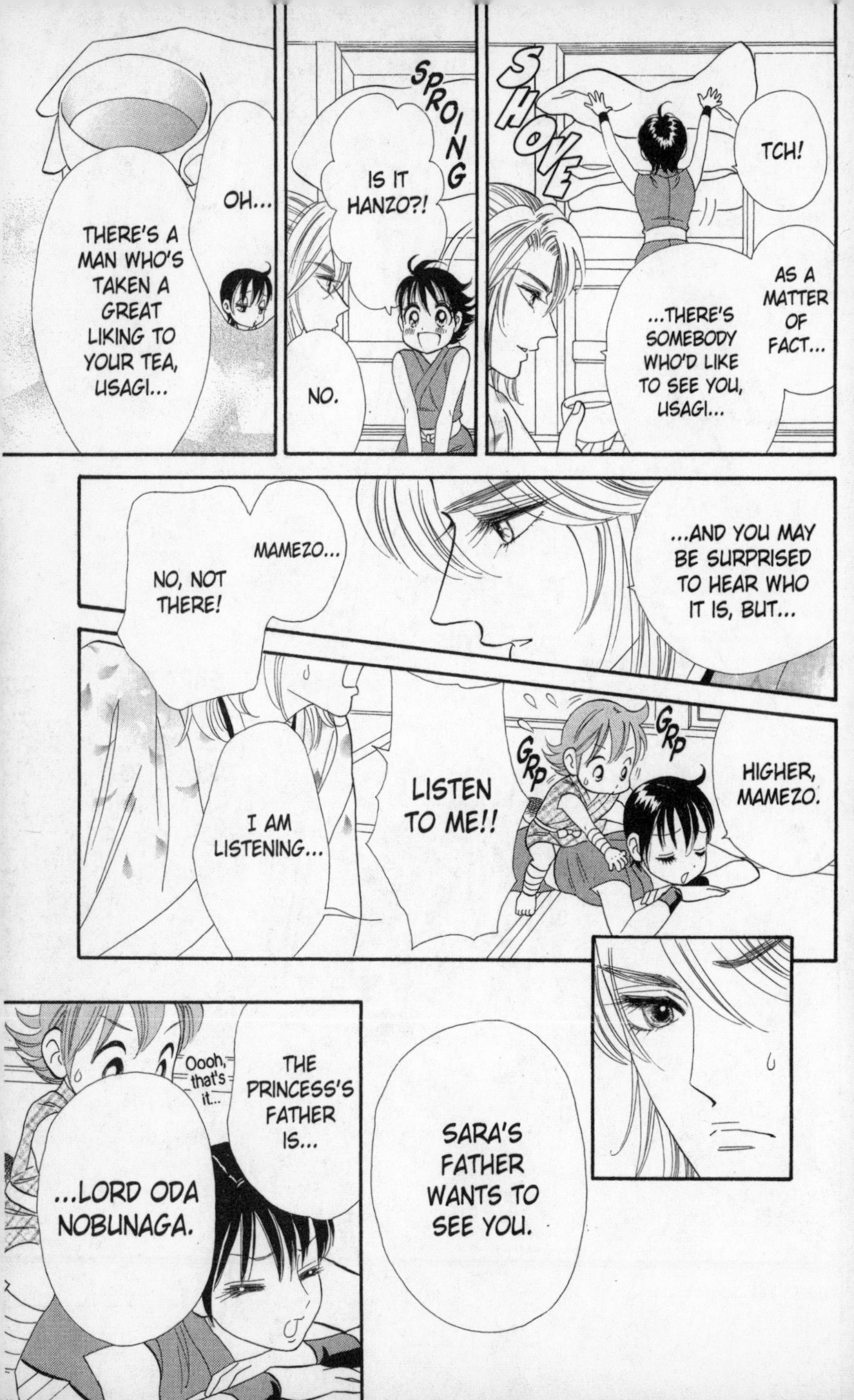
SHOVE
TCH!
AS A MATTER OF FACT...
...THERE'S SOMEBODY WHO'D LIKE TO SEE YOU, USAGI...
SPROING
IS IT HANZO?!
NO.
OH...
THERE'S A MAN WHO'S TAKEN A GREAT LIKING TO YOUR TEA, USAGI...
...AND YOU MAY BE SURPRISED TO HEAR WHO IT IS, BUT...
MAMEZO...
NO, NOT THERE!
GRP
GRP
HIGHER, MAMEZO.
LISTEN TO ME!!
I AM LISTENING...
SARA'S FATHER WANTS TO SEE YOU.
THE PRINCESS'S FATHER IS...
Oooh, that's it...
...LORD ODA NOBUNAGA.

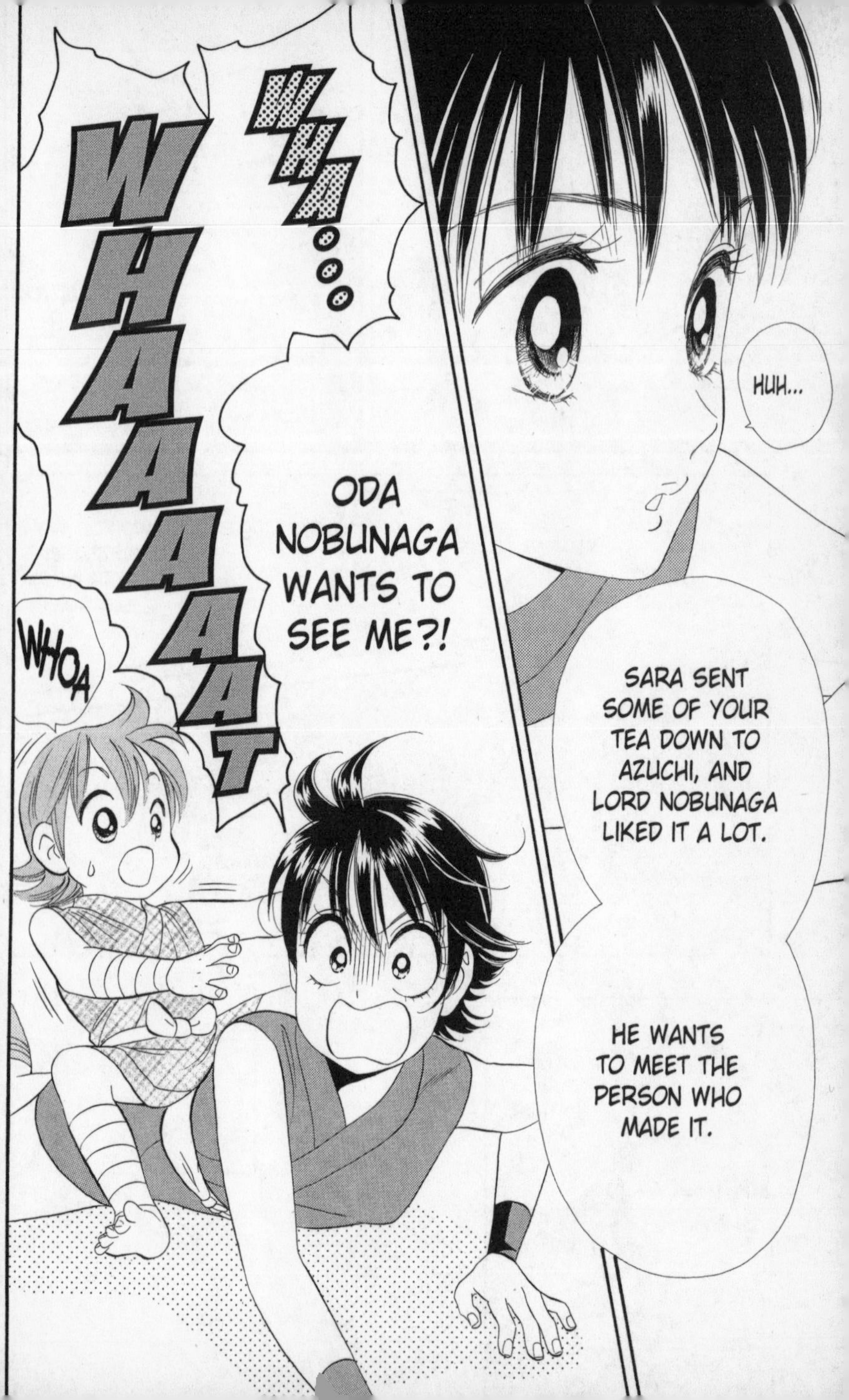
HUH...
SARA SENT SOME OF YOUR TEA DOWN TO AZUCHI, AND LORD NOBUNAGA LIKED IT A LOT.
HE WANTS TO MEET THE PERSON WHO MADE IT.
ODA NOBUNAGA WANTS TO SEE ME?!
WHA...
WHAAAAAT
WHOA

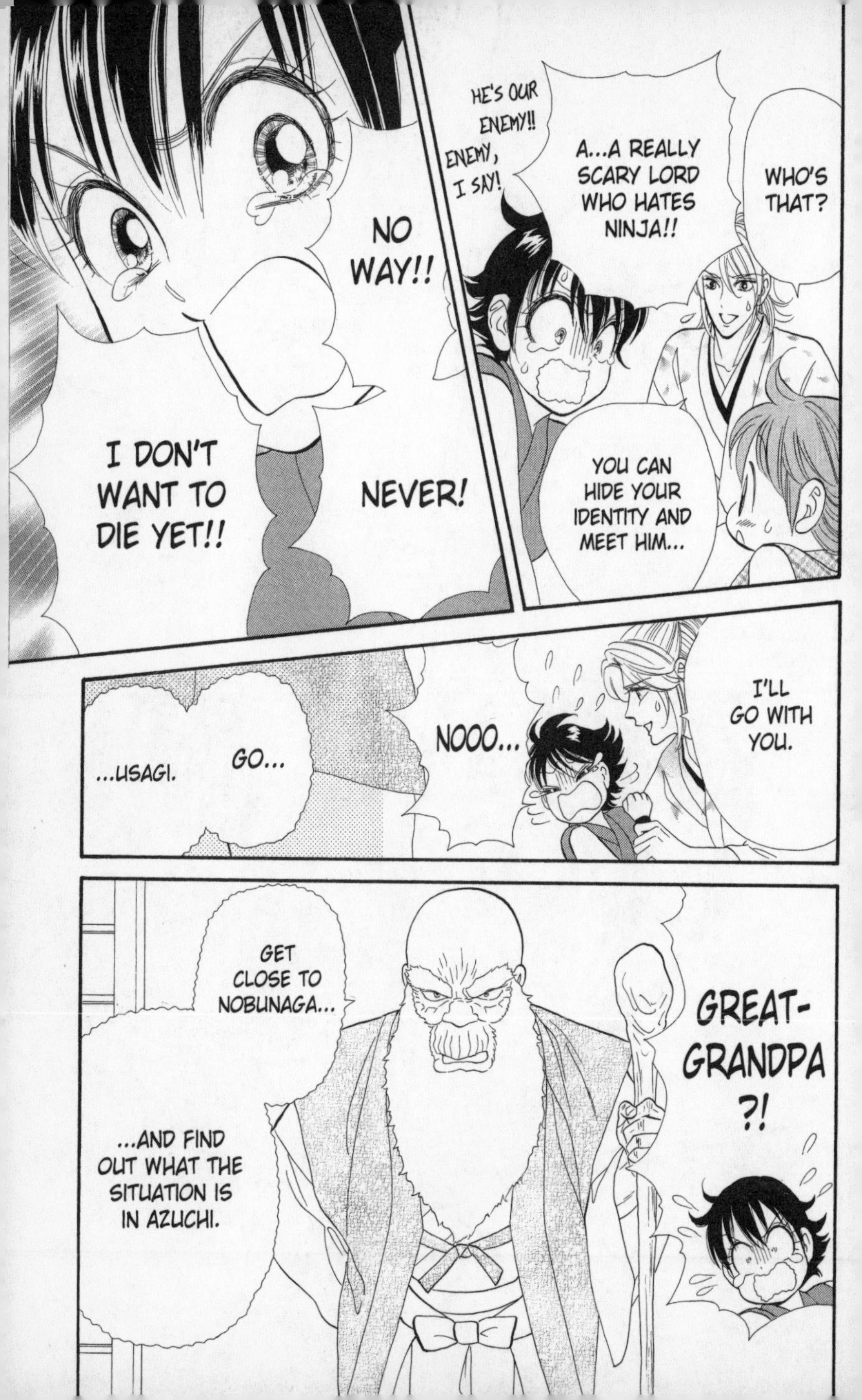
WHO'S THAT?
A...A REALLY SCARY LORD WHO HATES NINJA!!
HE'S OUR ENEMY!! ENEMY, I SAY!
YOU CAN HIDE YOUR IDENTITY AND MEET HIM...
NO WAY!!
NEVER!
I DON'T WANT TO DIE YET!!
I'LL GO WITH YOU.
NOOO...
GO...
...USAGI.
GREAT-GRANDPA?!
GET CLOSE TO NOBUNAGA...
...AND FIND OUT WHAT THE SITUATION IS IN AZUCHI.

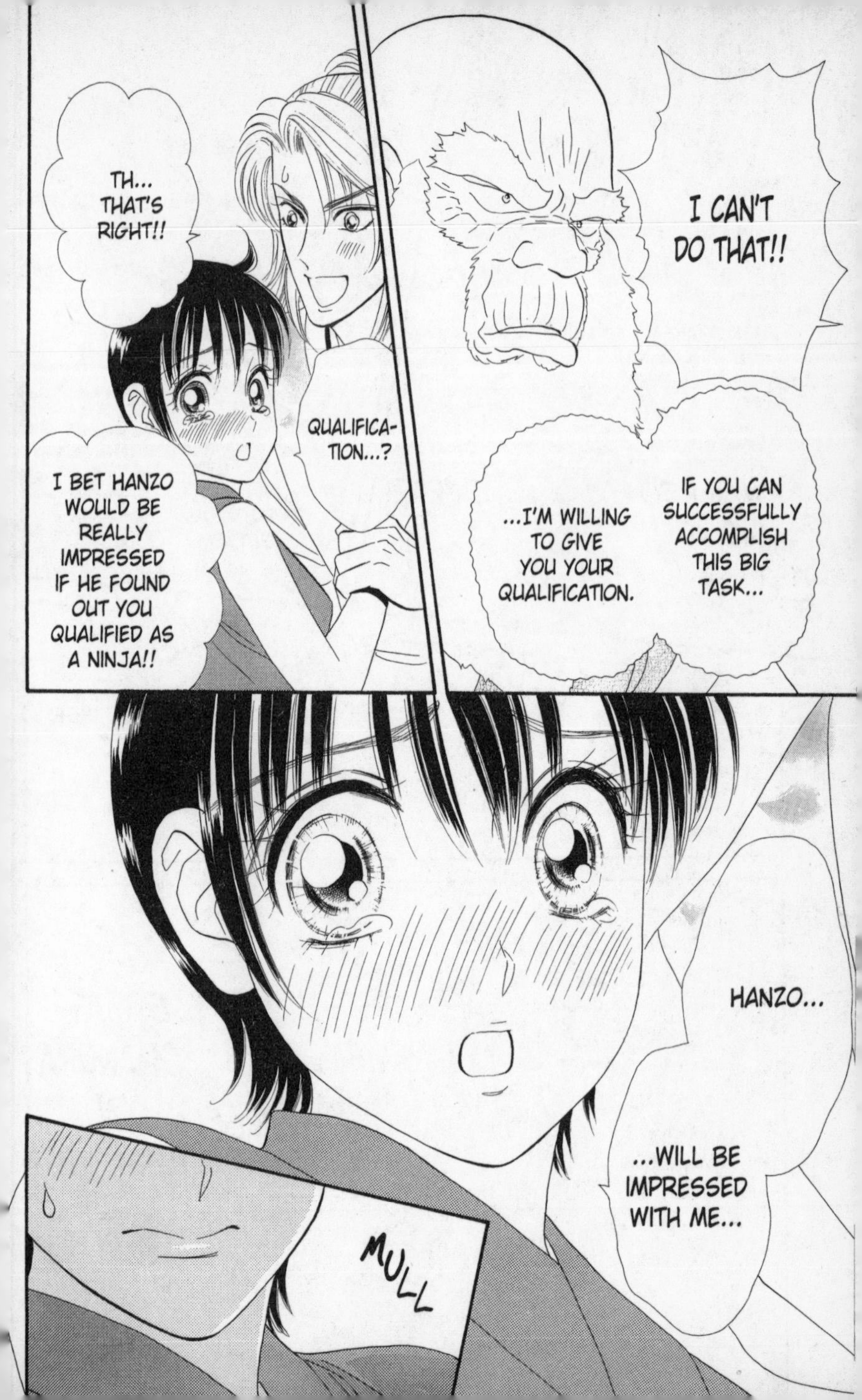
I CAN'T DO THAT!!
IF YOU CAN SUCCESSFULLY ACCOMPLISH THIS BIG TASK...
...I'M WILLING TO GIVE YOU YOUR QUALIFICATION.
QUALIFICA-TION...?
TH... THAT'S RIGHT!!
I BET HANZO WOULD BE REALLY IMPRESSED IF HE FOUND OUT YOU QUALIFIED AS A NINJA!!
HANZO...
...WILL BE IMPRESSED WITH ME...
MULL

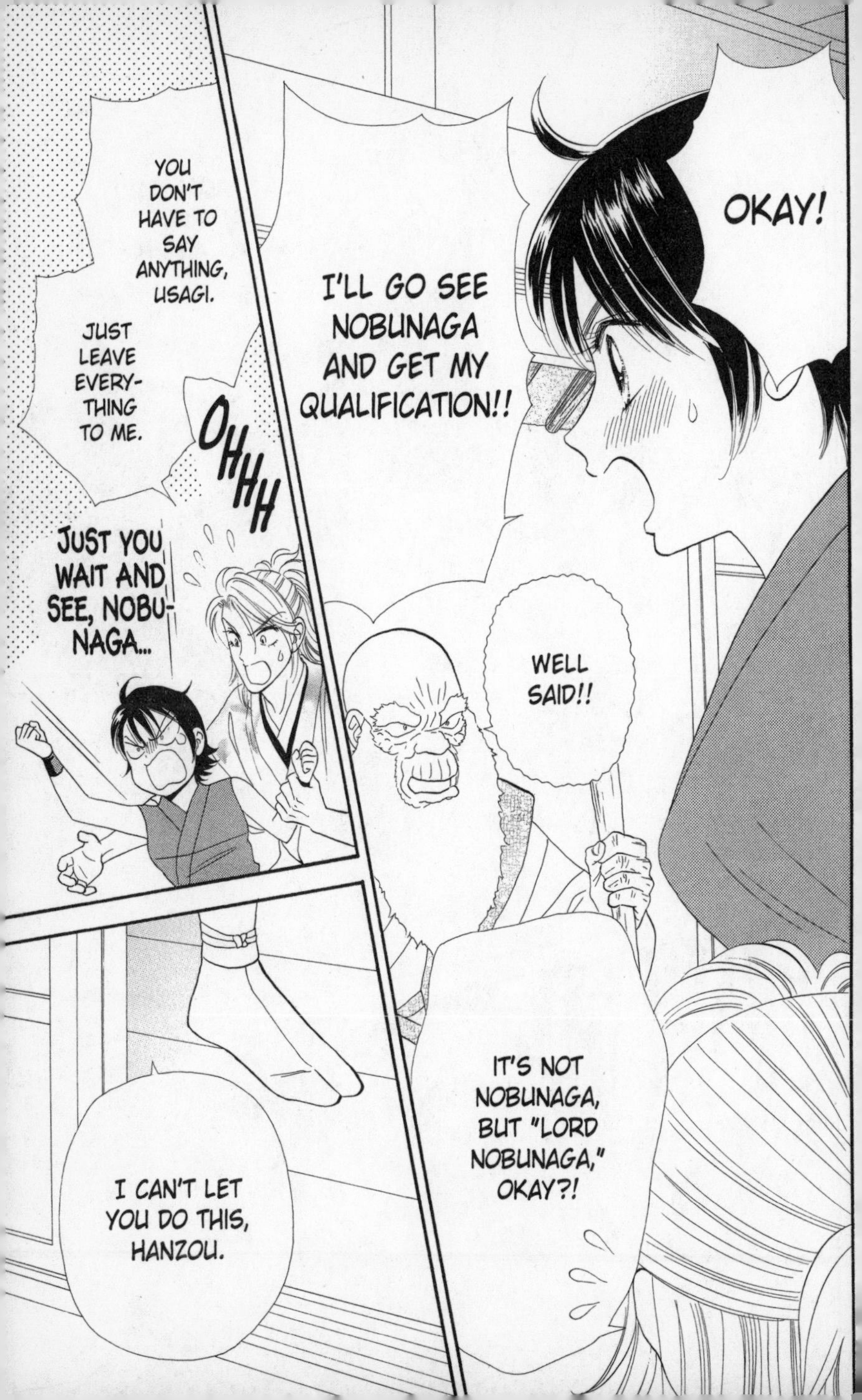
OKAY!
I'LL GO SEE NOBUNAGA AND GET MY QUALIFICATION!!
WELL SAID!!
IT'S NOT NOBUNAGA, BUT "LORD NOBUNAGA," OKAY?!
YOU DON'T HAVE TO SAY ANYTHING, USAGI.
JUST LEAVE EVERYTHING TO ME.
OHHHH
JUST YOU WAIT AND SEE, NOBUNAGA...
I CAN'T LET YOU DO THIS, HANZOU.

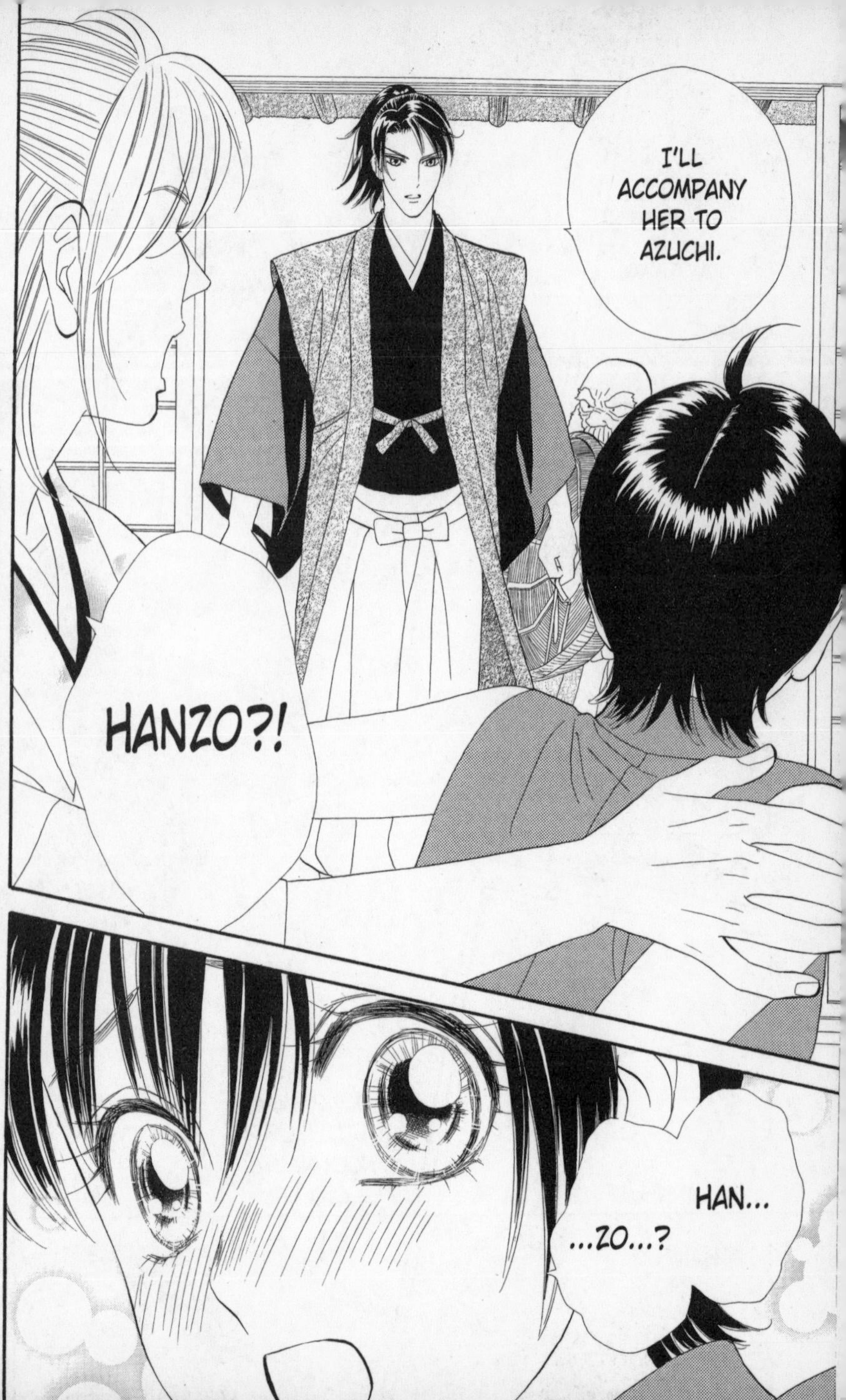
I'LL ACCOMPANY HER TO AZUCHI.
HANZO?!
HAN...
...ZO...?

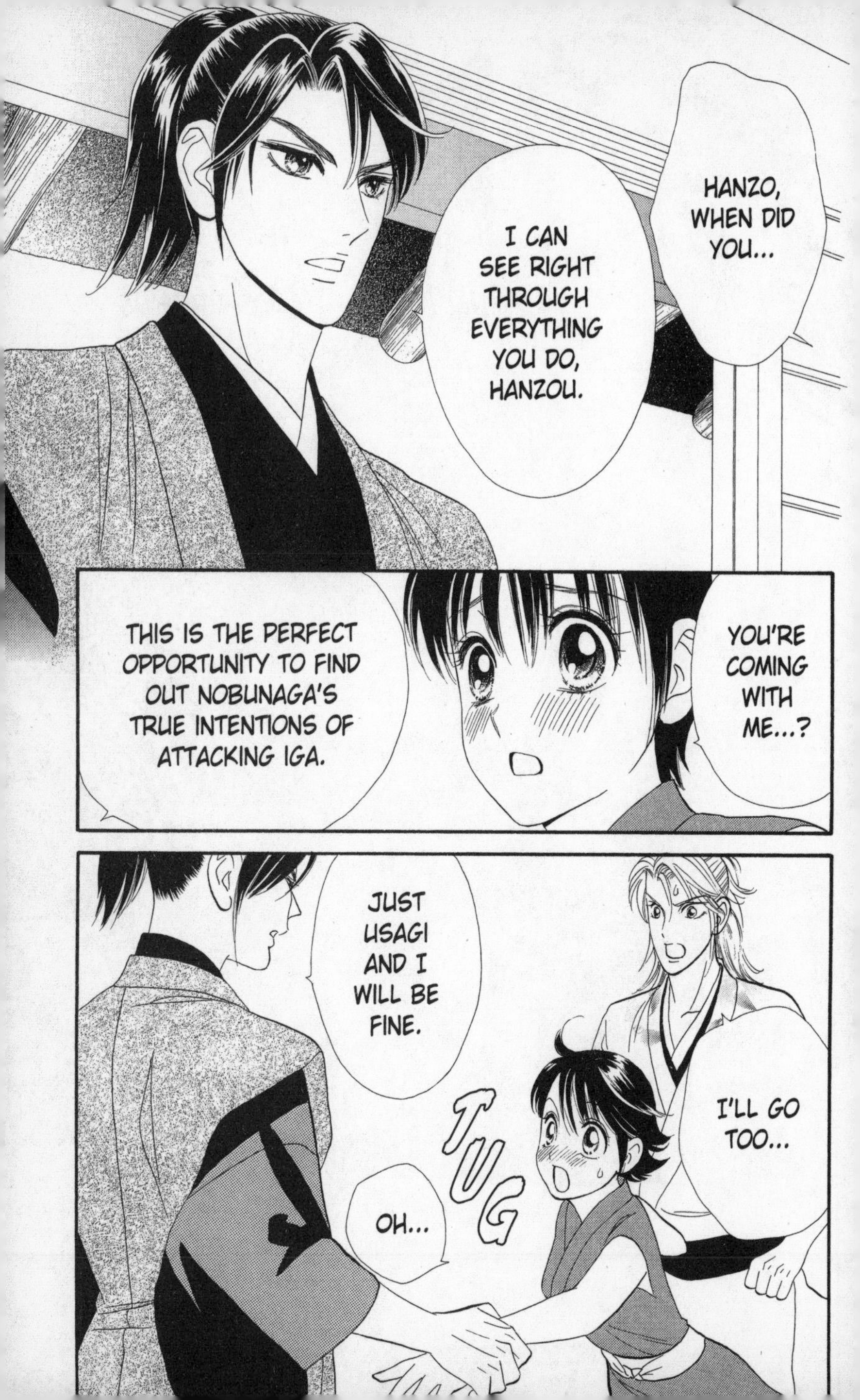
HANZO, WHEN DID YOU...
I CAN SEE RIGHT THROUGH EVERYTHING YOU DO, HANZOU.
YOU'RE COMING WITH ME...?
THIS IS THE PERFECT OPPORTUNITY TO FIND OUT NOBUNAGA'S TRUE INTENTIONS OF ATTACKING IGA.
I'LL GO TOO...
JUST USAGI AND I WILL BE FINE.
TUG
OH...

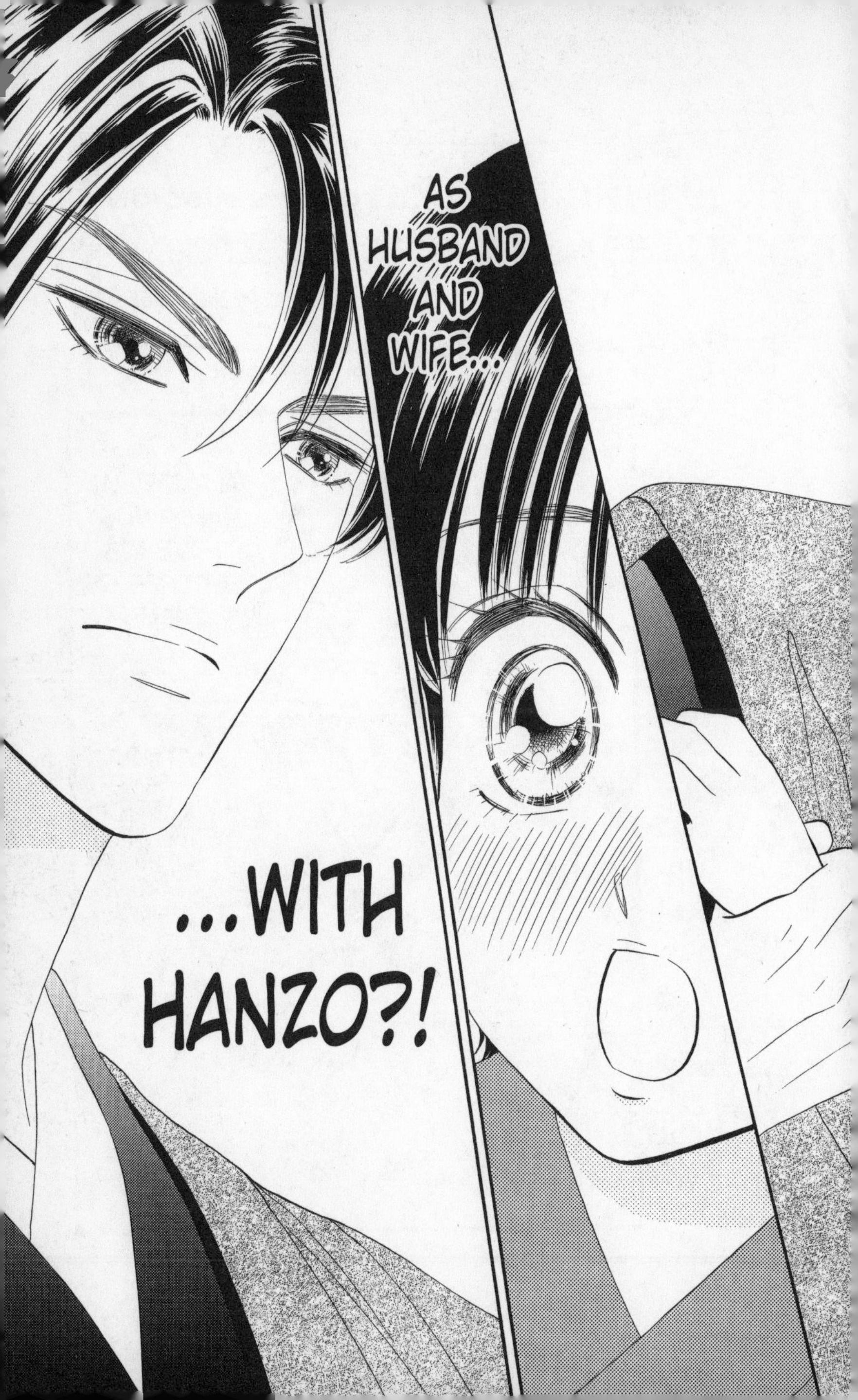
AS HUSBAND AND WIFE...
...WITH HANZO?!

TAIL OF THE MOON EXTRA: TODAY'S MISSION

"I WANT TO SEE HANZO IN A LITTLE LEAGUE LOOK."♡

-KYAKYA, SAITAMA PREFECTURE

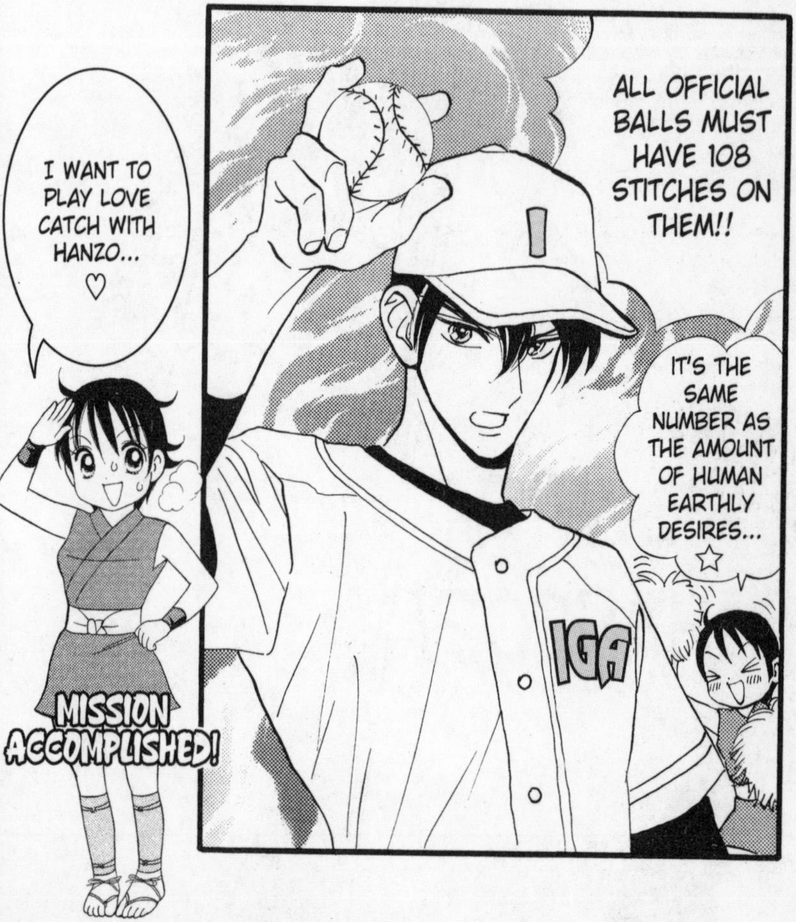
ALL OFFICIAL BALLS MUST HAVE 108 STITCHES ON THEM!!
IT'S THE SAME NUMBER AS THE AMOUNT OF HUMAN EARTHLY DESIRES... ☆
I WANT TO PLAY LOVE CATCH WITH HANZO... ♡
IGA
MISSION ACCOMPLISHED!

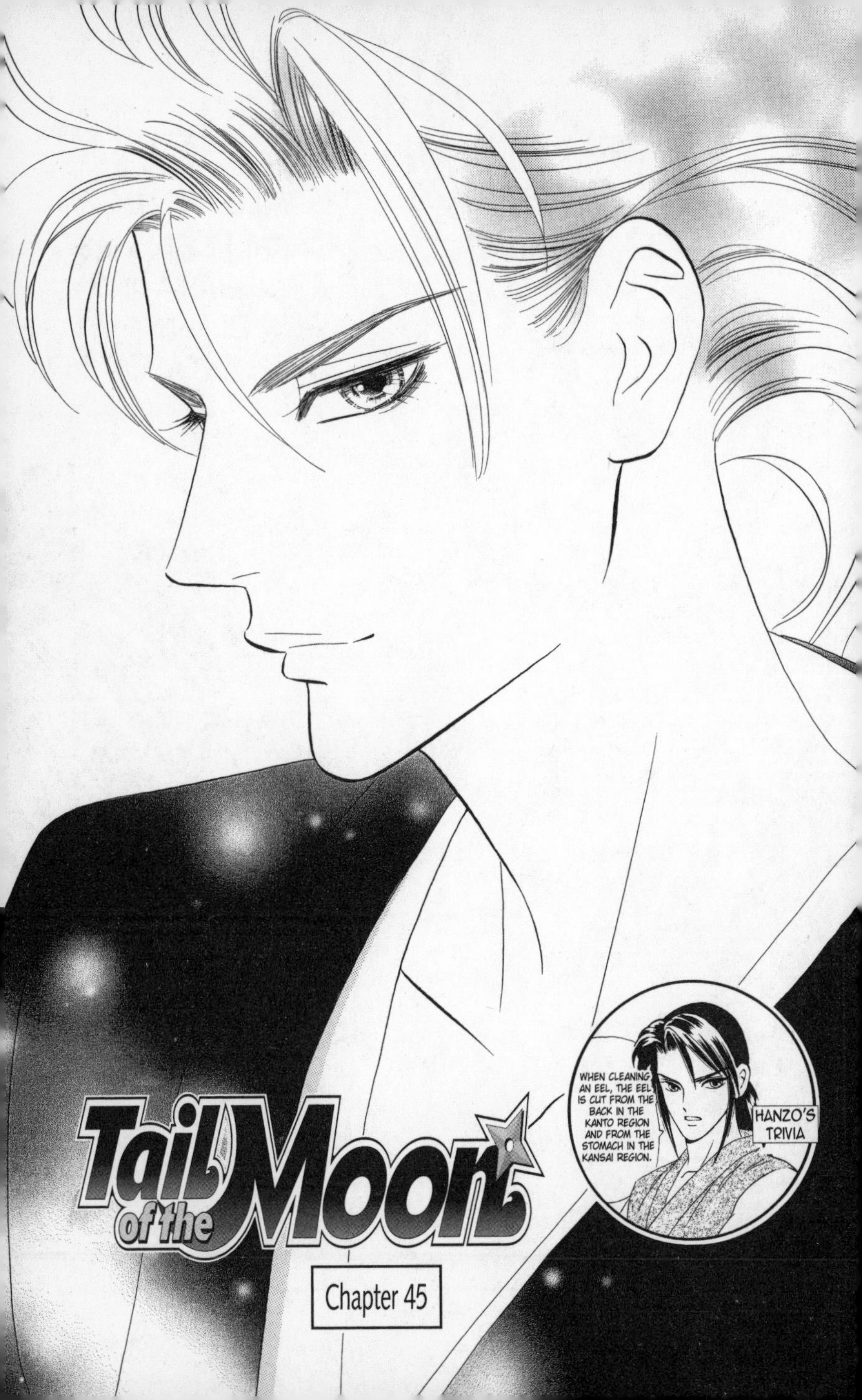
Tail of the Moon
Chapter 45
HANZO'S TRIVIA
WHEN CLEANING AN EEL, THE EEL IS CUT FROM THE BACK IN THE KANTO REGION AND FROM THE STOMACH IN THE KANSAI REGION.

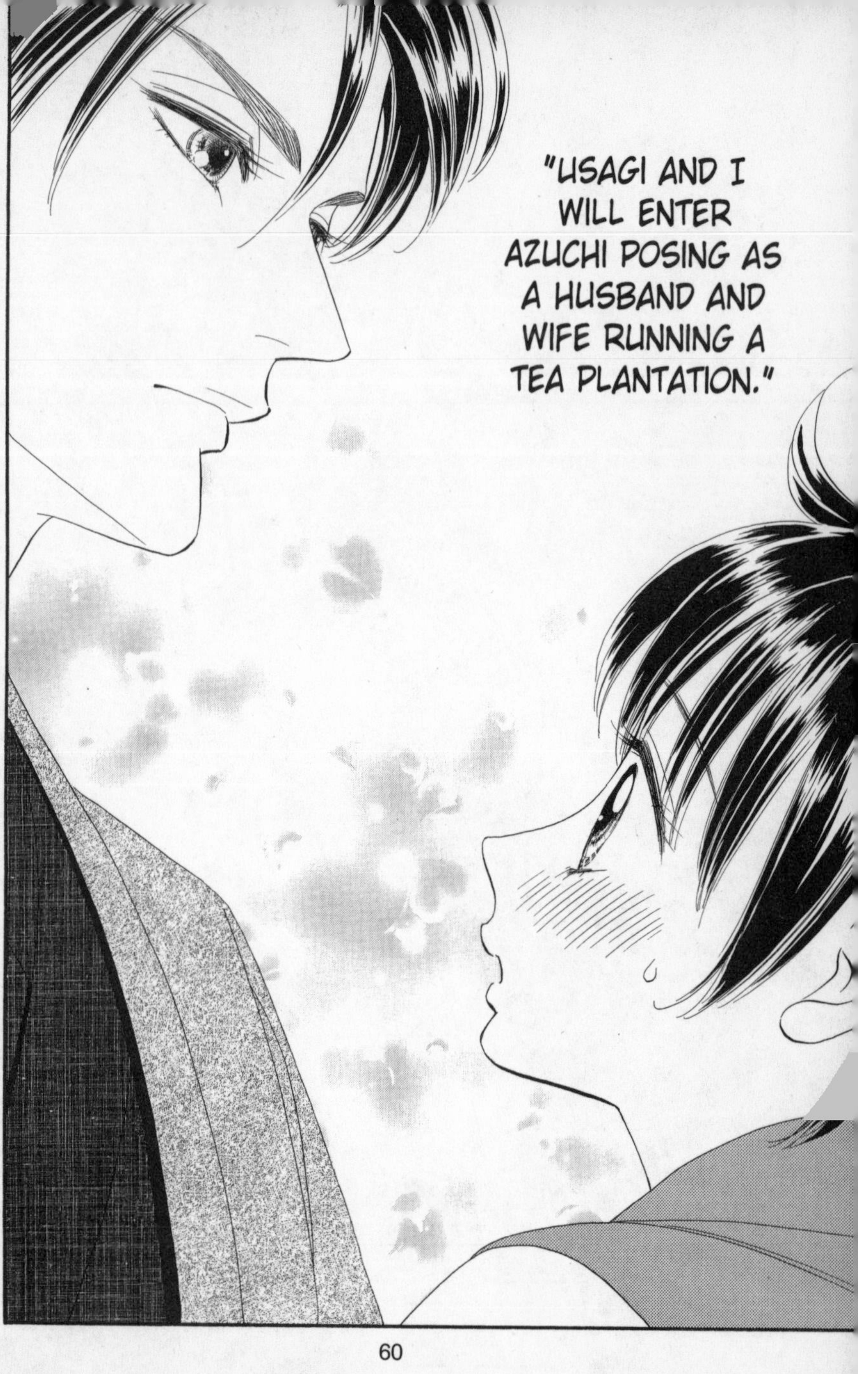
"USAGI AND I WILL ENTER AZUCHI POSING AS A HUSBAND AND WIFE RUNNING A TEA PLANTATION."

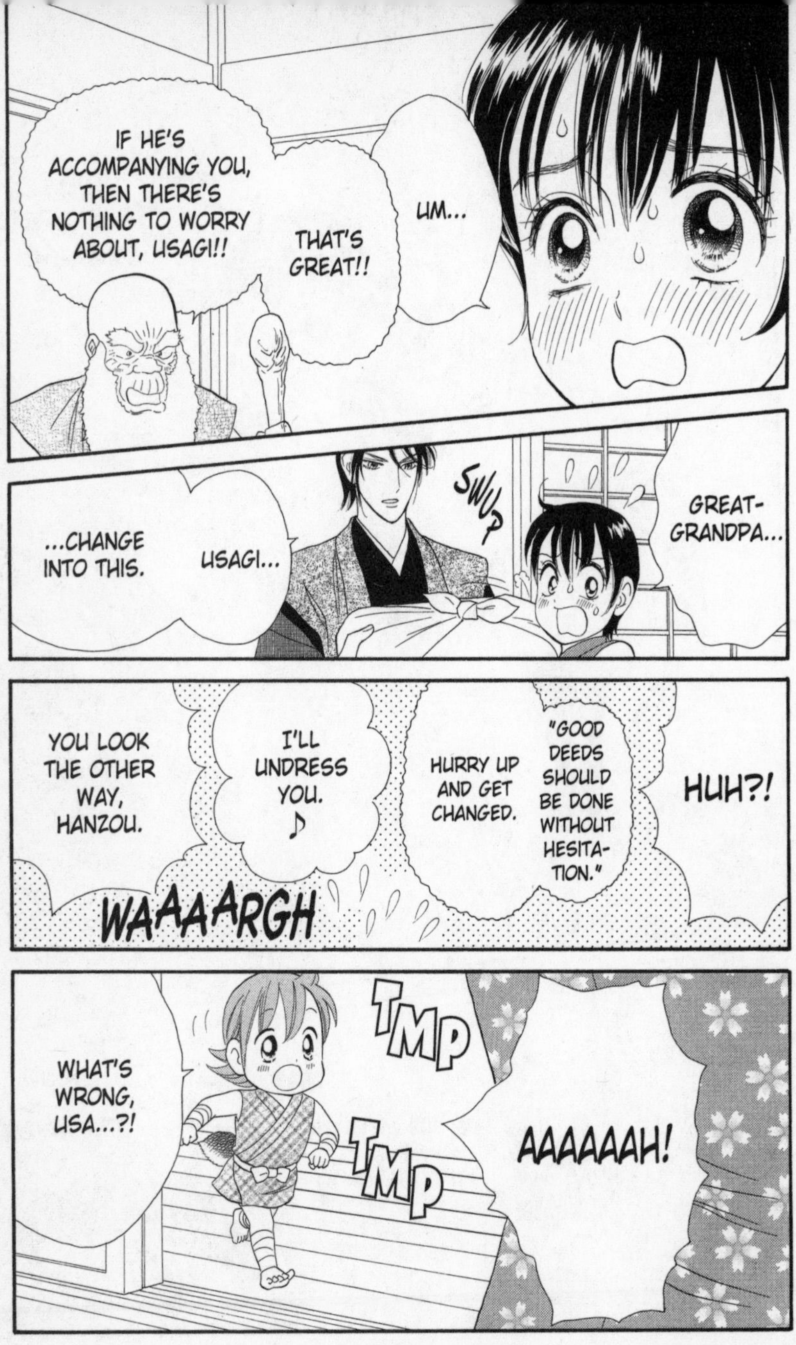
UM...
THAT'S GREAT!!
IF HE'S ACCOMPANYING YOU, THEN THERE'S NOTHING TO WORRY ABOUT, USAGI!!
GREAT-GRANDPA...
SWUP
USAGI...
...CHANGE INTO THIS.
HUH?!
"GOOD DEEDS SHOULD BE DONE WITHOUT HESITA-TION."
HURRY UP AND GET CHANGED.
I'LL UNDRESS YOU. ♪
YOU LOOK THE OTHER WAY, HANZOU.
WAAAARGH
AAAAAAH!
TMP
TMP
WHAT'S WRONG, USA...?!

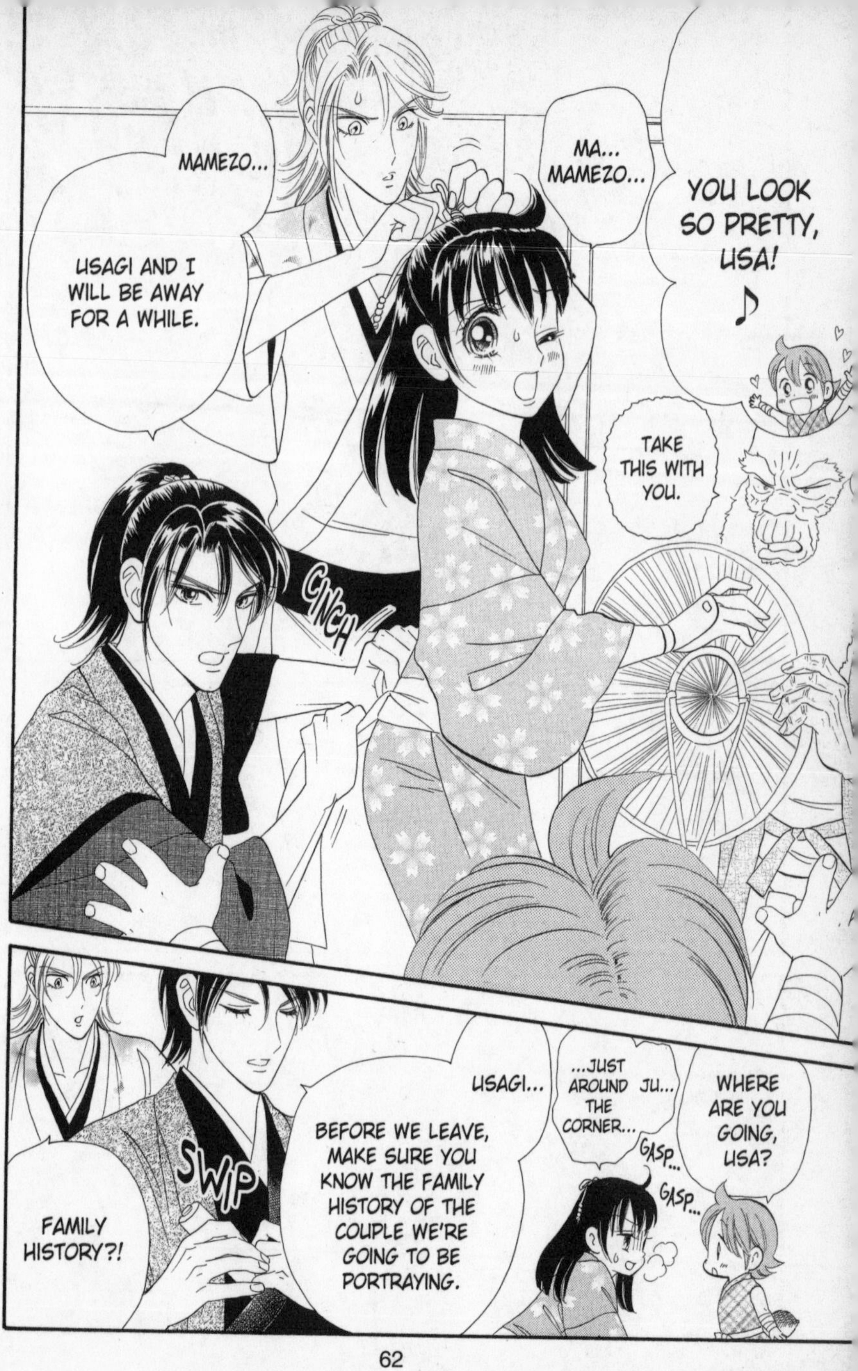
YOU LOOK SO PRETTY, USA! ♪
MA... MAMEZO...
MAMEZO...
USAGI AND I WILL BE AWAY FOR A WHILE.
TAKE THIS WITH YOU.
CINCH
WHERE ARE YOU GOING, USA?
GASP...
GASP...
...JUST AROUND JU... THE CORNER...
USAGI...
BEFORE WE LEAVE, MAKE SURE YOU KNOW THE FAMILY HISTORY OF THE COUPLE WE'RE GOING TO BE PORTRAYING.
SWIP
FAMILY HISTORY?!

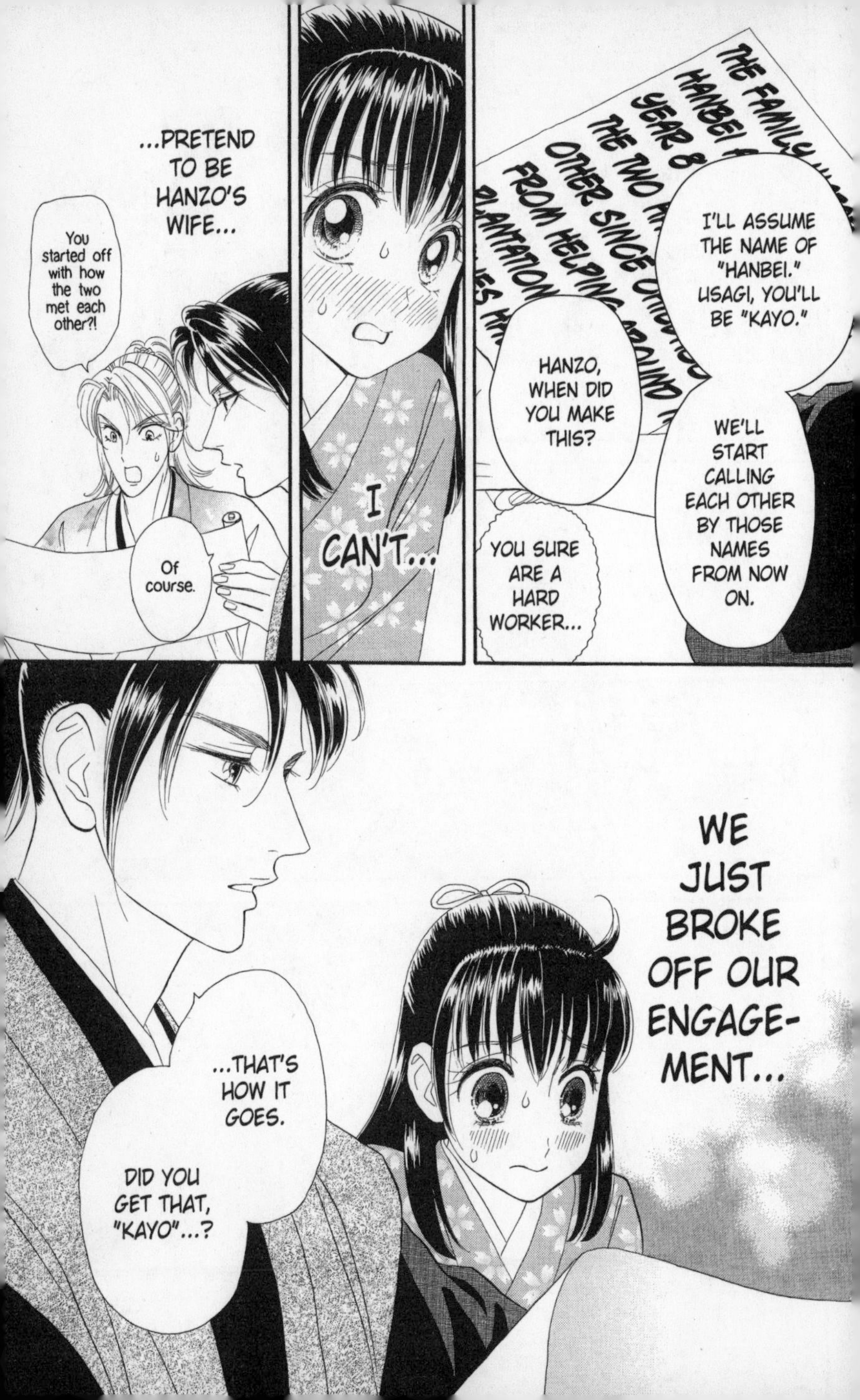
I'LL ASSUME THE NAME OF "HANBEI." USAGI, YOU'LL BE "KAYO."
WE'LL START CALLING EACH OTHER BY THOSE NAMES FROM NOW ON.
HANZO, WHEN DID YOU MAKE THIS?
YOU SURE ARE A HARD WORKER...
I CAN'T...
...PRETEND TO BE HANZO'S WIFE...
You started off with how the two met each other?!
Of course.
WE JUST BROKE OFF OUR ENGAGEMENT...
...THAT'S HOW IT GOES.
DID YOU GET THAT, "KAYO"...?

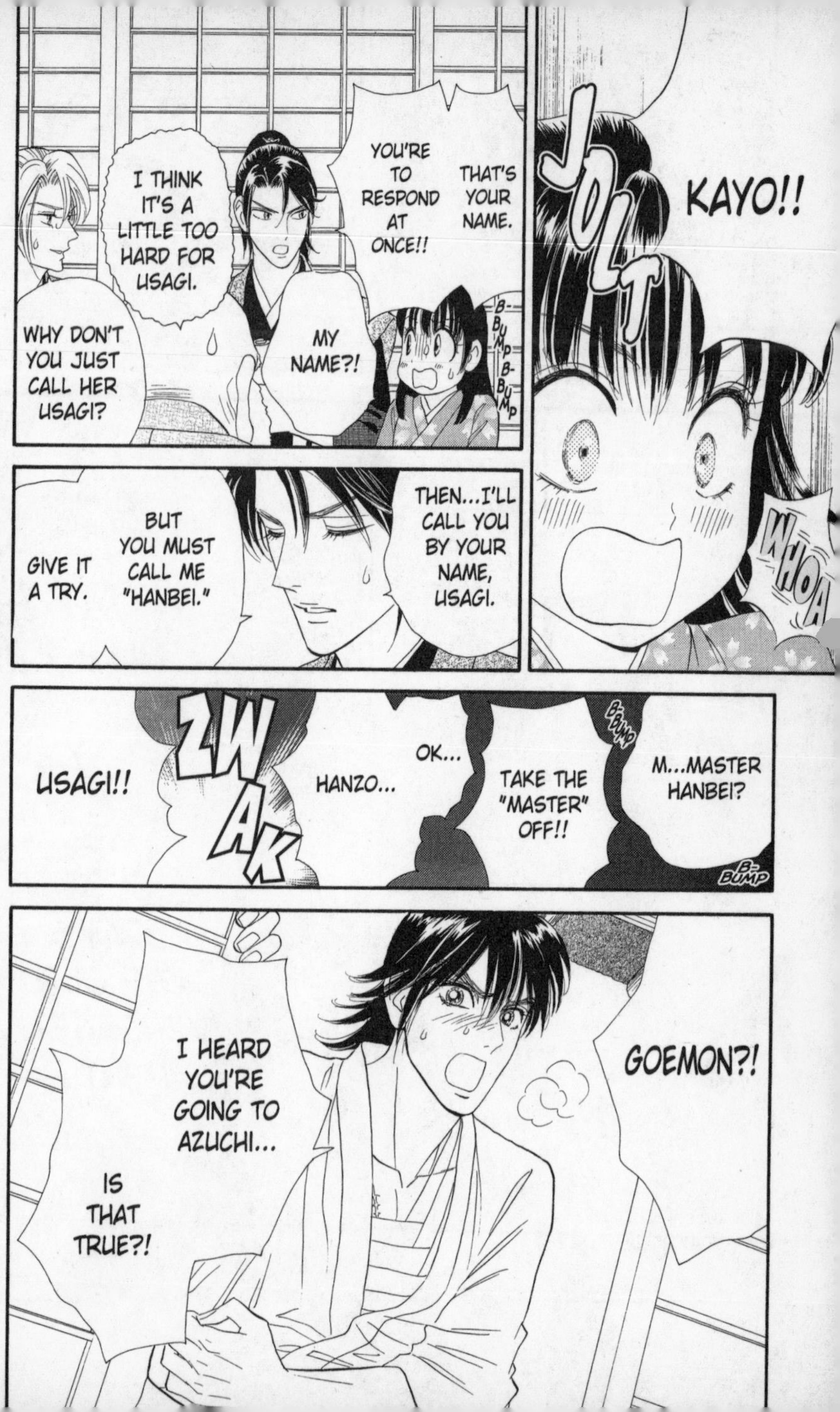
KAYO!!
JOLT
WHOA
THAT'S YOUR NAME.
YOU'RE TO RESPOND AT ONCE!!
MY NAME?!
B-BUMP B-BUMP
I THINK IT'S A LITTLE TOO HARD FOR USAGI.
WHY DON'T YOU JUST CALL HER USAGI?
THEN...I'LL CALL YOU BY YOUR NAME, USAGI.
BUT YOU MUST CALL ME "HANBEI."
GIVE IT A TRY.
B-BUMP
M...MASTER HANBEI?
B-BUMP
TAKE THE "MASTER" OFF!!
OK...
HANZO...
ZWAK
USAGI!!
GOEMON?!
I HEARD YOU'RE GOING TO AZUCHI...
IS THAT TRUE?!

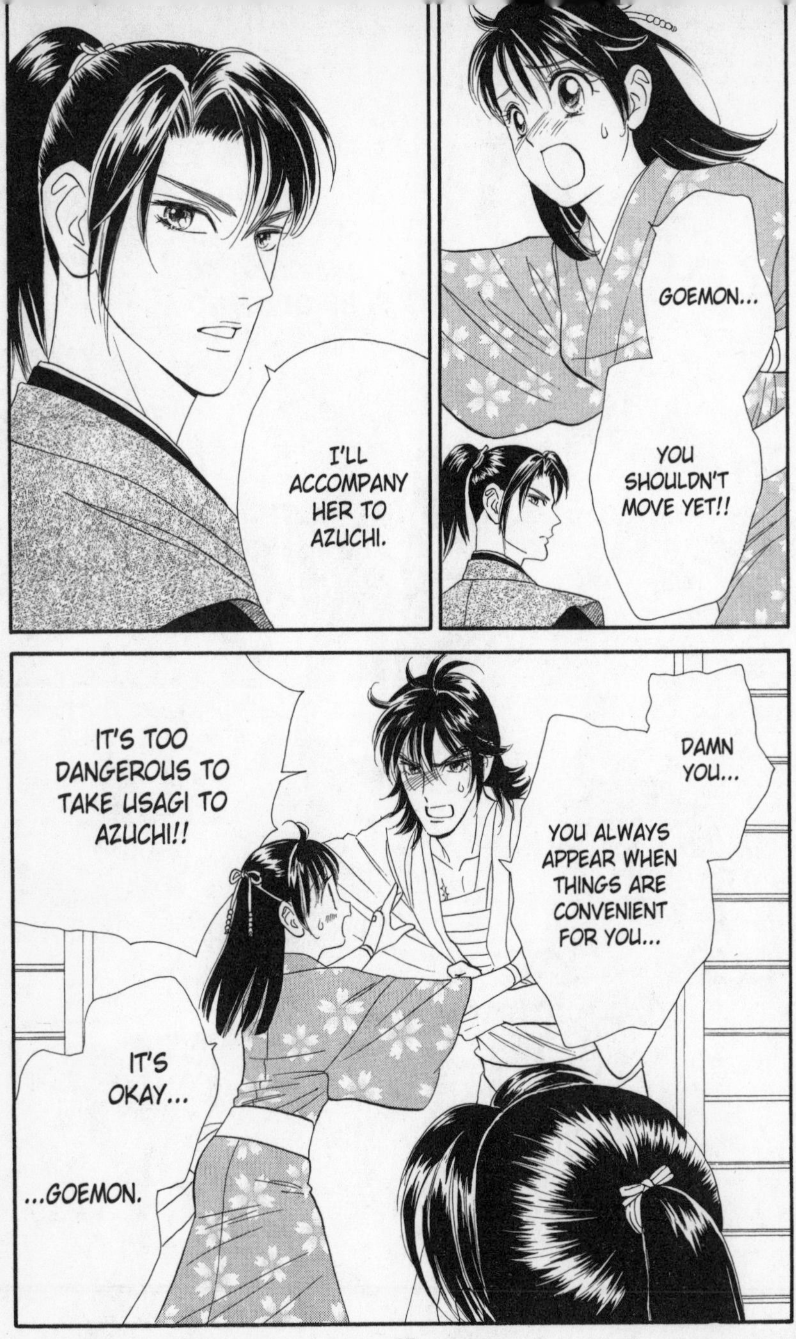
GOEMON...
YOU SHOULDN'T MOVE YET!!
I'LL ACCOMPANY HER TO AZUCHI.
DAMN YOU...
YOU ALWAYS APPEAR WHEN THINGS ARE CONVENIENT FOR YOU...
IT'S TOO DANGEROUS TO TAKE USAGI TO AZUCHI!!
IT'S OKAY...
...GOEMON.

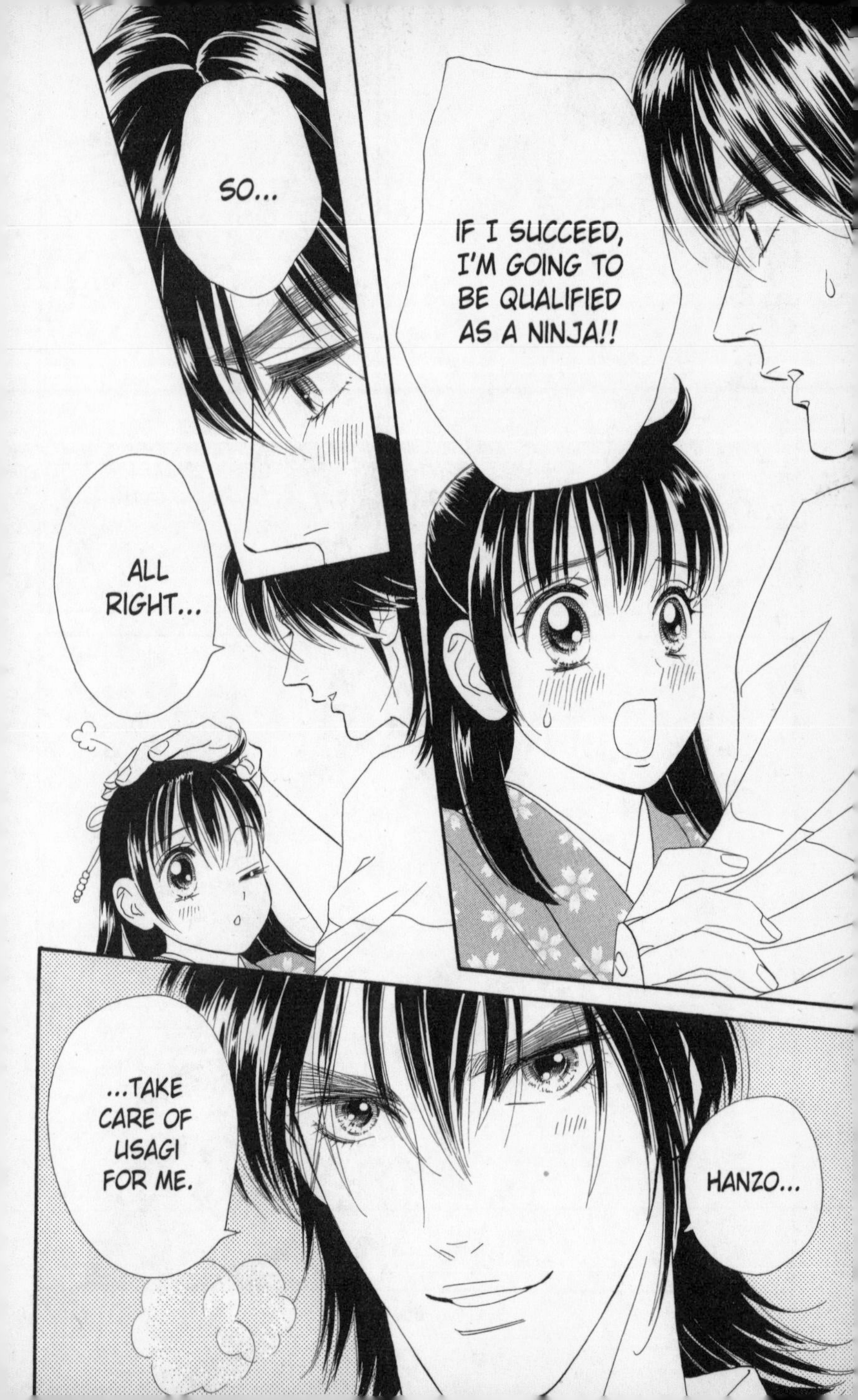
IF I SUCCEED, I'M GOING TO BE QUALIFIED AS A NINJA!!
SO...
ALL RIGHT...
HANZO...
...TAKE CARE OF USAGI FOR ME.

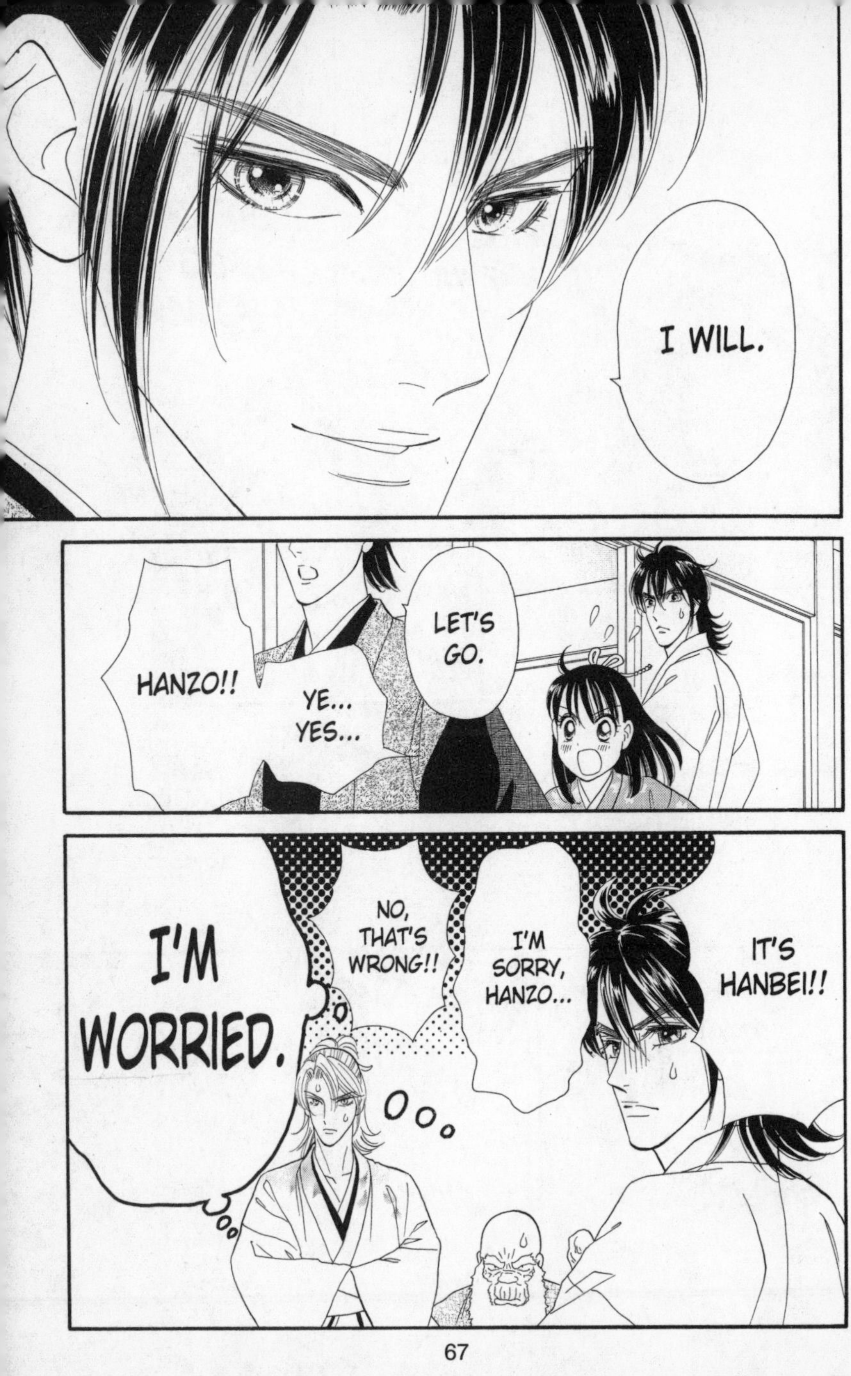
I WILL.
LET'S GO.
HANZO!!
YE... YES...
IT'S HANBEI!!
I'M SORRY, HANZO...
NO, THAT'S WRONG!!
I'M WORRIED.

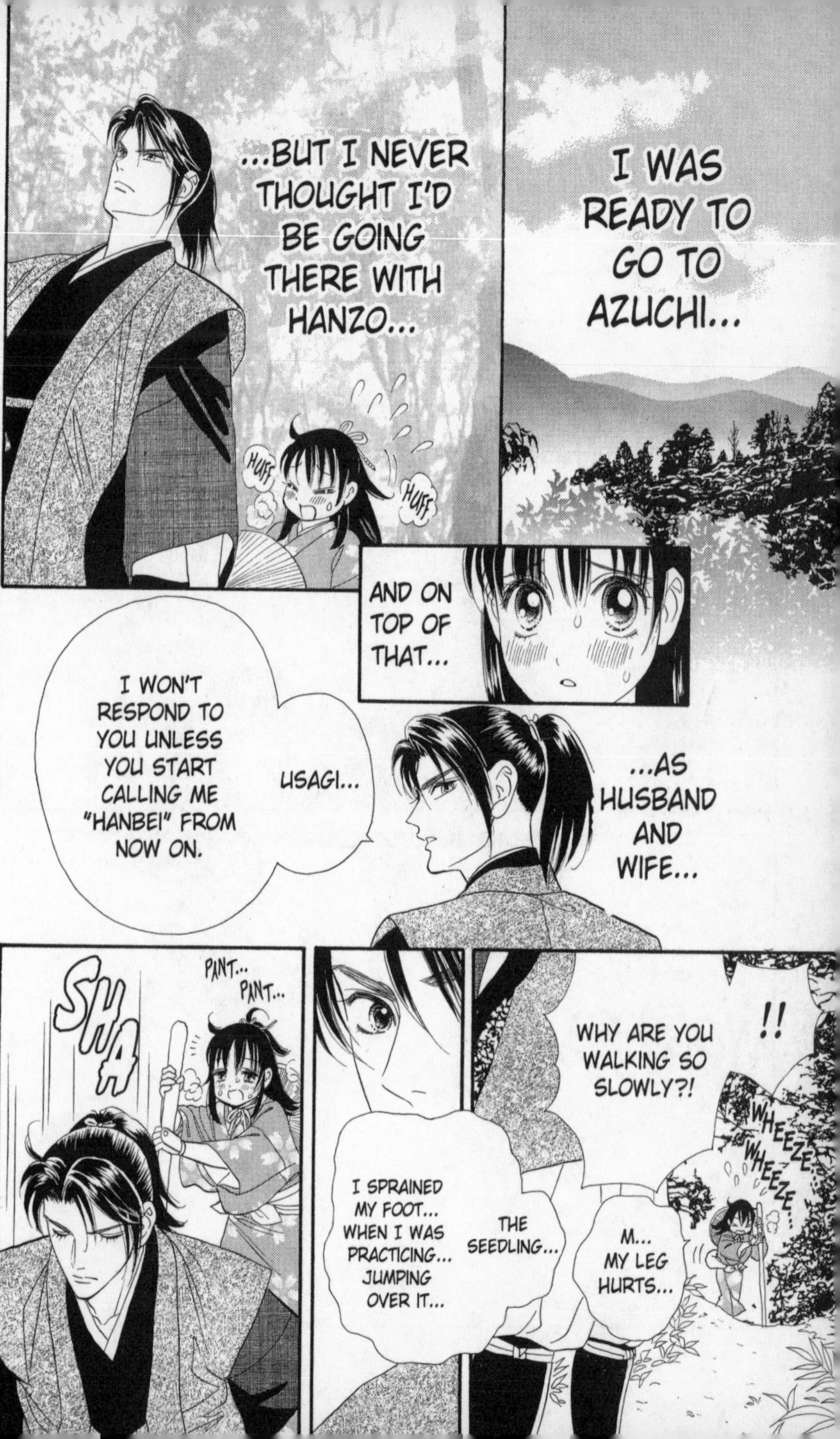
I WAS READY TO GO TO AZUCHI...
...BUT I NEVER THOUGHT I'D BE GOING THERE WITH HANZO...
HUFF
HUFF
AND ON TOP OF THAT...
...AS HUSBAND AND WIFE...
USAGI...
I WON'T RESPOND TO YOU UNLESS YOU START CALLING ME "HANBEI" FROM NOW ON.
!!
WHY ARE YOU WALKING SO SLOWLY?!
WHEEZE
WHEEZE
M... MY LEG HURTS...
THE SEEDLING...
I SPRAINED MY FOOT... WHEN I WAS PRACTICING... JUMPING OVER IT...
SHA
PANT... PANT...

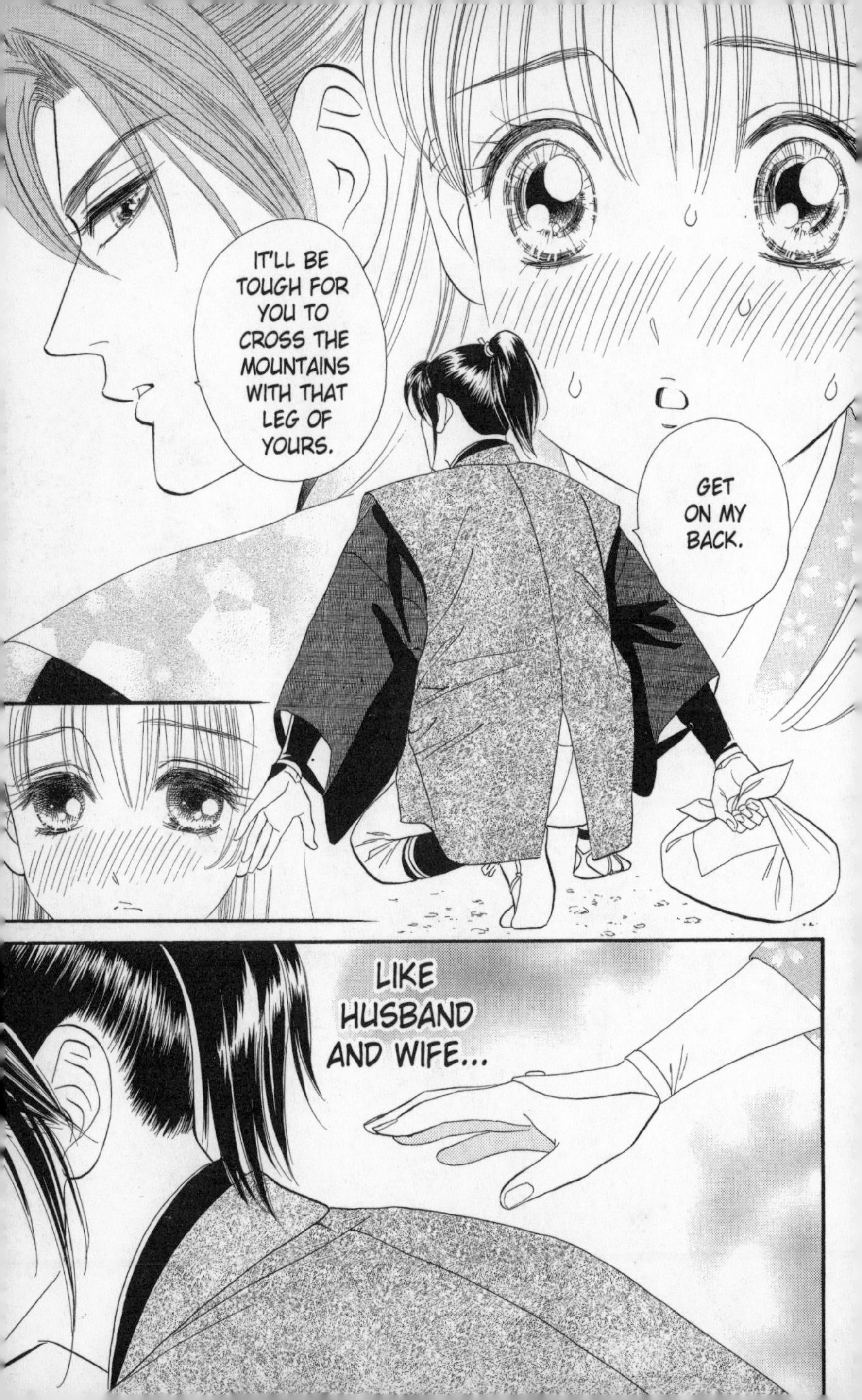
GET ON MY BACK.
IT'LL BE TOUGH FOR YOU TO CROSS THE MOUNTAINS WITH THAT LEG OF YOURS.
LIKE HUSBAND AND WIFE...

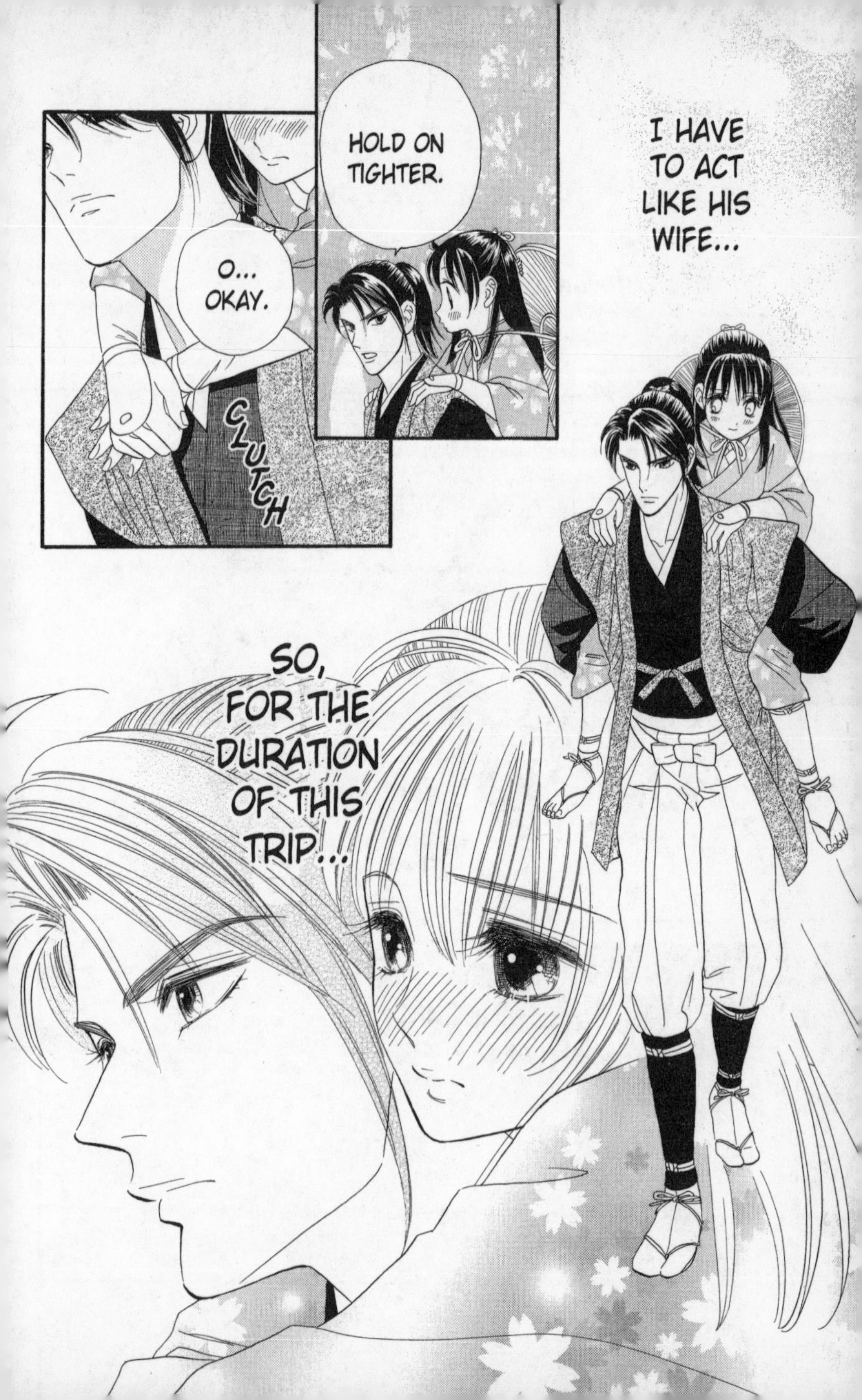
HOLD ON TIGHTER.
O... OKAY.
CLUTCH
I HAVE TO ACT LIKE HIS WIFE...
SO, FOR THE DURATION OF THIS TRIP...

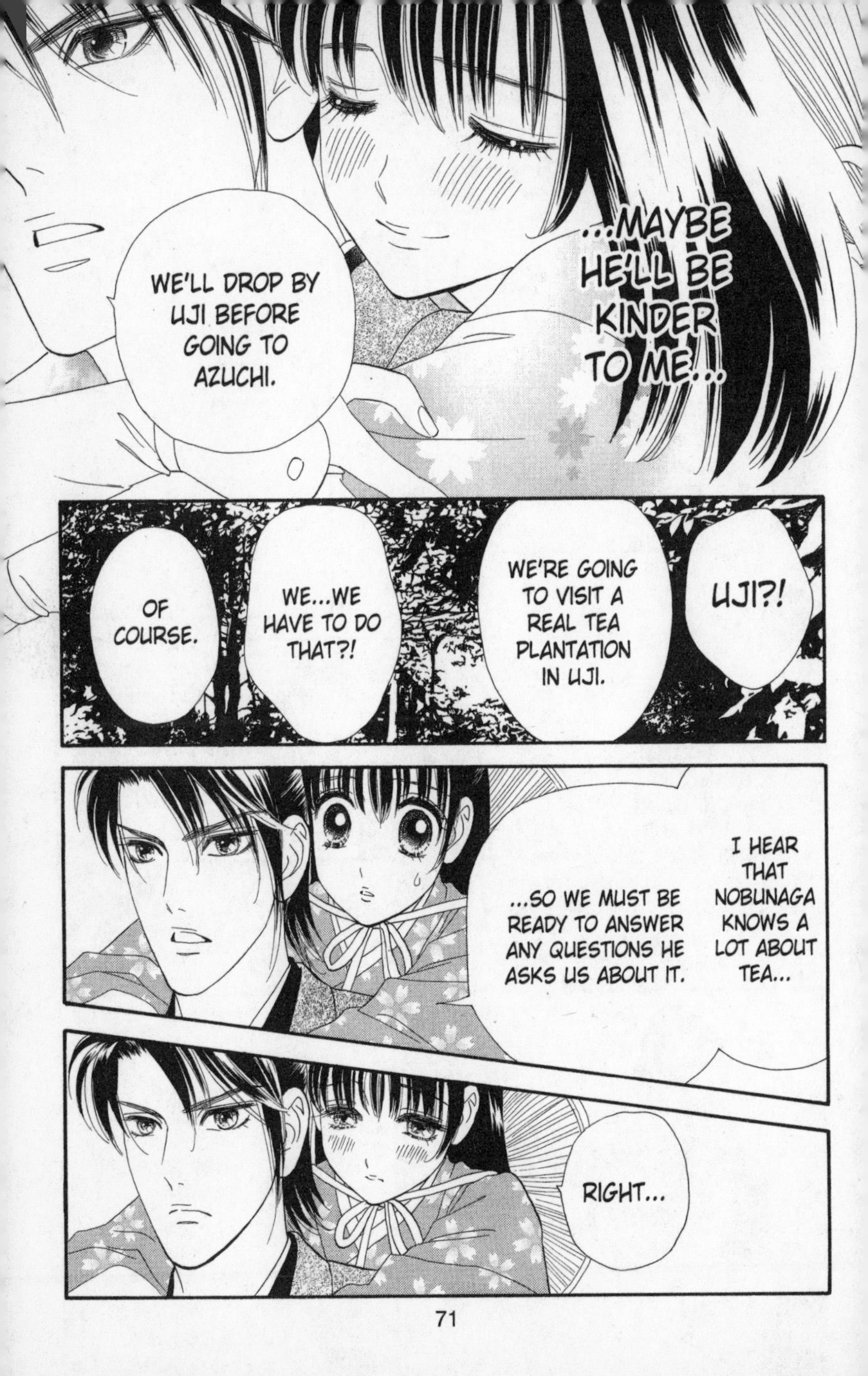
...MAYBE HE'LL BE KINDER TO ME...
WE'LL DROP BY UJI BEFORE GOING TO AZUCHI.
UJI?!
WE'RE GOING TO VISIT A REAL TEA PLANTATION IN UJI.
WE...WE HAVE TO DO THAT?!
OF COURSE.
I HEAR THAT NOBUNAGA KNOWS A LOT ABOUT TEA...
...SO WE MUST BE READY TO ANSWER ANY QUESTIONS HE ASKS US ABOUT IT.
RIGHT...

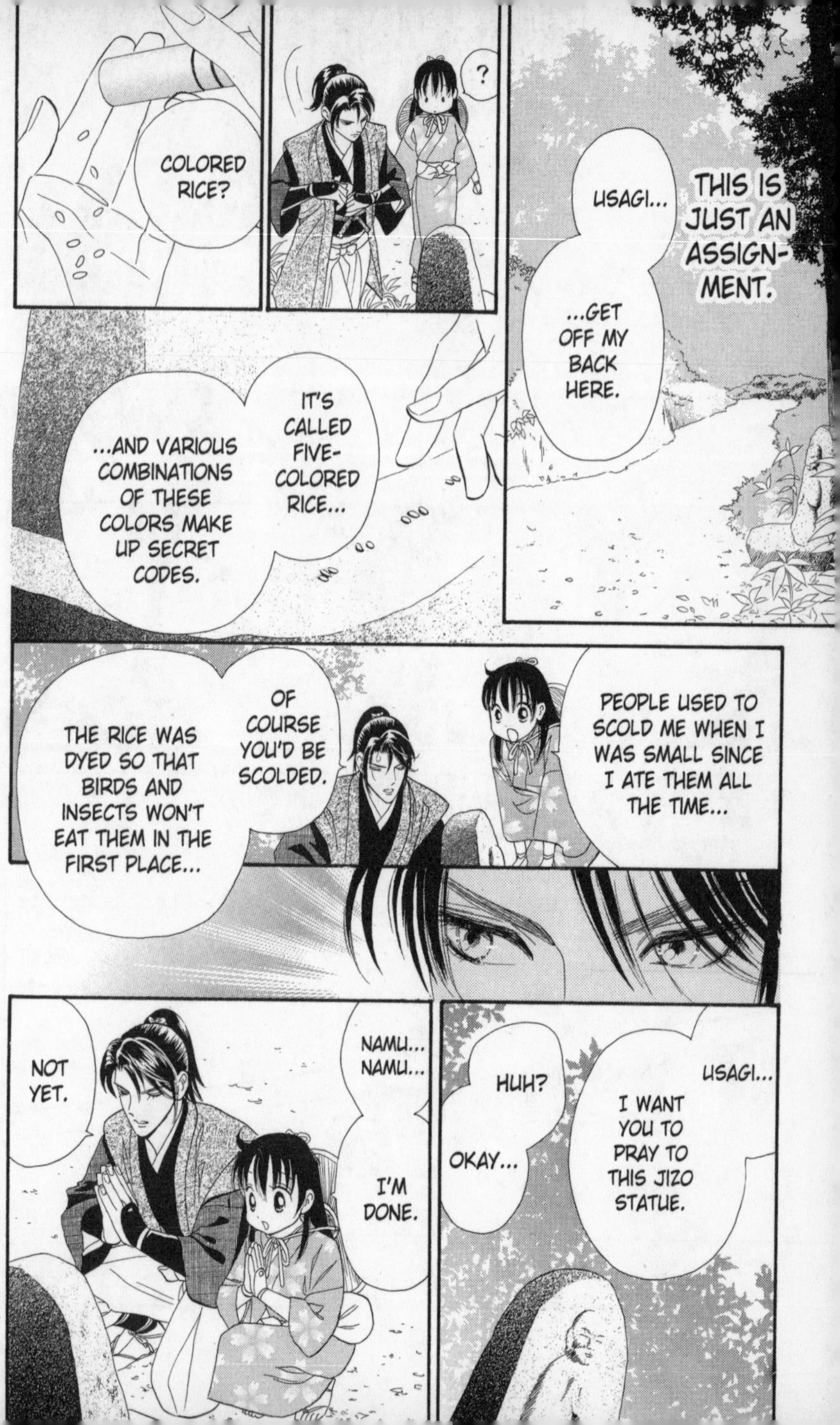
THIS IS JUST AN ASSIGNMENT.
USAGI...
...GET OFF MY BACK HERE.
?
COLORED RICE?
IT'S CALLED FIVE-COLORED RICE...
...AND VARIOUS COMBINATIONS OF THESE COLORS MAKE UP SECRET CODES.
PEOPLE USED TO SCOLD ME WHEN I WAS SMALL SINCE I ATE THEM ALL THE TIME...
OF COURSE YOU'D BE SCOLDED.
THE RICE WAS DYED SO THAT BIRDS AND INSECTS WON'T EAT THEM IN THE FIRST PLACE...
USAGI...
I WANT YOU TO PRAY TO THIS JIZO STATUE.
HUH?
OKAY...
NAMU... NAMU...
I'M DONE.
NOT YET.

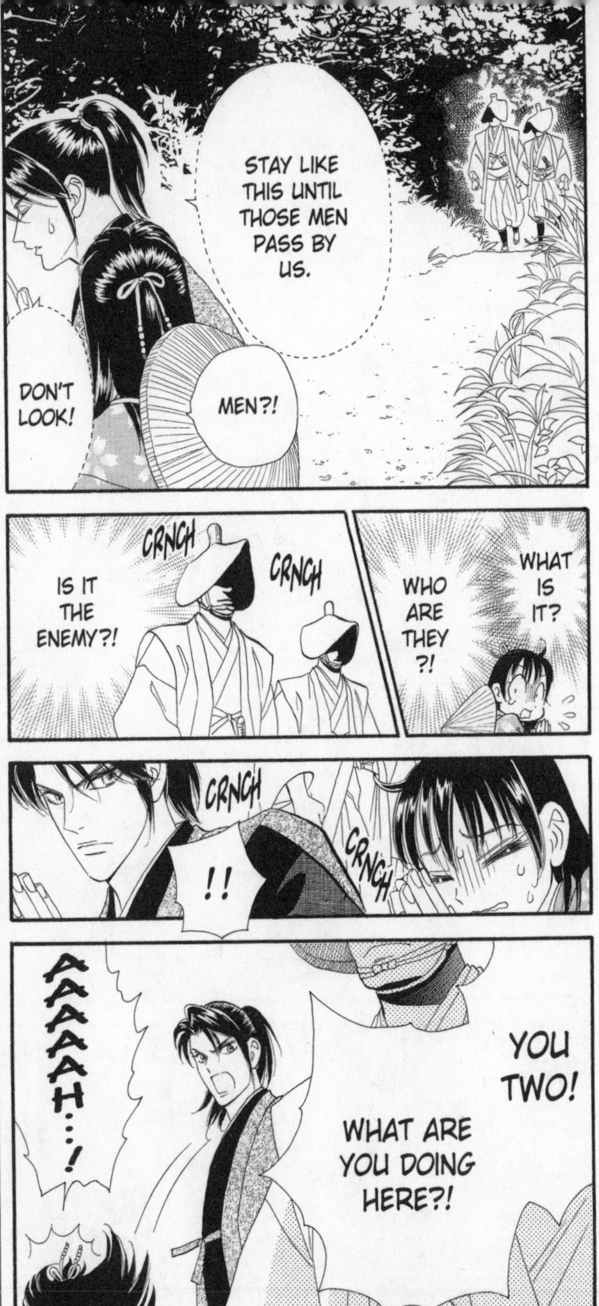
STAY LIKE THIS UNTIL THOSE MEN PASS BY US.
MEN?!
DON'T LOOK!
WHAT IS IT?
WHO ARE THEY ?!
CRNCH
CRNCH
IS IT THE ENEMY?!
CRNCH
!!
CRNCH
YOU TWO!
WHAT ARE YOU DOING HERE?!
AAAAAH...!

UE-RIN'S WAY OF THE MANGA ⑦

"Making my debut with the first manga I sent" ♪

Not only did that dream not come true, but I was faced with a huge sense of loss as well. I decided to take a good look at the reason behind my failure.

My current self + What I lack = Final result

Though I was one of the better drawers at school, there were a lot of people who were far better than me out in the world. Even if I work ten times as hard as those people, I may never be able to get half as good as them...but I'll do what I can!!

Come to think of it, I was a pretty passionate middle schooler...

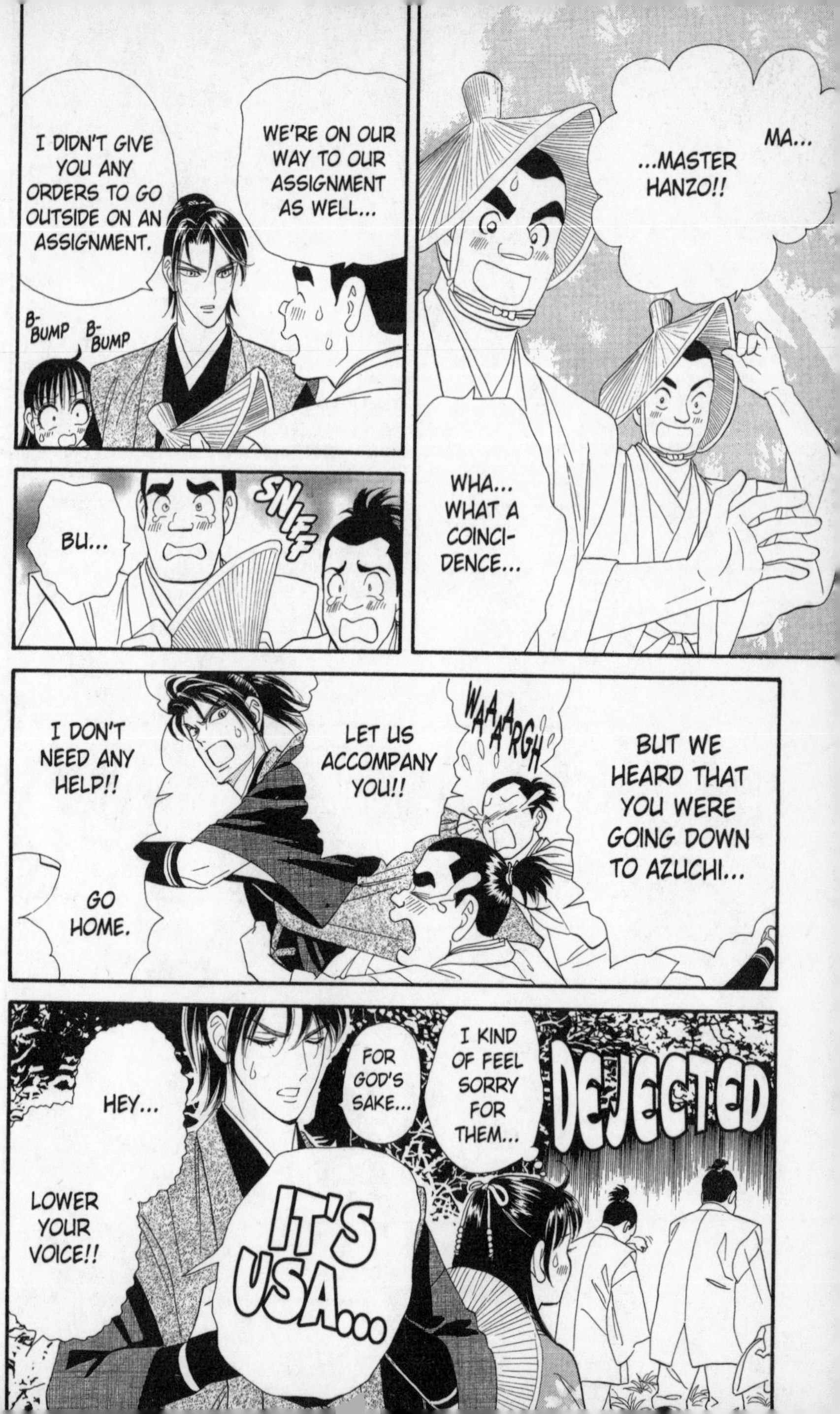
MA...
...MASTER HANZO!!
WHA... WHAT A COINCIDENCE...
WE'RE ON OUR WAY TO OUR ASSIGNMENT AS WELL...
I DIDN'T GIVE YOU ANY ORDERS TO GO OUTSIDE ON AN ASSIGNMENT.
B-BUMP B-BUMP
SNIFF
BU...
BUT WE HEARD THAT YOU WERE GOING DOWN TO AZUCHI...
WAAARGH
LET US ACCOMPANY YOU!!
I DON'T NEED ANY HELP!!
GO HOME.
DEJECTED
I KIND OF FEEL SORRY FOR THEM...
FOR GOD'S SAKE...
HEY...
IT'S USA...
LOWER YOUR VOICE!!

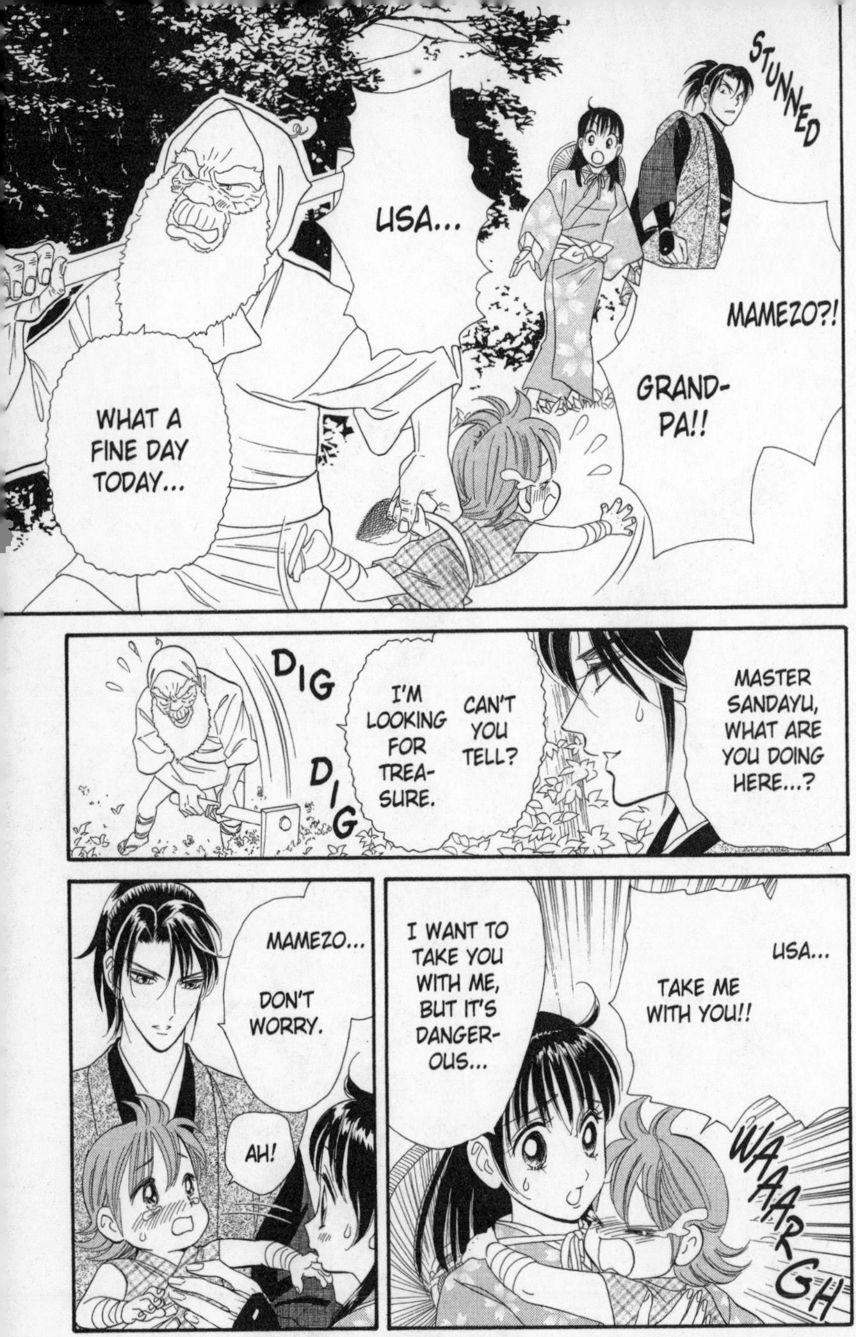
STUNNED
MAMEZO?!
GRAND-PA!!
USA...
WHAT A FINE DAY TODAY...
MASTER SANDAYU, WHAT ARE YOU DOING HERE...?
CAN'T YOU TELL?
I'M LOOKING FOR TREA-SURE.
DIG DIG DIG
USA...
TAKE ME WITH YOU!!
I WANT TO TAKE YOU WITH ME, BUT IT'S DANGER-OUS...
WAAARGH
MAMEZO...
DON'T WORRY.
AH!

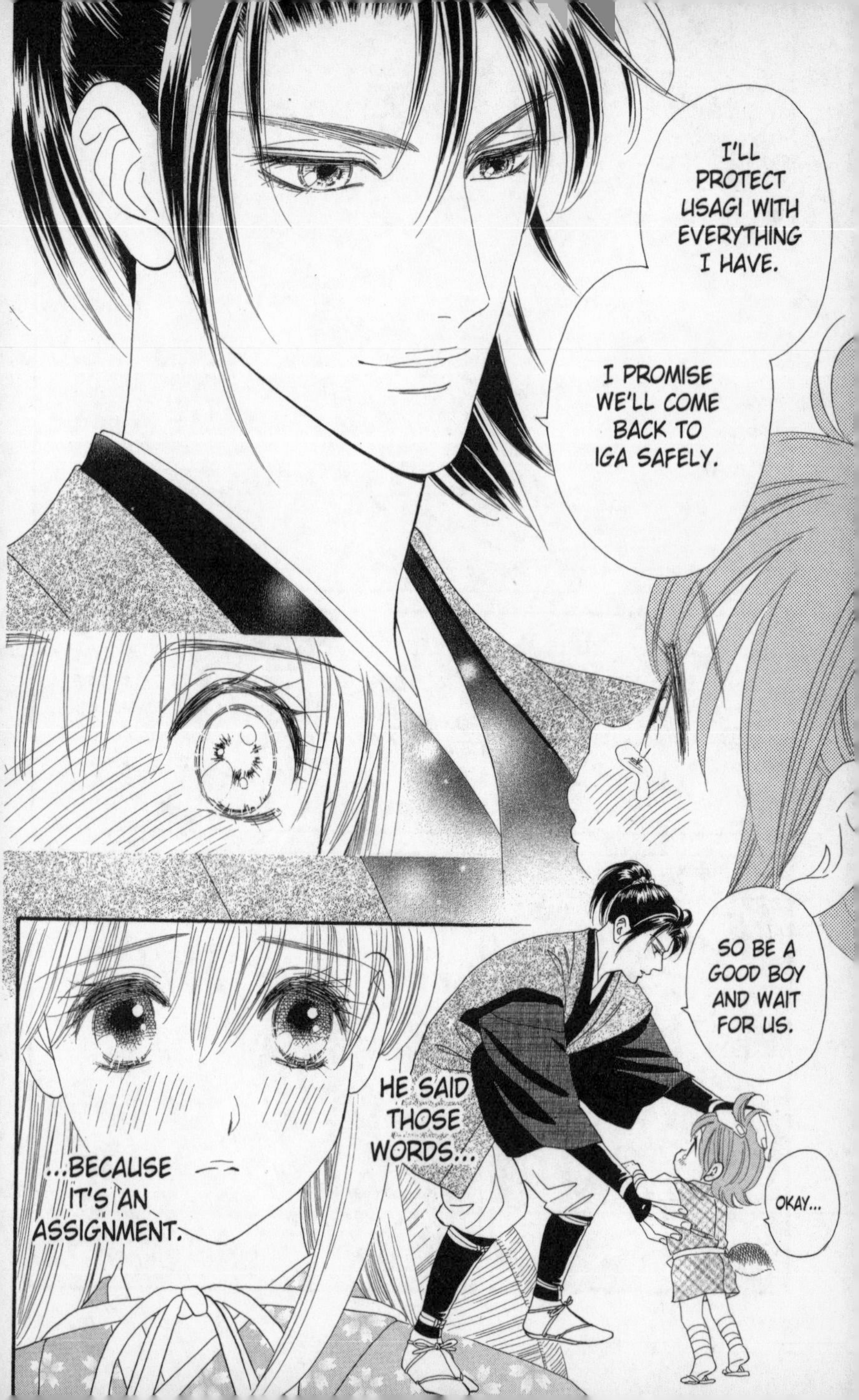
I'LL PROTECT USAGI WITH EVERYTHING I HAVE.
I PROMISE WE'LL COME BACK TO IGA SAFELY.
SO BE A GOOD BOY AND WAIT FOR US.
OKAY...
HE SAID THOSE WORDS...
...BECAUSE IT'S AN ASSIGNMENT.

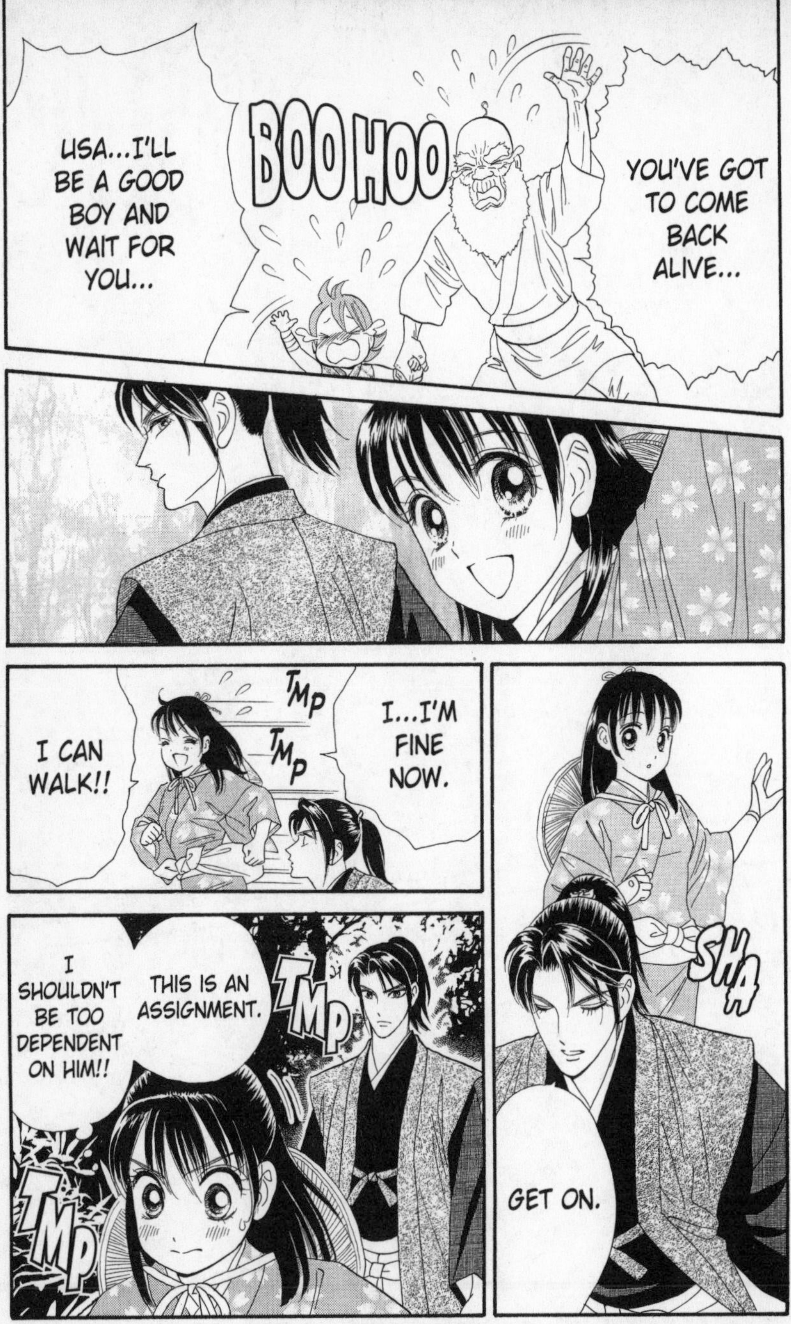
YOU'VE GOT TO COME BACK ALIVE...
BOO HOO
USA...I'LL BE A GOOD BOY AND WAIT FOR YOU...
SHA
GET ON.
I...I'M FINE NOW.
TMP
TMP
I CAN WALK!!
THIS IS AN ASSIGNMENT.
TMP
I SHOULDN'T BE TOO DEPENDENT ON HIM!!
TMP

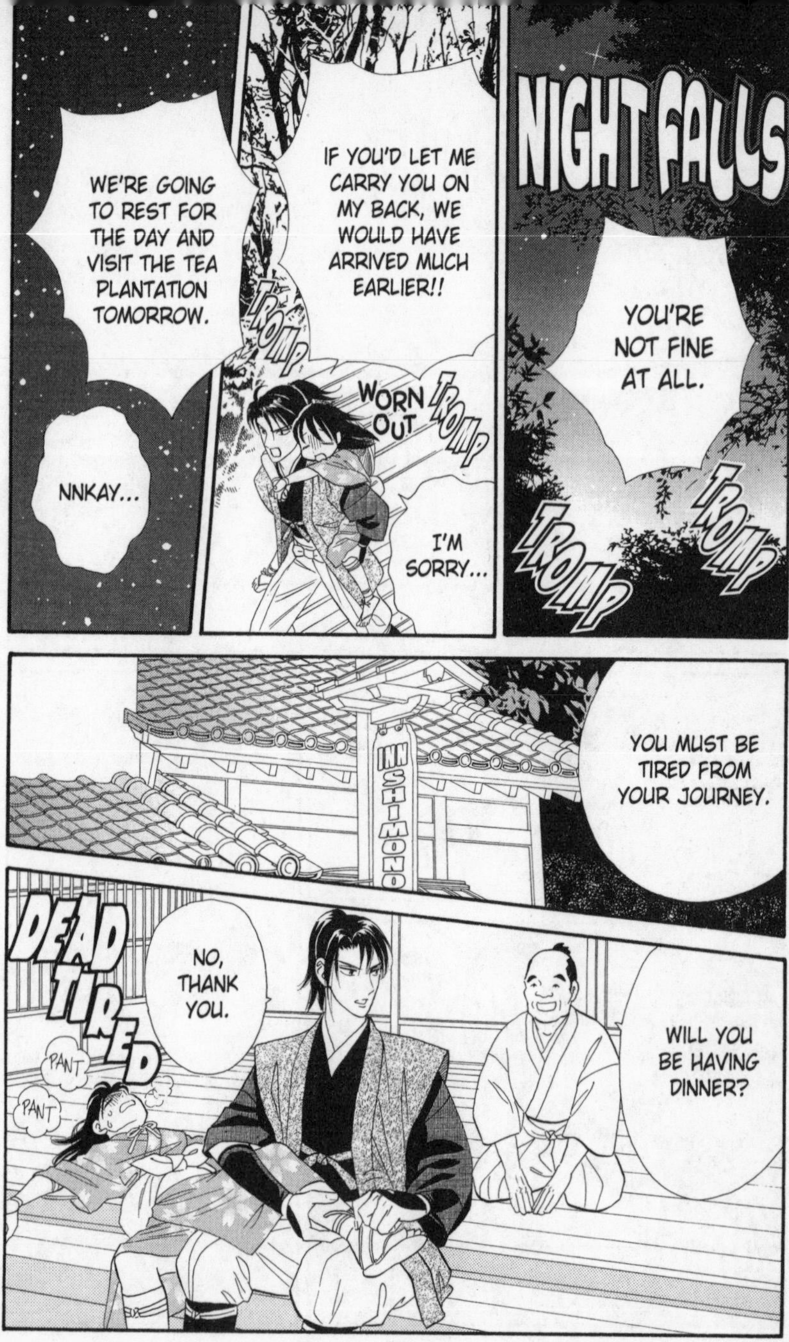
NIGHT FALLS
YOU'RE NOT FINE AT ALL.
TROMP
TROMP
IF YOU'D LET ME CARRY YOU ON MY BACK, WE WOULD HAVE ARRIVED MUCH EARLIER!!
TROMP
WORN OUT
TROMP
I'M SORRY...
WE'RE GOING TO REST FOR THE DAY AND VISIT THE TEA PLANTATION TOMORROW.
NNKAY...
YOU MUST BE TIRED FROM YOUR JOURNEY.
INN SHIMONO
WILL YOU BE HAVING DINNER?
NO, THANK YOU.
DEAD TIRED
PANT
PANT

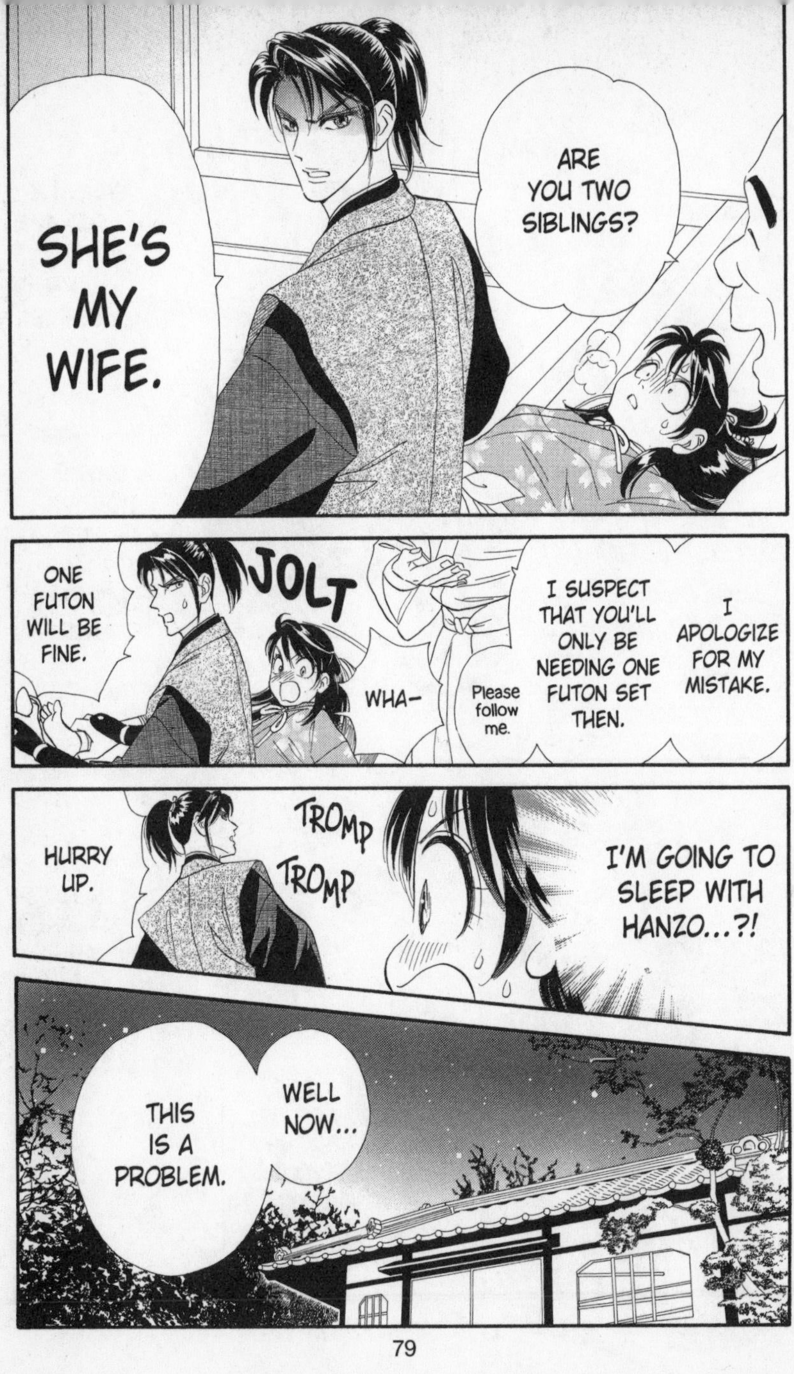
ARE YOU TWO SIBLINGS?
SHE'S MY WIFE.
I APOLOGIZE FOR MY MISTAKE.
I SUSPECT THAT YOU'LL ONLY BE NEEDING ONE FUTON SET THEN.
Please follow me.
WHA-
JOLT
ONE FUTON WILL BE FINE.
I'M GOING TO SLEEP WITH HANZO...?!
TROMP
TROMP
HURRY UP.
WELL NOW...
THIS IS A PROBLEM.

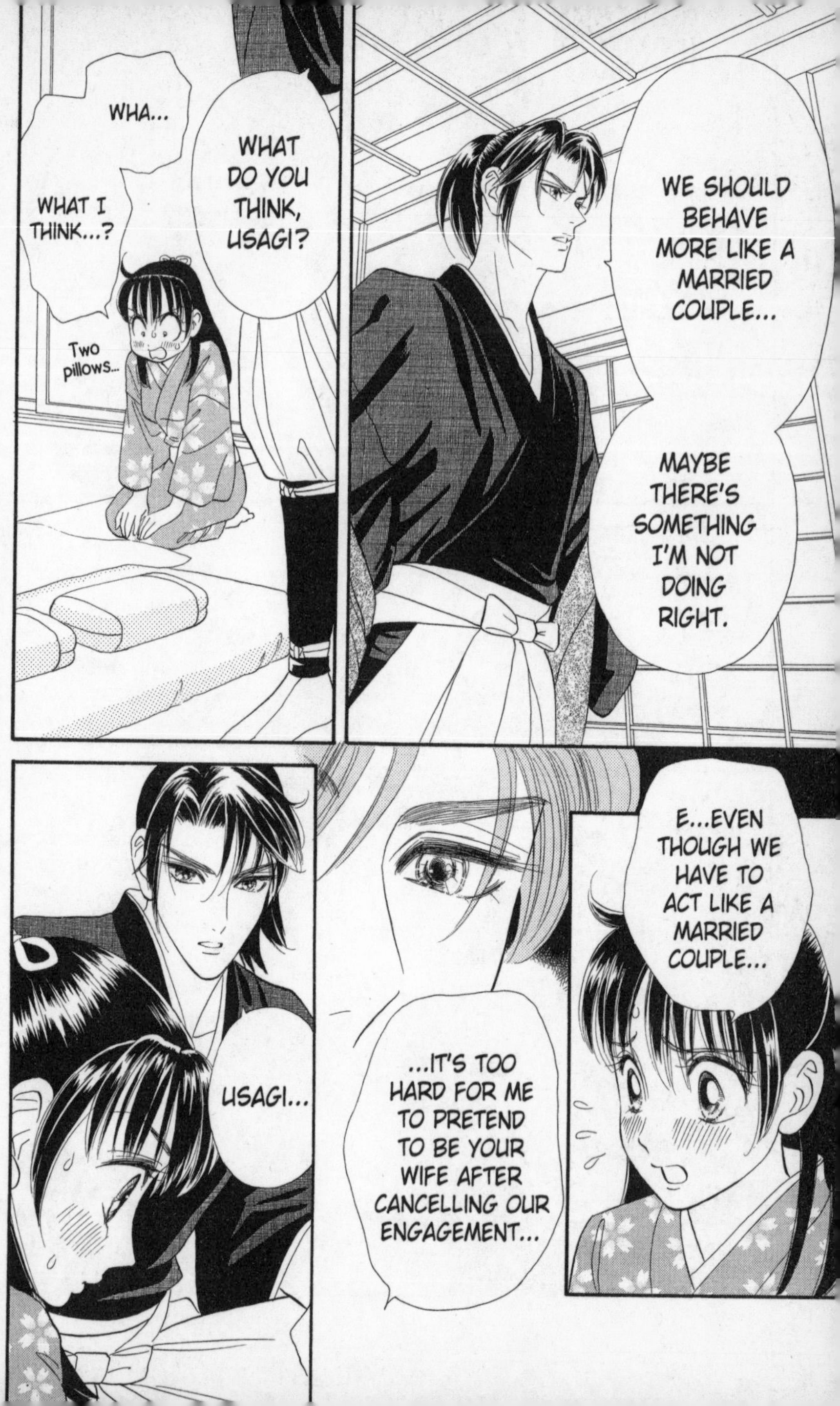
WE SHOULD BEHAVE MORE LIKE A MARRIED COUPLE...
MAYBE THERE'S SOMETHING I'M NOT DOING RIGHT.
WHAT DO YOU THINK, USAGI?
WHA...
WHAT I THINK...?
Two pillows...
E...EVEN THOUGH WE HAVE TO ACT LIKE A MARRIED COUPLE...
...IT'S TOO HARD FOR ME TO PRETEND TO BE YOUR WIFE AFTER CANCELLING OUR ENGAGEMENT...
USAGI...

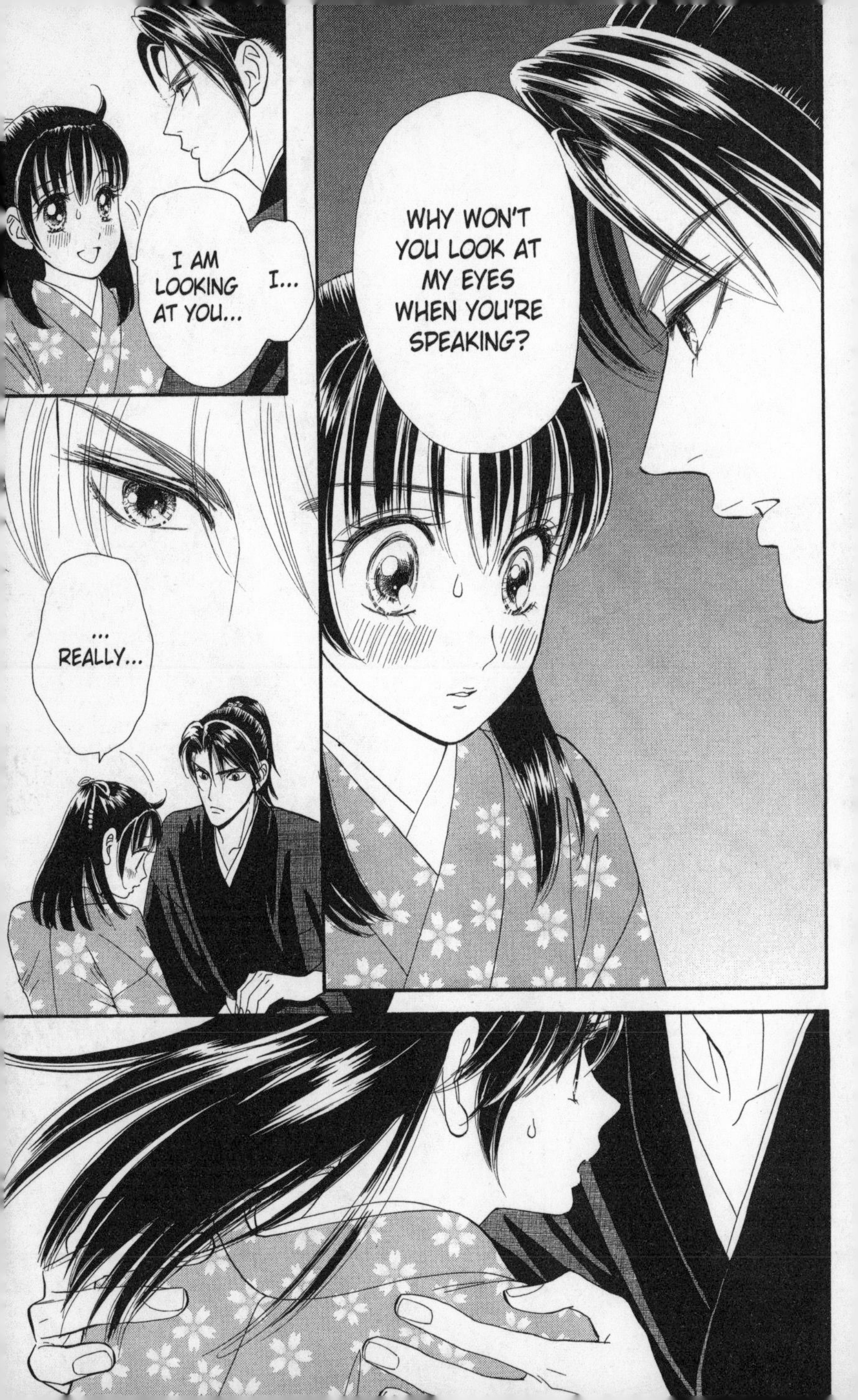
WHY WON'T YOU LOOK AT MY EYES WHEN YOU'RE SPEAKING?
I...
I AM LOOKING AT YOU...
... REALLY...

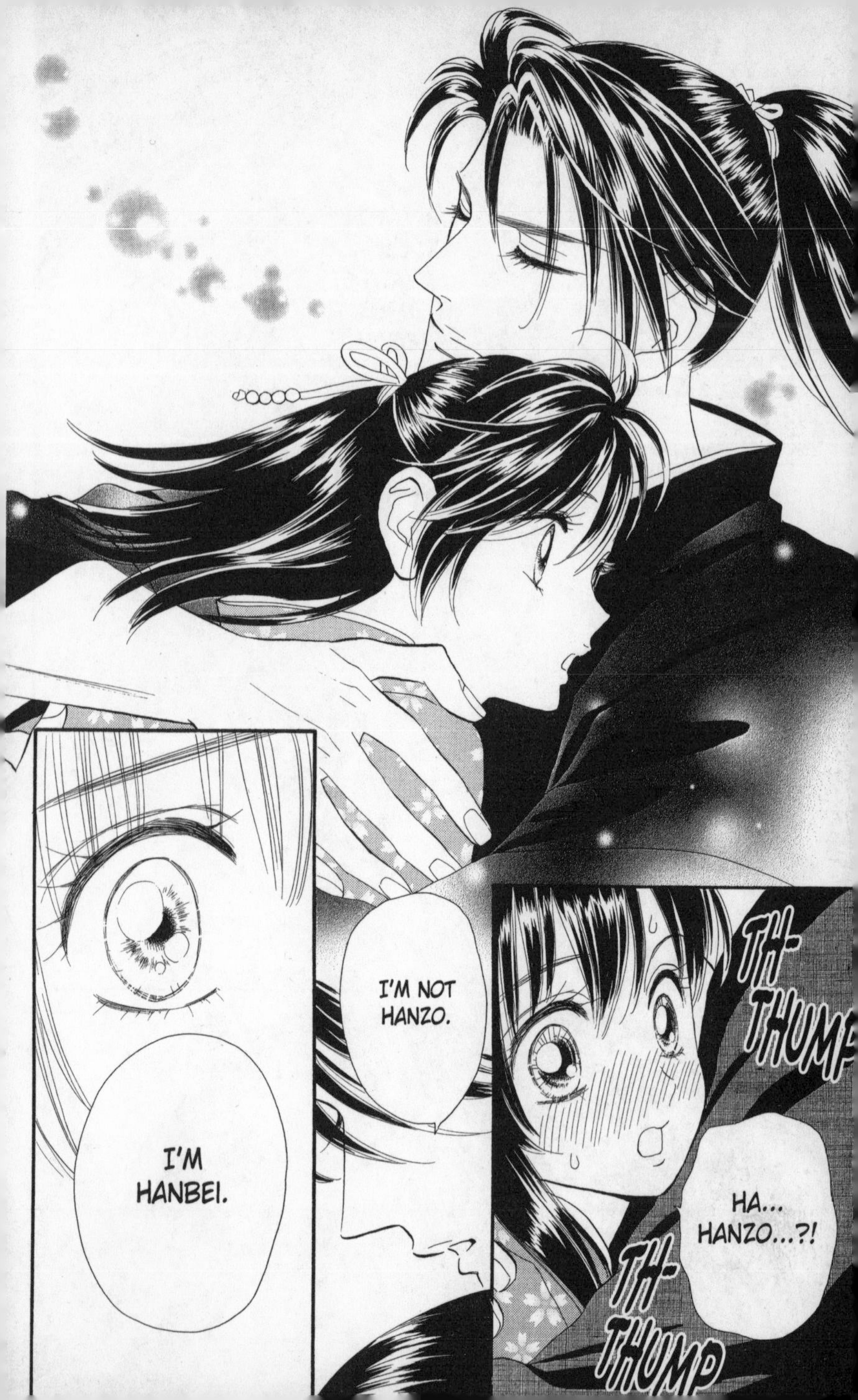
TH-THUMP
HA... HANZO...?!
TH-THUMP
I'M NOT HANZO.
I'M HANBEI.

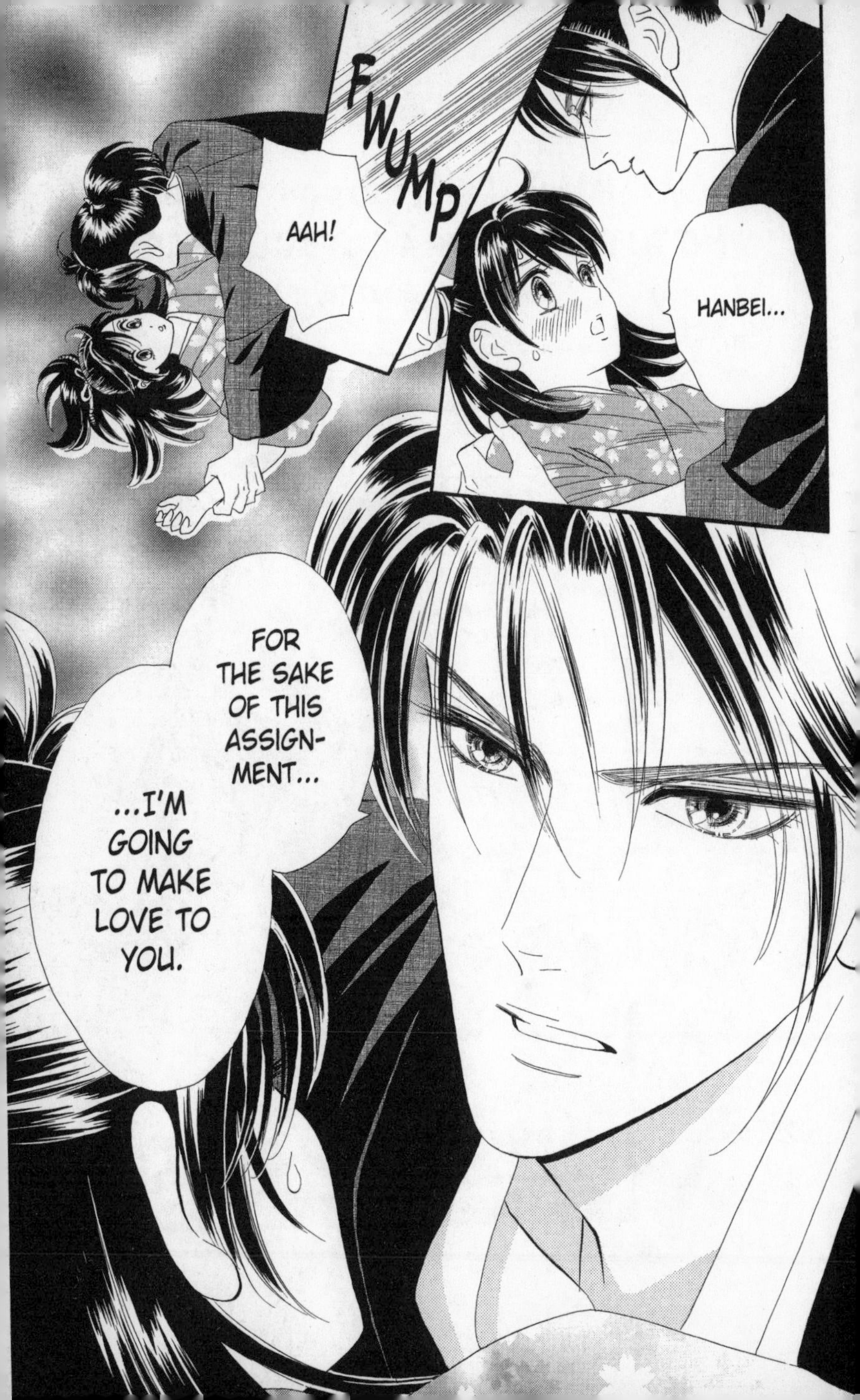
FWUMP
HANBEI...
AAH!
FOR THE SAKE OF THIS ASSIGNMENT...
...I'M GOING TO MAKE LOVE TO YOU.

TAIL OF THE MOON EXTRA: TODAY'S MISSION

"I WANT TO SEE HANZO IN A CARPENTER'S OUTFIT!"

-"MAMEZO IS SO CUTE," SAGA PREFECTURE

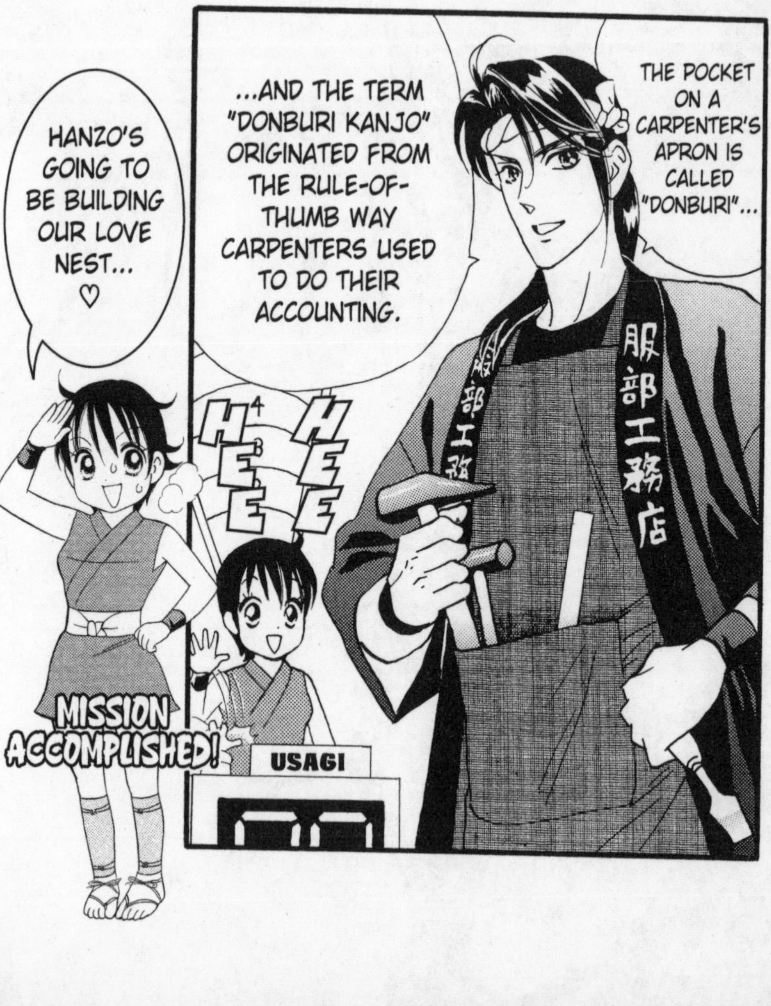

THE POCKET ON A CARPENTER'S APRON IS CALLED "DONBURI"...
...AND THE TERM "DONBURI KANJO" ORIGINATED FROM THE RULE-OF-THUMB WAY CARPENTERS USED TO DO THEIR ACCOUNTING.
服部工務店
HEEE
HEEE
HANZO'S GOING TO BE BUILDING OUR LOVE NEST... ♡
USAGI
MISSION ACCOMPLISHED!

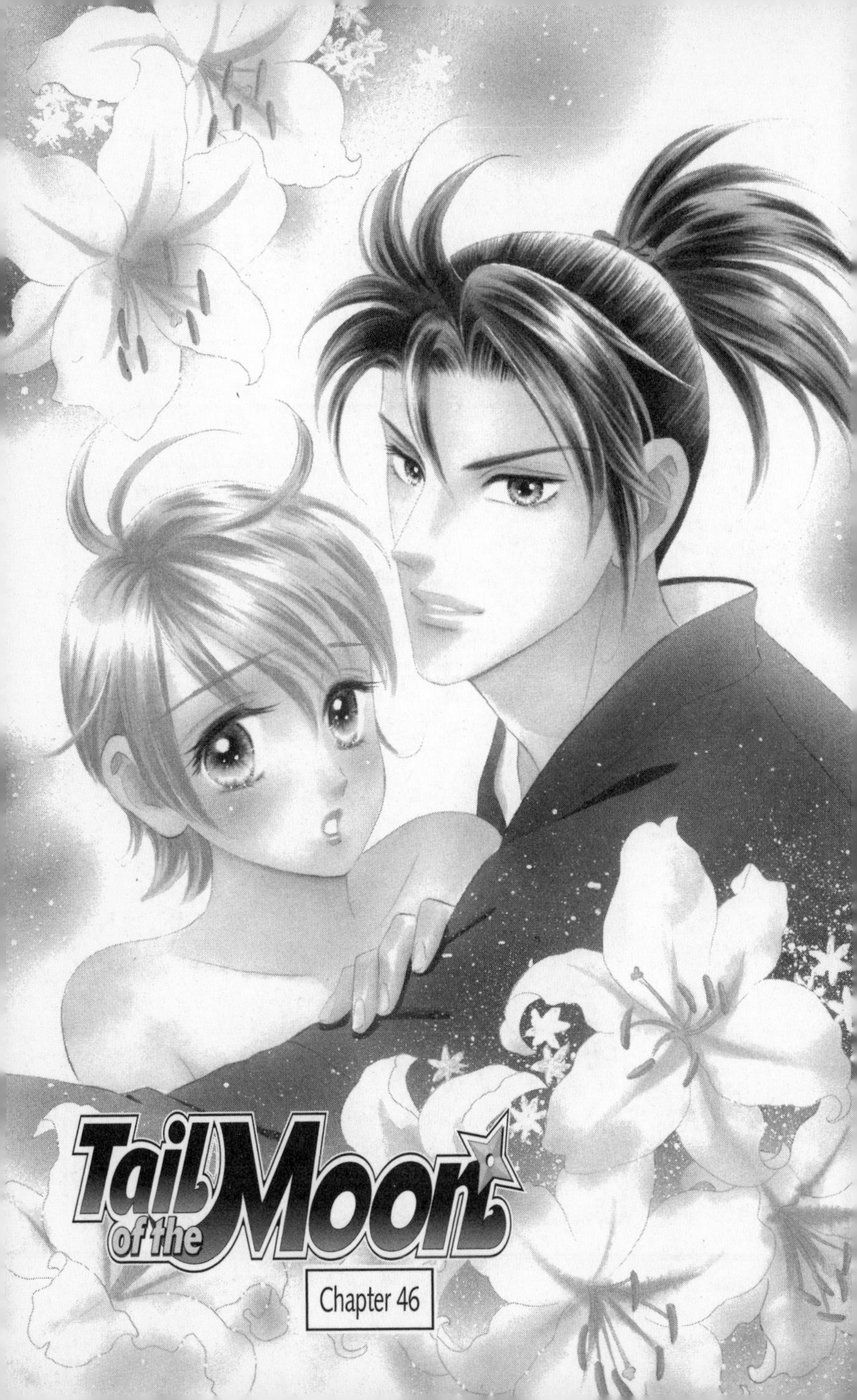
Tail of the Moon
Chapter 46

TAIL OF THE MOON EXTRA: TODAY'S MISSION

"I WANT TO SEE HANZO AND HANZOU MAKING PASSES AT GIRLS!!"

-AKIZAKURA, KUMAMOTO PREFECTURE

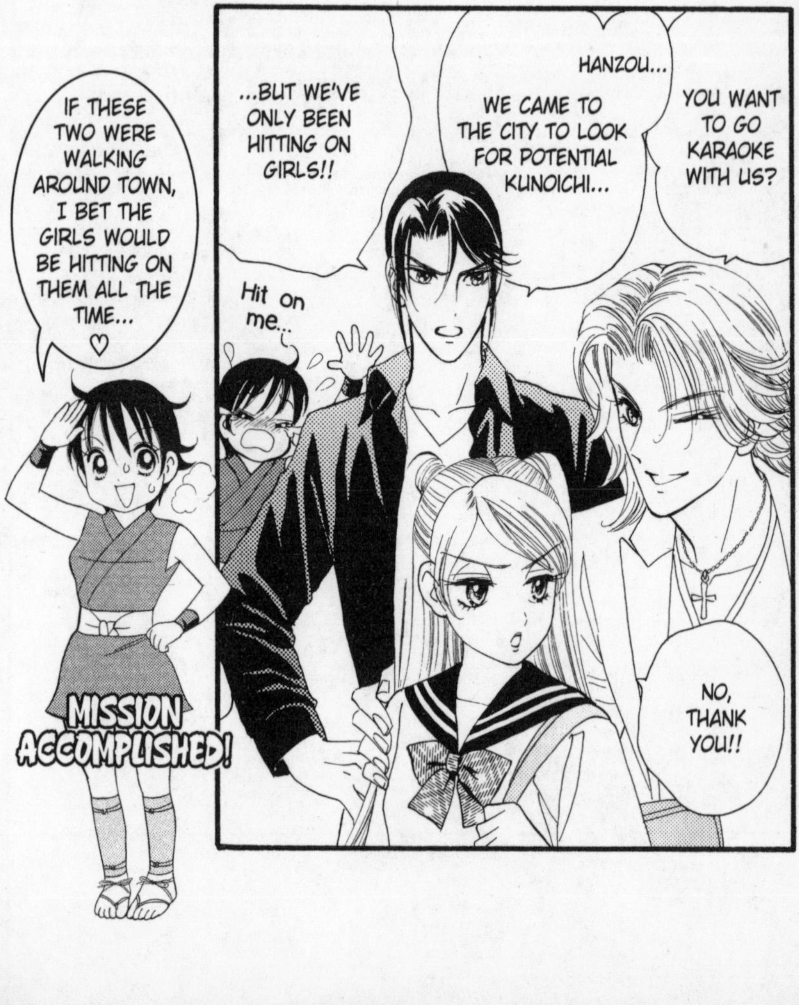

YOU WANT TO GO KARAOKE WITH US?
HANZOU...
WE CAME TO THE CITY TO LOOK FOR POTENTIAL KUNOICHI...
...BUT WE'VE ONLY BEEN HITTING ON GIRLS!!
Hit on me...
NO, THANK YOU!!
IF THESE TWO WERE WALKING AROUND TOWN, I BET THE GIRLS WOULD BE HITTING ON THEM ALL THE TIME... ♡
MISSION ACCOMPLISHED!

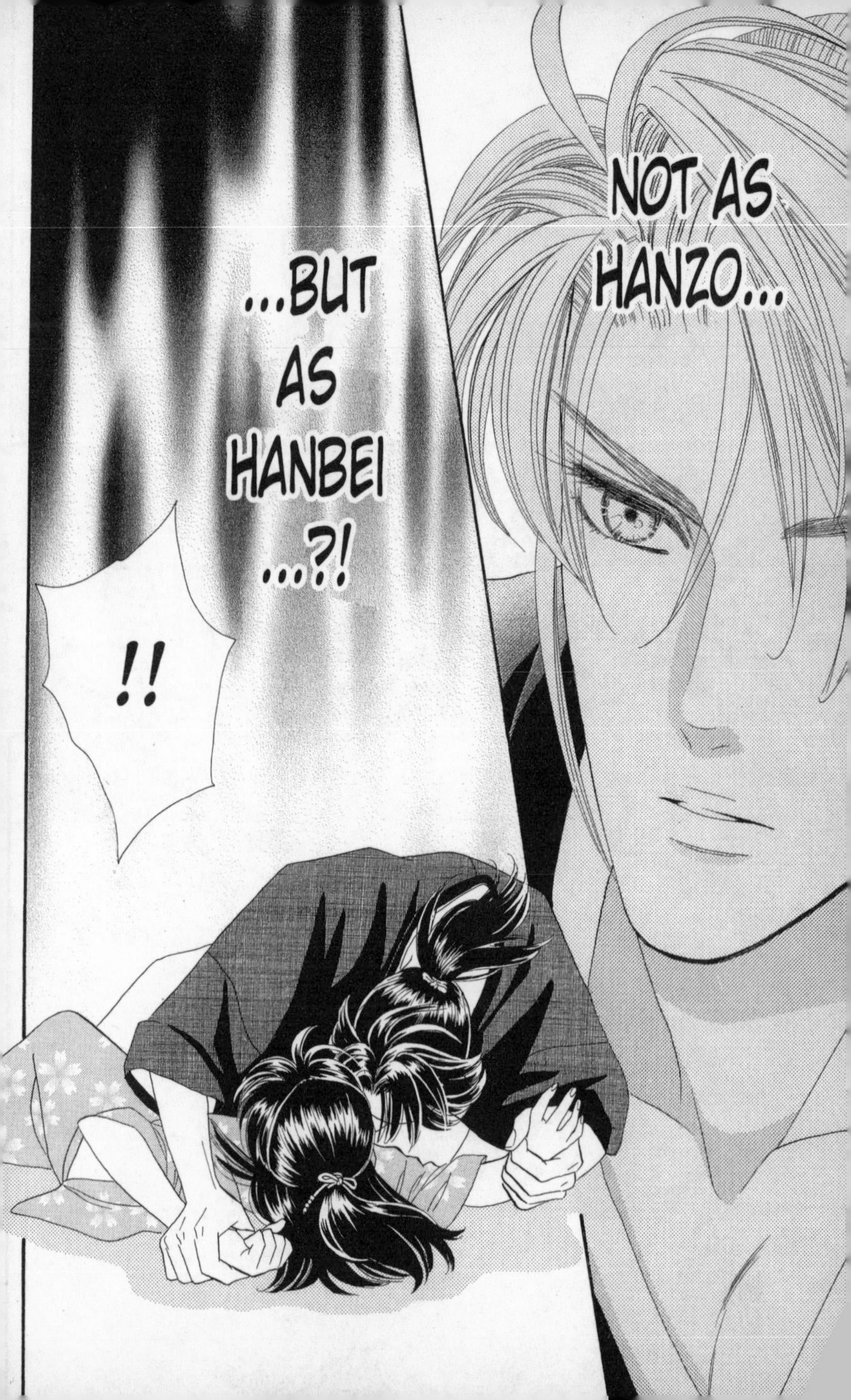
NOT AS HANZO...
...BUT AS HANBEI ...?!
!!

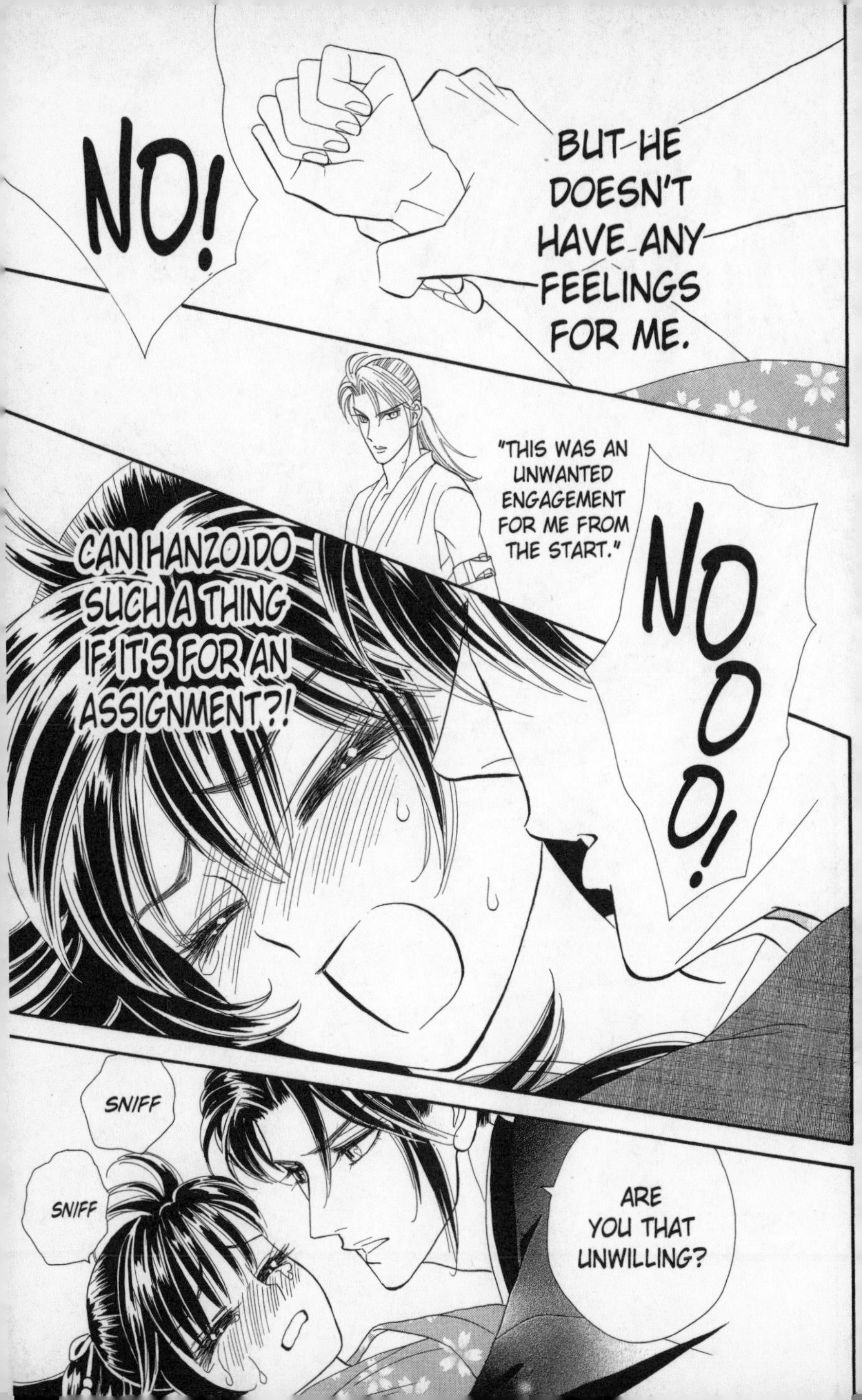
BUT HE DOESN'T HAVE ANY FEELINGS FOR ME.
NO!
"THIS WAS AN UNWANTED ENGAGEMENT FOR ME FROM THE START."
NOOOO!
CAN HANZO DO SUCH A THING IF IT'S FOR AN ASSIGNMENT?!
ARE YOU THAT UNWILLING?
SNIFF
SNIFF

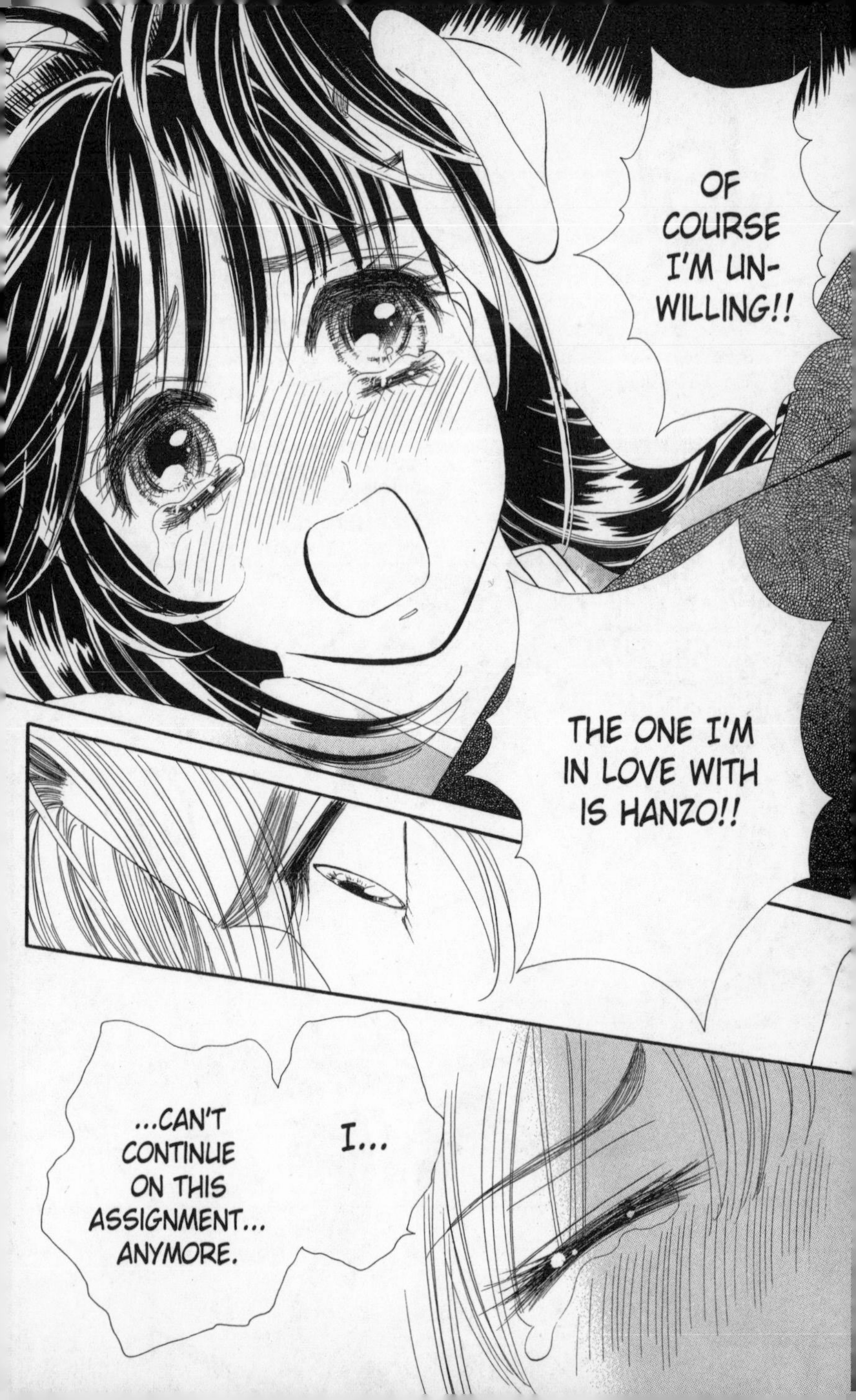
OF COURSE I'M UN-WILLING!!
THE ONE I'M IN LOVE WITH IS HANZO!!
I...
...CAN'T CONTINUE ON THIS ASSIGNMENT... ANYMORE.

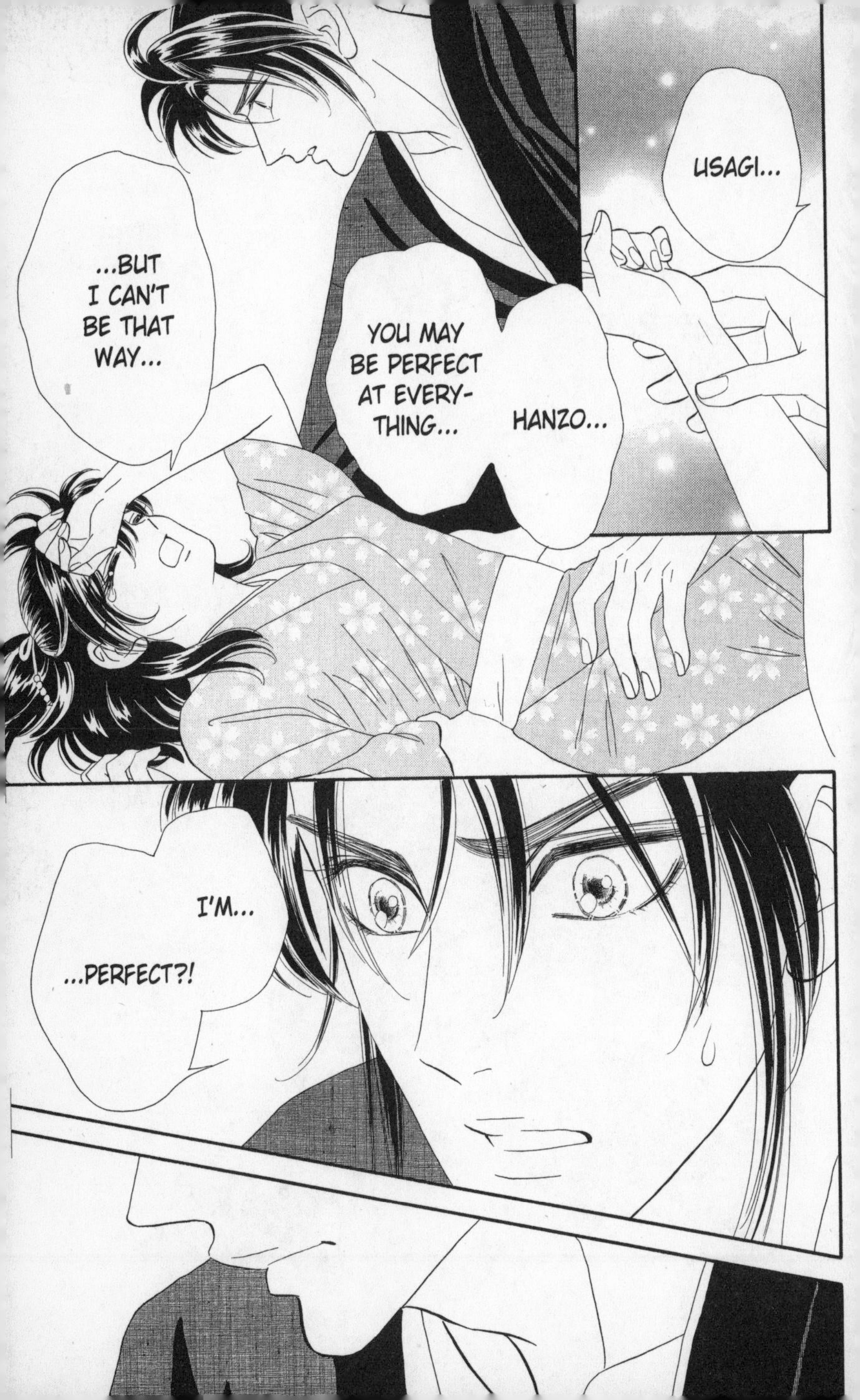
USAGI...
HANZO...
YOU MAY BE PERFECT AT EVERY-THING...
...BUT I CAN'T BE THAT WAY...
I'M...
...PERFECT?!

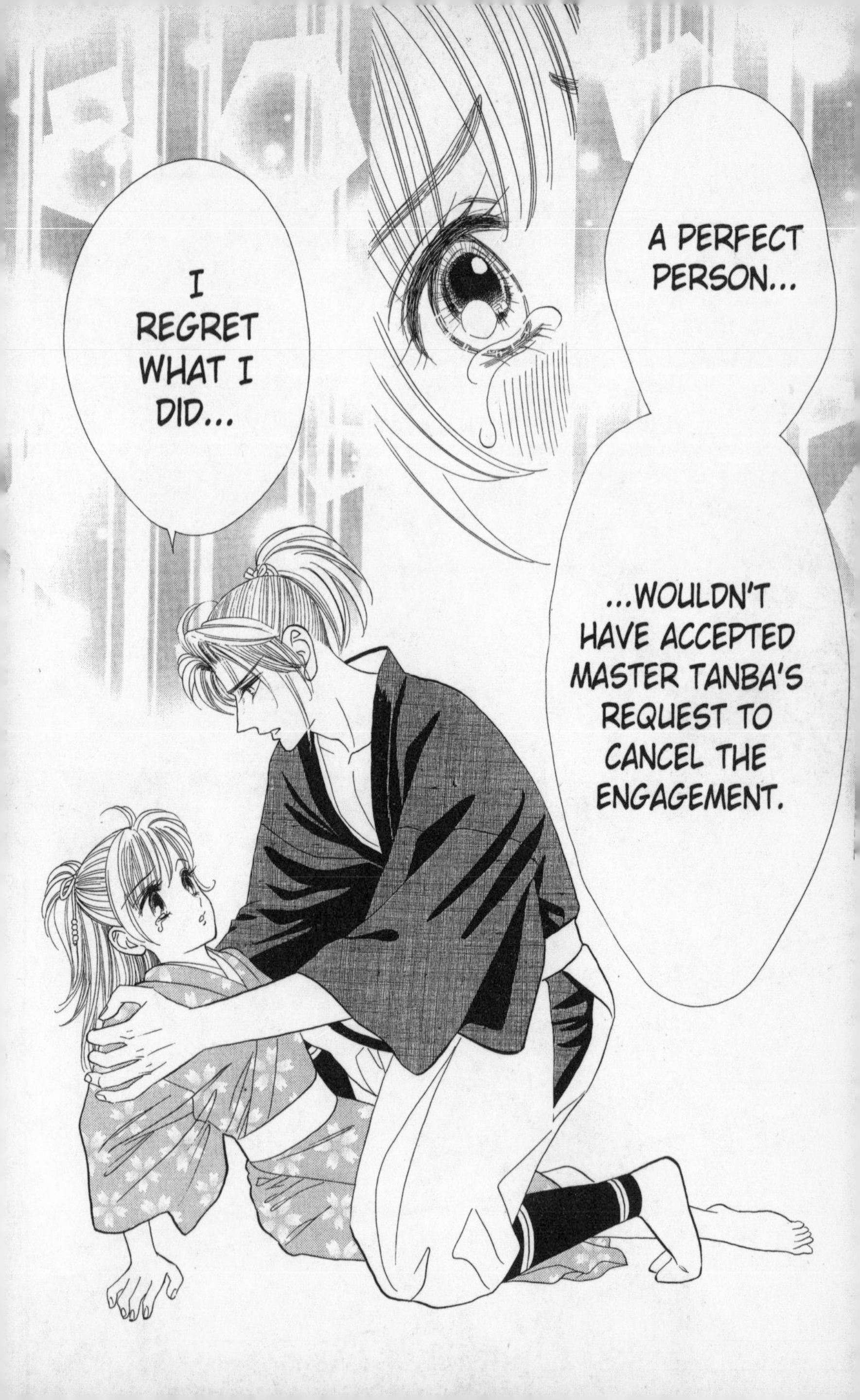
A PERFECT PERSON...
I REGRET WHAT I DID...
...WOULDN'T HAVE ACCEPTED MASTER TANBA'S REQUEST TO CANCEL THE ENGAGEMENT.

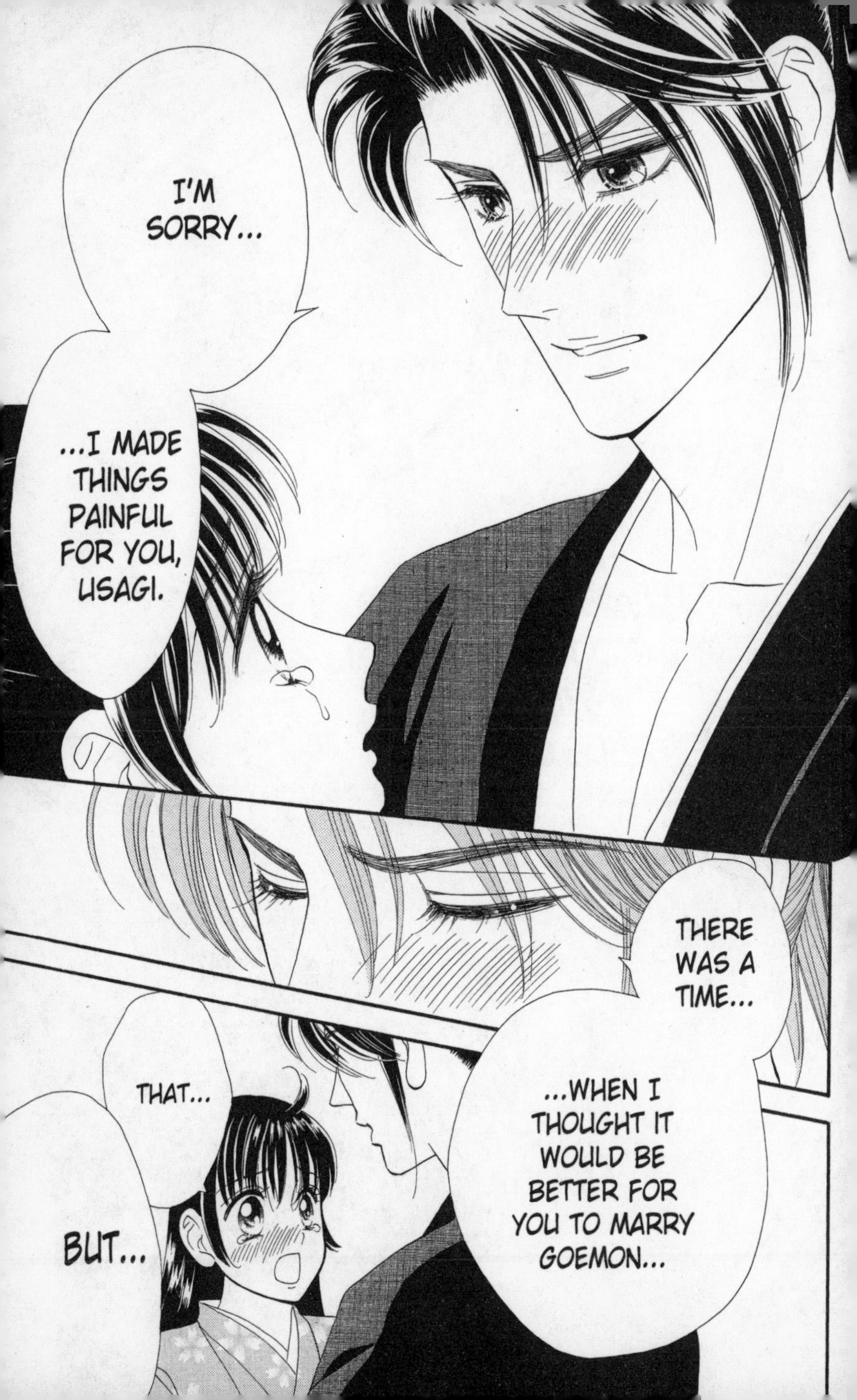
I'M SORRY...
...I MADE THINGS PAINFUL FOR YOU, USAGI.
THERE WAS A TIME...
...WHEN I THOUGHT IT WOULD BE BETTER FOR YOU TO MARRY GOEMON...
THAT...
BUT...

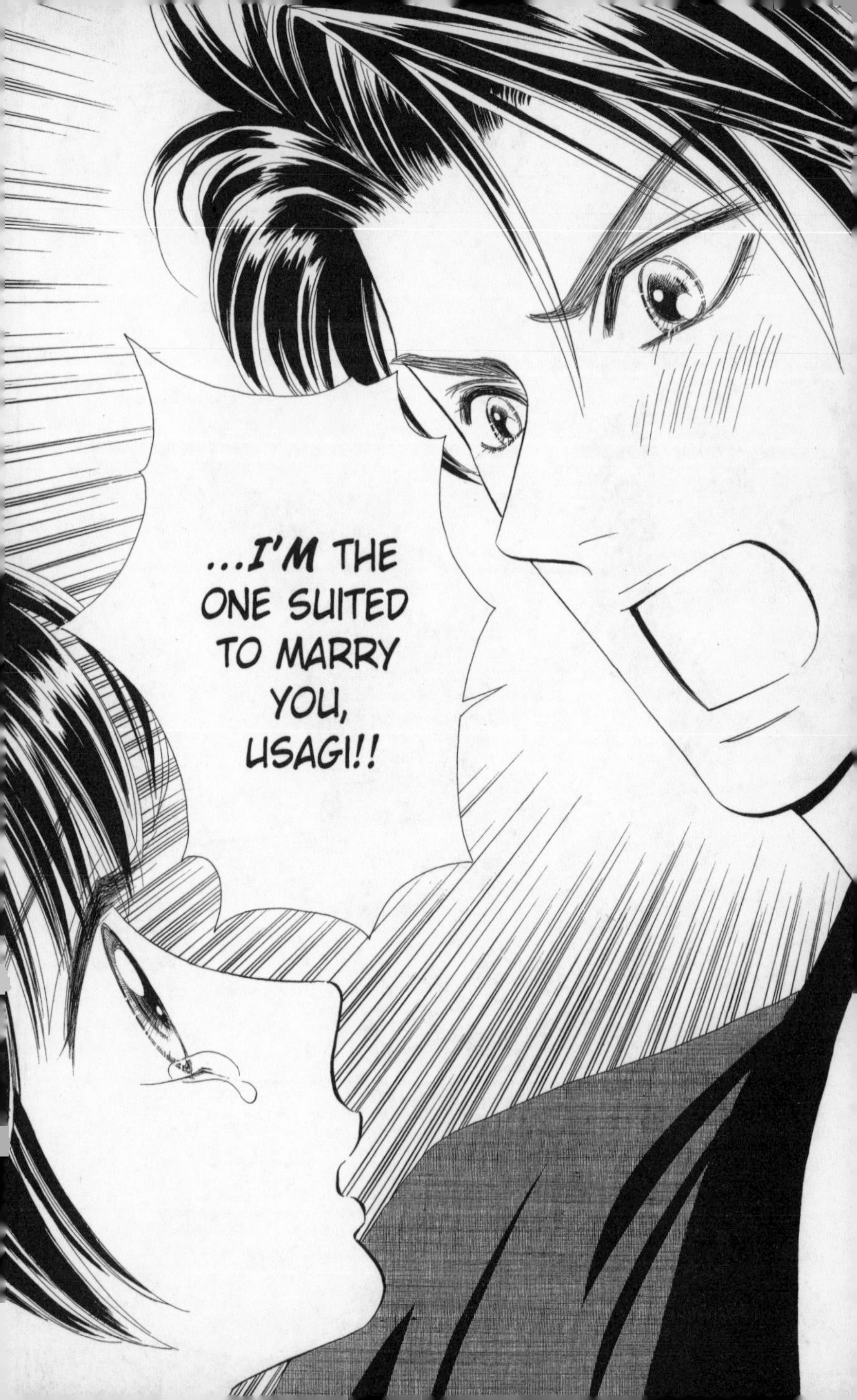
...I'M THE ONE SUITED TO MARRY YOU, USAGI!!

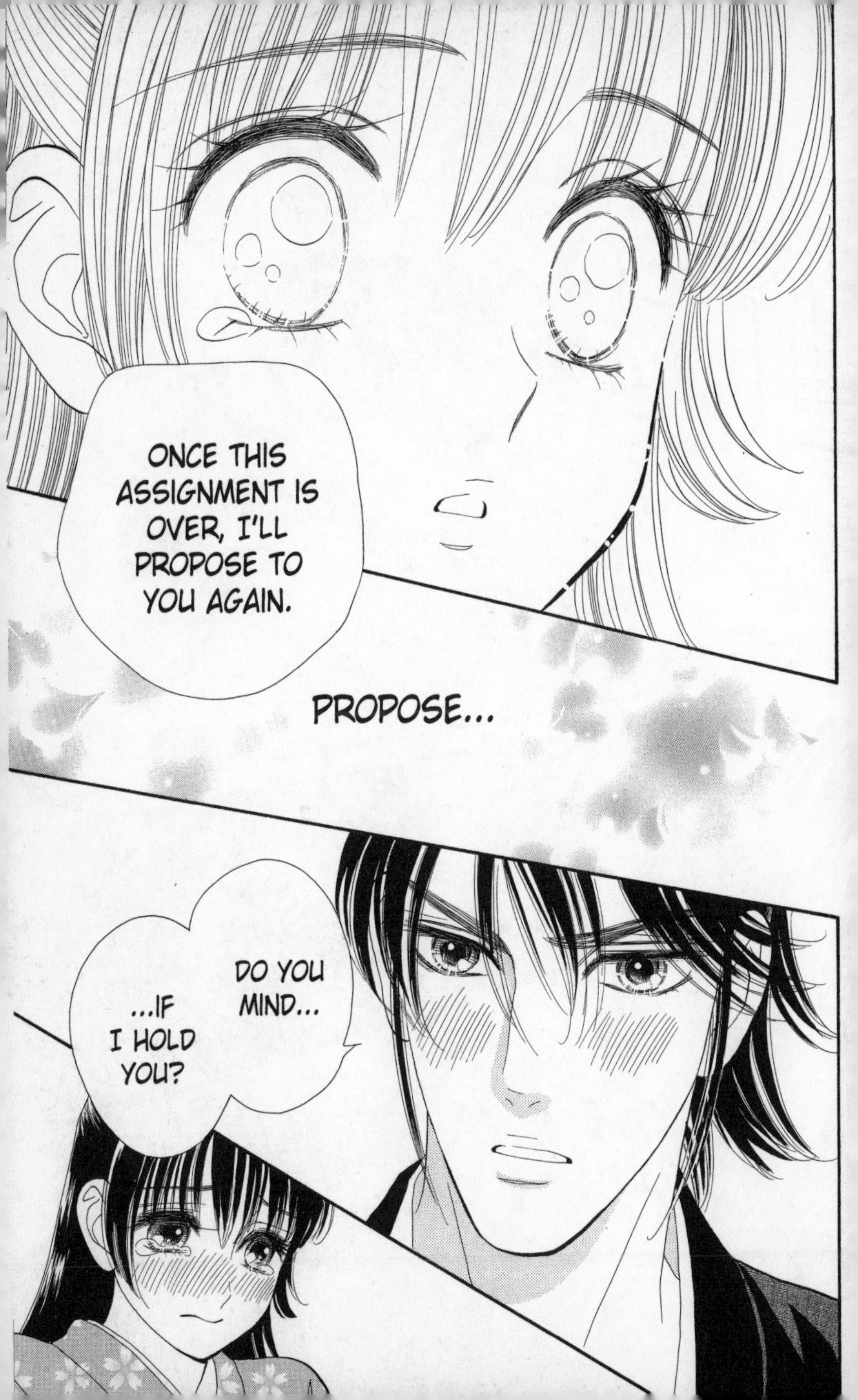
ONCE THIS ASSIGNMENT IS OVER, I'LL PROPOSE TO YOU AGAIN.
PROPOSE...
DO YOU MIND...
...IF I HOLD YOU?

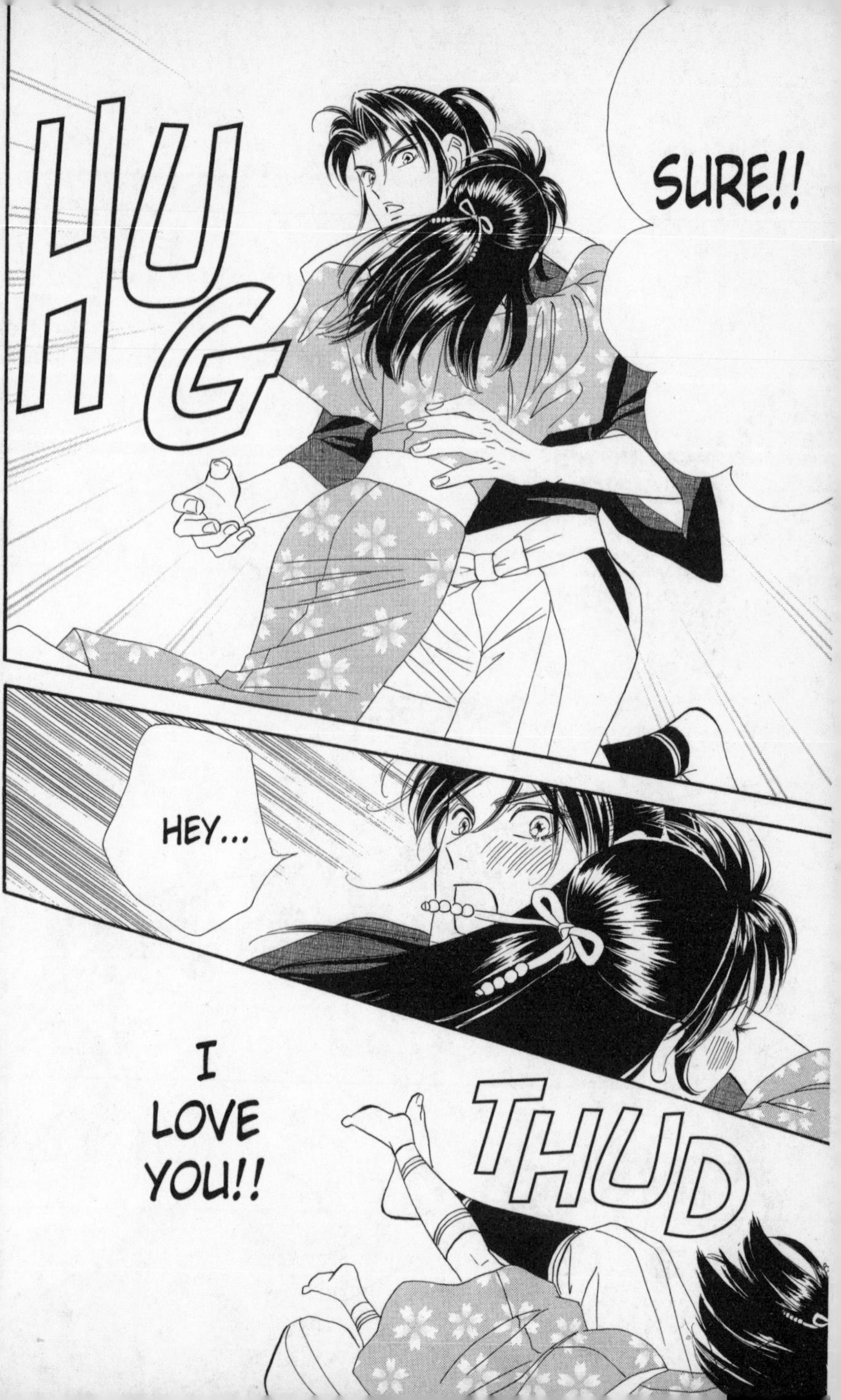
SURE!!
HUG
HEY...
THUD
I LOVE YOU!!

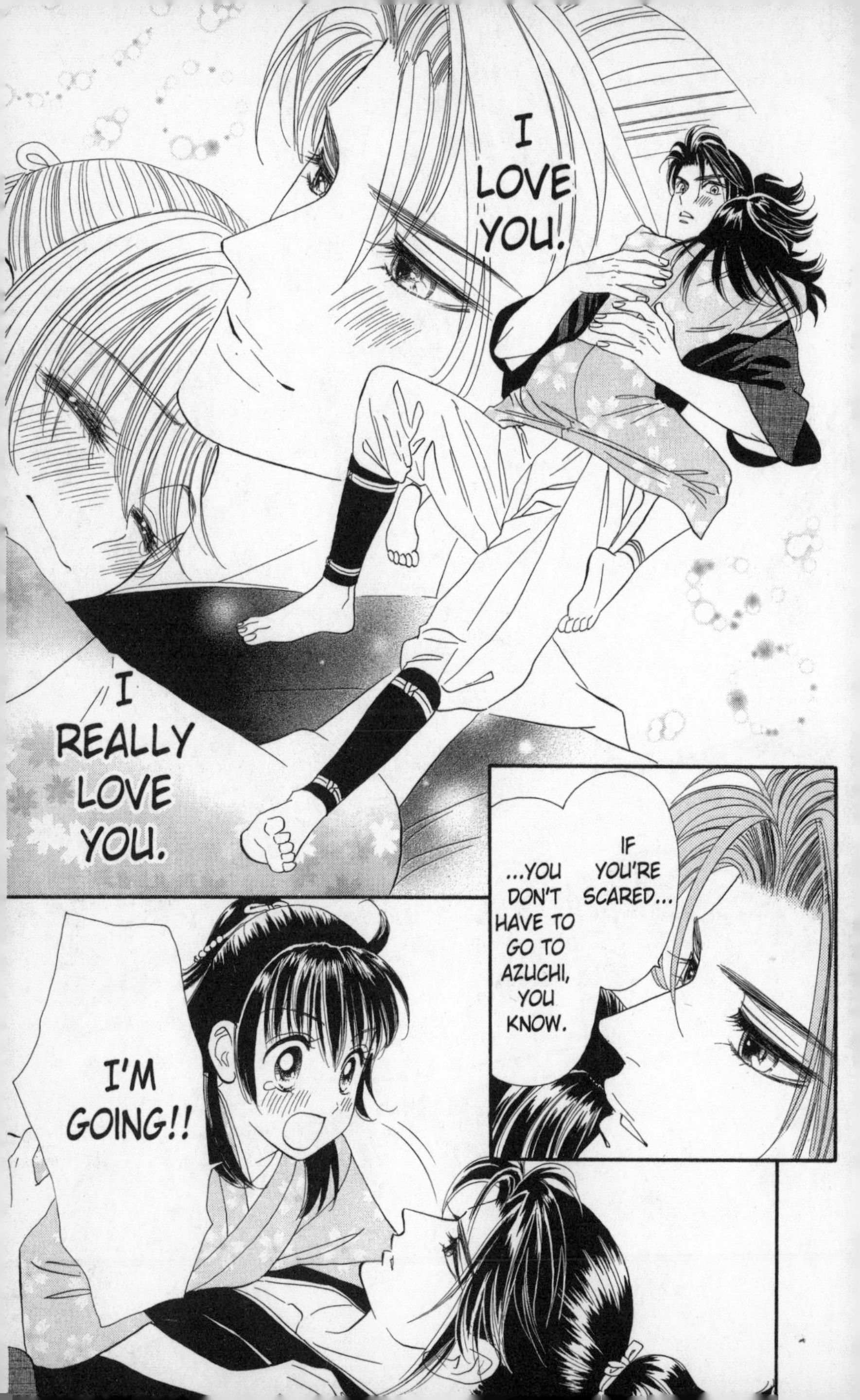
I LOVE YOU!
I REALLY LOVE YOU.
IF YOU'RE SCARED...
...YOU DON'T HAVE TO GO TO AZUCHI, YOU KNOW.
I'M GOING!!

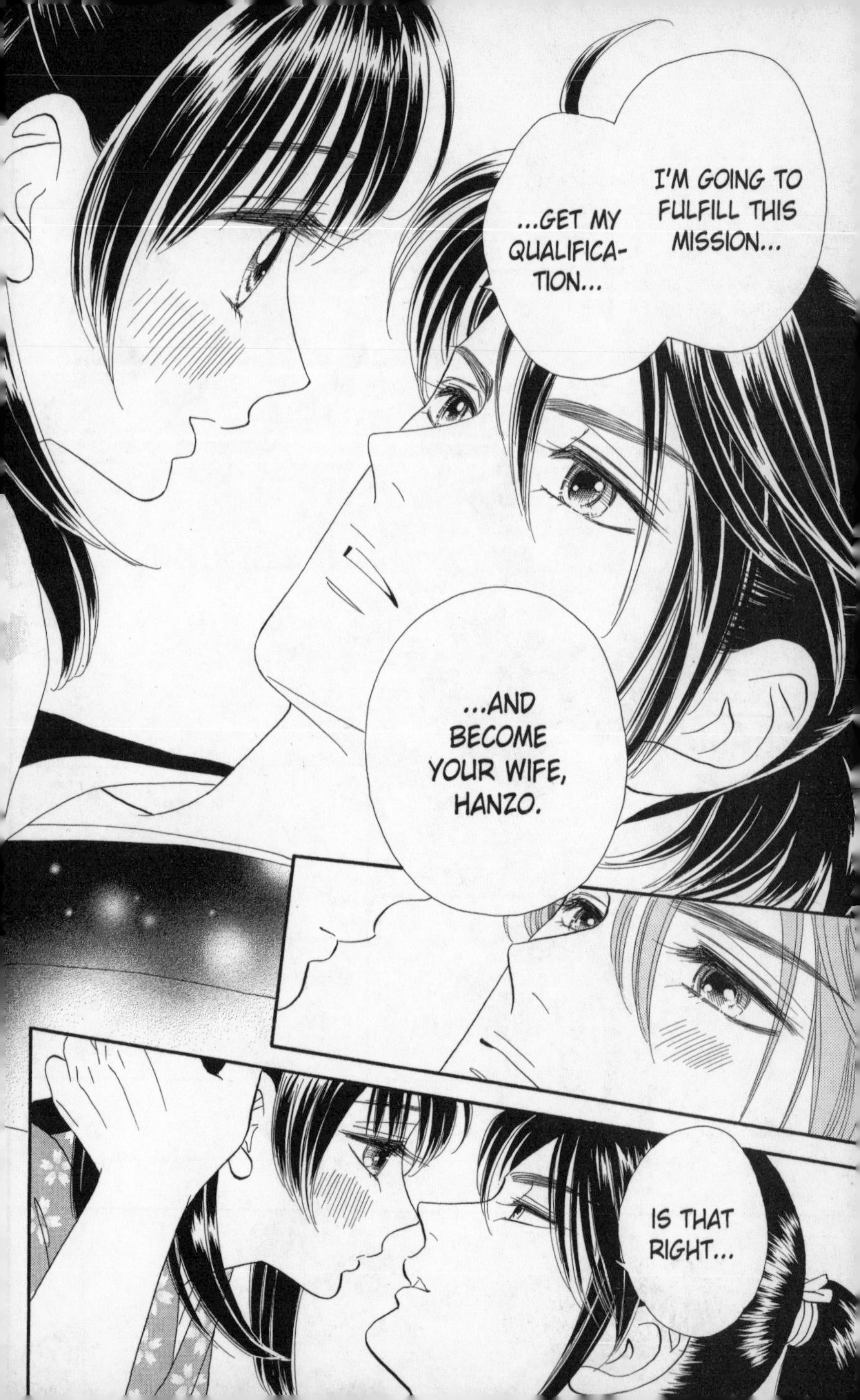
I'M GOING TO FULFILL THIS MISSION...
...GET MY QUALIFICA-TION...
...AND BECOME YOUR WIFE, HANZO.
IS THAT RIGHT...

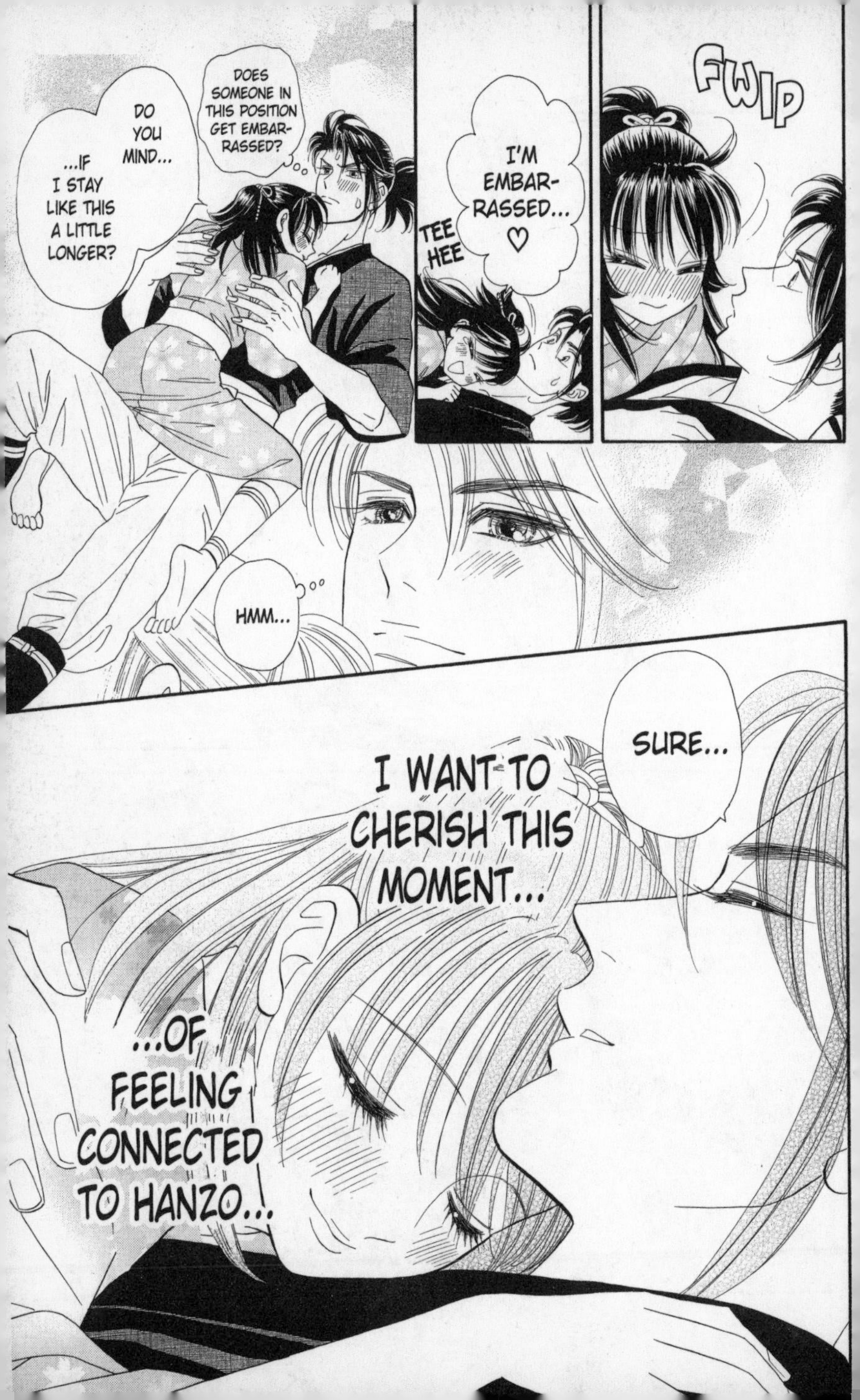
FWIP
I'M EMBARRASSED... ♡
TEE HEE
DOES SOMEONE IN THIS POSITION GET EMBARRASSED?
DO YOU MIND...
...IF I STAY LIKE THIS A LITTLE LONGER?
HMM...
SURE...
I WANT TO CHERISH THIS MOMENT...
...OF FEELING CONNECTED TO HANZO...

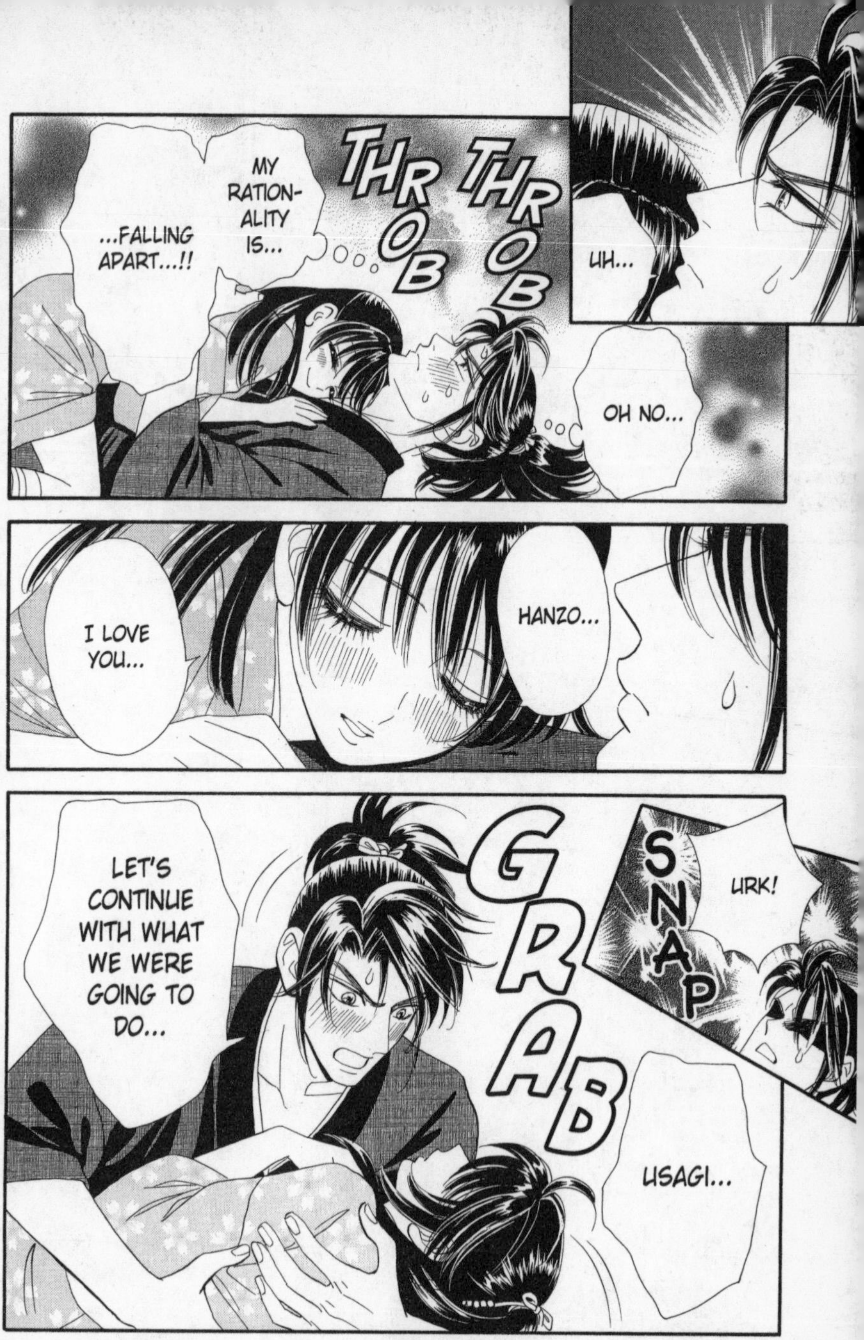
UH...
THROB THROB
OH NO...
MY RATION-ALITY IS...
...FALLING APART...!!
HANZO...
I LOVE YOU...
SNAP
URK!
GRAB
USAGI...
LET'S CONTINUE WITH WHAT WE WERE GOING TO DO...

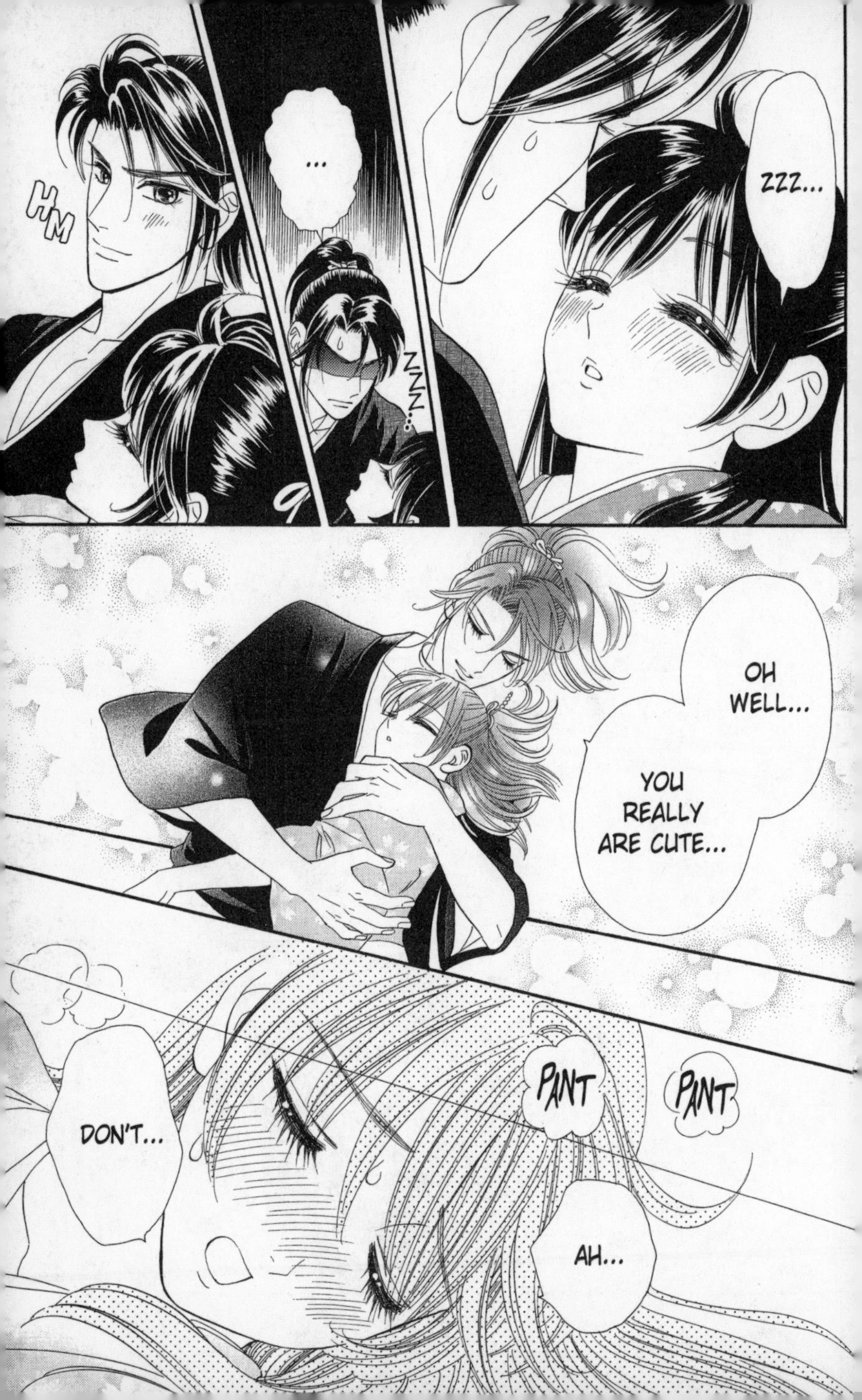
ZZZ...
...
ZZZ...
HM
OH WELL...
YOU REALLY ARE CUTE...
PANT
PANT
AH...
DON'T...

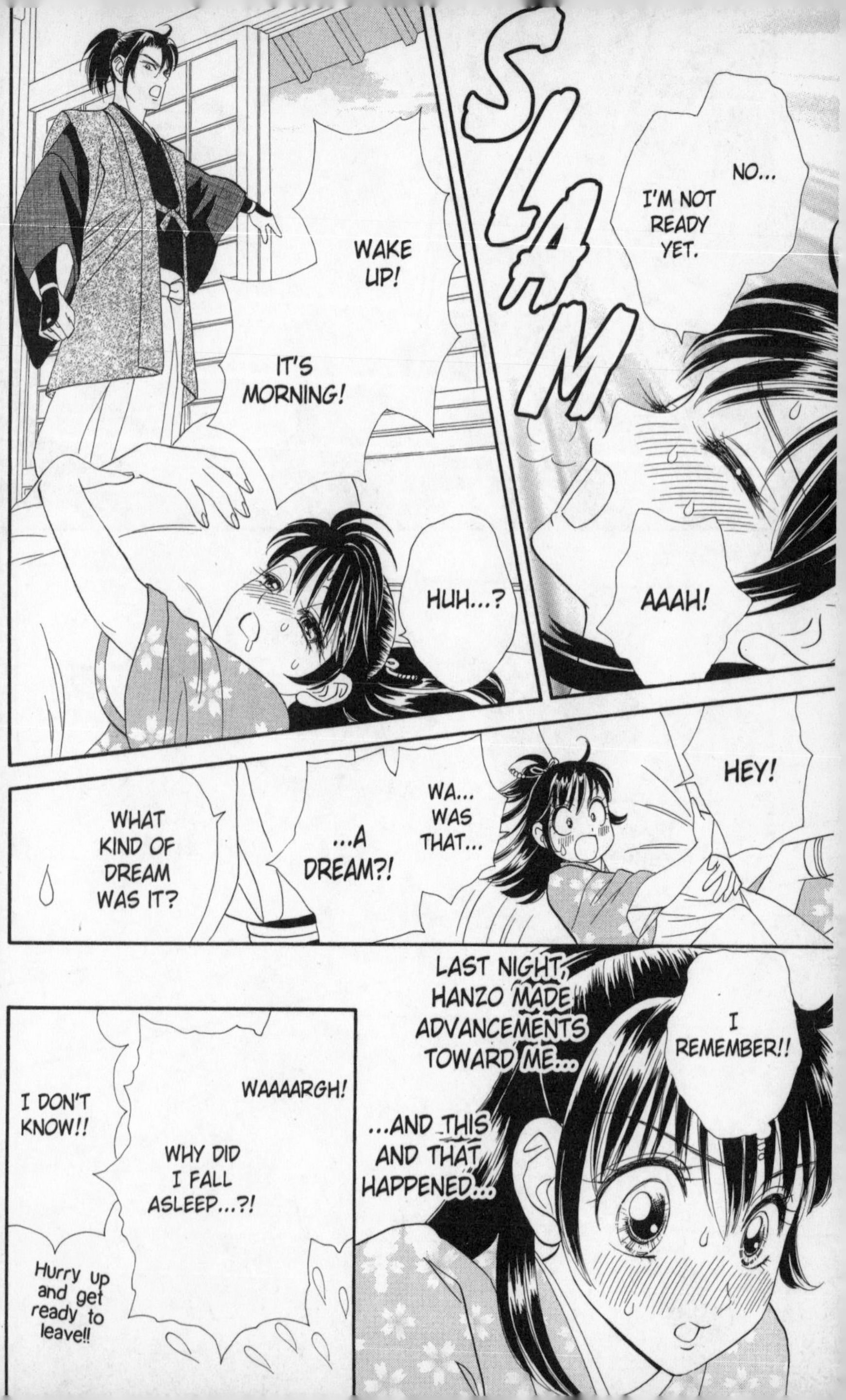
NO... I'M NOT READY YET.
SLAM
AAAH!
WAKE UP!
IT'S MORNING!
HUH...?
HEY!
WA... WAS THAT...
...A DREAM?!
WHAT KIND OF DREAM WAS IT?
I REMEMBER!!
LAST NIGHT, HANZO MADE ADVANCEMENTS TOWARD ME...
...AND THIS AND THAT HAPPENED...
WAAAARGH!
WHY DID I FALL ASLEEP...?!
I DON'T KNOW!!
Hurry up and get ready to leave!!

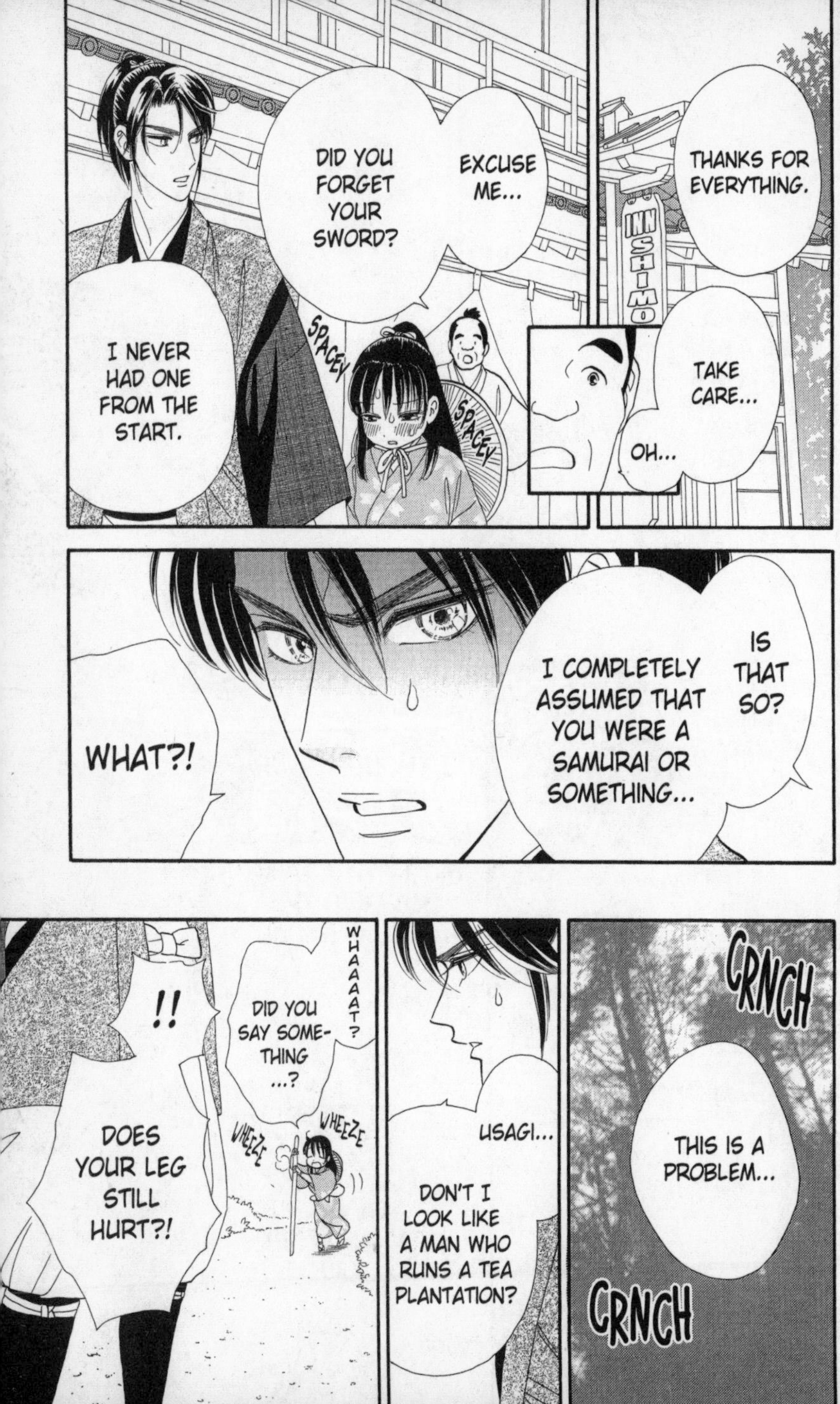
THANKS FOR EVERYTHING.
INN SHIMO
TAKE CARE...
OH...
EXCUSE ME...
DID YOU FORGET YOUR SWORD?
SPACEY
SPACEY
I NEVER HAD ONE FROM THE START.
IS THAT SO?
I COMPLETELY ASSUMED THAT YOU WERE A SAMURAI OR SOMETHING...
WHAT?!
CRNCH
THIS IS A PROBLEM...
CRNCH
USAGI...
DON'T I LOOK LIKE A MAN WHO RUNS A TEA PLANTATION?
WHAAAAAT?
DID YOU SAY SOME-THING ...?
WHEEZE
WHEEZE
!!
DOES YOUR LEG STILL HURT?!

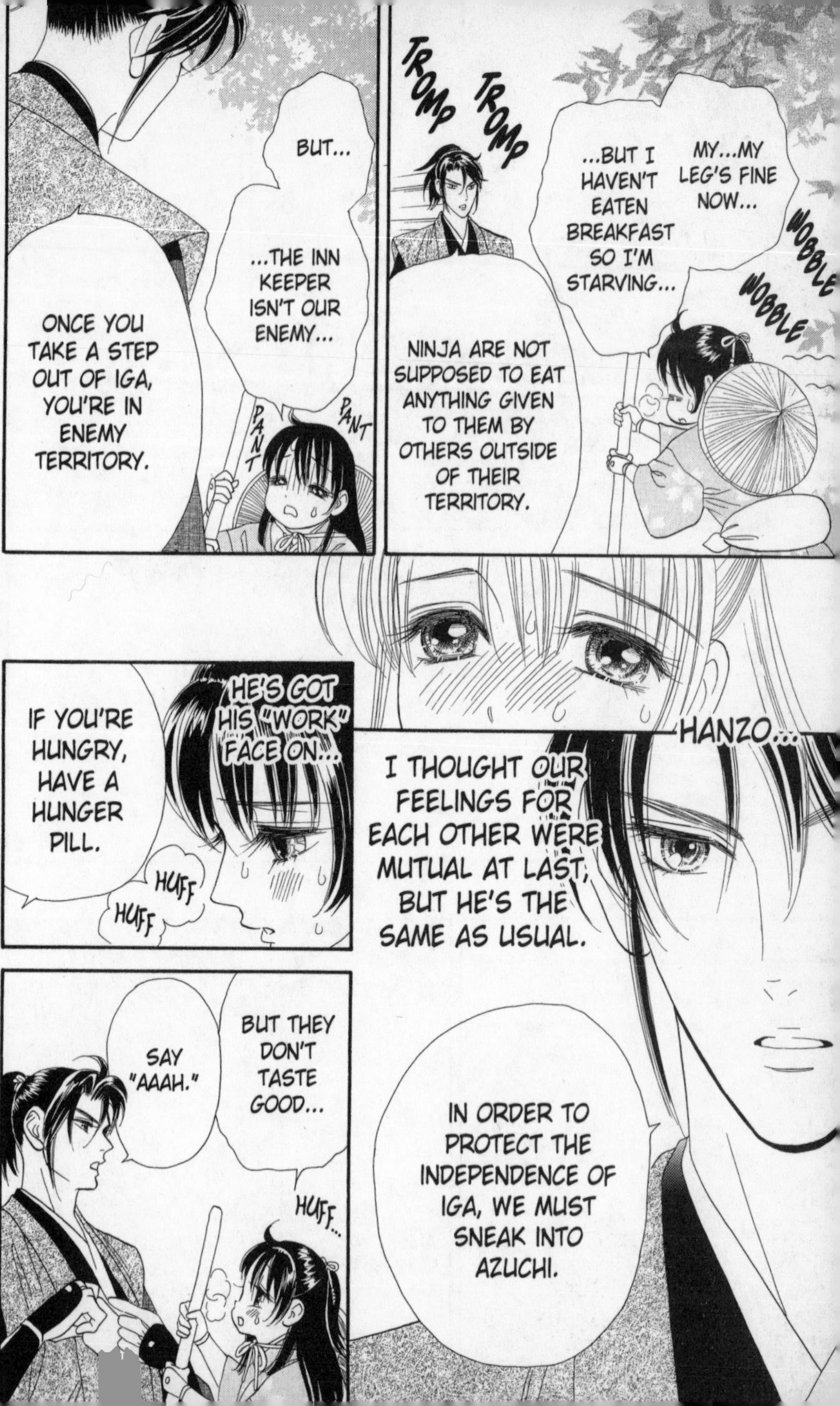
MY...MY LEG'S FINE NOW...
WOBBLE WOBBLE
...BUT I HAVEN'T EATEN BREAKFAST SO I'M STARVING...
TROMP TROMP
NINJA ARE NOT SUPPOSED TO EAT ANYTHING GIVEN TO THEM BY OTHERS OUTSIDE OF THEIR TERRITORY.
BUT...
...THE INN KEEPER ISN'T OUR ENEMY...
PANT PANT
ONCE YOU TAKE A STEP OUT OF IGA, YOU'RE IN ENEMY TERRITORY.
HANZO...
I THOUGHT OUR FEELINGS FOR EACH OTHER WERE MUTUAL AT LAST, BUT HE'S THE SAME AS USUAL.
IN ORDER TO PROTECT THE INDEPENDENCE OF IGA, WE MUST SNEAK INTO AZUCHI.
HE'S GOT HIS "WORK" FACE ON...
IF YOU'RE HUNGRY, HAVE A HUNGER PILL.
HUFF HUFF
BUT THEY DON'T TASTE GOOD...
SAY "AAAH."
HUFF...

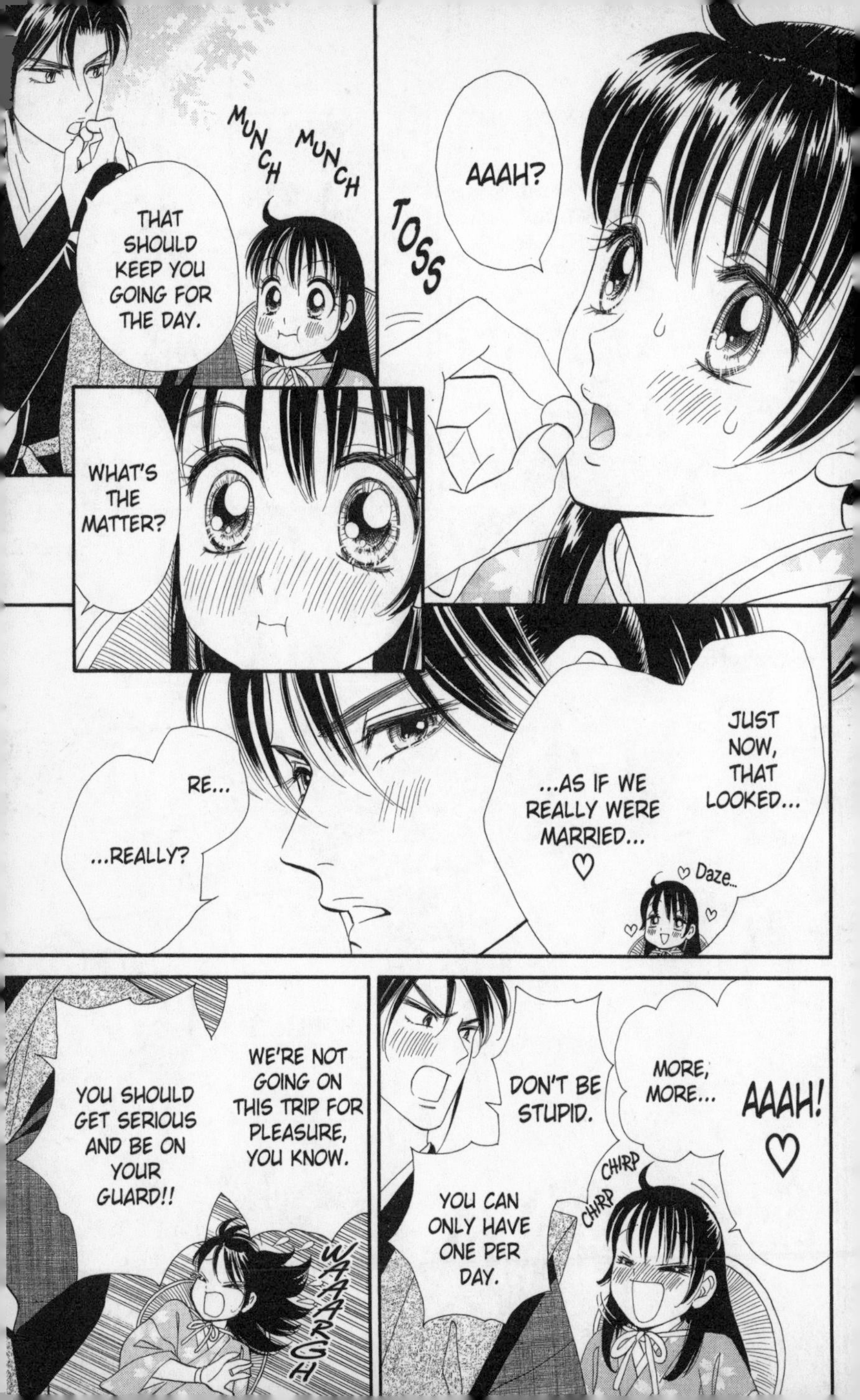
AAAH?
TOSS
MUNCH MUNCH
THAT SHOULD KEEP YOU GOING FOR THE DAY.
WHAT'S THE MATTER?
JUST NOW, THAT LOOKED...
...AS IF WE REALLY WERE MARRIED... ♡
♡ Daze...
RE...
...REALLY?
MORE, MORE...
AAAH! ♡
CHIRP CHIRP
DON'T BE STUPID.
YOU CAN ONLY HAVE ONE PER DAY.
WE'RE NOT GOING ON THIS TRIP FOR PLEASURE, YOU KNOW.
YOU SHOULD GET SERIOUS AND BE ON YOUR GUARD!!
WAAAARGH

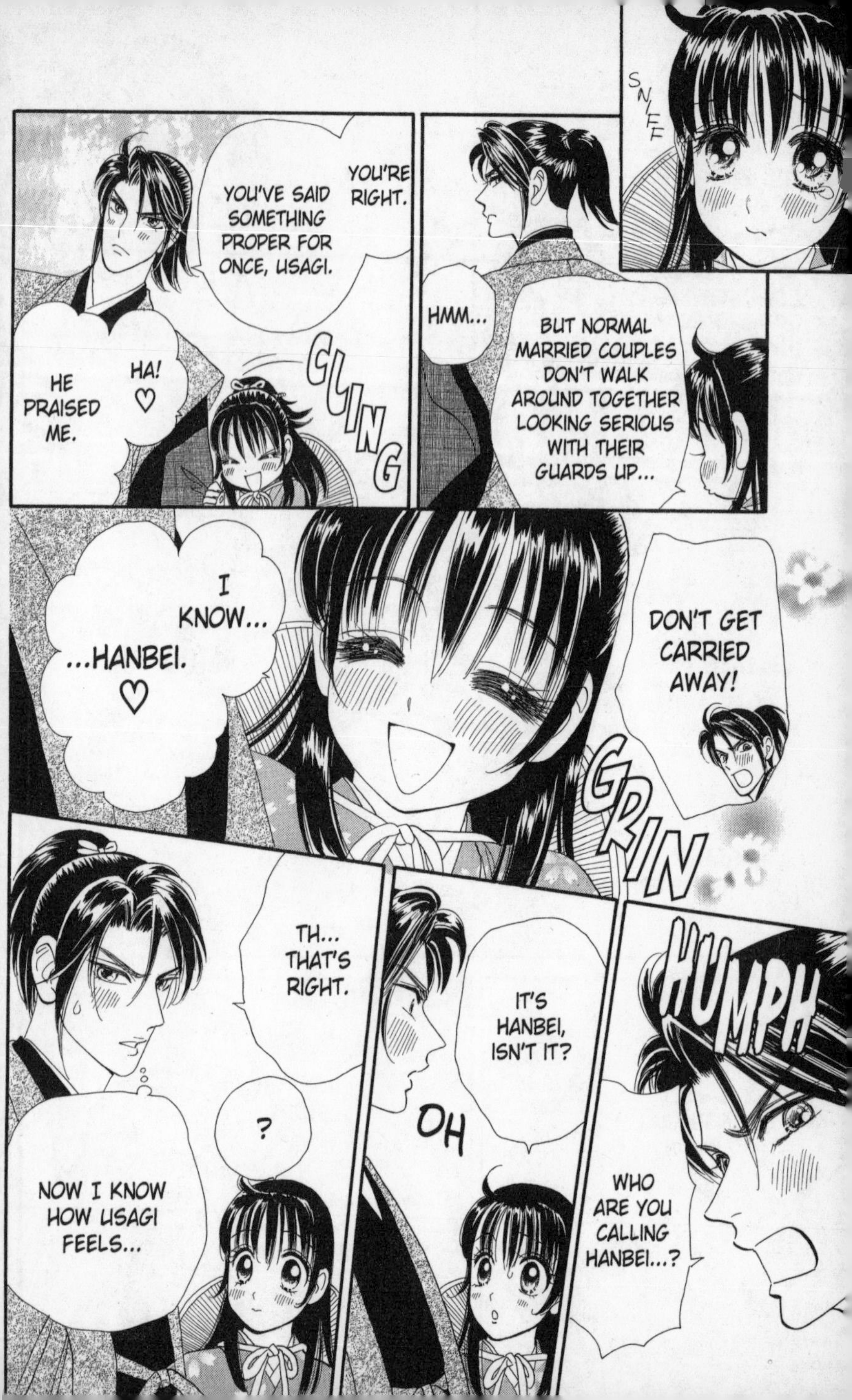
SNIFF
HMM...
BUT NORMAL MARRIED COUPLES DON'T WALK AROUND TOGETHER LOOKING SERIOUS WITH THEIR GUARDS UP...
YOU'RE RIGHT.
YOU'VE SAID SOMETHING PROPER FOR ONCE, USAGI.
CLING
HA! ♡
HE PRAISED ME.
DON'T GET CARRIED AWAY!
GRIN
I KNOW...
...HANBEI. ♡
HUMPH
WHO ARE YOU CALLING HANBEI...?
IT'S HANBEI, ISN'T IT?
OH
TH... THAT'S RIGHT.
?
NOW I KNOW HOW USAGI FEELS...

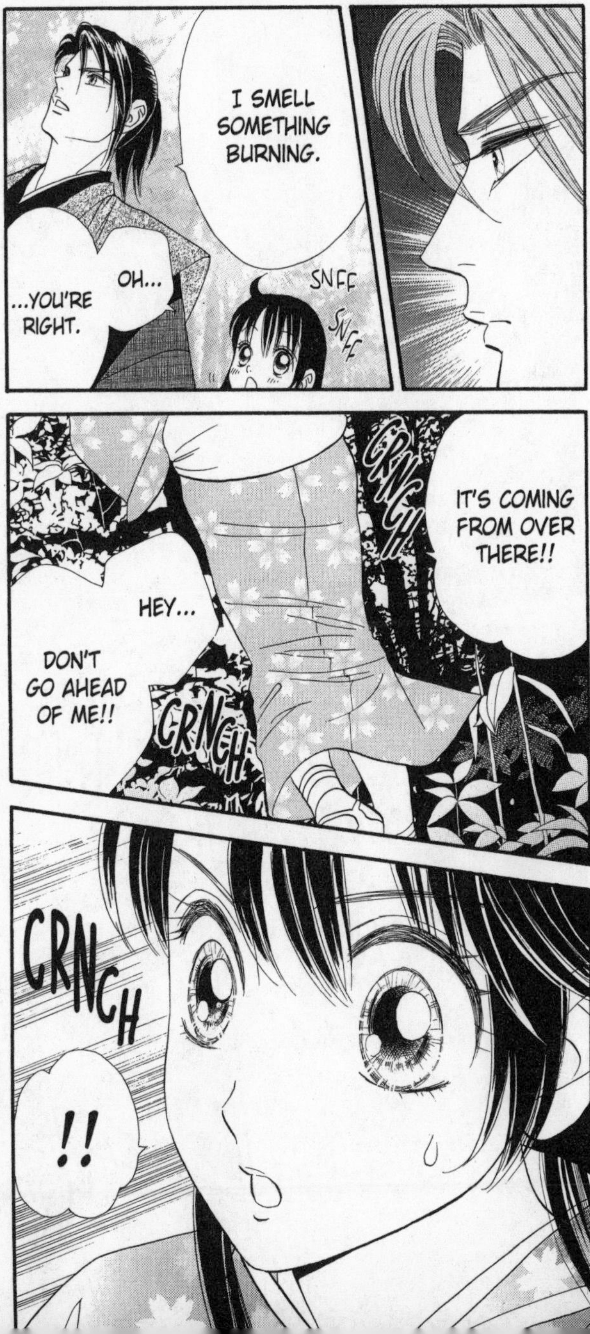
I SMELL SOMETHING BURNING.
SNFF
SNFF
OH...
...YOU'RE RIGHT.
CRNCH
IT'S COMING FROM OVER THERE!!
HEY...
DON'T GO AHEAD OF ME!!
CRNCH
CRNCH
!!

UE-RIN'S WAY OF THE MANGA ⑧

Back then, I was on the swimming team, so I would swim about 3km everyday after school, go to sleep right after coming home, and draw my manga in the middle of the night after my family members had all gone to bed.

I was really busy with my classes, extracurricular activities, and cram school, so finding time to draw manga was hard. I would draw manga happily until it was time for me to go to school.

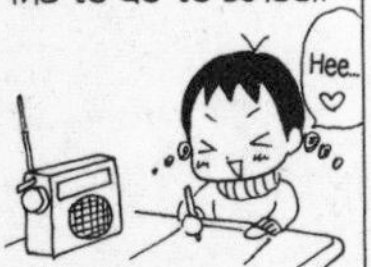
Hee... ♡

(This was around the time I got hooked on the radio.)

I also came up with a plan to improve my skills.

Plan ①

Overcome my weak points in focus lines and shadowing!

Plan ②

Draw a 30-page one-shot manga every month and submit them to magazines.

Well, I only had two plans...

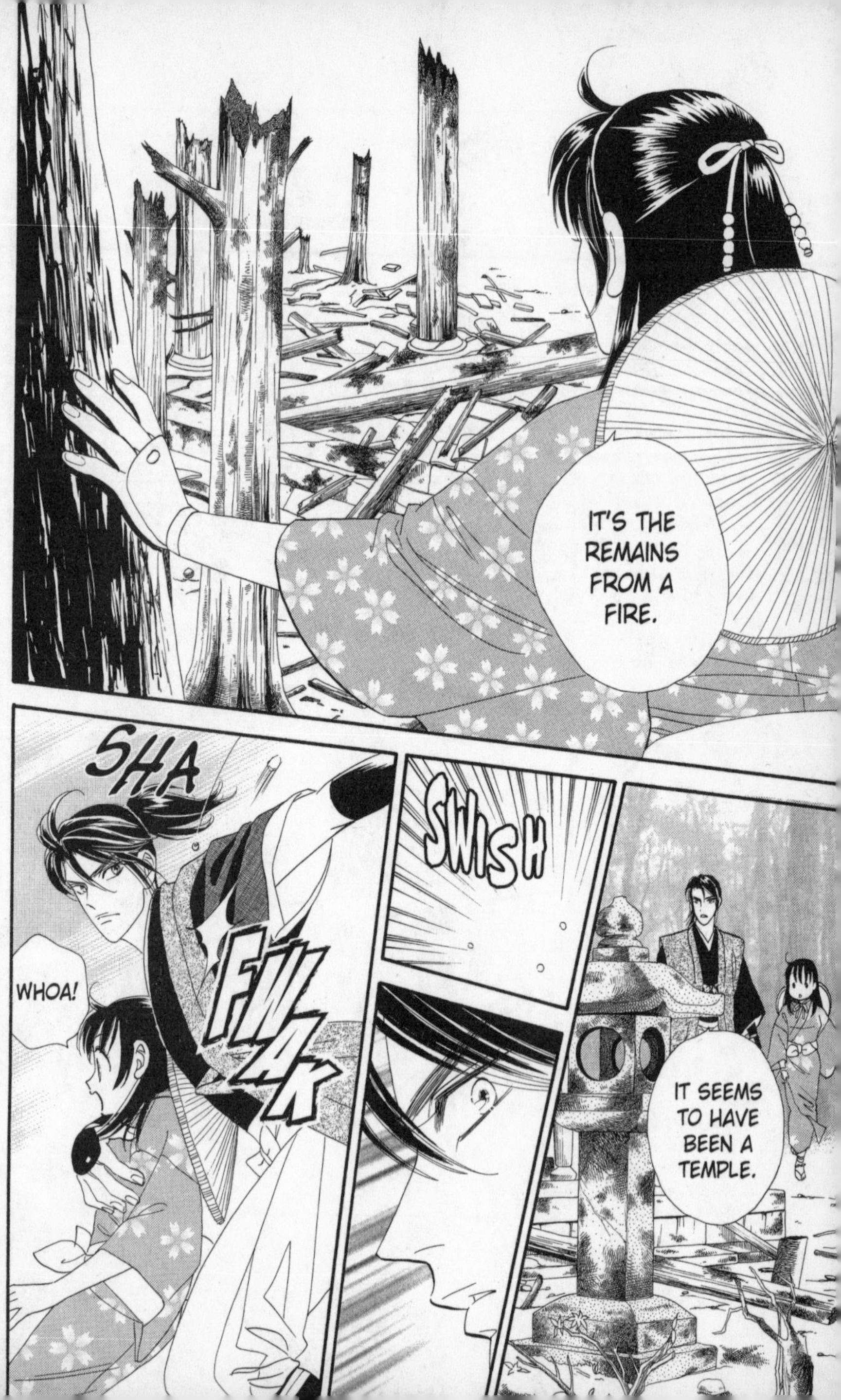
IT'S THE REMAINS FROM A FIRE.
IT SEEMS TO HAVE BEEN A TEMPLE.
SWISH
SHA
FWAK
WHOA!

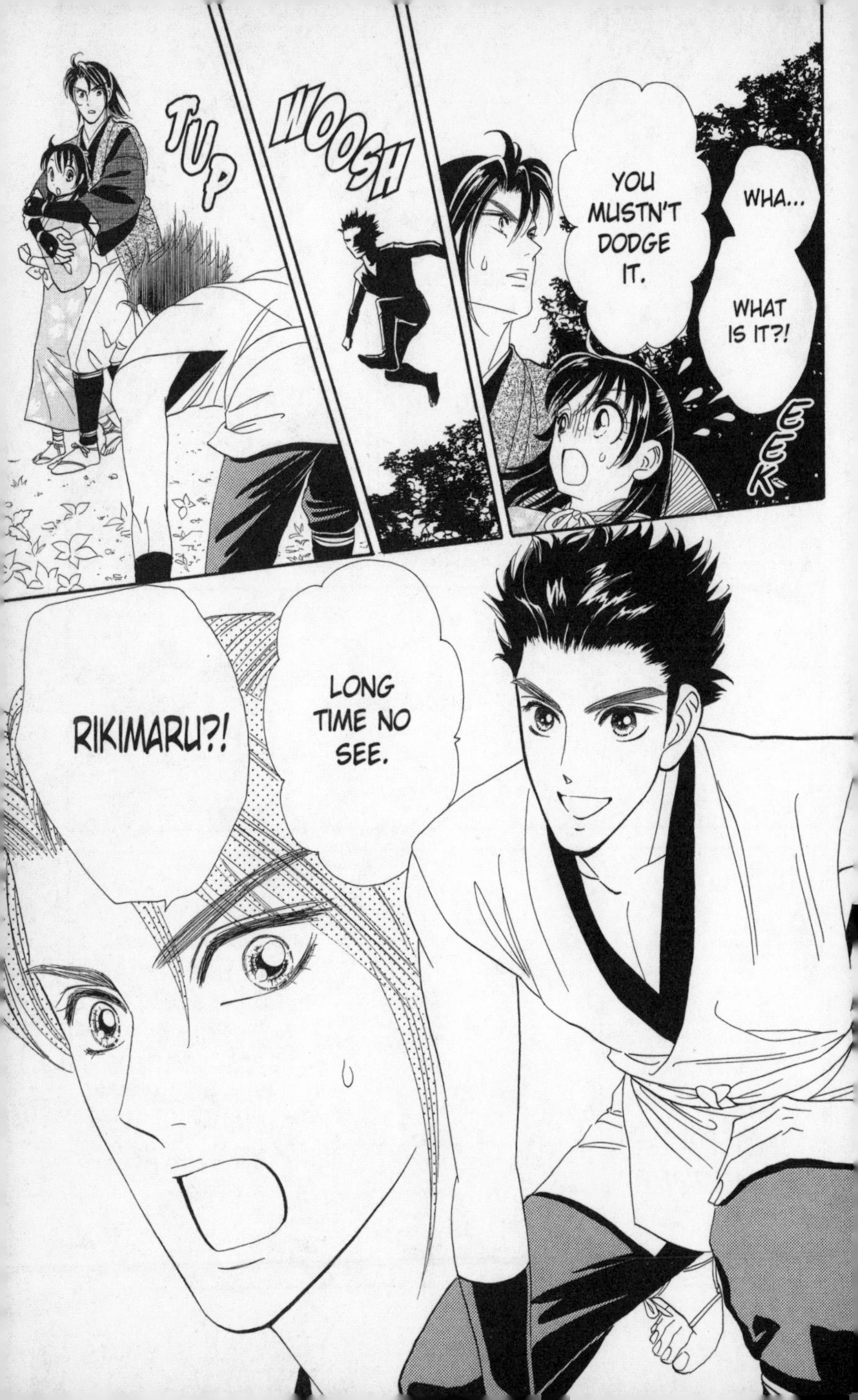
WHA... WHAT IS IT?!
YOU MUSTN'T DODGE IT.
EEK
WOOSH
TUP
LONG TIME NO SEE.
RIKIMARU?!

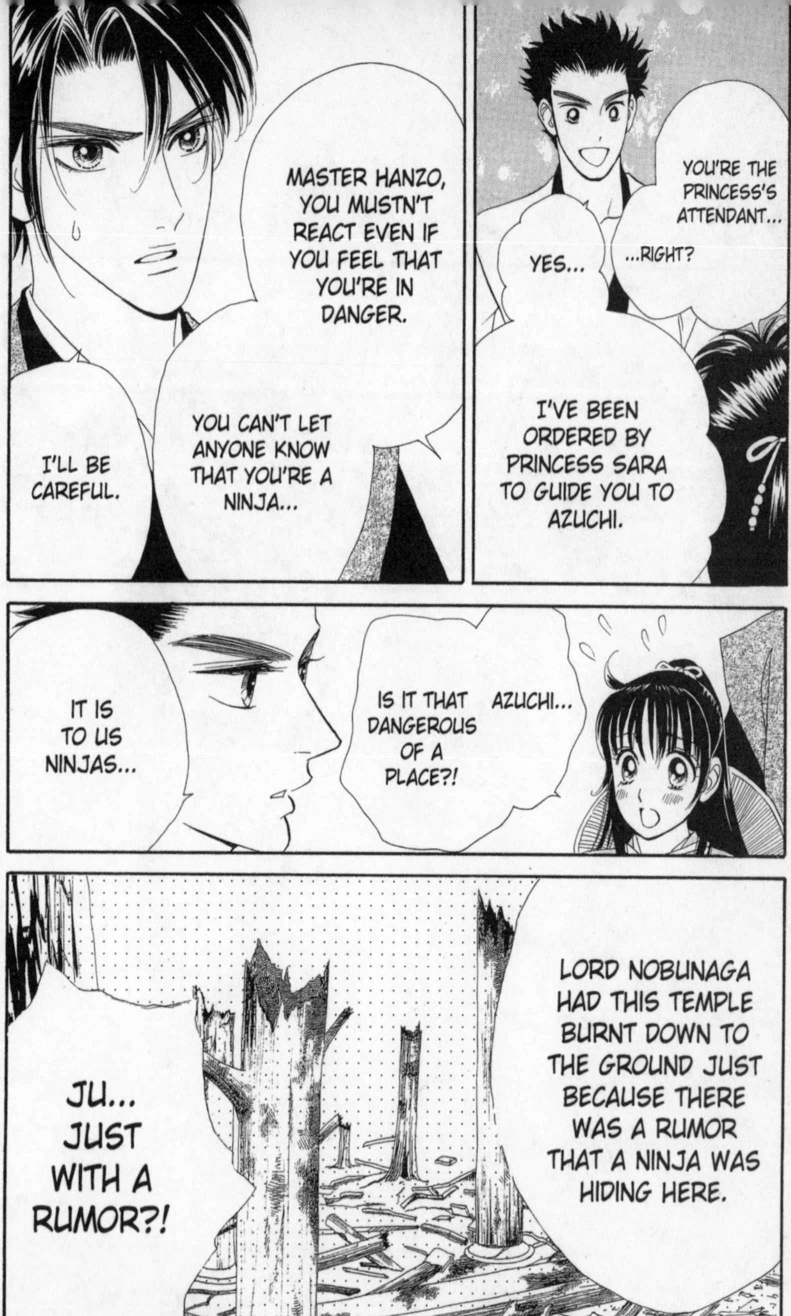
YOU'RE THE PRINCESS'S ATTENDANT...
...RIGHT?
YES...
I'VE BEEN ORDERED BY PRINCESS SARA TO GUIDE YOU TO AZUCHI.
MASTER HANZO, YOU MUSTN'T REACT EVEN IF YOU FEEL THAT YOU'RE IN DANGER.
YOU CAN'T LET ANYONE KNOW THAT YOU'RE A NINJA...
I'LL BE CAREFUL.
AZUCHI...
IS IT THAT DANGEROUS OF A PLACE?!
IT IS TO US NINJAS...
LORD NOBUNAGA HAD THIS TEMPLE BURNT DOWN TO THE GROUND JUST BECAUSE THERE WAS A RUMOR THAT A NINJA WAS HIDING HERE.
JU... JUST WITH A RUMOR?!

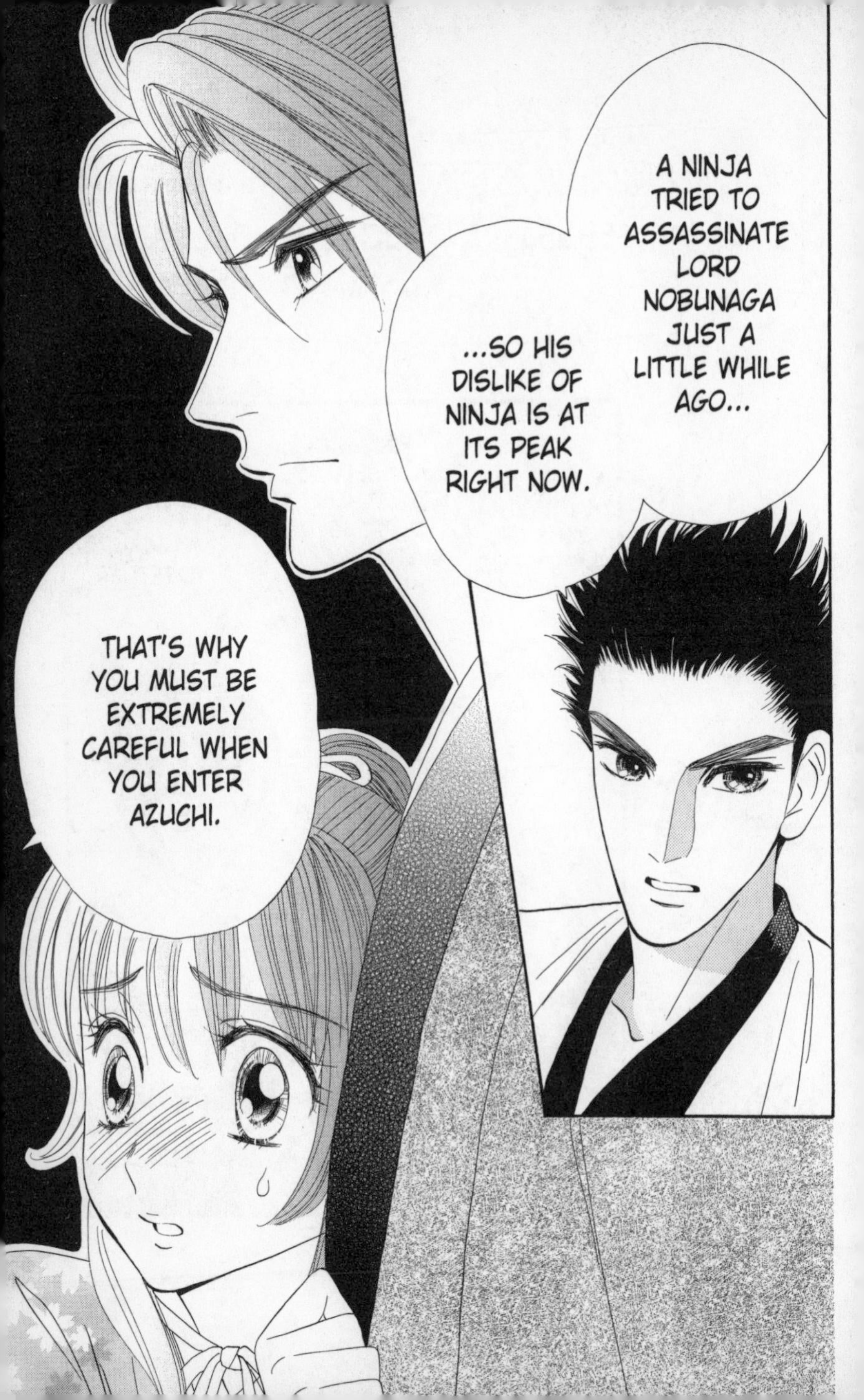
A NINJA TRIED TO ASSASSINATE LORD NOBUNAGA JUST A LITTLE WHILE AGO...
...SO HIS DISLIKE OF NINJA IS AT ITS PEAK RIGHT NOW.
THAT'S WHY YOU MUST BE EXTREMELY CAREFUL WHEN YOU ENTER AZUCHI.

TAIL OF THE MOON EXTRA: TODAY'S MISSION

"I WANT TO SEE USAGI AND YURI AS SCHOOL GIRLS."

-MIKAN, WAKAYAMA PREFECTURE

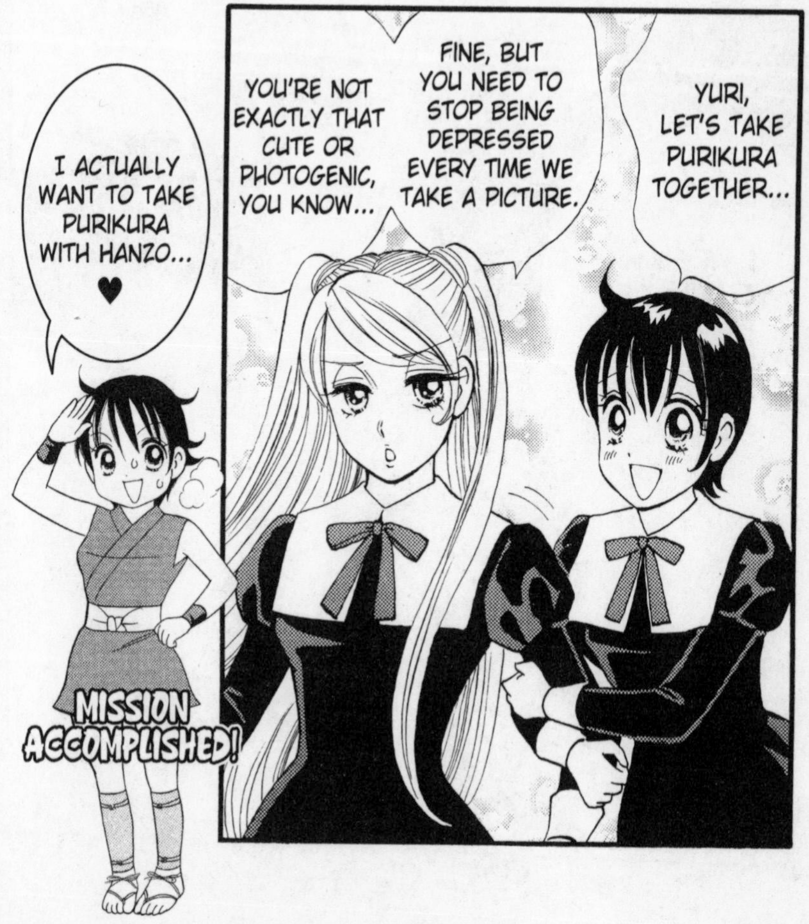
YURI, LET'S TAKE PURIKURA TOGETHER...
FINE, BUT YOU NEED TO STOP BEING DEPRESSED EVERY TIME WE TAKE A PICTURE.
YOU'RE NOT EXACTLY THAT CUTE OR PHOTOGENIC, YOU KNOW...
I ACTUALLY WANT TO TAKE PURIKURA WITH HANZO... ♥
MISSION ACCOMPLISHED!

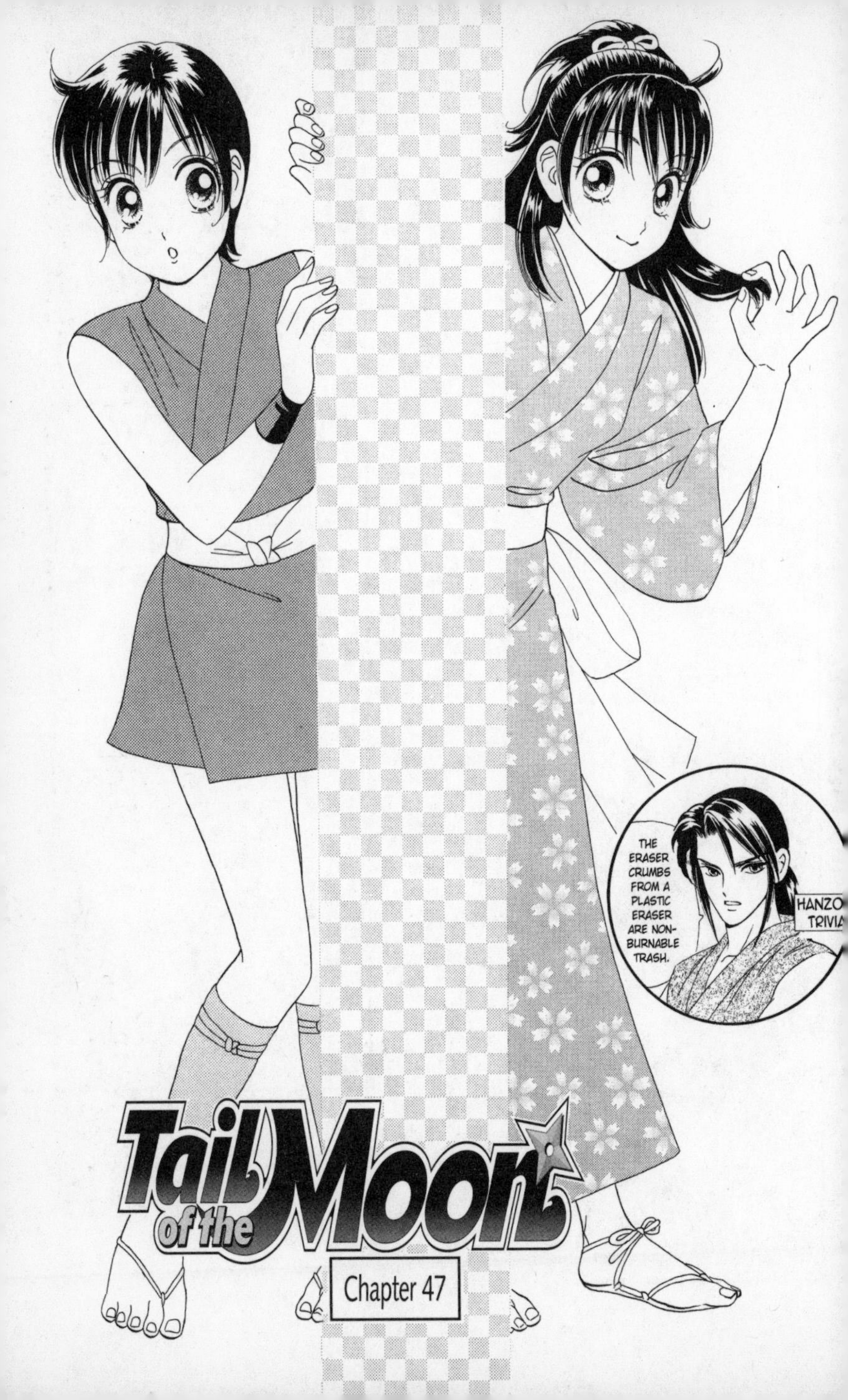
Tail of the Moon
Chapter 47
HANZO TRIVIA
THE ERASER CRUMBS FROM A PLASTIC ERASER ARE NON-BURNABLE TRASH.

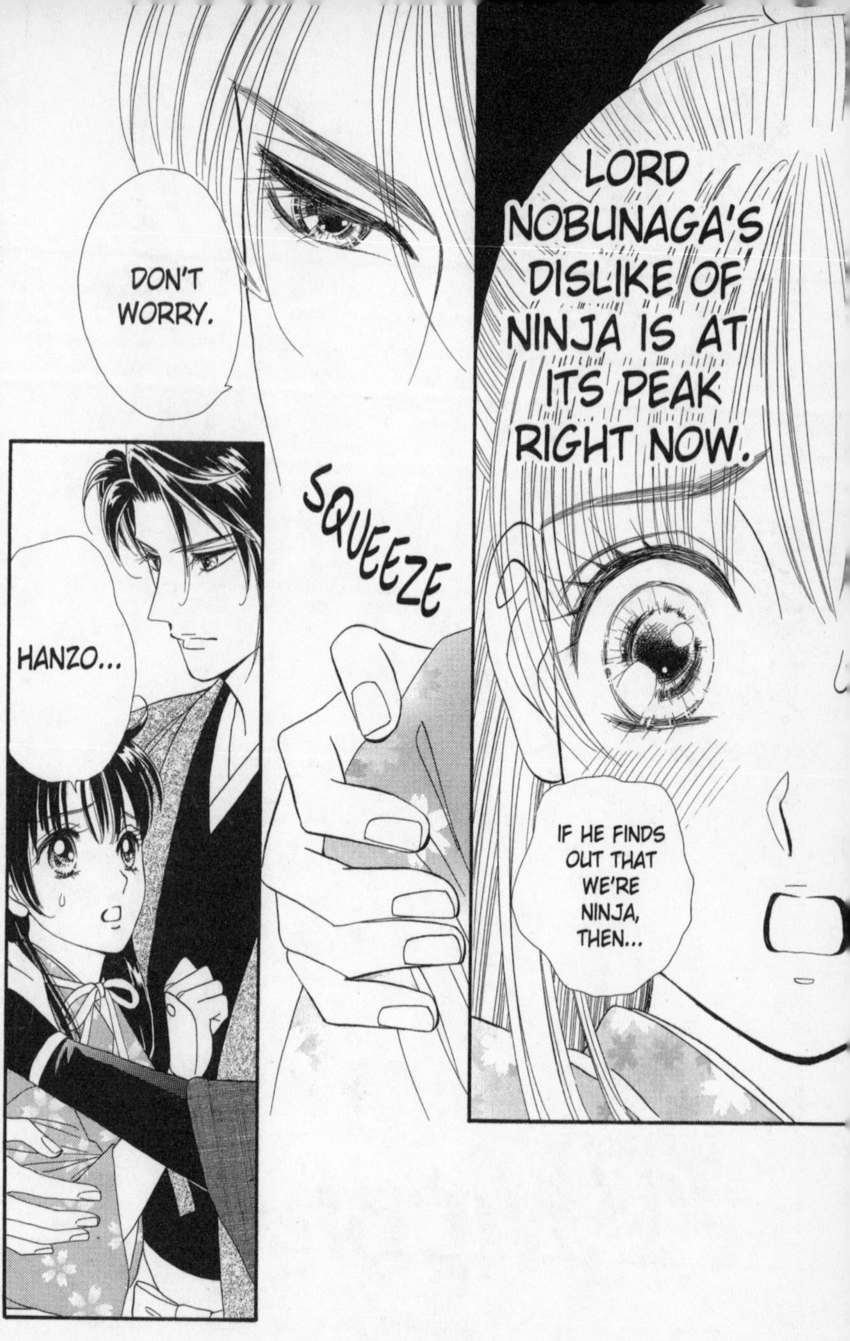
LORD NOBUNAGA'S DISLIKE OF NINJA IS AT ITS PEAK RIGHT NOW.
IF HE FINDS OUT THAT WE'RE NINJA, THEN...
DON'T WORRY.
SQUEEZE
HANZO...

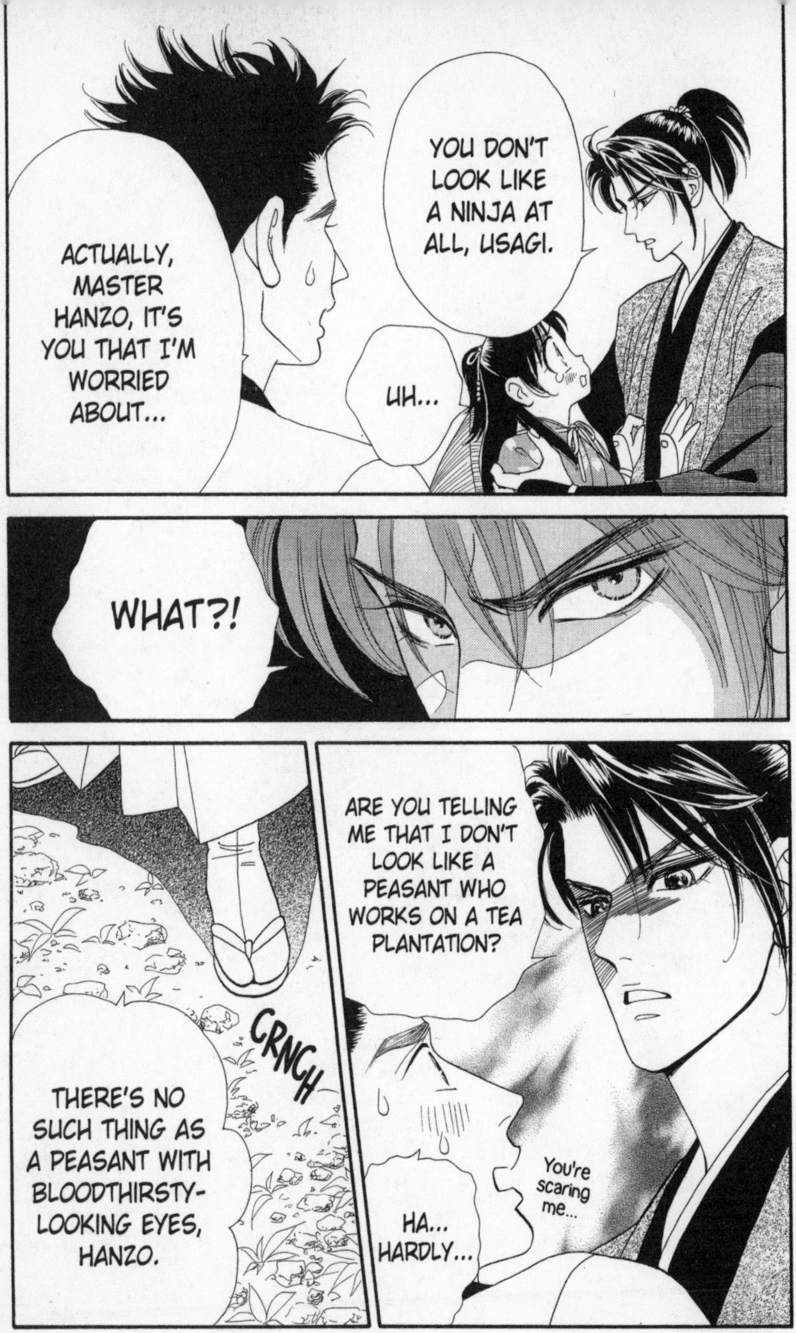
YOU DON'T LOOK LIKE A NINJA AT ALL, USAGI.
UH...
ACTUALLY, MASTER HANZO, IT'S YOU THAT I'M WORRIED ABOUT...
WHAT?!
ARE YOU TELLING ME THAT I DON'T LOOK LIKE A PEASANT WHO WORKS ON A TEA PLANTATION?
You're scaring me...
HA... HARDLY...
CRNCH
THERE'S NO SUCH THING AS A PEASANT WITH BLOODTHIRSTY-LOOKING EYES, HANZO.

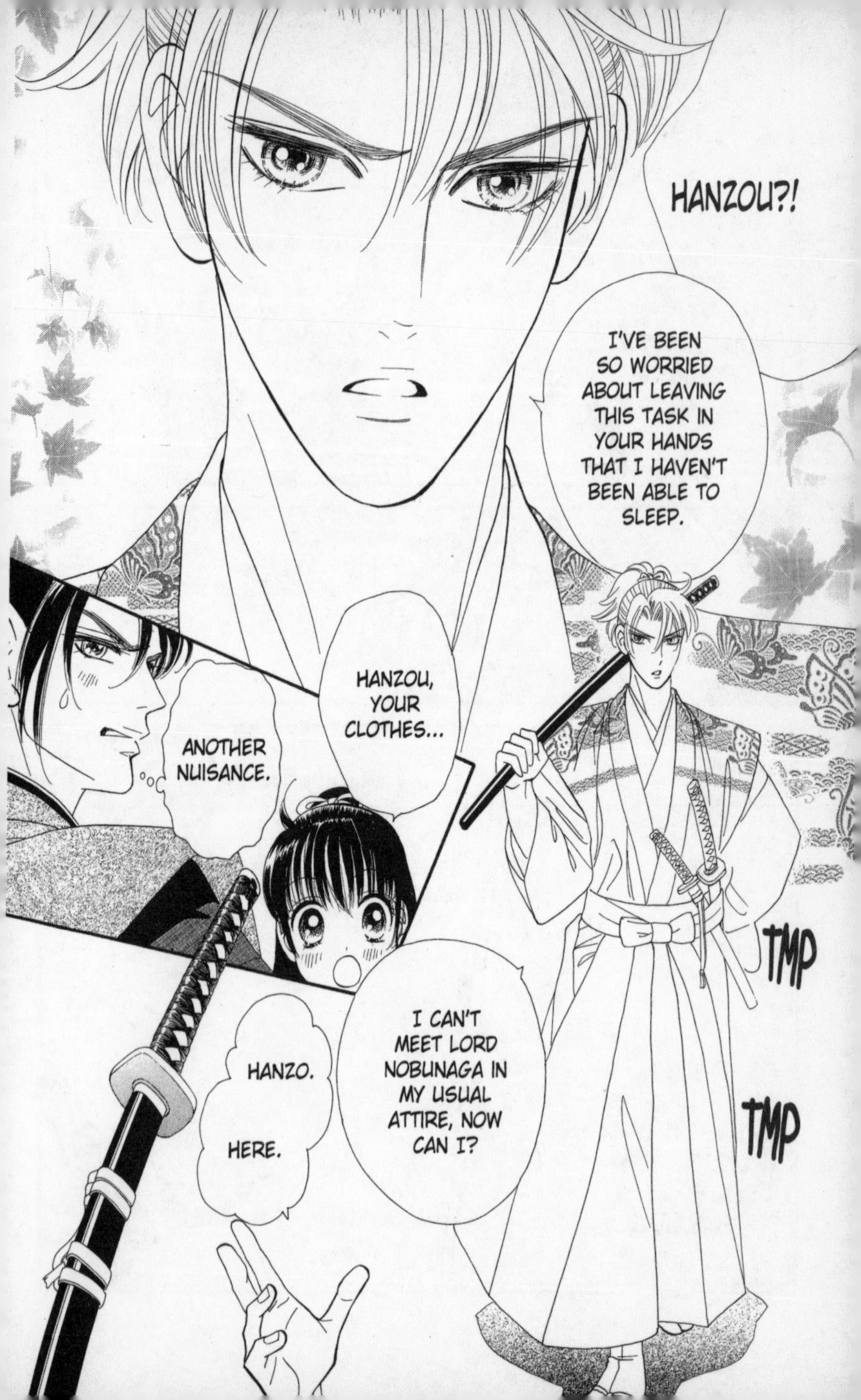
HANZOU?!
I'VE BEEN SO WORRIED ABOUT LEAVING THIS TASK IN YOUR HANDS THAT I HAVEN'T BEEN ABLE TO SLEEP.
HANZOU, YOUR CLOTHES...
ANOTHER NUISANCE.
TMP
TMP
I CAN'T MEET LORD NOBUNAGA IN MY USUAL ATTIRE, NOW CAN I?
HANZO.
HERE.

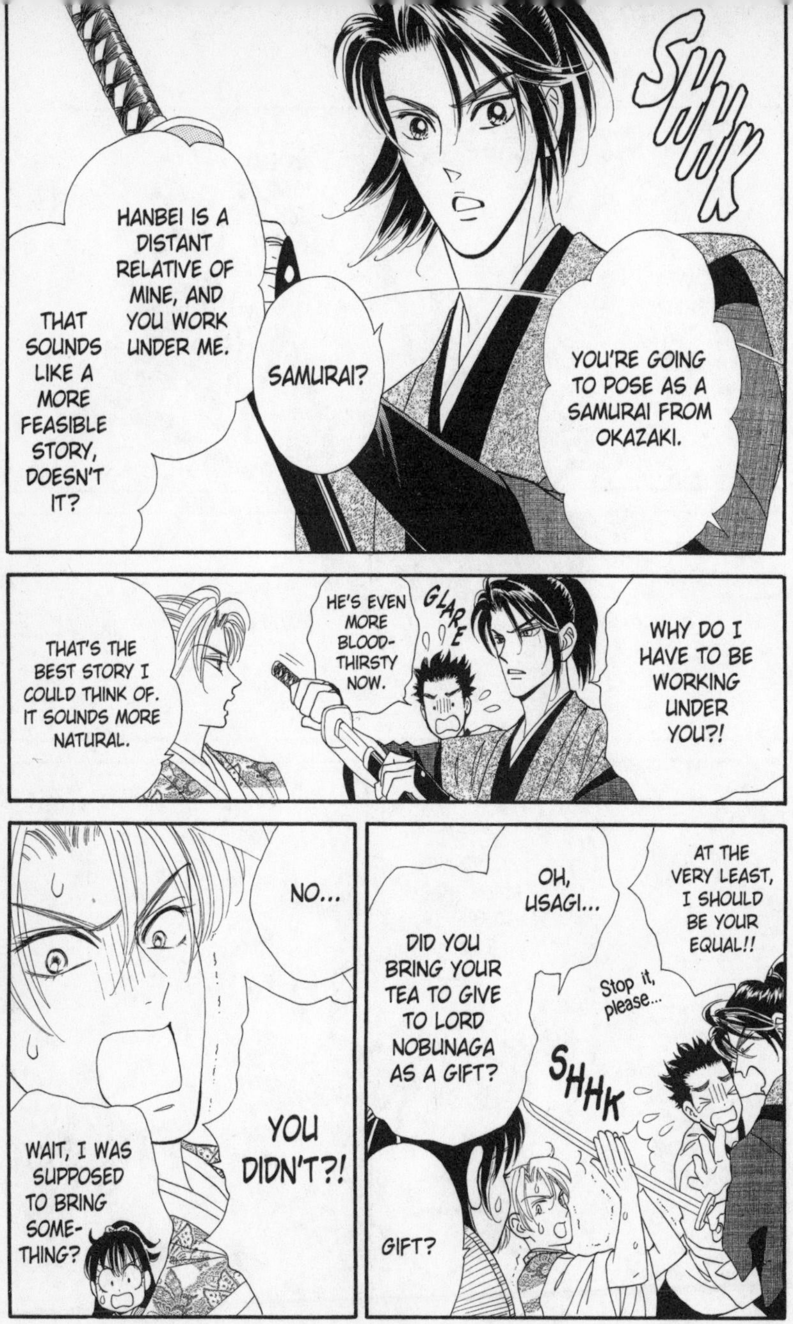
SHHK
YOU'RE GOING TO POSE AS A SAMURAI FROM OKAZAKI.
SAMURAI?
HANBEI IS A DISTANT RELATIVE OF MINE, AND YOU WORK UNDER ME.
THAT SOUNDS LIKE A MORE FEASIBLE STORY, DOESN'T IT?
WHY DO I HAVE TO BE WORKING UNDER YOU?!
GLARE
HE'S EVEN MORE BLOOD-THIRSTY NOW.
THAT'S THE BEST STORY I COULD THINK OF. IT SOUNDS MORE NATURAL.
AT THE VERY LEAST, I SHOULD BE YOUR EQUAL!!
OH, USAGI...
DID YOU BRING YOUR TEA TO GIVE TO LORD NOBUNAGA AS A GIFT?
Stop it, please...
SHHK
GIFT?
NO...
YOU DIDN'T?!
WAIT, I WAS SUPPOSED TO BRING SOME-THING?

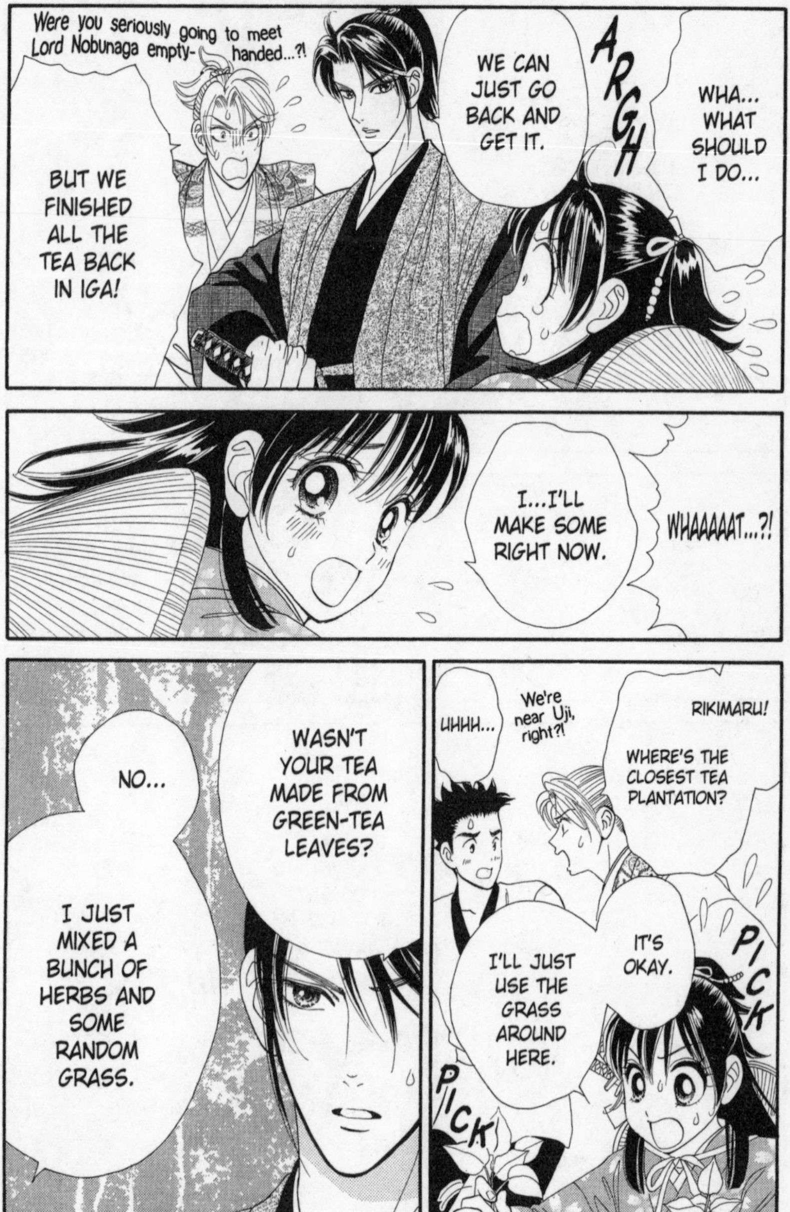
WHA... WHAT SHOULD I DO...
ARGH
WE CAN JUST GO BACK AND GET IT.
Were you seriously going to meet Lord Nobunaga empty-handed...?!
BUT WE FINISHED ALL THE TEA BACK IN IGA!
WHAAAAAT...?!
I...I'LL MAKE SOME RIGHT NOW.
RIKIMARU!
WHERE'S THE CLOSEST TEA PLANTATION?
We're near Uji, right?!
UHHH...
PICK
IT'S OKAY.
I'LL JUST USE THE GRASS AROUND HERE.
PICK
WASN'T YOUR TEA MADE FROM GREEN-TEA LEAVES?
NO...
I JUST MIXED A BUNCH OF HERBS AND SOME RANDOM GRASS.

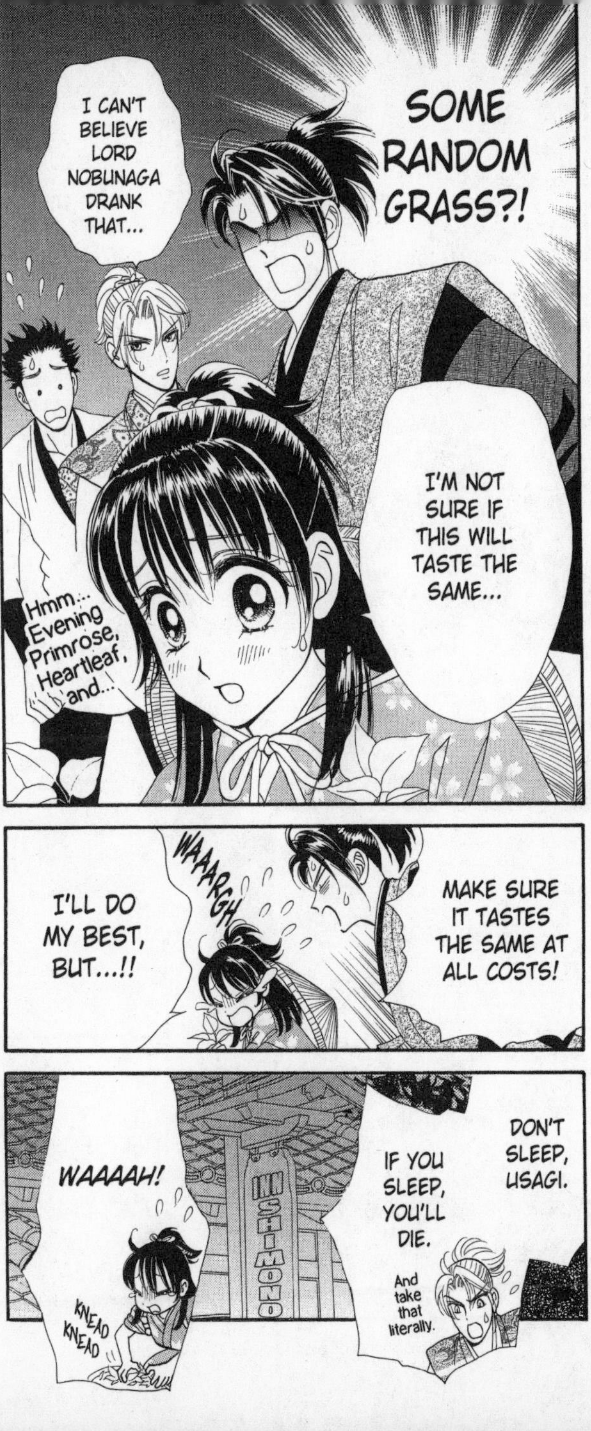
SOME RANDOM GRASS?!
I CAN'T BELIEVE LORD NOBUNAGA DRANK THAT...
I'M NOT SURE IF THIS WILL TASTE THE SAME...
Hmm... Evening Primrose, Heartleaf, and...
MAKE SURE IT TASTES THE SAME AT ALL COSTS!
WAAARGH
I'LL DO MY BEST, BUT...!!
DON'T SLEEP, USAGI.
IF YOU SLEEP, YOU'LL DIE.
And take that literally.
INN SHIMONO
WAAAAH!
KNEAD KNEAD

UE-RIN'S WAY OF THE MANGA 9

I had a lot of fun drawing focus lines and shadowing, but I had to practice hard every day to overcome my "I don't like it because I'm not good at it" sentiment.

I kept my promise of sending in one manga per month, and I finally received a small award around my third work. Gradually, I began to toddle up the thin "Manga Path" with the help of a supervisor.

Back then, the editor in charge of "Manga School" visited Osaka and decided to hold a meeting with several of the people in the Kansai region who had submitted their work. So for the first time, I went to the big city of Osaka from the great countryside of Nara. Alhough it was a prefecture right next to mine (well, a city), Osaka felt like a huge metropolis that was far, far away.

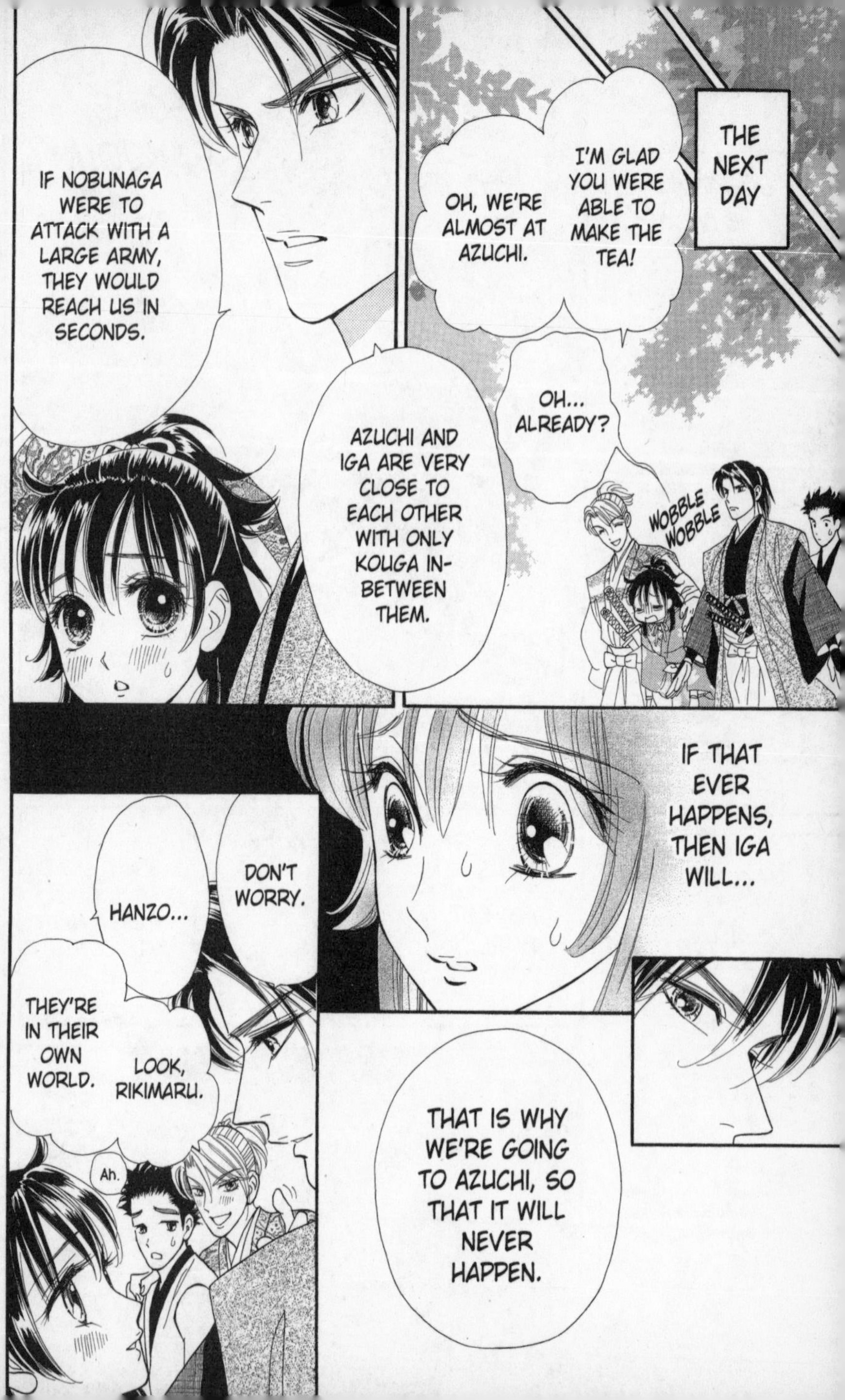
THE NEXT DAY
I'M GLAD YOU WERE ABLE TO MAKE THE TEA!
OH, WE'RE ALMOST AT AZUCHI.
OH... ALREADY?
WOBBLE WOBBLE
AZUCHI AND IGA ARE VERY CLOSE TO EACH OTHER WITH ONLY KOUGA IN-BETWEEN THEM.
IF NOBUNAGA WERE TO ATTACK WITH A LARGE ARMY, THEY WOULD REACH US IN SECONDS.
IF THAT EVER HAPPENS, THEN IGA WILL...
THAT IS WHY WE'RE GOING TO AZUCHI, SO THAT IT WILL NEVER HAPPEN.
DON'T WORRY.
HANZO...
LOOK, RIKIMARU.
THEY'RE IN THEIR OWN WORLD.
Ah.

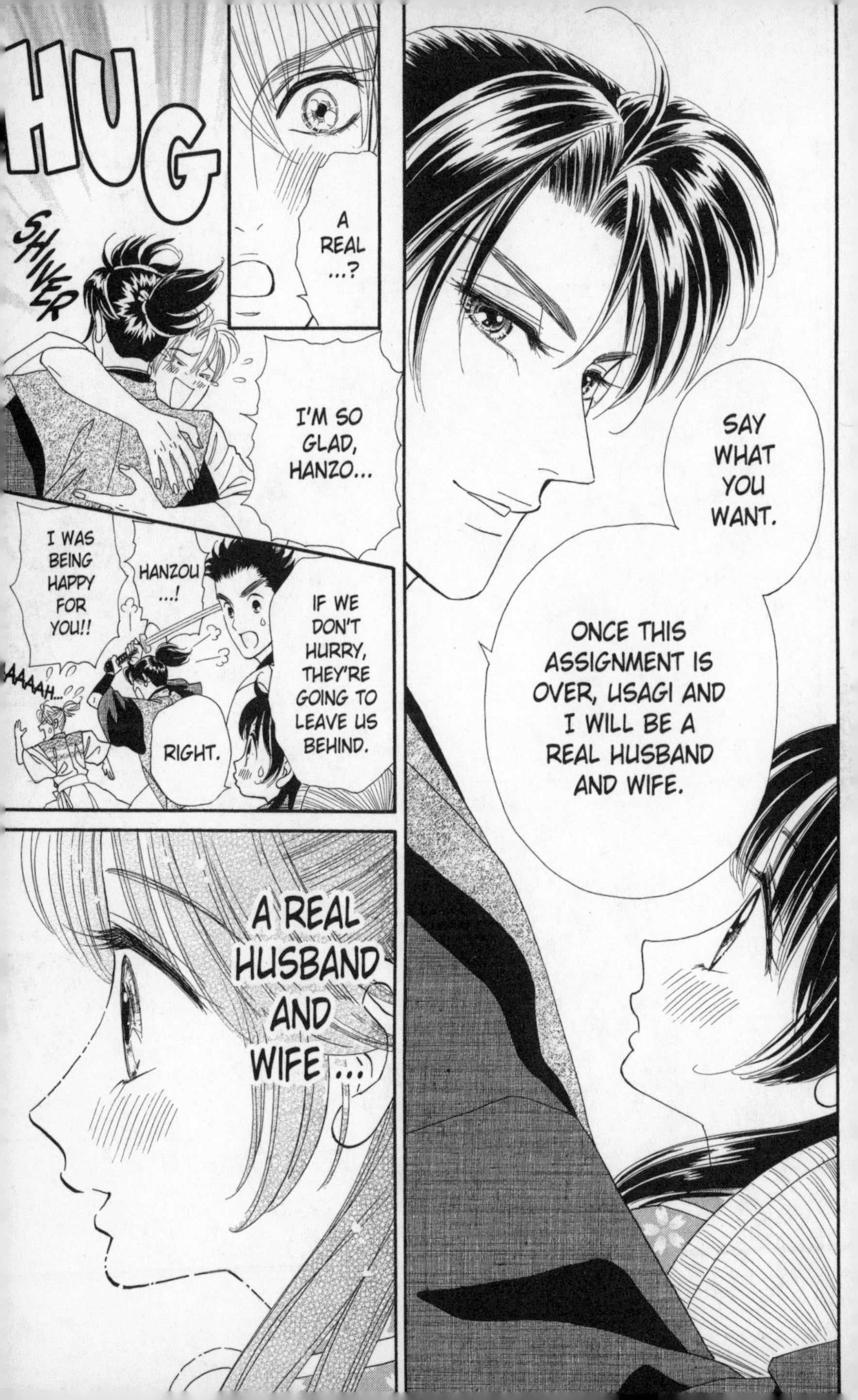
SAY WHAT YOU WANT.
ONCE THIS ASSIGNMENT IS OVER, USAGI AND I WILL BE A REAL HUSBAND AND WIFE.
A REAL ...?
HUG
SHIVER
I'M SO GLAD, HANZO...
IF WE DON'T HURRY, THEY'RE GOING TO LEAVE US BEHIND.
RIGHT.
HANZOU ...!
I WAS BEING HAPPY FOR YOU!!
AAAAAH...
A REAL HUSBAND AND WIFE ...!

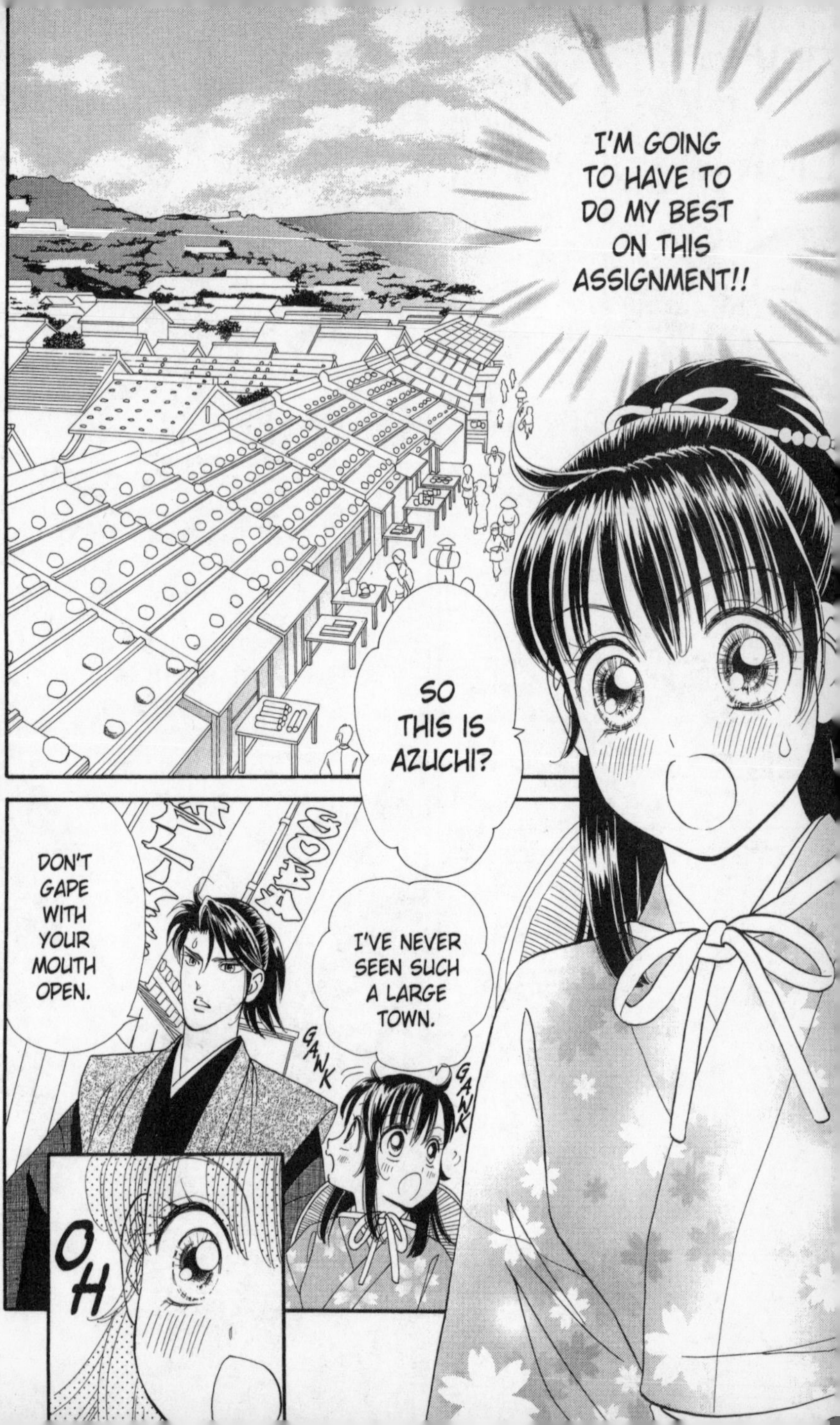
I'M GOING TO HAVE TO DO MY BEST ON THIS ASSIGNMENT!!
SO THIS IS AZUCHI?
I'VE NEVER SEEN SUCH A LARGE TOWN.
DON'T GAPE WITH YOUR MOUTH OPEN.
GANK
GANK
OH

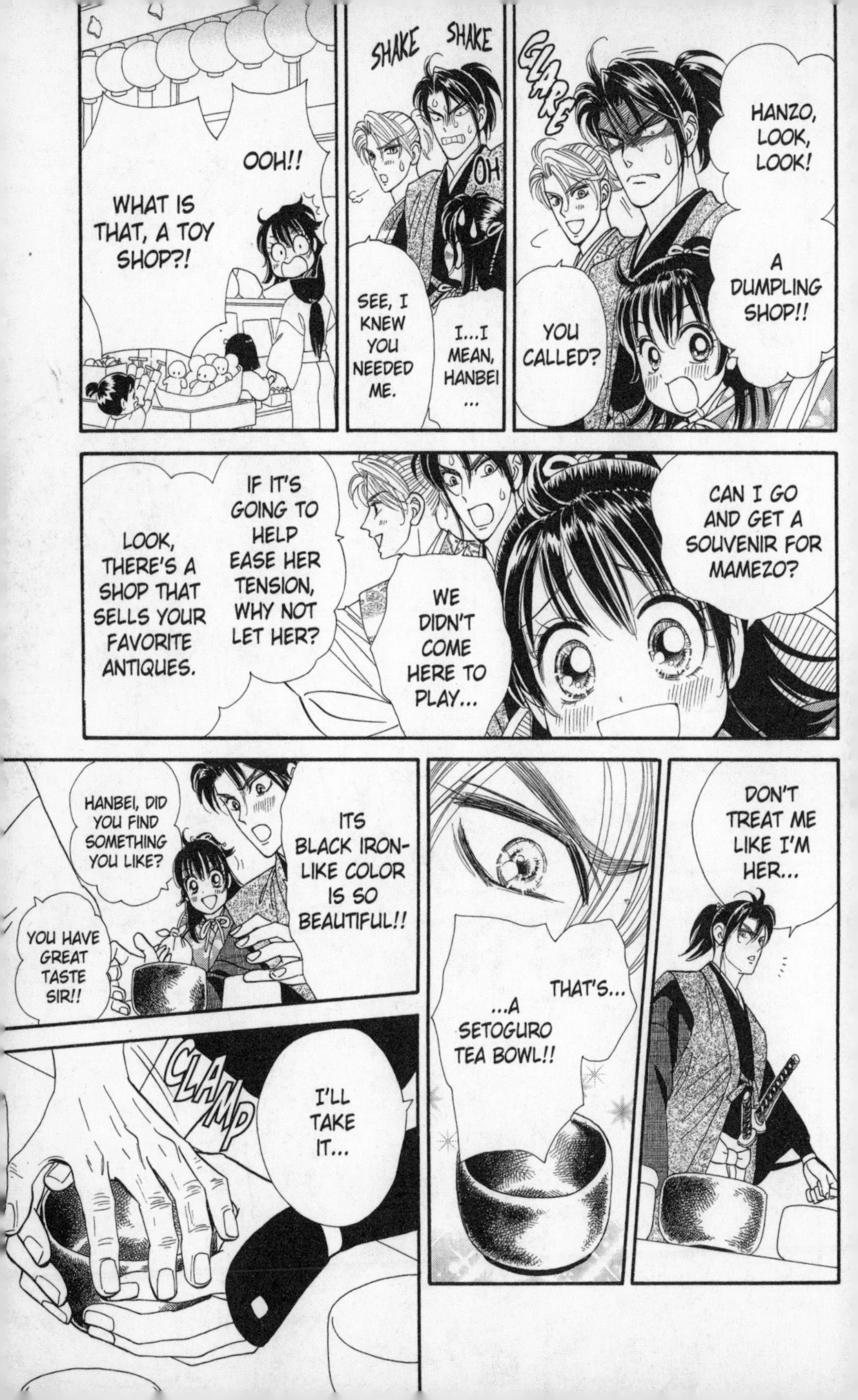
GLARE
HANZO, LOOK, LOOK!
A DUMPLING SHOP!!
YOU CALLED?
SHAKE
SHAKE
OH
I...I MEAN, HANBEI ...
SEE, I KNEW YOU NEEDED ME.
OOH!!
WHAT IS THAT, A TOY SHOP?!
CAN I GO AND GET A SOUVENIR FOR MAMEZO?
WE DIDN'T COME HERE TO PLAY...
IF IT'S GOING TO HELP EASE HER TENSION, WHY NOT LET HER?
LOOK, THERE'S A SHOP THAT SELLS YOUR FAVORITE ANTIQUES.
DON'T TREAT ME LIKE I'M HER...
THAT'S...
...A SETOGURO TEA BOWL!!
HANBEI, DID YOU FIND SOMETHING YOU LIKE?
ITS BLACK IRON-LIKE COLOR IS SO BEAUTIFUL!!
YOU HAVE GREAT TASTE SIR!!
CLAMP
I'LL TAKE IT...

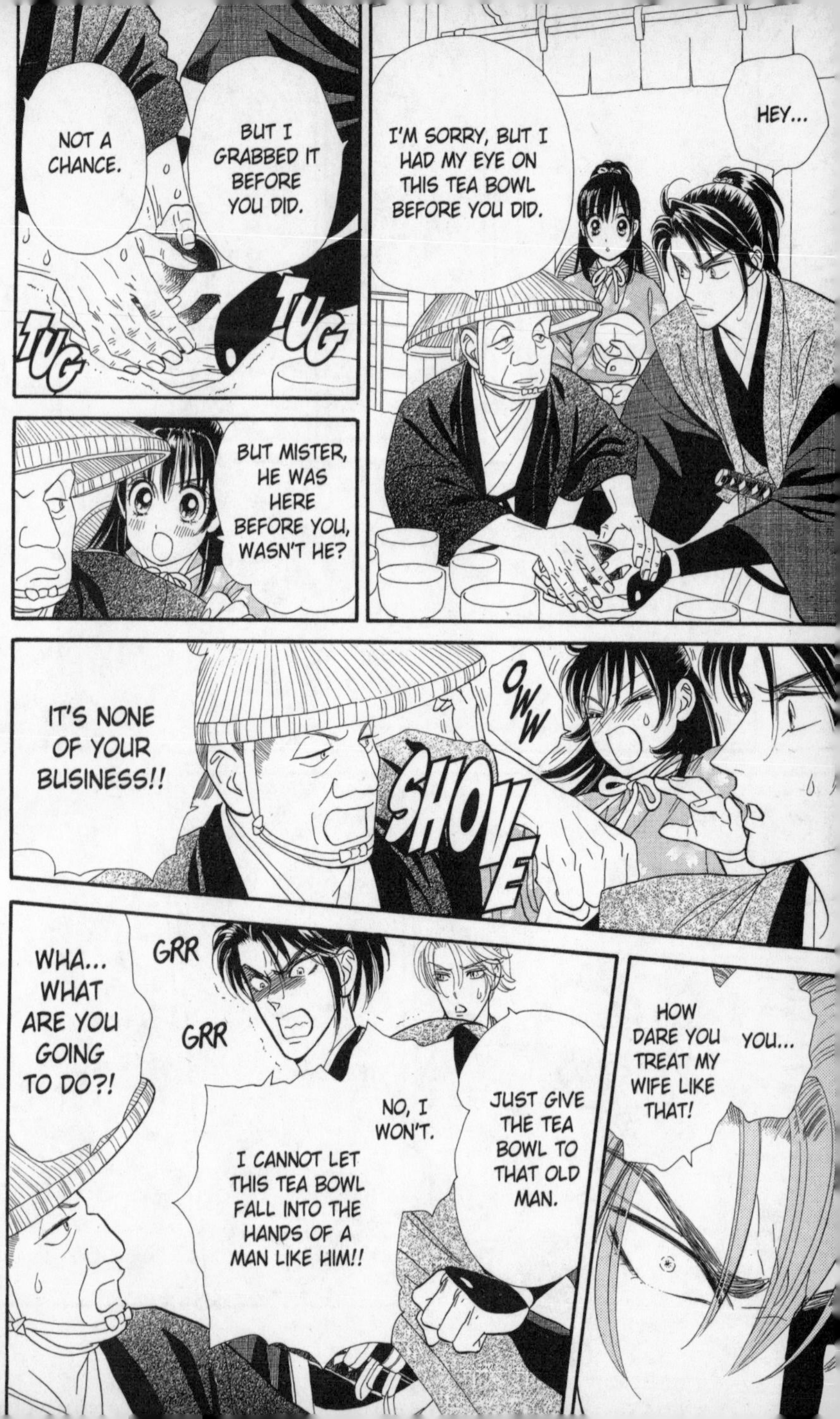
HEY...
I'M SORRY, BUT I HAD MY EYE ON THIS TEA BOWL BEFORE YOU DID.
BUT I GRABBED IT BEFORE YOU DID.
NOT A CHANCE.
TUG
TUG
BUT MISTER, HE WAS HERE BEFORE YOU, WASN'T HE?
OWW
SHOVE
IT'S NONE OF YOUR BUSINESS!!
YOU...
HOW DARE YOU TREAT MY WIFE LIKE THAT!
JUST GIVE THE TEA BOWL TO THAT OLD MAN.
NO, I WON'T.
I CANNOT LET THIS TEA BOWL FALL INTO THE HANDS OF A MAN LIKE HIM!!
GRR
GRR
WHA... WHAT ARE YOU GOING TO DO?!

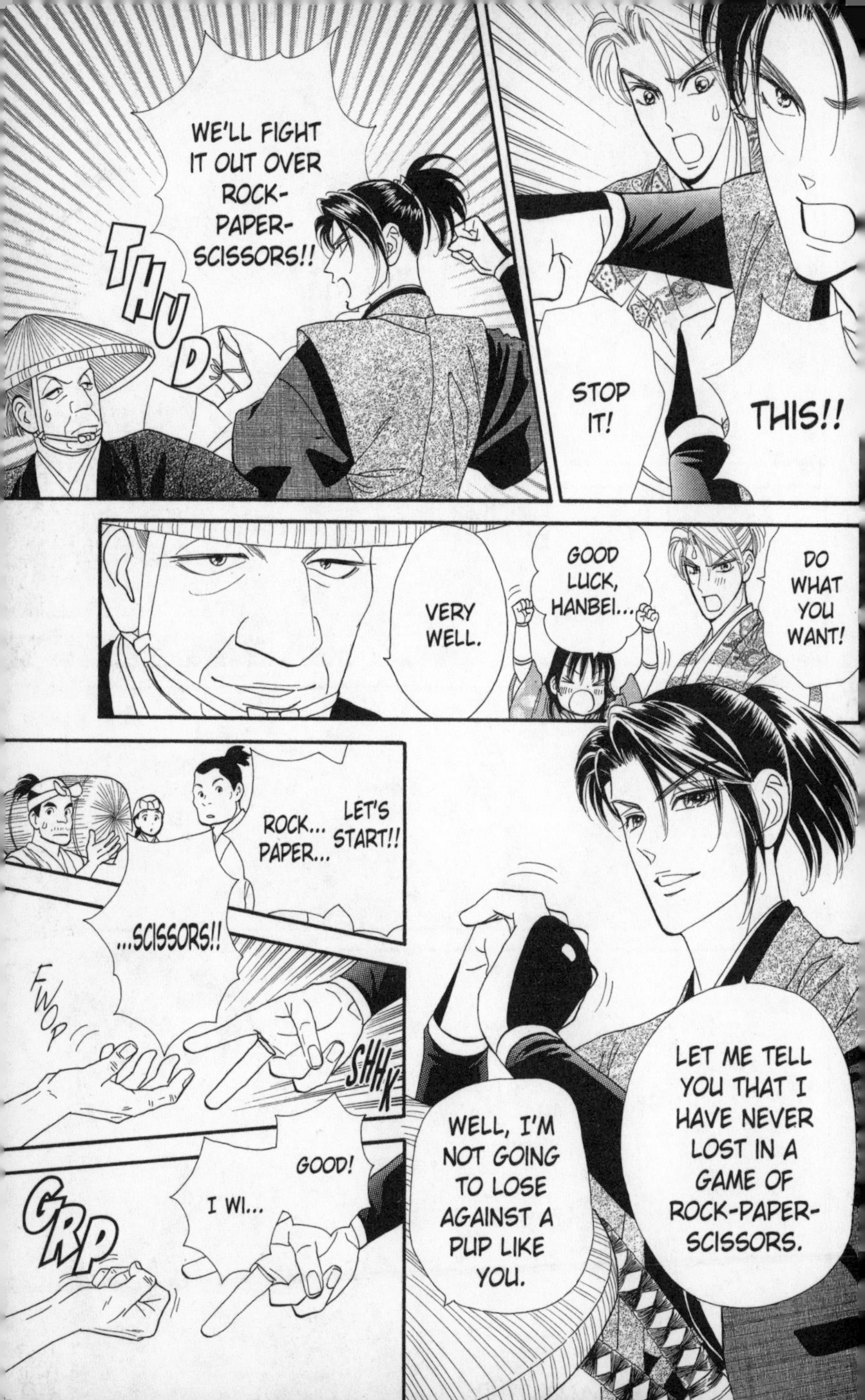
THIS!!
STOP IT!
WE'LL FIGHT IT OUT OVER ROCK-PAPER-SCISSORS!!
THUD
DO WHAT YOU WANT!
GOOD LUCK, HANBEI...
VERY WELL.
LET ME TELL YOU THAT I HAVE NEVER LOST IN A GAME OF ROCK-PAPER-SCISSORS.
WELL, I'M NOT GOING TO LOSE AGAINST A PUP LIKE YOU.
LET'S START!!
ROCK... PAPER...
...SCISSORS!!
FWOP
SHHK
GOOD!
I WI...
GRP

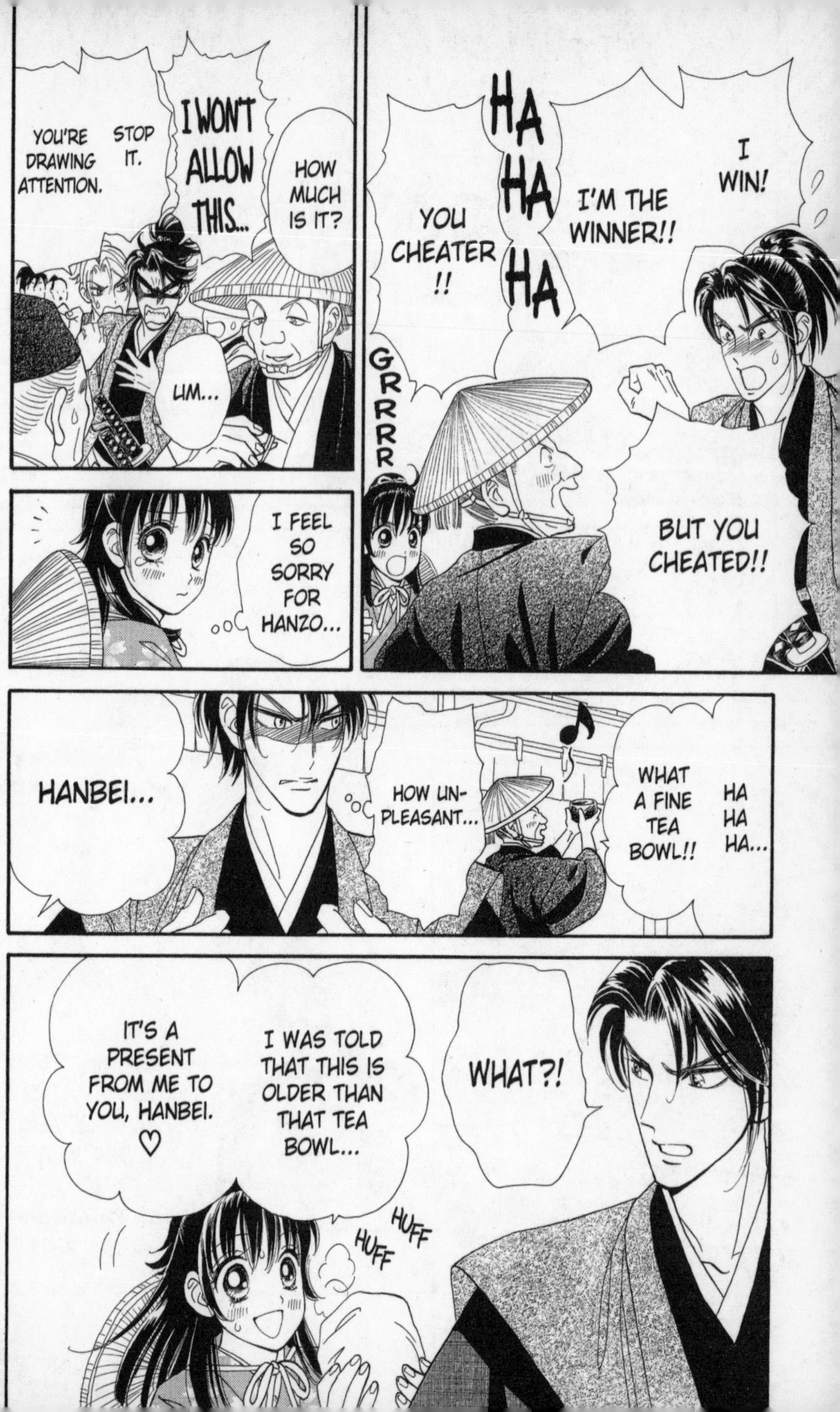
I WIN!
I'M THE WINNER!!
HA HA HA
YOU CHEATER !!
GRRRR
BUT YOU CHEATED!!
HOW MUCH IS IT?
I WON'T ALLOW THIS...
STOP IT.
YOU'RE DRAWING ATTENTION.
UM...
I FEEL SO SORRY FOR HANZO...
HA HA HA...
WHAT A FINE TEA BOWL!!
HOW UN-PLEASANT...
HANBEI...
WHAT?!
I WAS TOLD THAT THIS IS OLDER THAN THAT TEA BOWL...
IT'S A PRESENT FROM ME TO YOU, HANBEI. ♡
HUFF HUFF

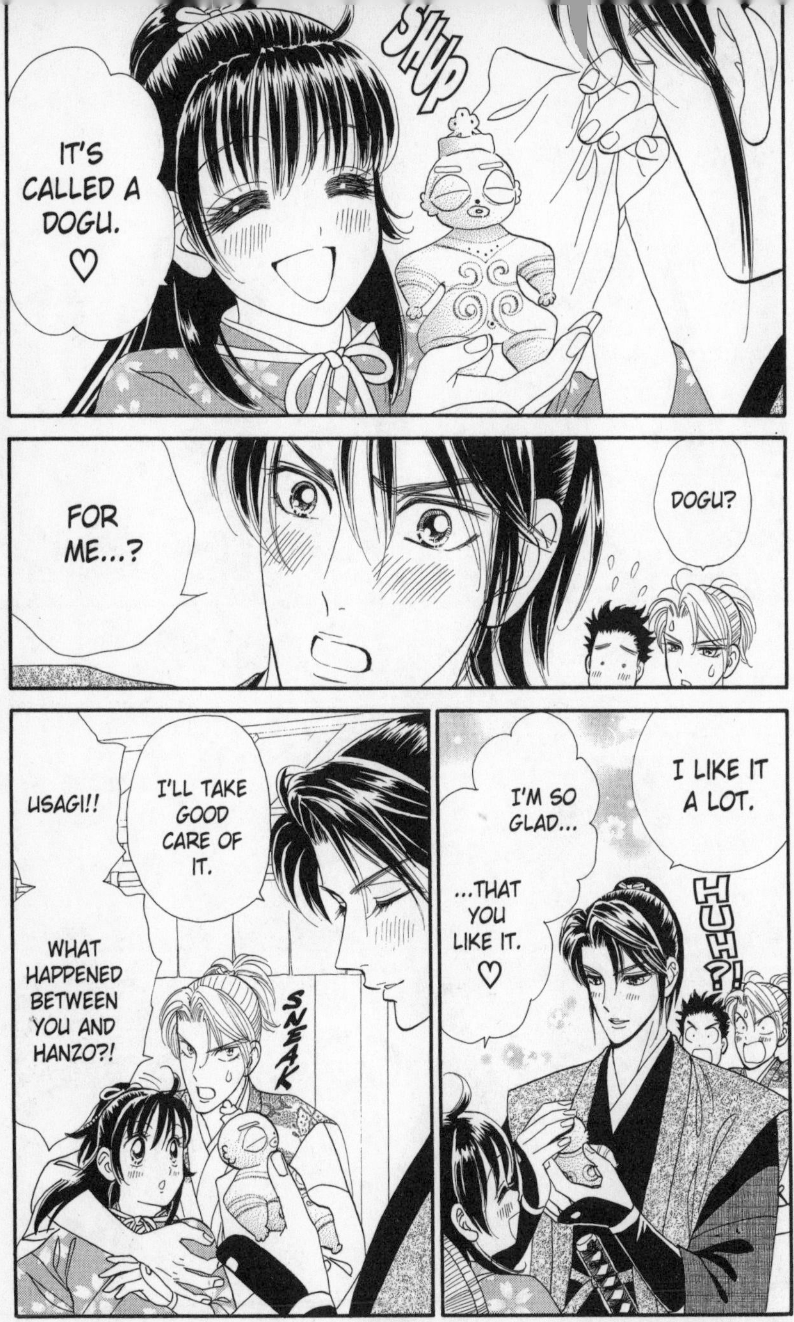
SHUP
IT'S CALLED A DOGU. ♡
DOGU?
FOR ME...?
I LIKE IT A LOT.
HUH?!
I'M SO GLAD...
...THAT YOU LIKE IT. ♡
I'LL TAKE GOOD CARE OF IT.
USAGI!!
SNEAK
WHAT HAPPENED BETWEEN YOU AND HANZO?!

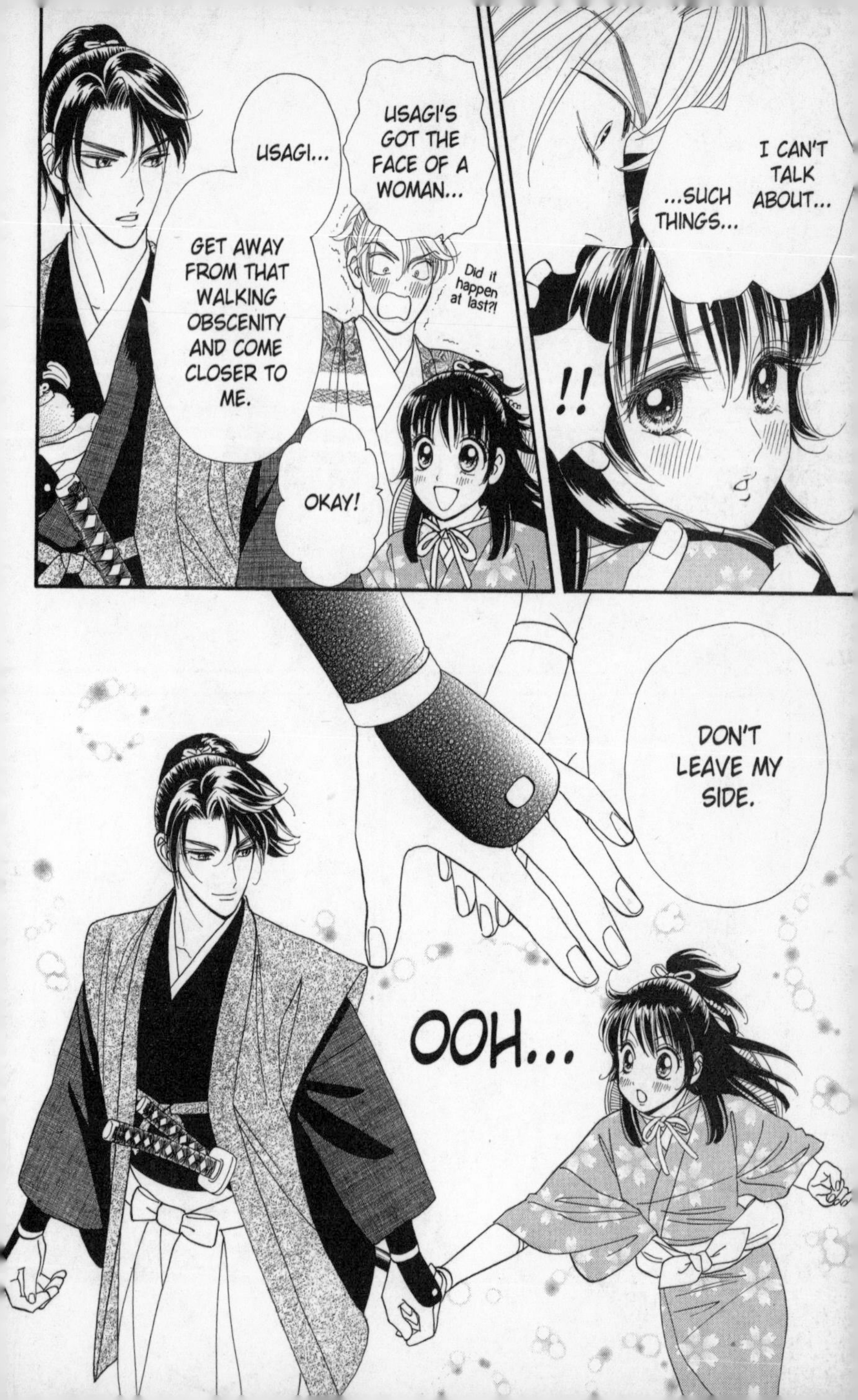
I CAN'T TALK ABOUT...
...SUCH THINGS...
!!
USAGI'S GOT THE FACE OF A WOMAN...
USAGI...
Did it happen at last?!
GET AWAY FROM THAT WALKING OBSCENITY AND COME CLOSER TO ME.
OKAY!
DON'T LEAVE MY SIDE.
OOH...

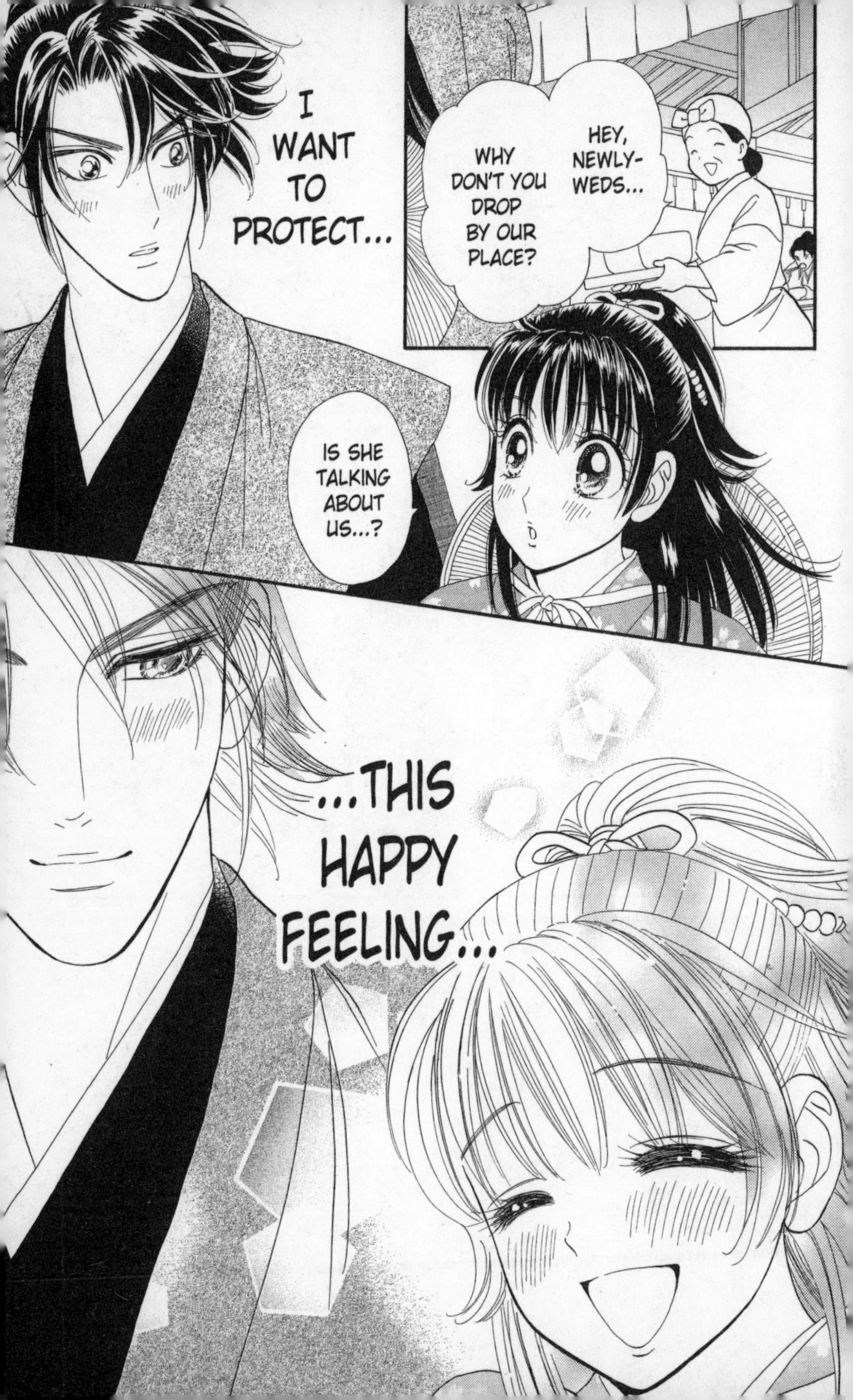
HEY, NEWLY-WEDS...
WHY DON'T YOU DROP BY OUR PLACE?
IS SHE TALKING ABOUT US...?
I WANT TO PROTECT...
...THIS HAPPY FEELING...

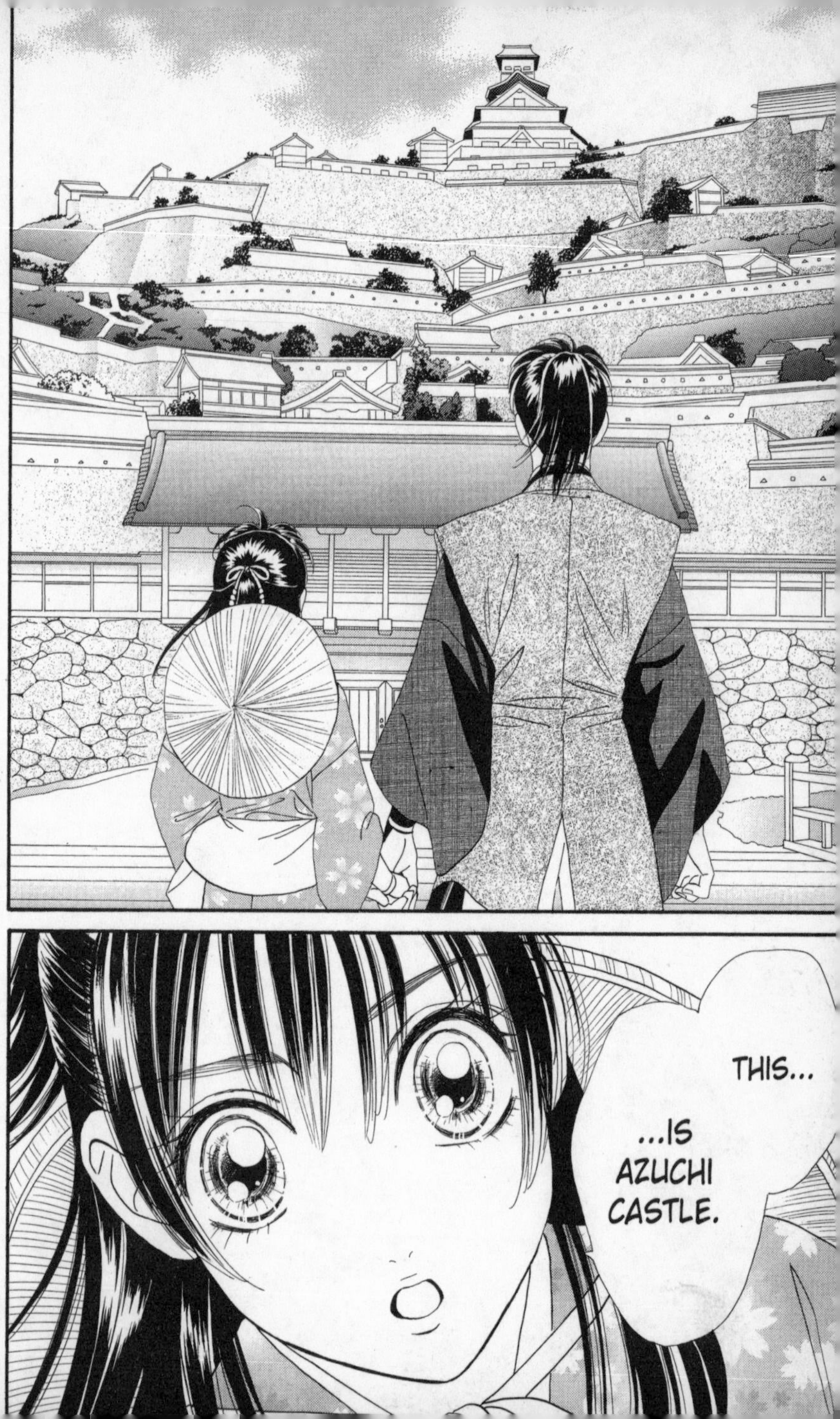
THIS...
...IS AZUCHI CASTLE.

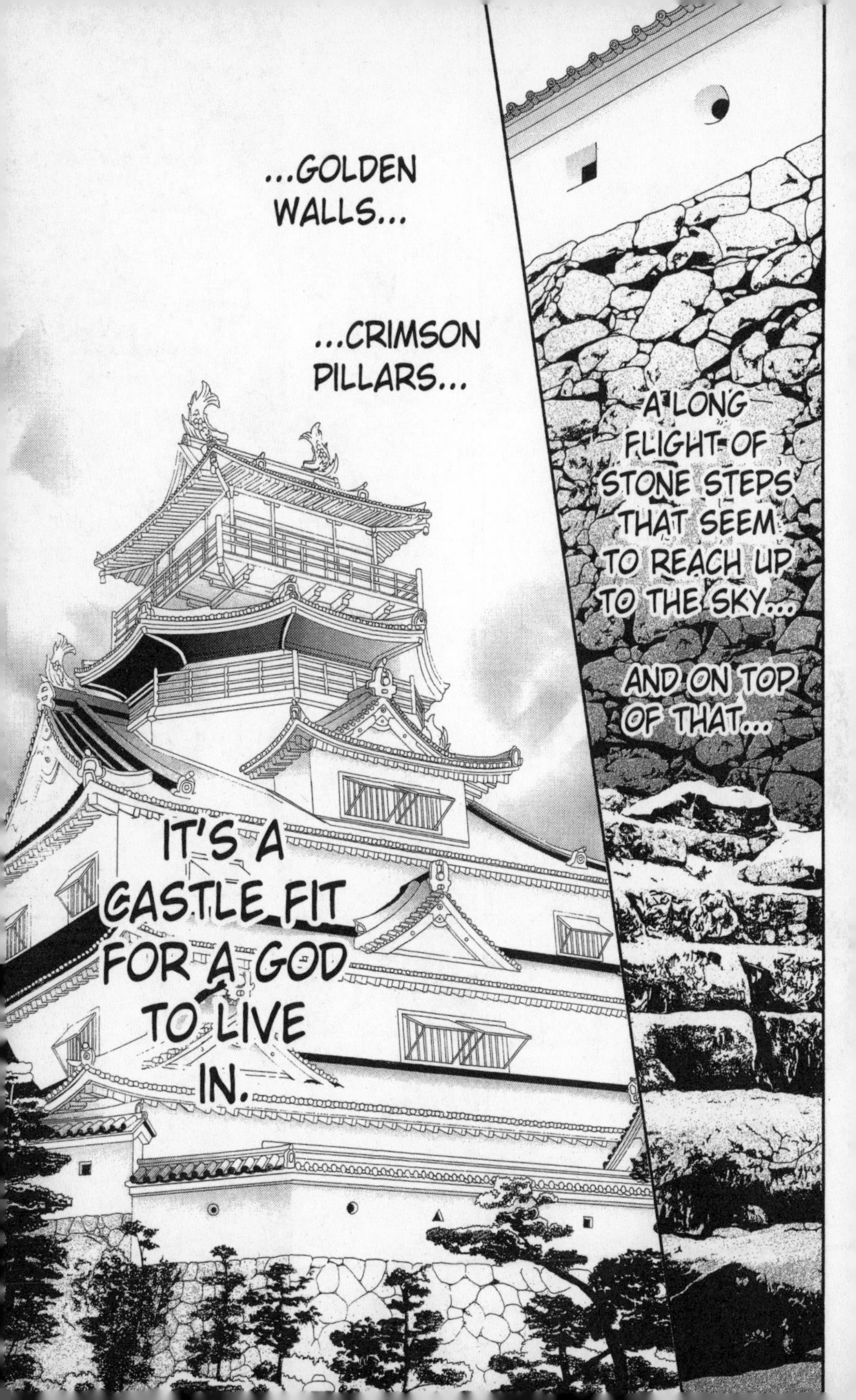
A LONG FLIGHT OF STONE STEPS THAT SEEM TO REACH UP TO THE SKY...
AND ON TOP OF THAT...
...GOLDEN WALLS...
...CRIMSON PILLARS...
IT'S A CASTLE FIT FOR A GOD TO LIVE IN.

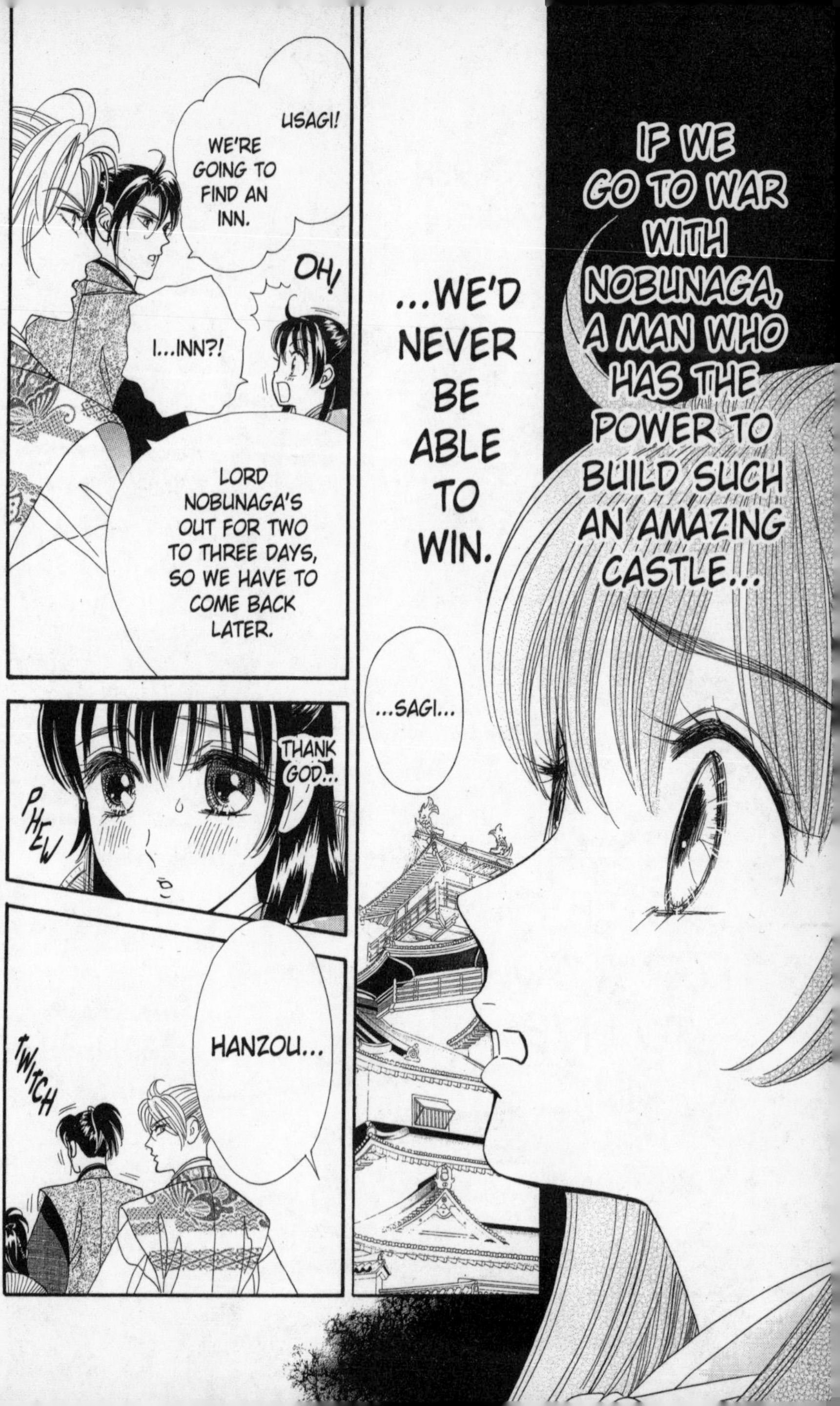
IF WE GO TO WAR WITH NOBUNAGA, A MAN WHO HAS THE POWER TO BUILD SUCH AN AMAZING CASTLE...
...WE'D NEVER BE ABLE TO WIN.
...SAGI...
USAGI!
WE'RE GOING TO FIND AN INN.
OH!
I...INN?!
LORD NOBUNAGA'S OUT FOR TWO TO THREE DAYS, SO WE HAVE TO COME BACK LATER.
THANK GOD...
PHEW
HANZOU...
TWITCH

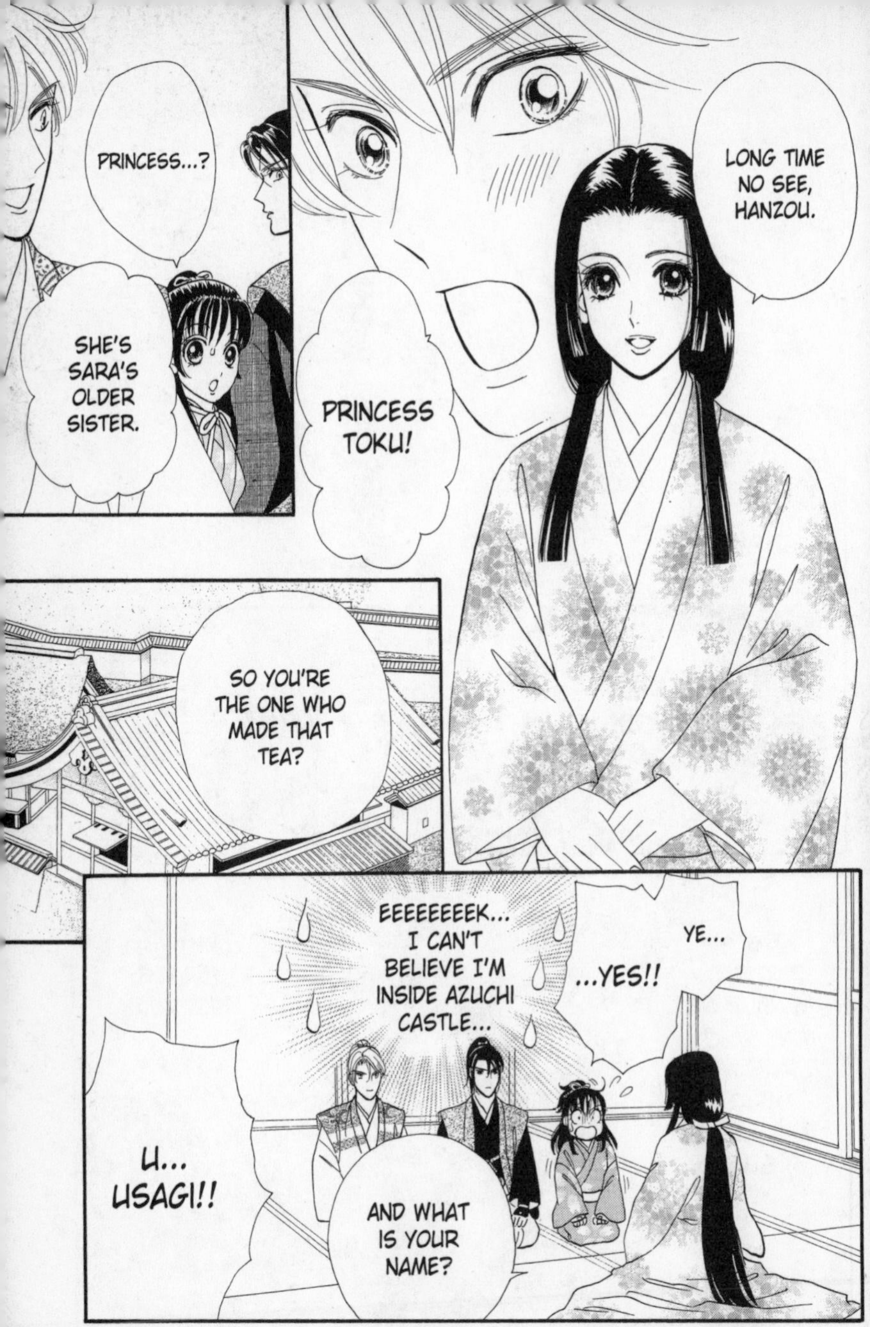
LONG TIME NO SEE, HANZOU.
PRINCESS TOKU!
PRINCESS...?
SHE'S SARA'S OLDER SISTER.
SO YOU'RE THE ONE WHO MADE THAT TEA?
YE... ...YES!!
EEEEEEEEK... I CAN'T BELIEVE I'M INSIDE AZUCHI CASTLE...
AND WHAT IS YOUR NAME?
U... USAGI!!

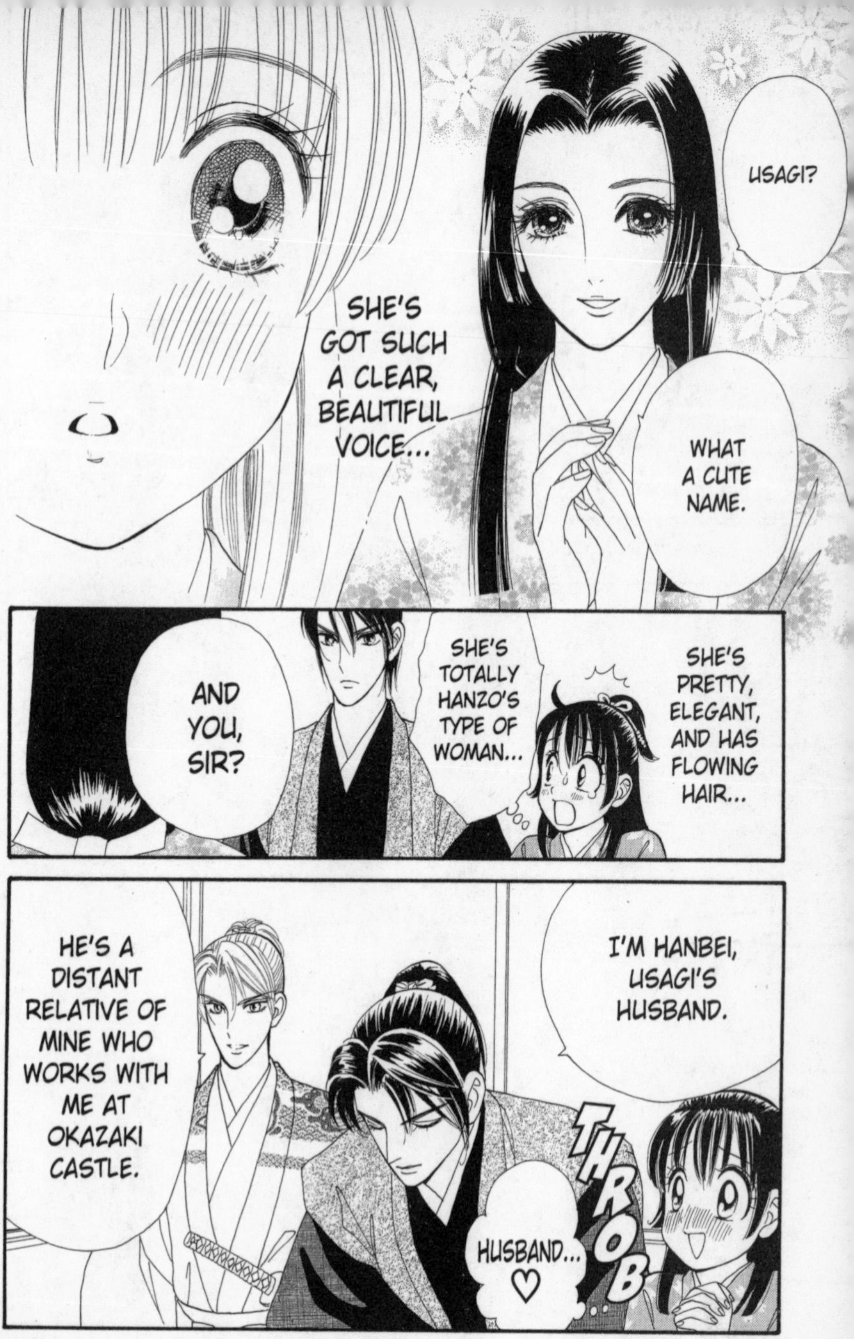
USAGI?
WHAT A CUTE NAME.
SHE'S GOT SUCH A CLEAR, BEAUTIFUL VOICE...
SHE'S PRETTY, ELEGANT, AND HAS FLOWING HAIR...
SHE'S TOTALLY HANZO'S TYPE OF WOMAN...
AND YOU, SIR?
I'M HANBEI, USAGI'S HUSBAND.
THROB
HUSBAND... ♥
HE'S A DISTANT RELATIVE OF MINE WHO WORKS WITH ME AT OKAZAKI CASTLE.

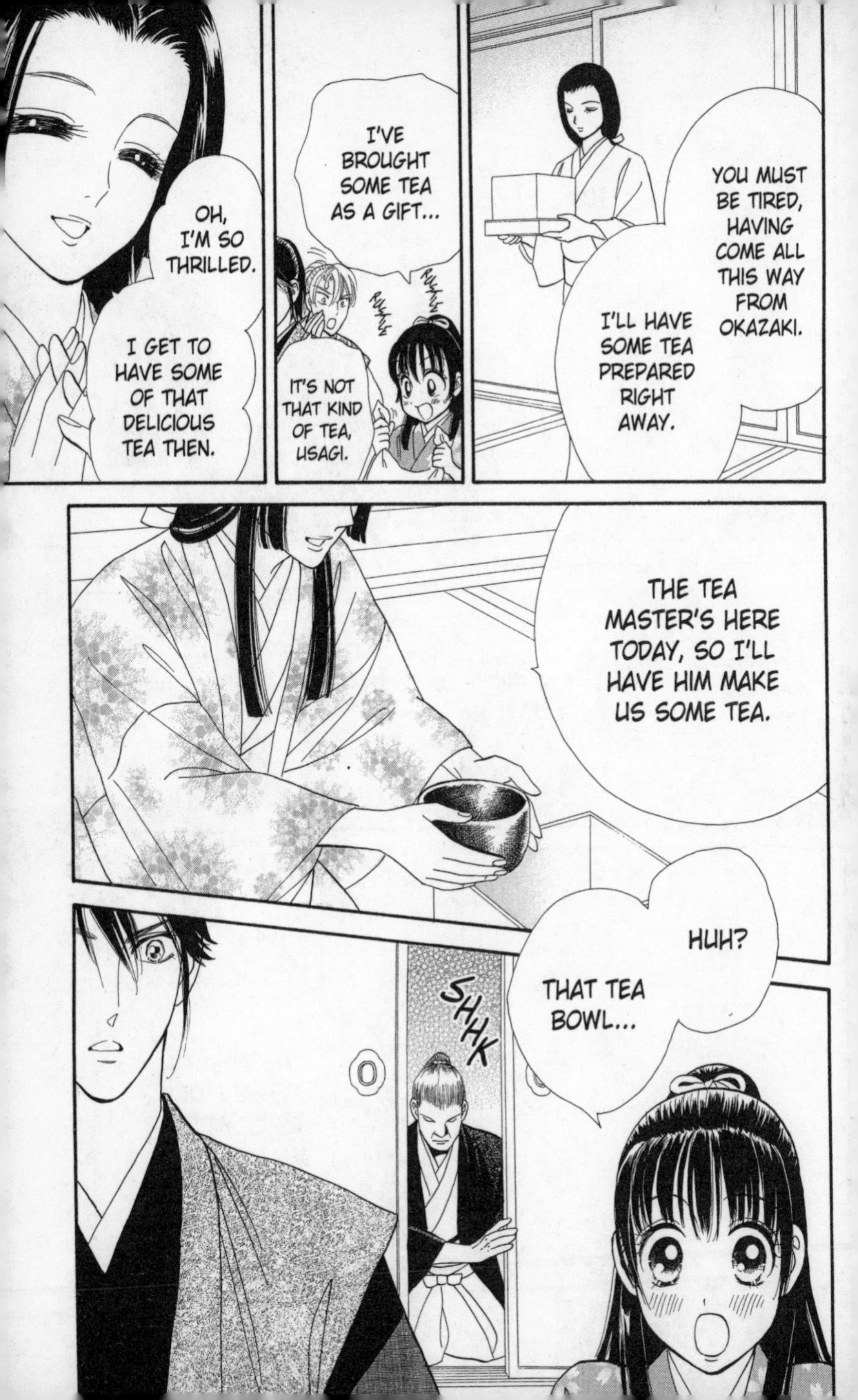
YOU MUST BE TIRED, HAVING COME ALL THIS WAY FROM OKAZAKI.
I'LL HAVE SOME TEA PREPARED RIGHT AWAY.
I'VE BROUGHT SOME TEA AS A GIFT...
IT'S NOT THAT KIND OF TEA, USAGI.
OH, I'M SO THRILLED.
I GET TO HAVE SOME OF THAT DELICIOUS TEA THEN.
THE TEA MASTER'S HERE TODAY, SO I'LL HAVE HIM MAKE US SOME TEA.
HUH?
THAT TEA BOWL...
SHHK

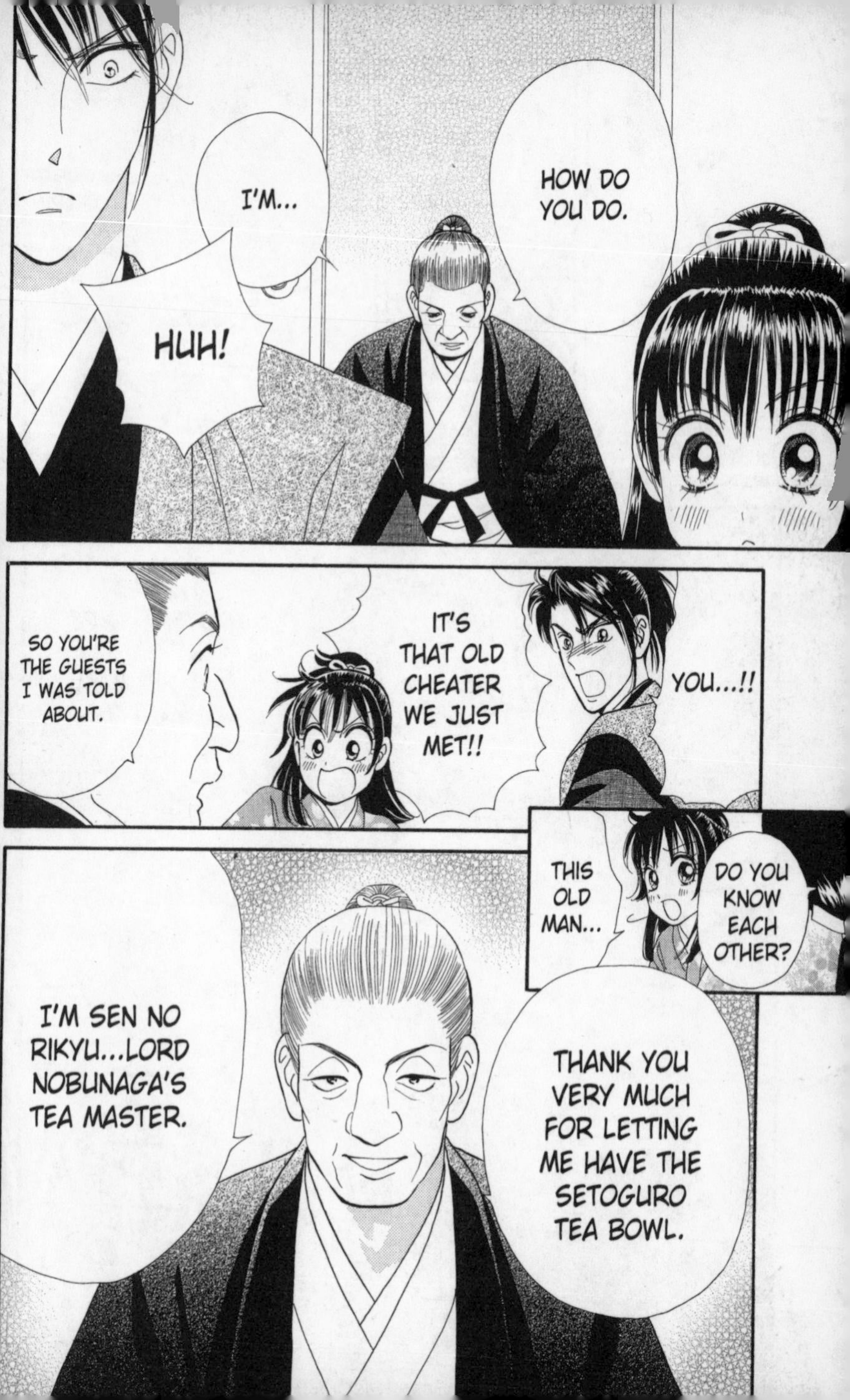
HOW DO YOU DO.
I'M...
HUH!
YOU...!!
IT'S THAT OLD CHEATER WE JUST MET!!
SO YOU'RE THE GUESTS I WAS TOLD ABOUT.
DO YOU KNOW EACH OTHER?
THIS OLD MAN...
I'M SEN NO RIKYU...LORD NOBUNAGA'S TEA MASTER.
THANK YOU VERY MUCH FOR LETTING ME HAVE THE SETOGURO TEA BOWL.

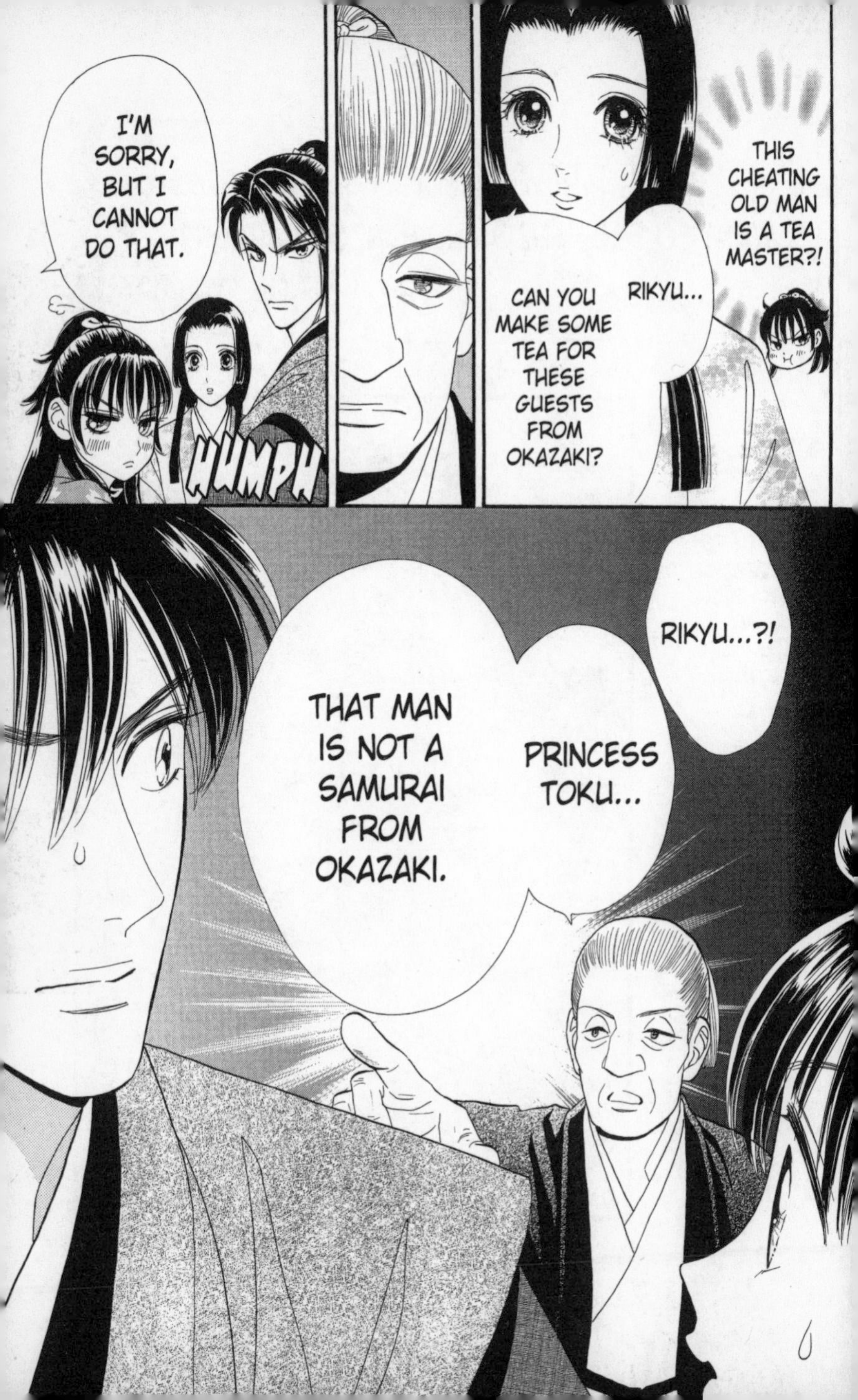
THIS CHEATING OLD MAN IS A TEA MASTER?!
RIKYU...
CAN YOU MAKE SOME TEA FOR THESE GUESTS FROM OKAZAKI?
I'M SORRY, BUT I CANNOT DO THAT.
HUMPH
RIKYU...?!
PRINCESS TOKU...
THAT MAN IS NOT A SAMURAI FROM OKAZAKI.

TAIL OF THE MOON EXTRA: TODAY'S MISSION
"I WANT TO SEE HANZO AND HANZOU BABYSITTING!"

-SAORI ASAI, AICHI PREFECTURE

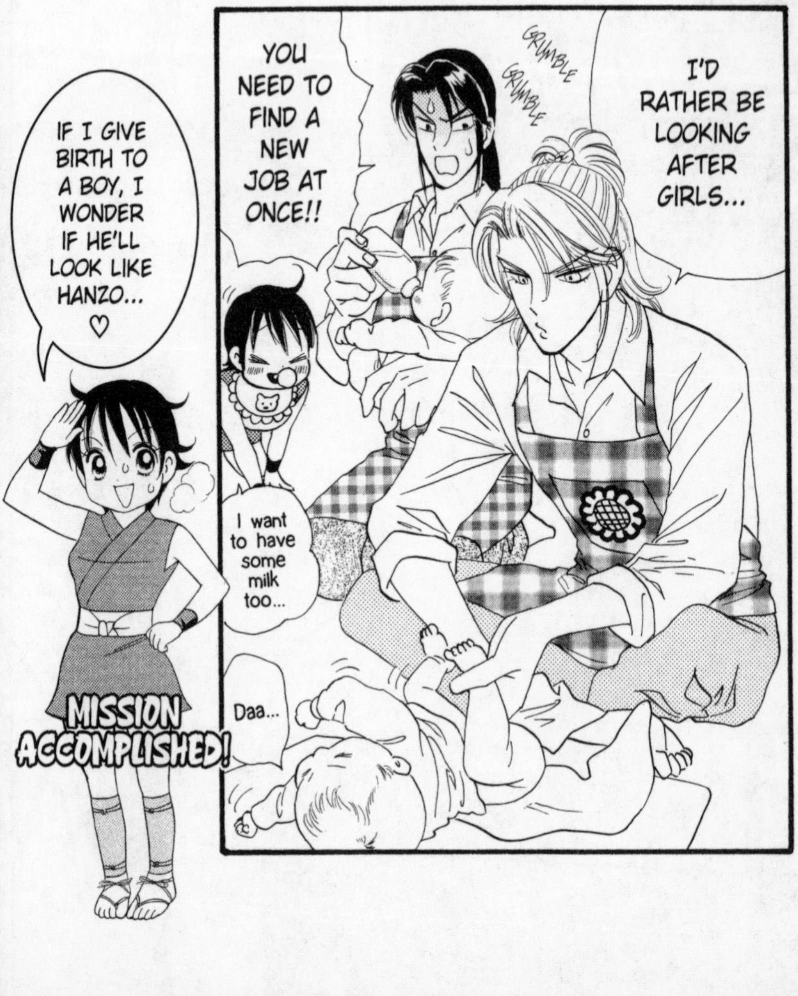
I'D RATHER BE LOOKING AFTER GIRLS...
GRUMBLE GRUMBLE
YOU NEED TO FIND A NEW JOB AT ONCE!!
I want to have some milk too...
Daa...
IF I GIVE BIRTH TO A BOY, I WONDER IF HE'LL LOOK LIKE HANZO... ♡
MISSION ACCOMPLISHED!

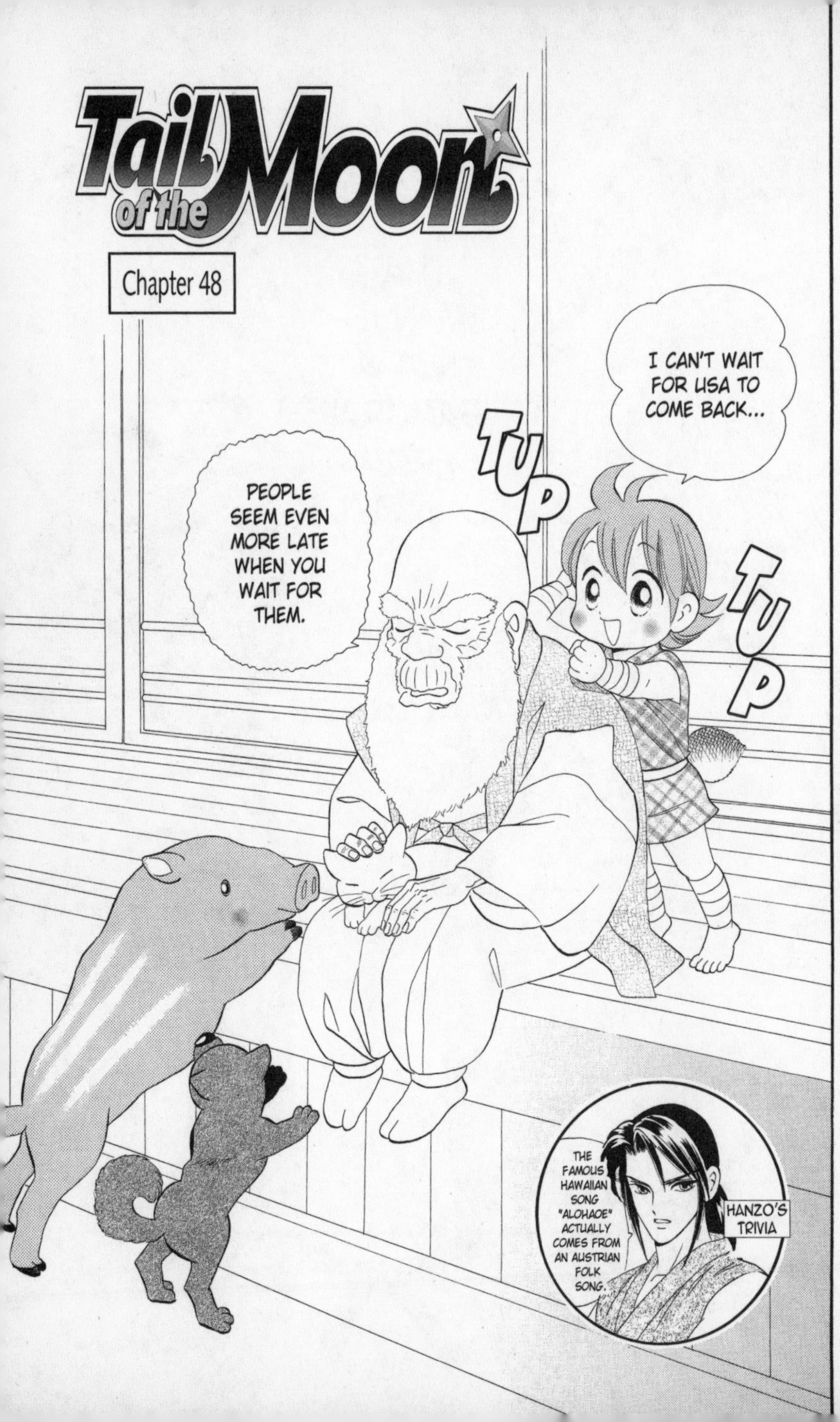
Tail of the Moon
Chapter 48
I CAN'T WAIT FOR USA TO COME BACK...
TUP
TUP
PEOPLE SEEM EVEN MORE LATE WHEN YOU WAIT FOR THEM.
TUP
TUP
HANZO'S TRIVIA
THE FAMOUS HAWAIIAN SONG "ALOHAOE" ACTUALLY COMES FROM AN AUSTRIAN FOLK SONG.

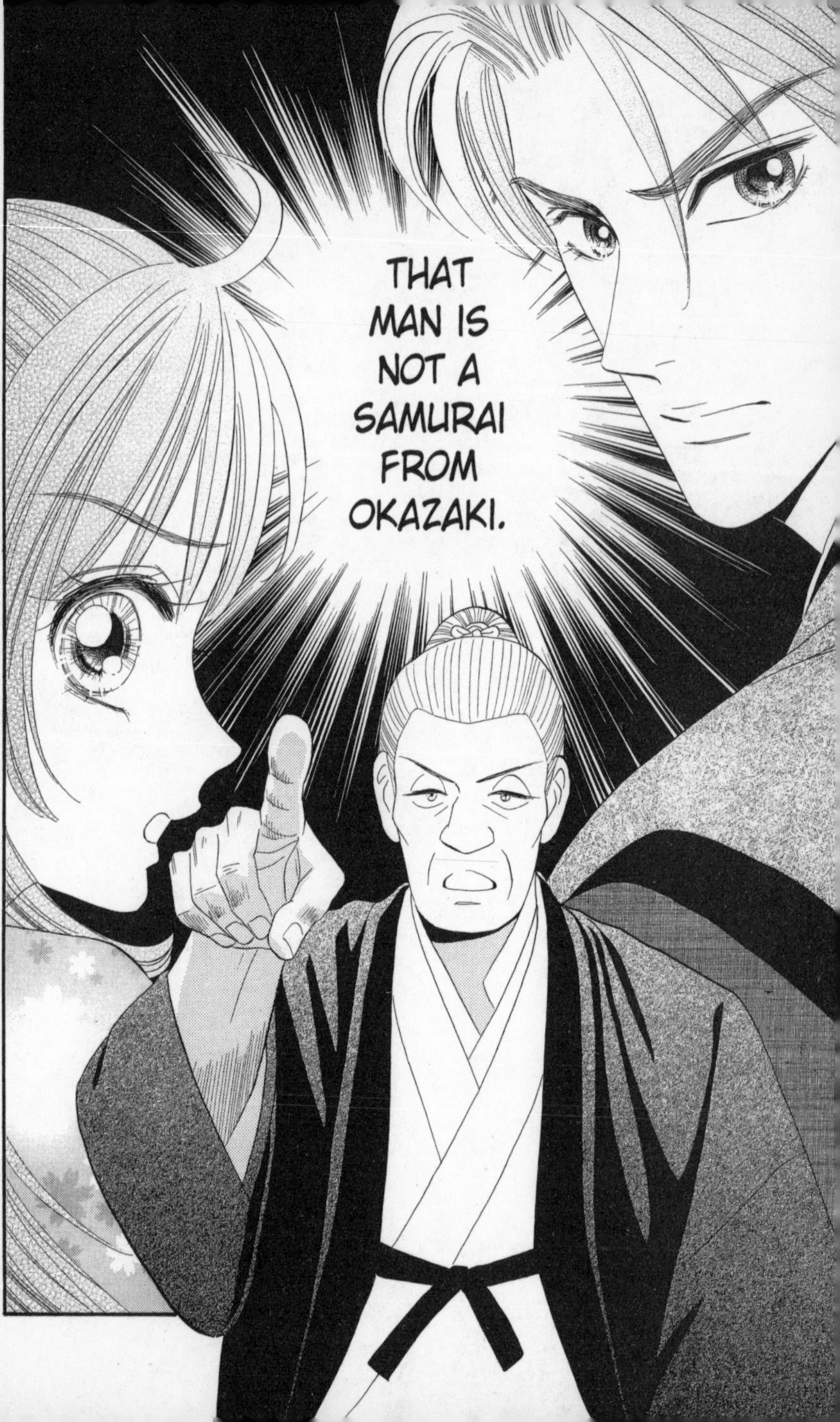
THAT MAN IS NOT A SAMURAI FROM OKAZAKI.

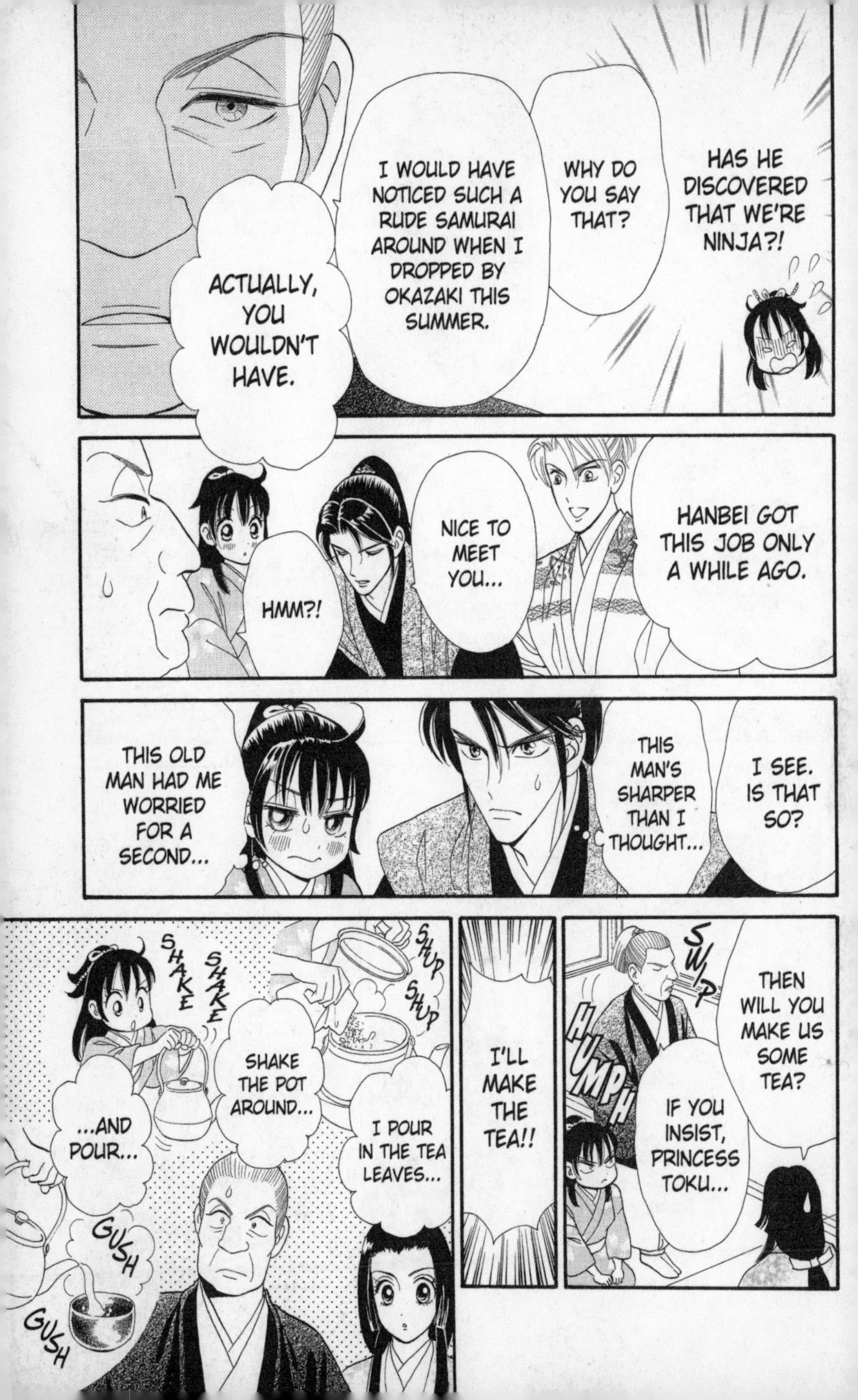
HAS HE DISCOVERED THAT WE'RE NINJA?!
WHY DO YOU SAY THAT?
I WOULD HAVE NOTICED SUCH A RUDE SAMURAI AROUND WHEN I DROPPED BY OKAZAKI THIS SUMMER.
ACTUALLY, YOU WOULDN'T HAVE.
HANBEI GOT THIS JOB ONLY A WHILE AGO.
NICE TO MEET YOU...
HMM?!
I SEE. IS THAT SO?
THIS MAN'S SHARPER THAN I THOUGHT...
THIS OLD MAN HAD ME WORRIED FOR A SECOND...
SWIP
THEN WILL YOU MAKE US SOME TEA?
HUMPH
IF YOU INSIST, PRINCESS TOKU...
I'LL MAKE THE TEA!!
SHUP SHUP
I POUR IN THE TEA LEAVES...
SHAKE THE POT AROUND...
SHAKE SHAKE
...AND POUR...
GUSH GUSH

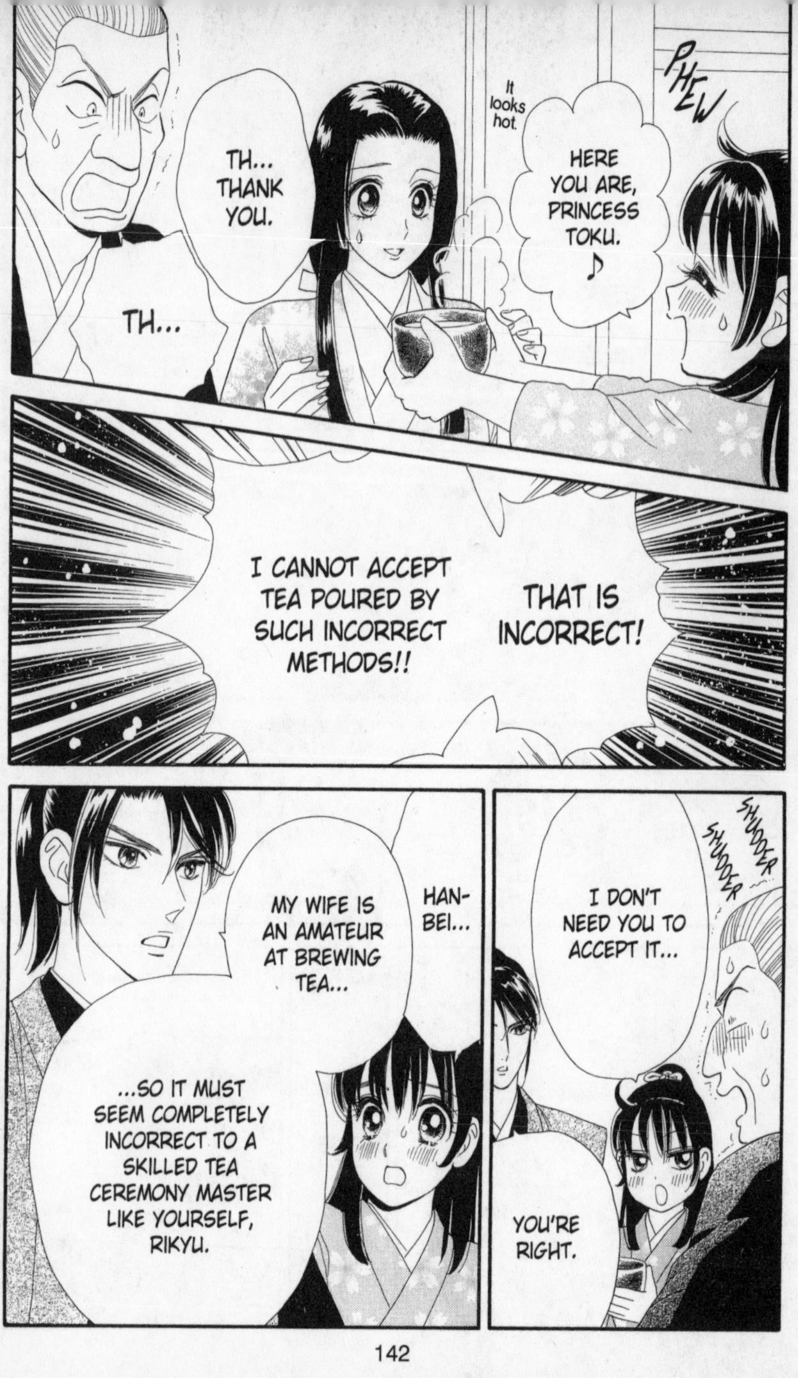
PHEW
It looks hot.
HERE YOU ARE, PRINCESS TOKU. ♪
TH... THANK YOU.
TH...
THAT IS INCORRECT!
I CANNOT ACCEPT TEA POURED BY SUCH INCORRECT METHODS!!
SHUDDER SHUDDER
I DON'T NEED YOU TO ACCEPT IT...
YOU'RE RIGHT.
HAN-BEI...
MY WIFE IS AN AMATEUR AT BREWING TEA...
...SO IT MUST SEEM COMPLETELY INCORRECT TO A SKILLED TEA CEREMONY MASTER LIKE YOURSELF, RIKYU.

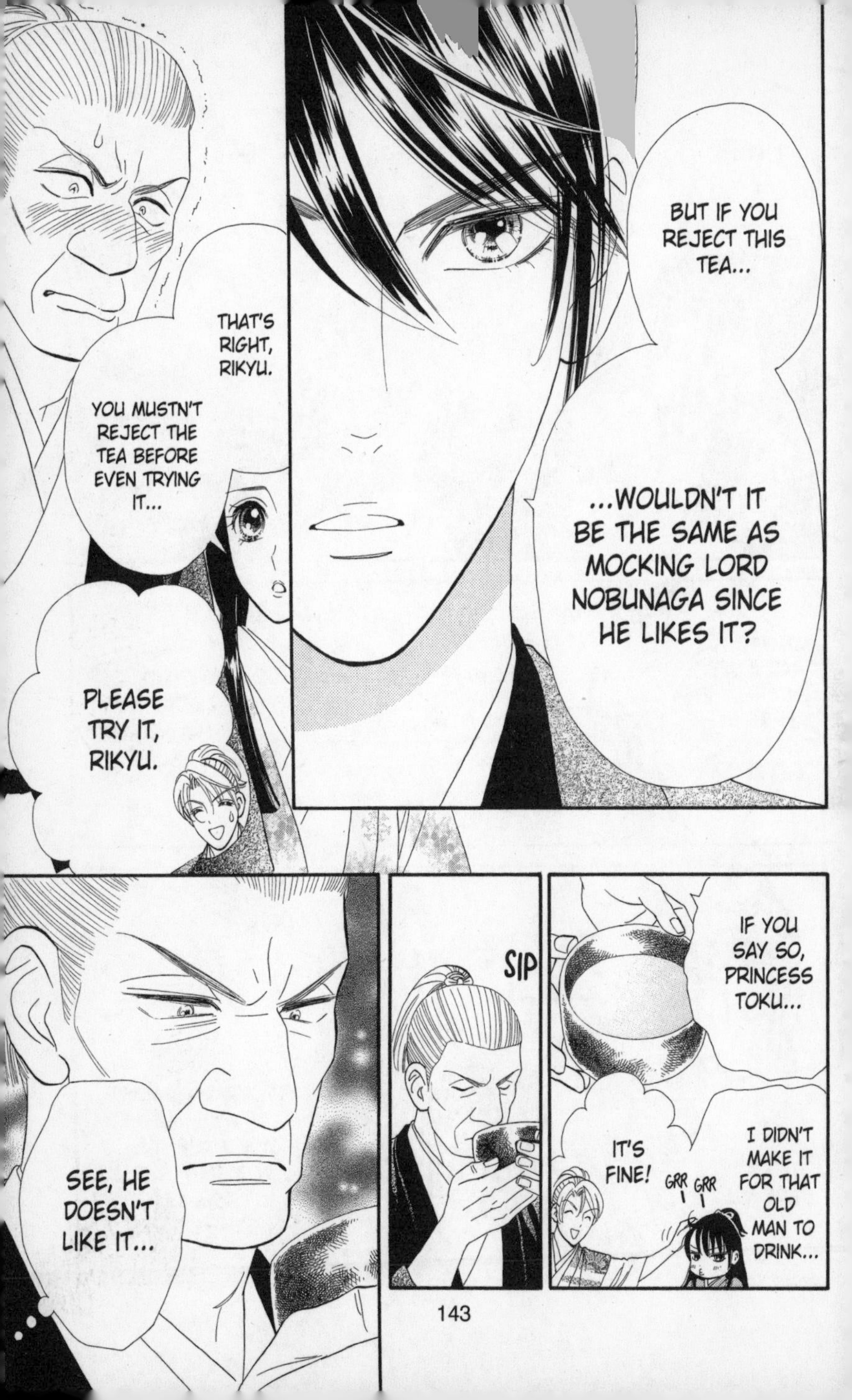
BUT IF YOU REJECT THIS TEA...
...WOULDN'T IT BE THE SAME AS MOCKING LORD NOBUNAGA SINCE HE LIKES IT?
THAT'S RIGHT, RIKYU.
YOU MUSTN'T REJECT THE TEA BEFORE EVEN TRYING IT...
PLEASE TRY IT, RIKYU.
IF YOU SAY SO, PRINCESS TOKU...
I DIDN'T MAKE IT FOR THAT OLD MAN TO DRINK...
GRR GRR
IT'S FINE!
SIP
SEE, HE DOESN'T LIKE IT...

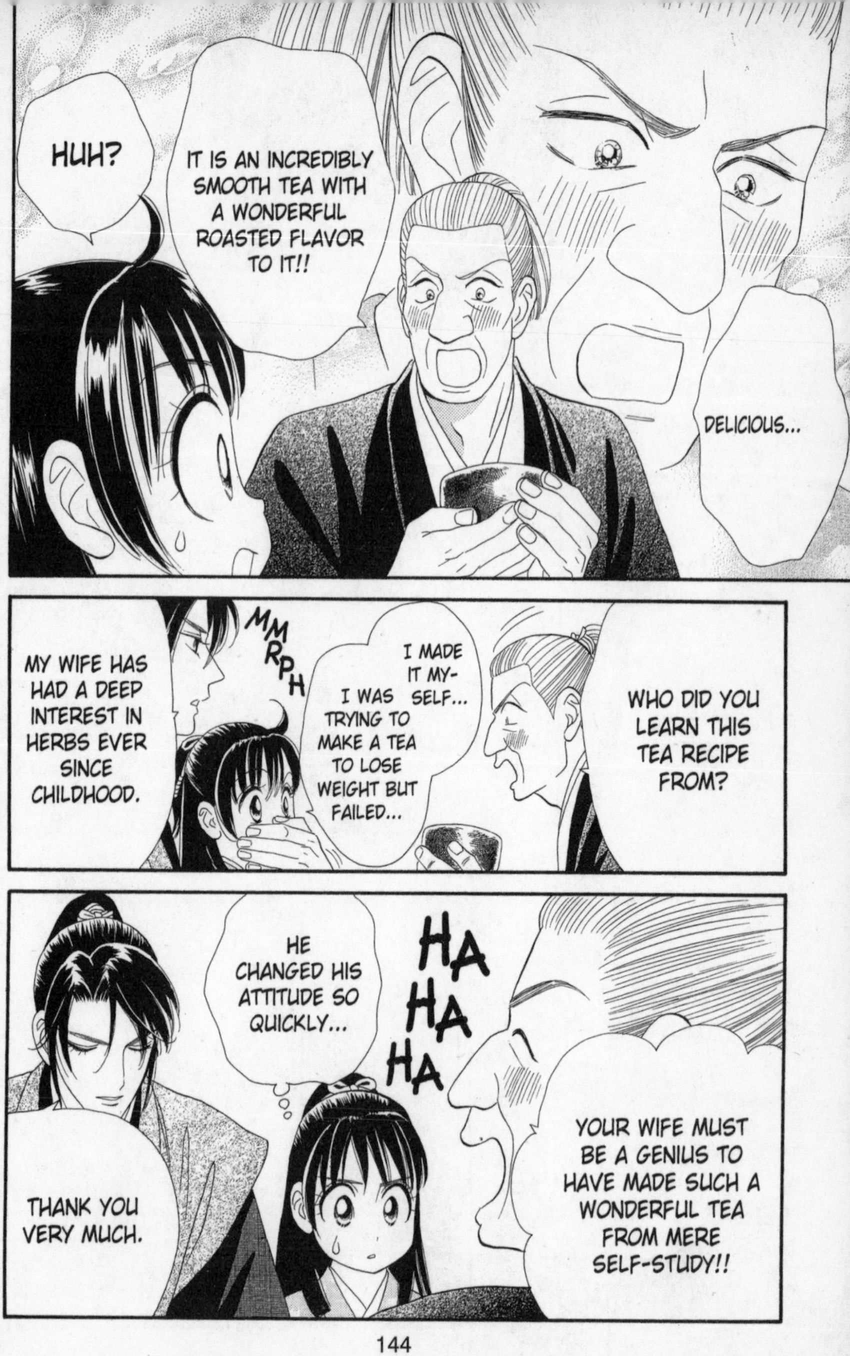
DELICIOUS...
IT IS AN INCREDIBLY SMOOTH TEA WITH A WONDERFUL ROASTED FLAVOR TO IT!!
HUH?
WHO DID YOU LEARN THIS TEA RECIPE FROM?
I MADE IT MYSELF... I WAS TRYING TO MAKE A TEA TO LOSE WEIGHT BUT FAILED...
MMRPH
MY WIFE HAS HAD A DEEP INTEREST IN HERBS EVER SINCE CHILDHOOD.
YOUR WIFE MUST BE A GENIUS TO HAVE MADE SUCH A WONDERFUL TEA FROM MERE SELF-STUDY!!
HA HA HA
HE CHANGED HIS ATTITUDE SO QUICKLY...
THANK YOU VERY MUCH.

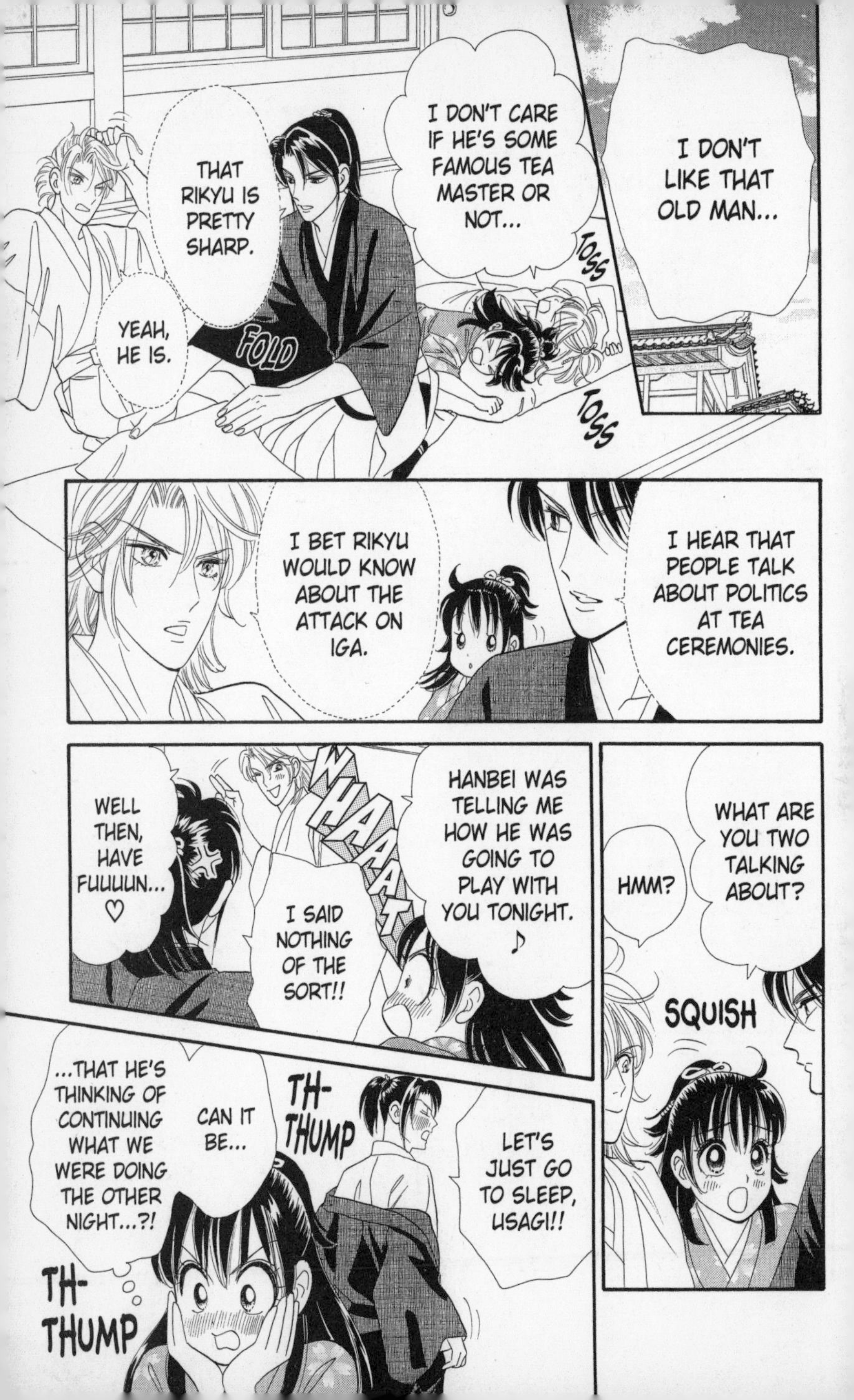
I DON'T LIKE THAT OLD MAN...
I DON'T CARE IF HE'S SOME FAMOUS TEA MASTER OR NOT...
TOSS
THAT RIKYU IS PRETTY SHARP.
TOSS
FOLD
YEAH, HE IS.
I HEAR THAT PEOPLE TALK ABOUT POLITICS AT TEA CEREMONIES.
I BET RIKYU WOULD KNOW ABOUT THE ATTACK ON IGA.
WHAT ARE YOU TWO TALKING ABOUT?
HMM?
SQUISH
HANBEI WAS TELLING ME HOW HE WAS GOING TO PLAY WITH YOU TONIGHT. ♪
WHAAAT
WELL THEN, HAVE FUUUUN... ♡
I SAID NOTHING OF THE SORT!!
LET'S JUST GO TO SLEEP, USAGI!!
TH-THUMP
CAN IT BE...
...THAT HE'S THINKING OF CONTINUING WHAT WE WERE DOING THE OTHER NIGHT...?!
TH-THUMP

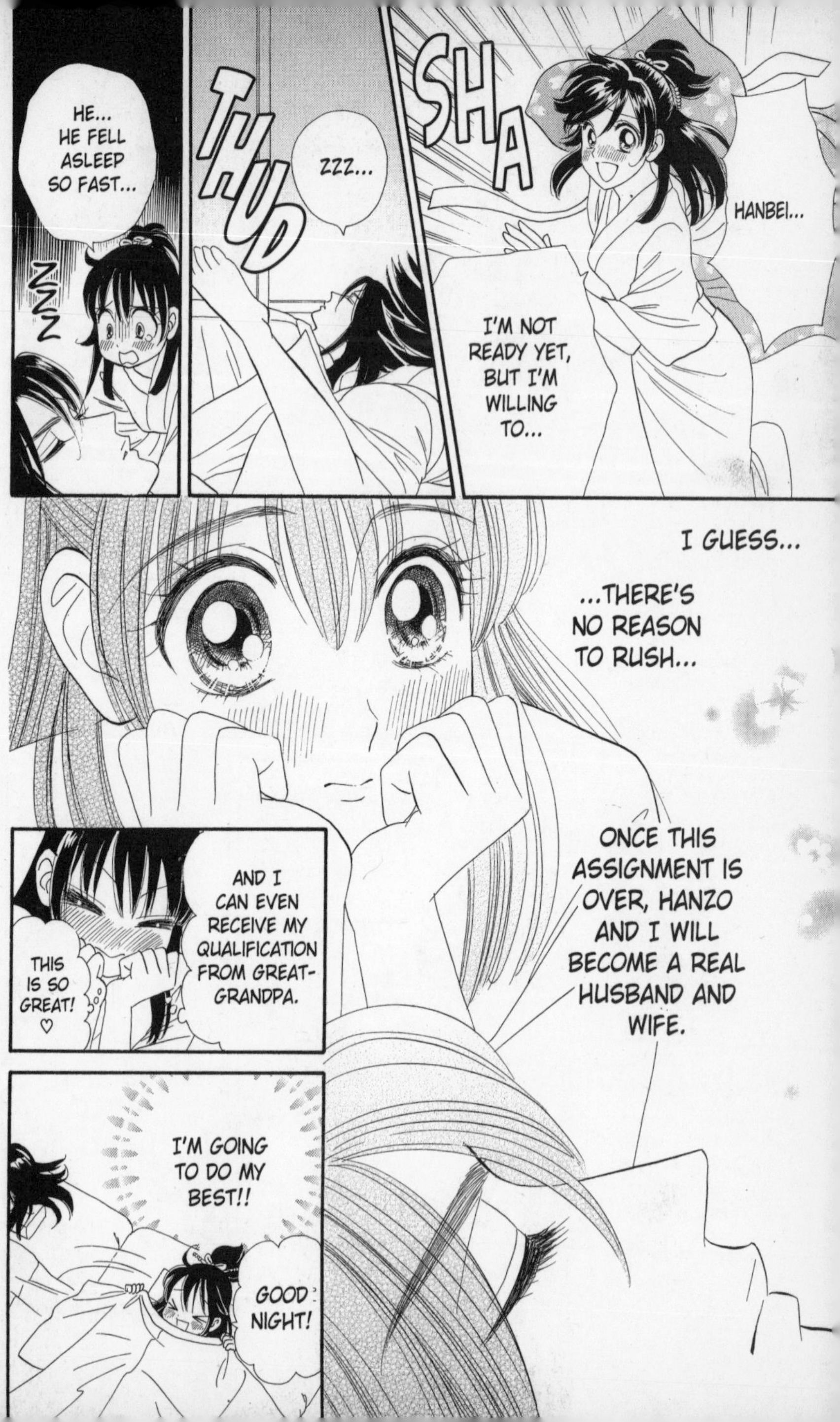
SHA
HANBEI...
I'M NOT READY YET, BUT I'M WILLING TO...
THUD
ZZZ...
HE... HE FELL ASLEEP SO FAST...
ZZZ
I GUESS...
...THERE'S NO REASON TO RUSH...
ONCE THIS ASSIGNMENT IS OVER, HANZO AND I WILL BECOME A REAL HUSBAND AND WIFE.
AND I CAN EVEN RECEIVE MY QUALIFICATION FROM GREAT-GRANDPA.
THIS IS SO GREAT! ♡
I'M GOING TO DO MY BEST!!
GOOD NIGHT!

UE-RIN'S WAY OF THE MANGA ⑩

My best memory of meeting the editor for the first time was how I was able to take a look at a real draft of an author who had a series in the magazine back then.

It was so beautiful!!

"Do you have to be so detailed with the backgrounds?!"

"I love these effects!!"

"How can you draw the reflection of light in the eyes and hair so beautifully?!"

It really was an eye-opener for me!!

My confidence and pride just got flushed away and I felt really embarrassed of myself.

The images I saw in the magazine and the real thing were totally different. It was ten times as beautiful...no, even more beautiful than that!!

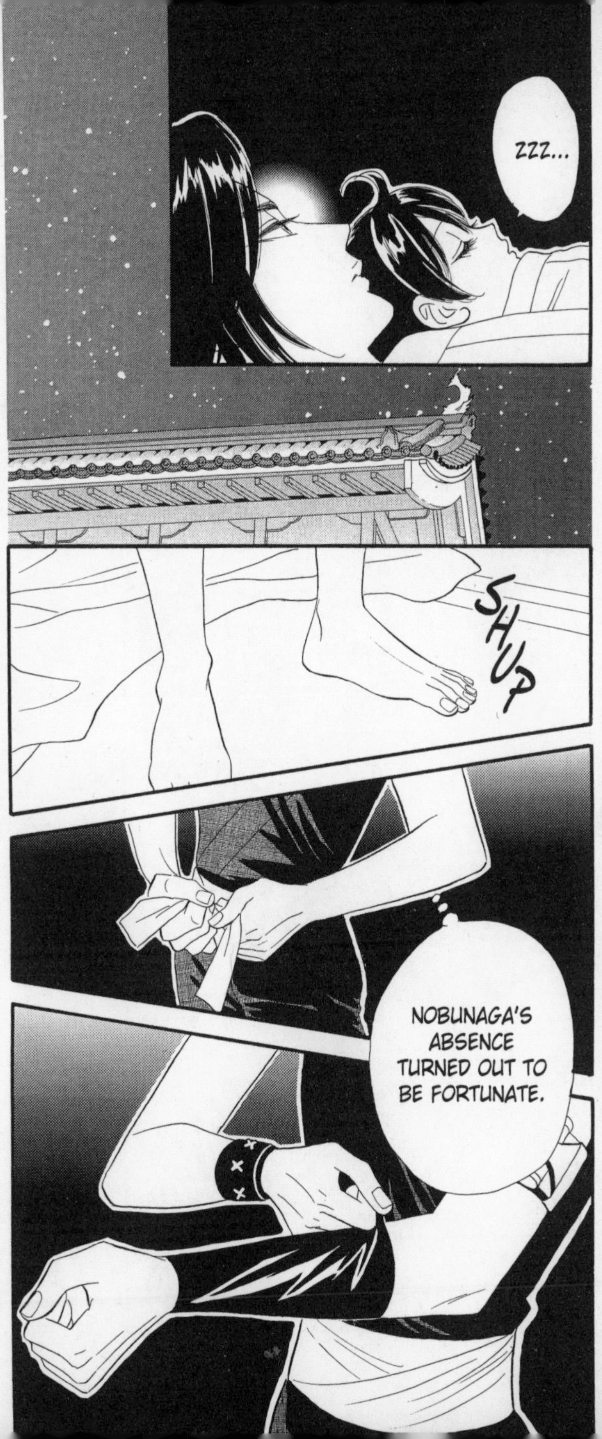
ZZZ...
SHUP
NOBUNAGA'S ABSENCE TURNED OUT TO BE FORTUNATE.

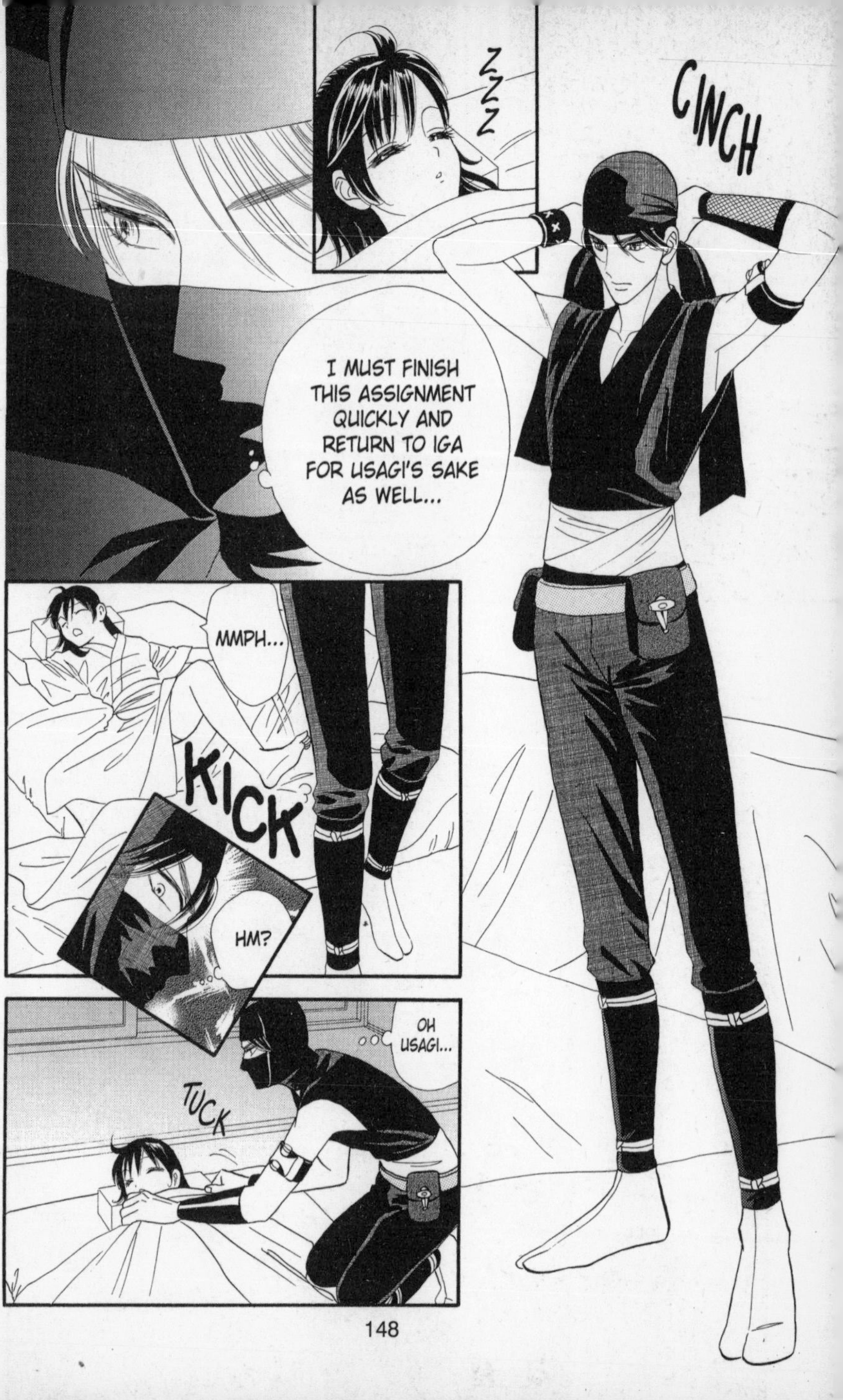
CINCH
ZZZ
I MUST FINISH THIS ASSIGNMENT QUICKLY AND RETURN TO IGA FOR USAGI'S SAKE AS WELL...
MMPH...
KICK
HM?
OH USAGI...
TUCK

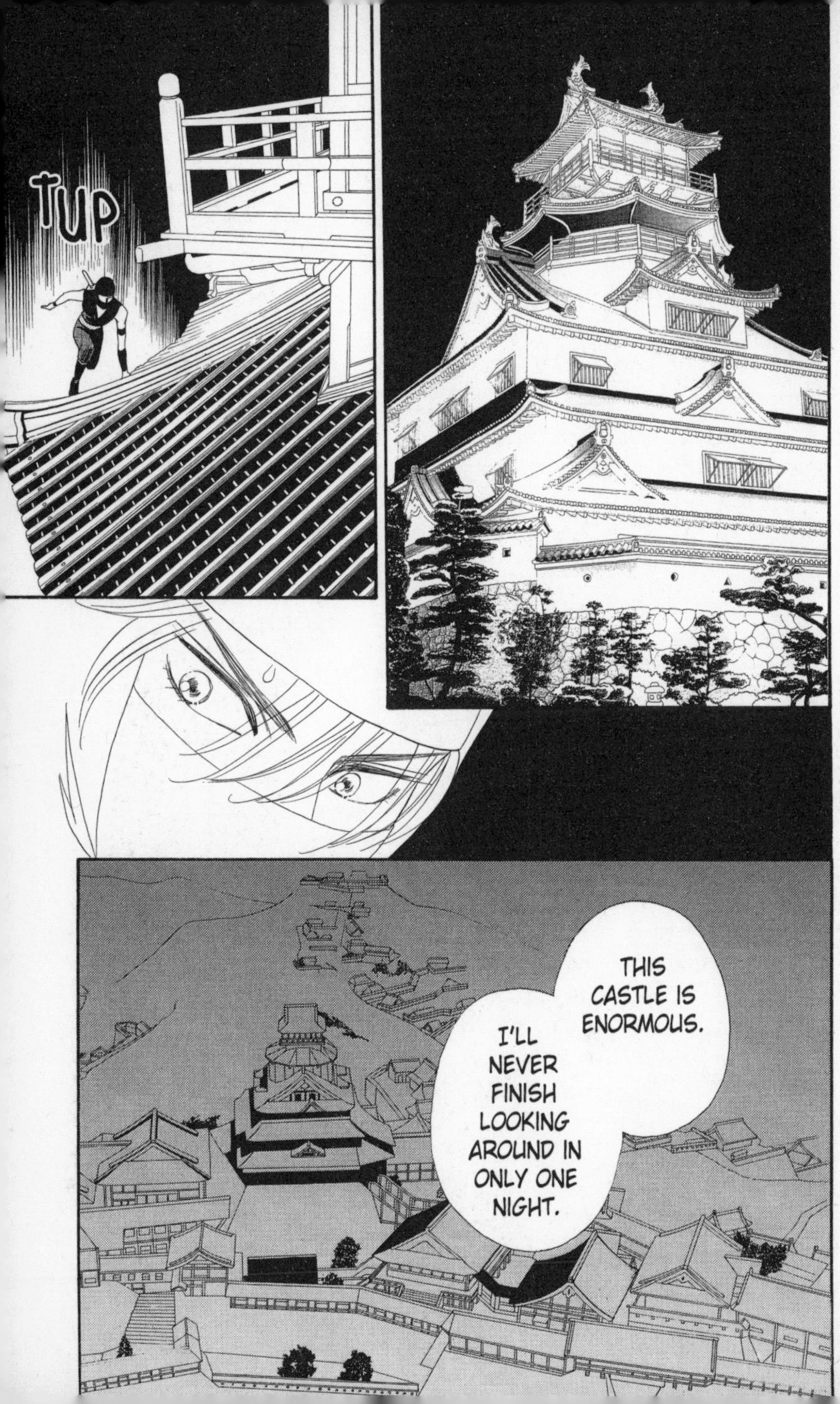
TUP
THIS CASTLE IS ENORMOUS.
I'LL NEVER FINISH LOOKING AROUND IN ONLY ONE NIGHT.

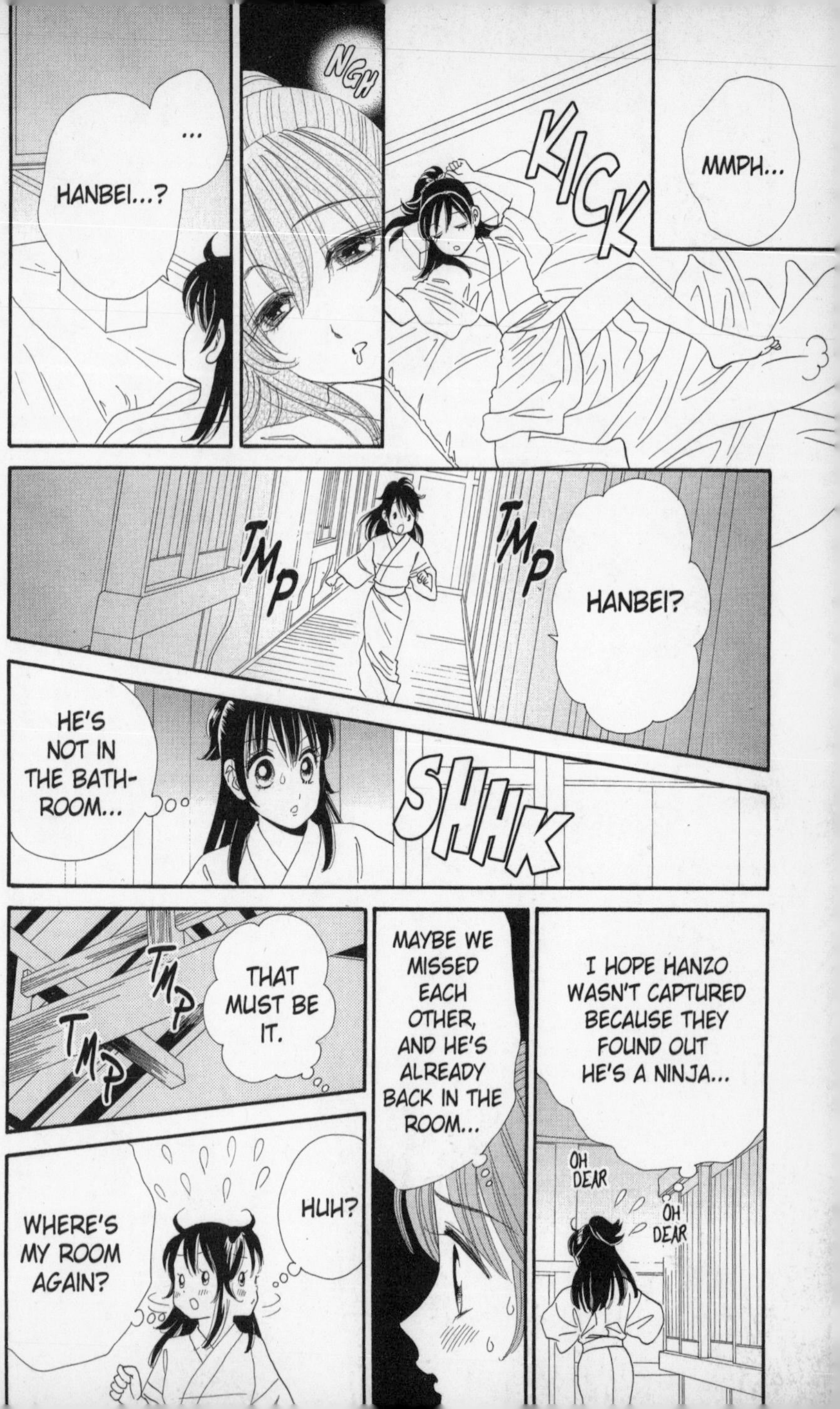
MMPH...
KICK
NGH
...
HANBEI...?
HANBEI?
TMP
TMP
SHHK
HE'S NOT IN THE BATH-ROOM...
I HOPE HANZO WASN'T CAPTURED BECAUSE THEY FOUND OUT HE'S A NINJA...
OH DEAR
OH DEAR
MAYBE WE MISSED EACH OTHER, AND HE'S ALREADY BACK IN THE ROOM...
THAT MUST BE IT.
TMP
TMP
HUH?
WHERE'S MY ROOM AGAIN?

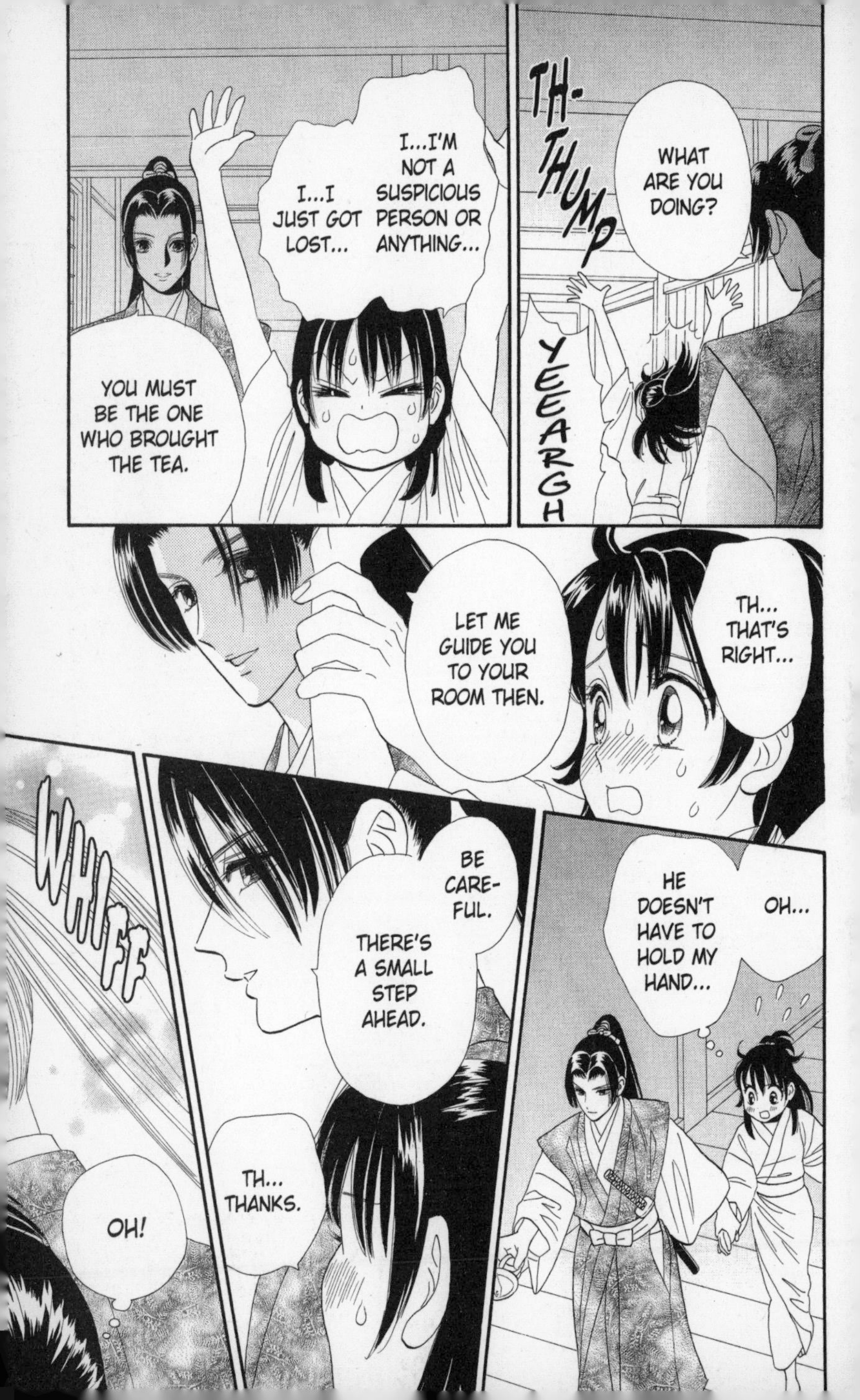
TH-THUMP
WHAT ARE YOU DOING?
YEEEARGH
I...I'M NOT A SUSPICIOUS PERSON OR ANYTHING...
I...I JUST GOT LOST...
YOU MUST BE THE ONE WHO BROUGHT THE TEA.
TH... THAT'S RIGHT...
LET ME GUIDE YOU TO YOUR ROOM THEN.
OH...
HE DOESN'T HAVE TO HOLD MY HAND...
BE CARE-FUL.
THERE'S A SMALL STEP AHEAD.
TH... THANKS.
WHIFF
OH!

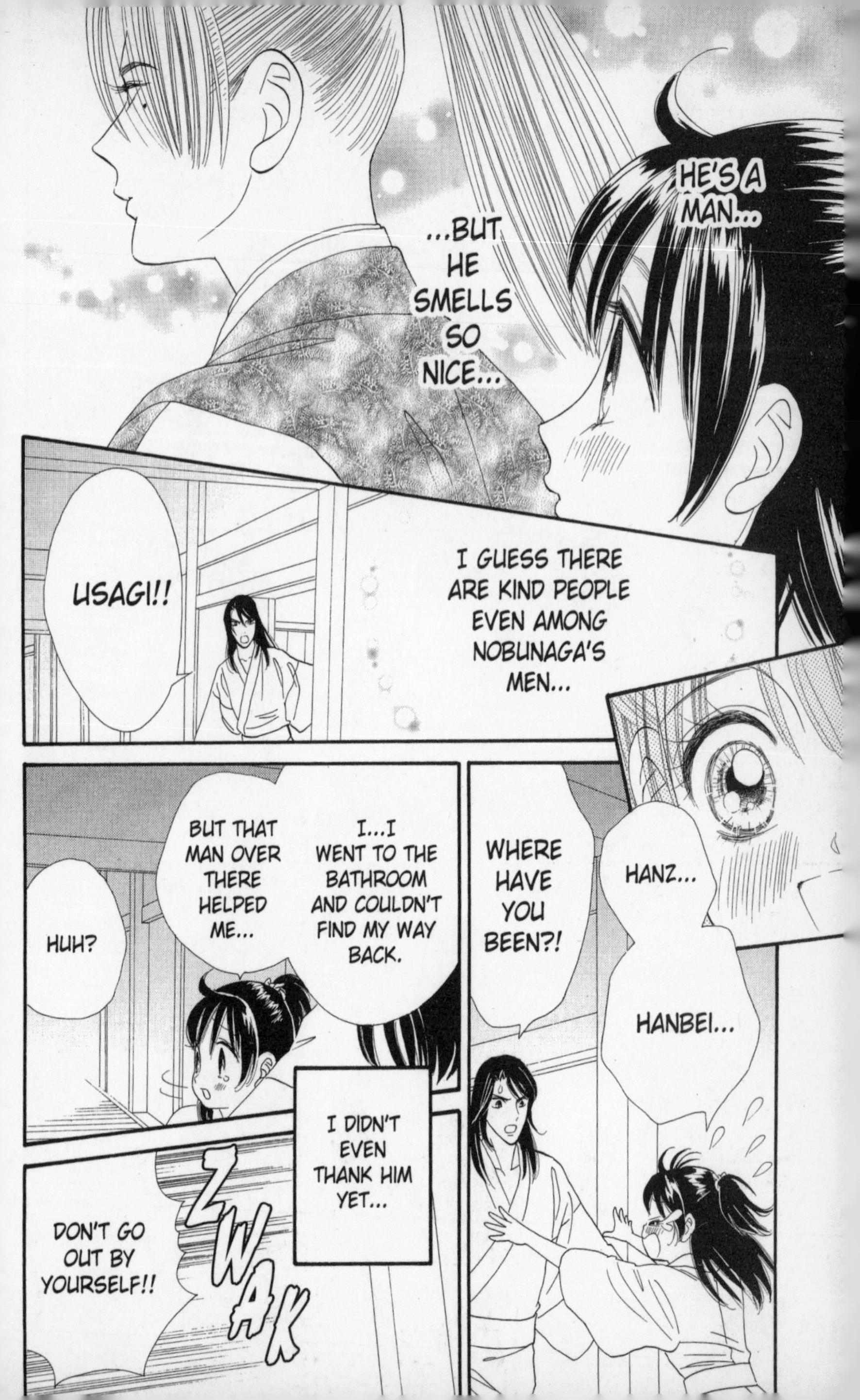
HE'S A MAN...
...BUT HE SMELLS SO NICE...
I GUESS THERE ARE KIND PEOPLE EVEN AMONG NOBUNAGA'S MEN...
USAGI!!
HANZ...
HANBEI...
WHERE HAVE YOU BEEN?!
I...I WENT TO THE BATHROOM AND COULDN'T FIND MY WAY BACK.
BUT THAT MAN OVER THERE HELPED ME...
HUH?
I DIDN'T EVEN THANK HIM YET...
ZWAK
DON'T GO OUT BY YOURSELF!!

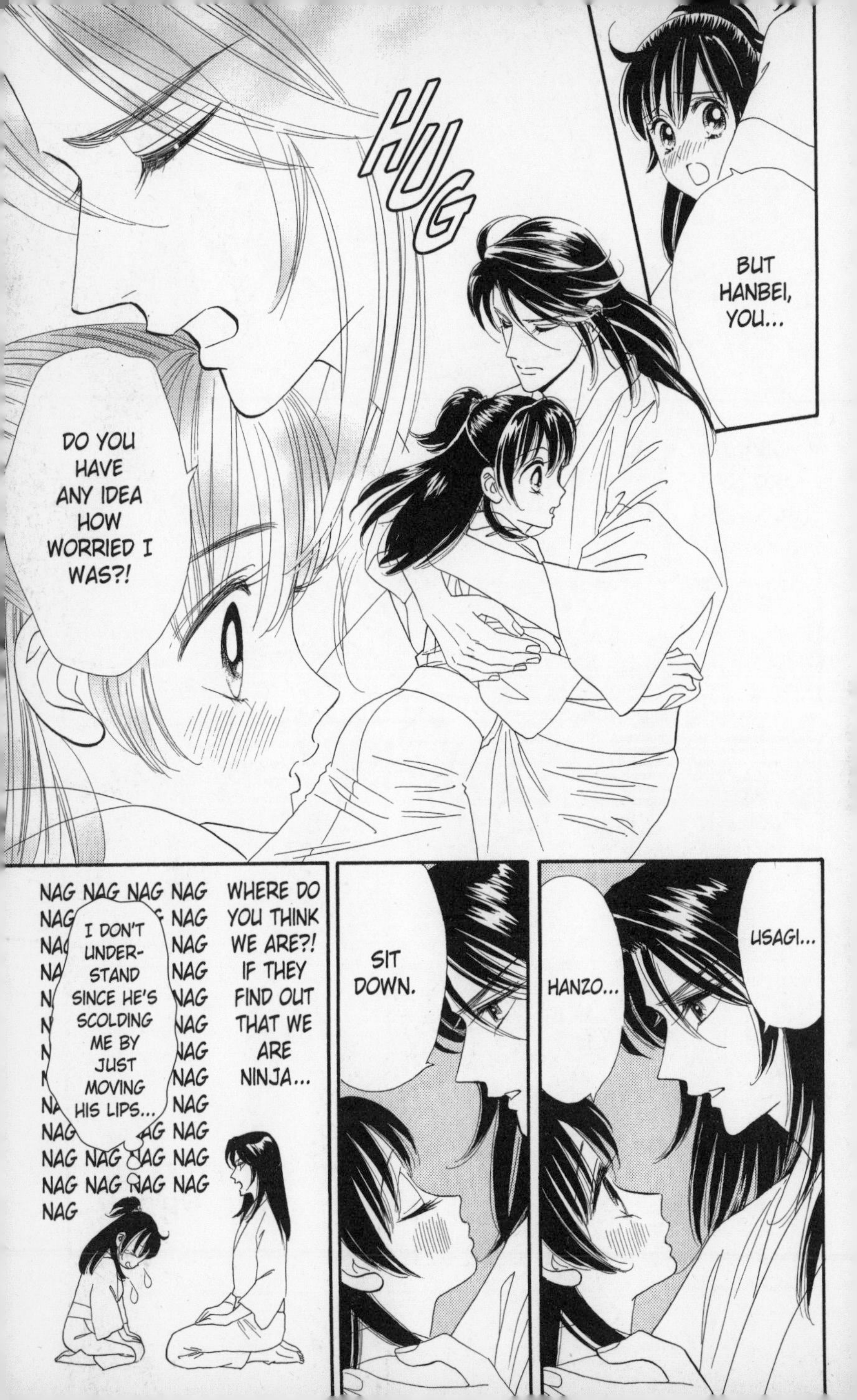
BUT HANBEI, YOU...
HUG
DO YOU HAVE ANY IDEA HOW WORRIED I WAS?!
USAGI...
HANZO...
SIT DOWN.
WHERE DO YOU THINK WE ARE?! IF THEY FIND OUT THAT WE ARE NINJA...
NAG NAG NAG NAG NAG NAG NAG NAG NAG NAG NAG NAG NAG NAG NAG NAG NAG NAG NAG NAG NAG NAG NAG NAG NAG NAG NAG
I DON'T UNDERSTAND SINCE HE'S SCOLDING ME BY JUST MOVING HIS LIPS...

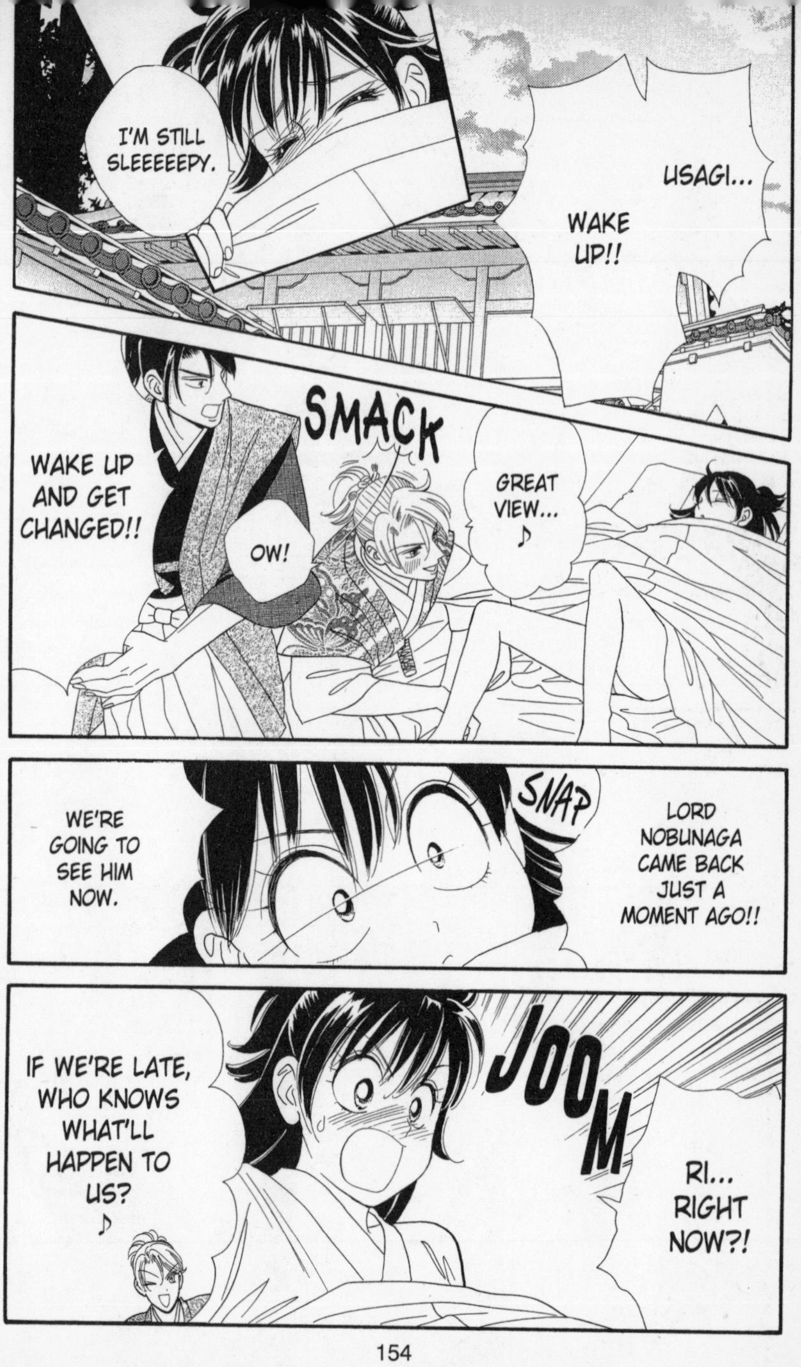
USAGI...
WAKE UP!!
I'M STILL SLEEEEEEPY.
GREAT VIEW... ♪
SMACK
OW!
WAKE UP AND GET CHANGED!!
LORD NOBUNAGA CAME BACK JUST A MOMENT AGO!!
SNAP
WE'RE GOING TO SEE HIM NOW.
RI... RIGHT NOW?!
JOOM
IF WE'RE LATE, WHO KNOWS WHAT'LL HAPPEN TO US? ♪

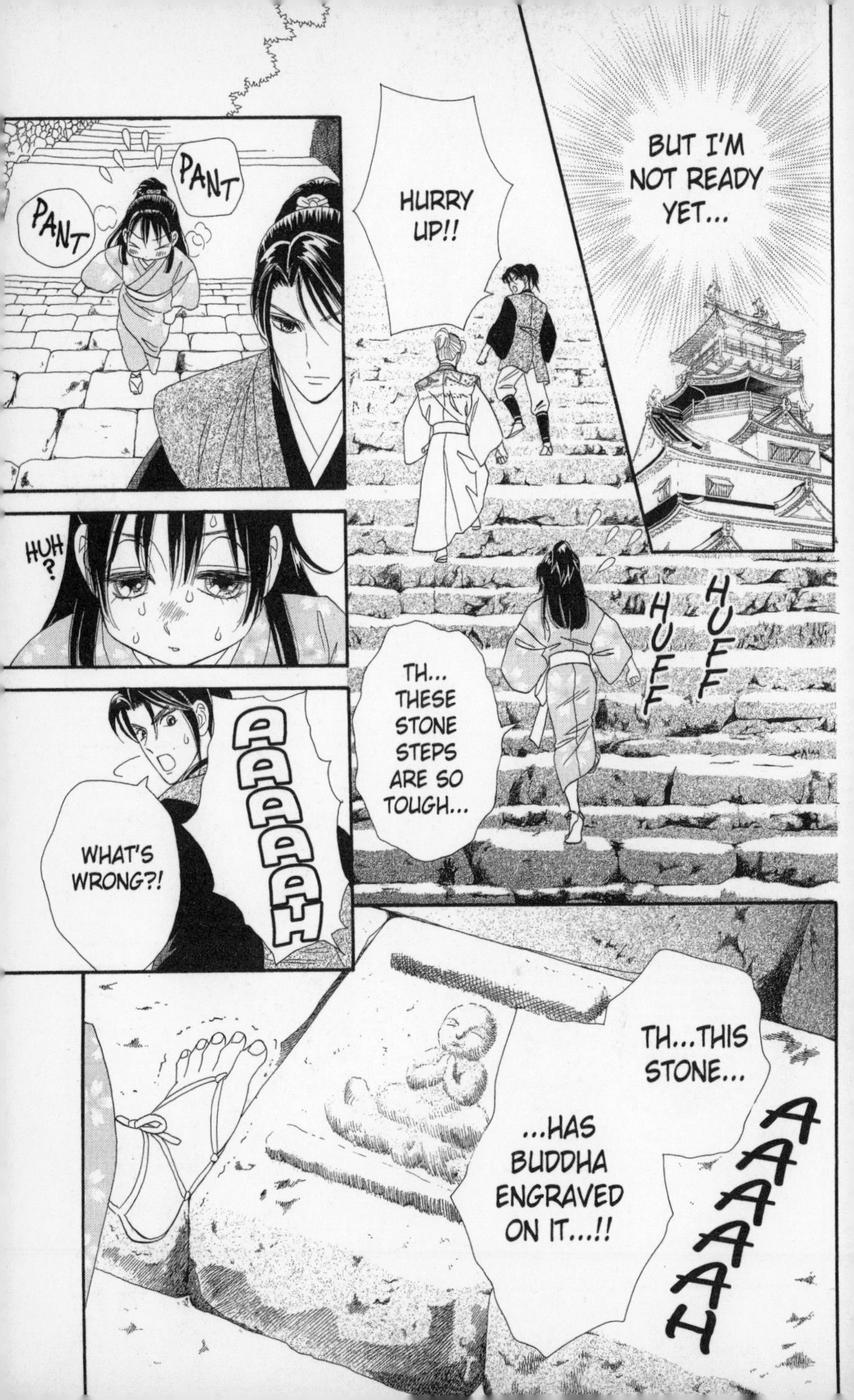
BUT I'M NOT READY YET...
HURRY UP!!
HUFF HUFF
TH... THESE STONE STEPS ARE SO TOUGH...
PANT
PANT
HUH?
AAAAAAH
WHAT'S WRONG?!
TH...THIS STONE...
...HAS BUDDHA ENGRAVED ON IT...!!
AAAAAAH

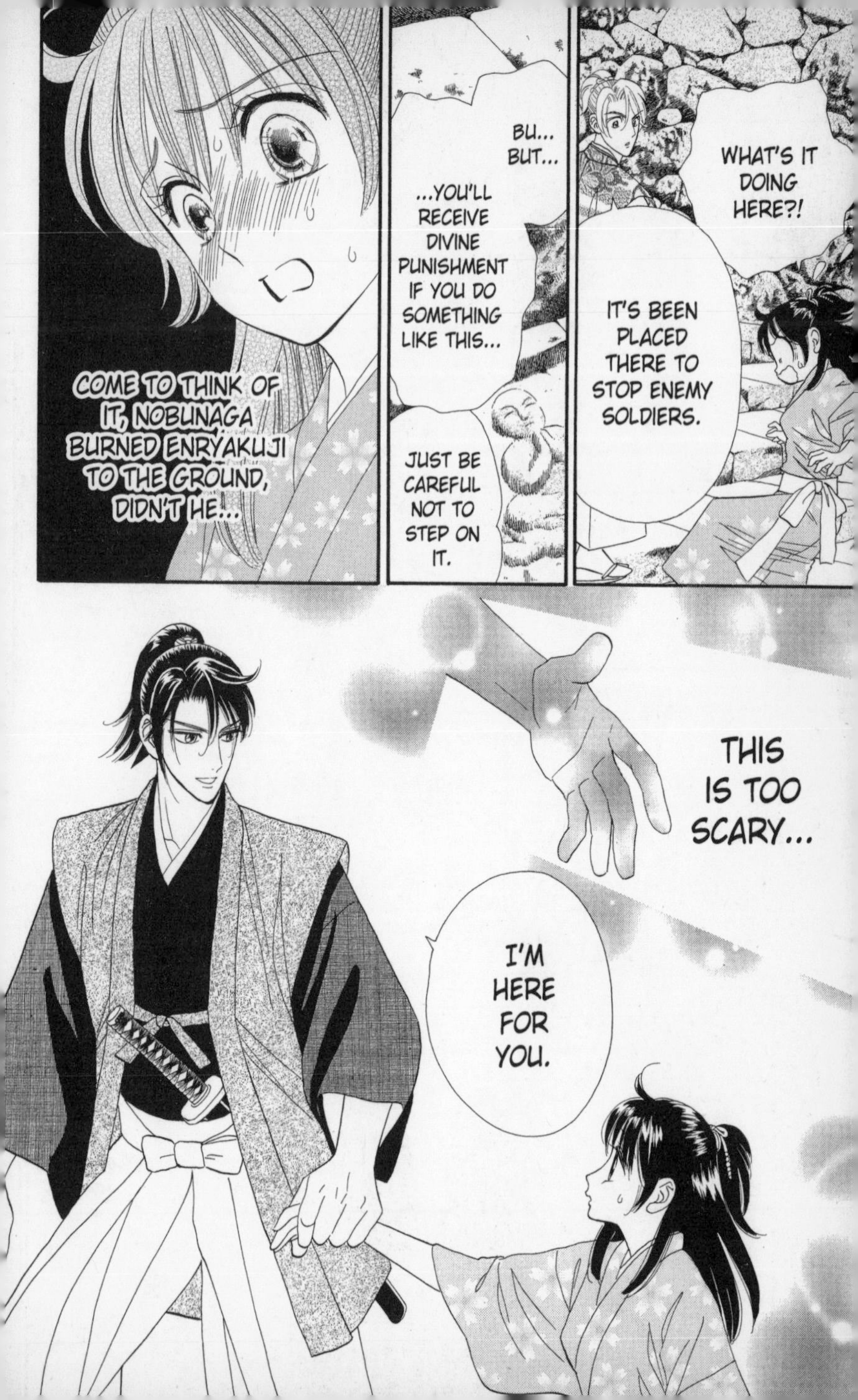
WHAT'S IT DOING HERE?!
IT'S BEEN PLACED THERE TO STOP ENEMY SOLDIERS.
BU... BUT...
...YOU'LL RECEIVE DIVINE PUNISHMENT IF YOU DO SOMETHING LIKE THIS...
JUST BE CAREFUL NOT TO STEP ON IT.
COME TO THINK OF IT, NOBUNAGA BURNED ENRYAKUJI TO THE GROUND, DIDN'T HE...
THIS IS TOO SCARY...
I'M HERE FOR YOU.

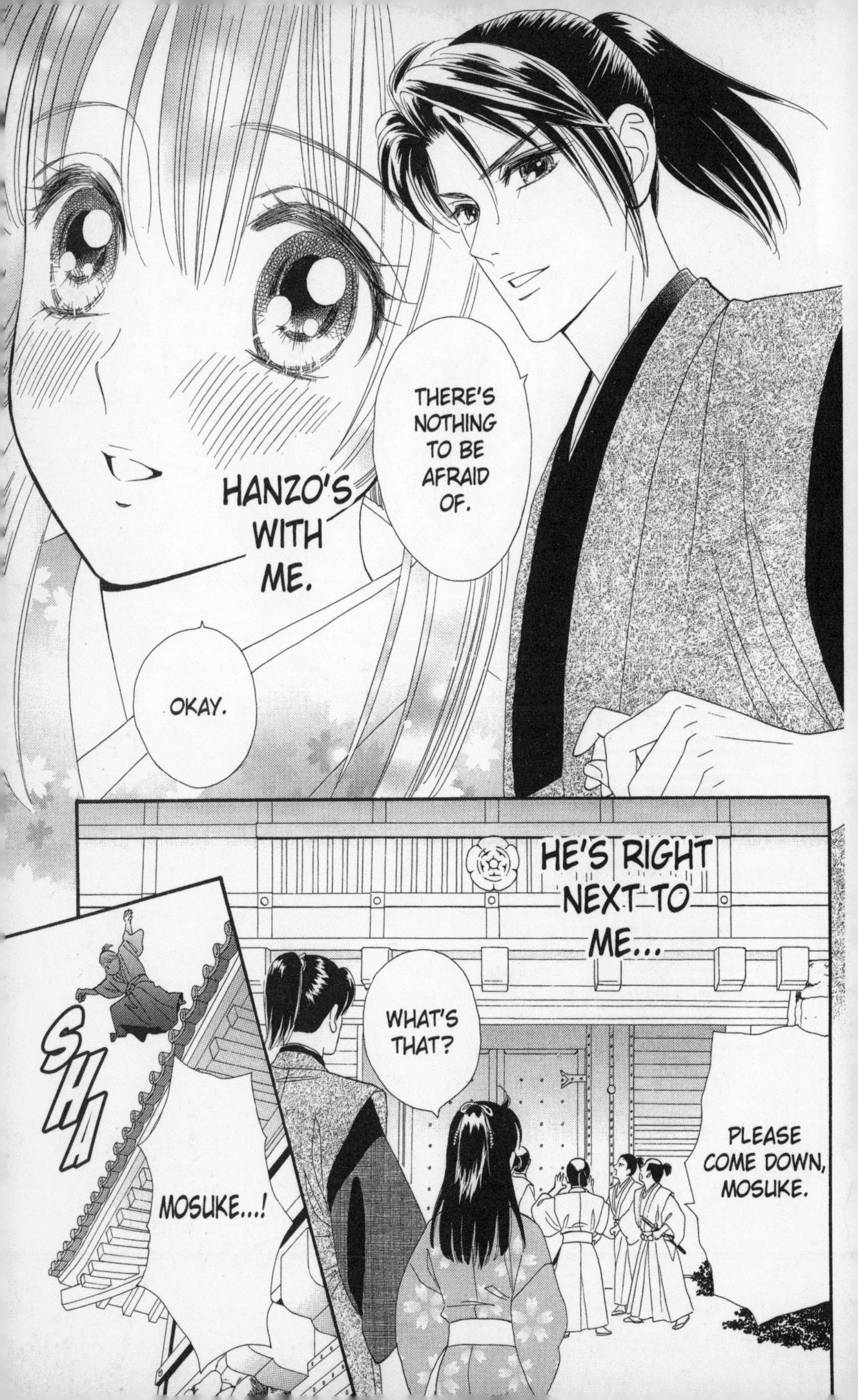
THERE'S NOTHING TO BE AFRAID OF.
HANZO'S WITH ME.
OKAY.
HE'S RIGHT NEXT TO ME...
WHAT'S THAT?
PLEASE COME DOWN, MOSUKE.
SHH
MOSUKE...!

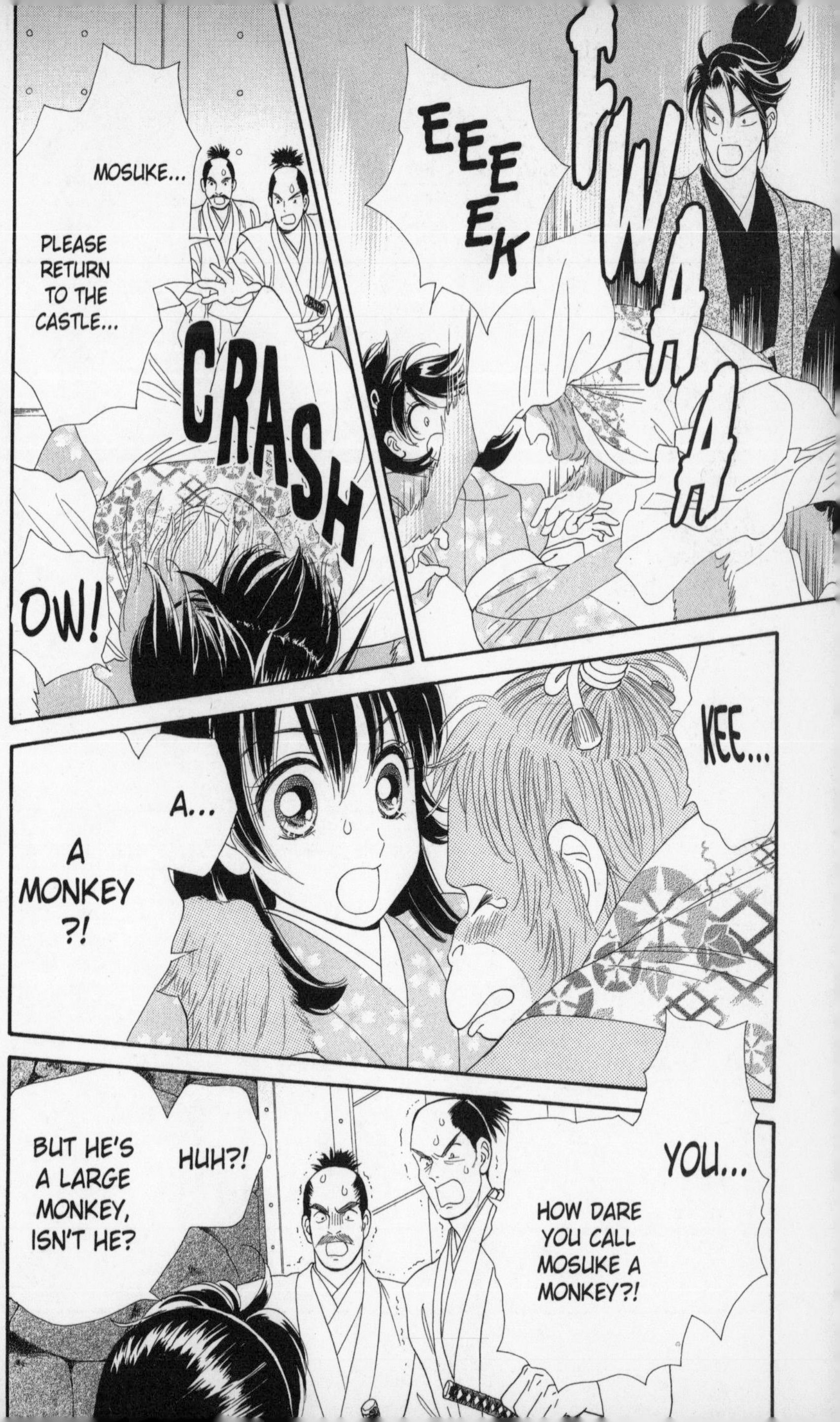
WAA
EEEEK
MOSUKE...
PLEASE RETURN TO THE CASTLE...
CRASH
OW!
KEE...
A...
A MONKEY ?!
YOU...
HOW DARE YOU CALL MOSUKE A MONKEY?!
HUH?!
BUT HE'S A LARGE MONKEY, ISN'T HE?

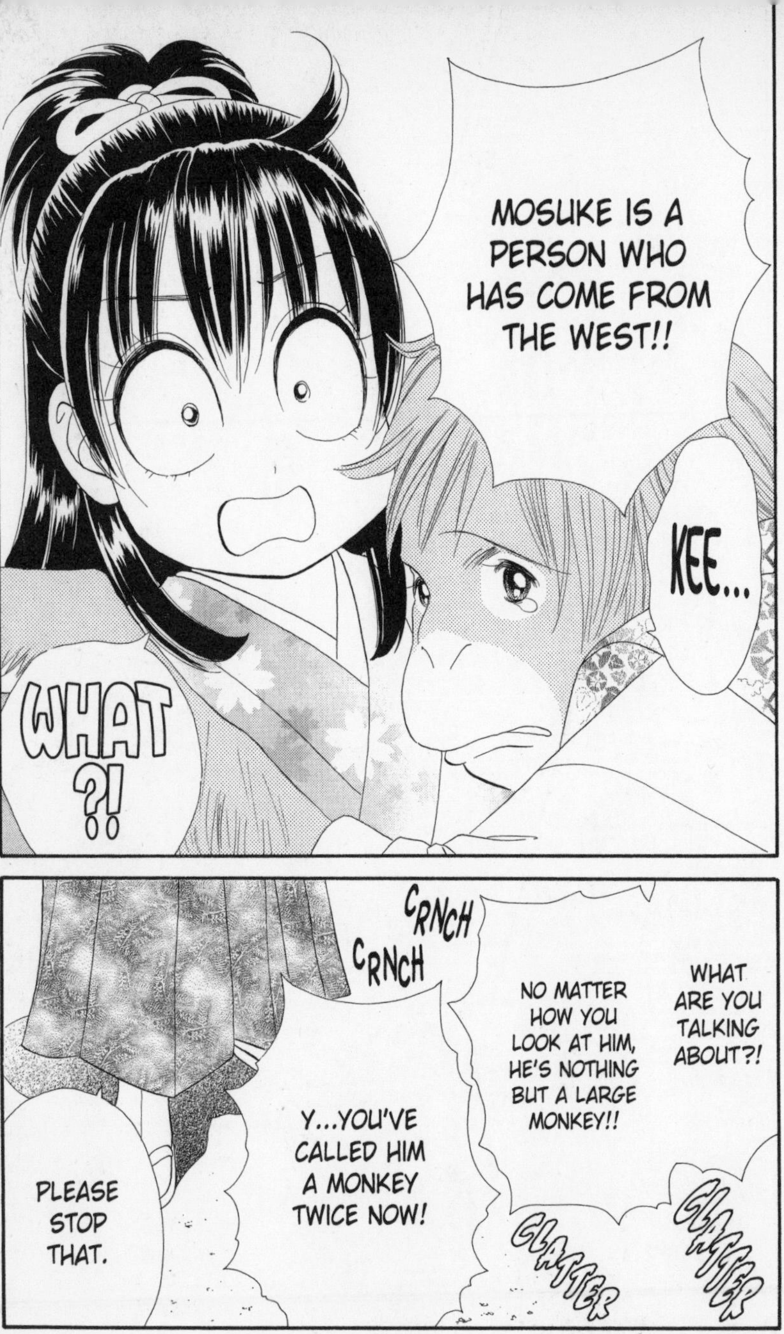
MOSUKE IS A PERSON WHO HAS COME FROM THE WEST!!
KEE...
WHAT ?!
CRNCH
CRNCH
WHAT ARE YOU TALKING ABOUT?!
NO MATTER HOW YOU LOOK AT HIM, HE'S NOTHING BUT A LARGE MONKEY!!
CLATTER
CLATTER
Y...YOU'VE CALLED HIM A MONKEY TWICE NOW!
PLEASE STOP THAT.

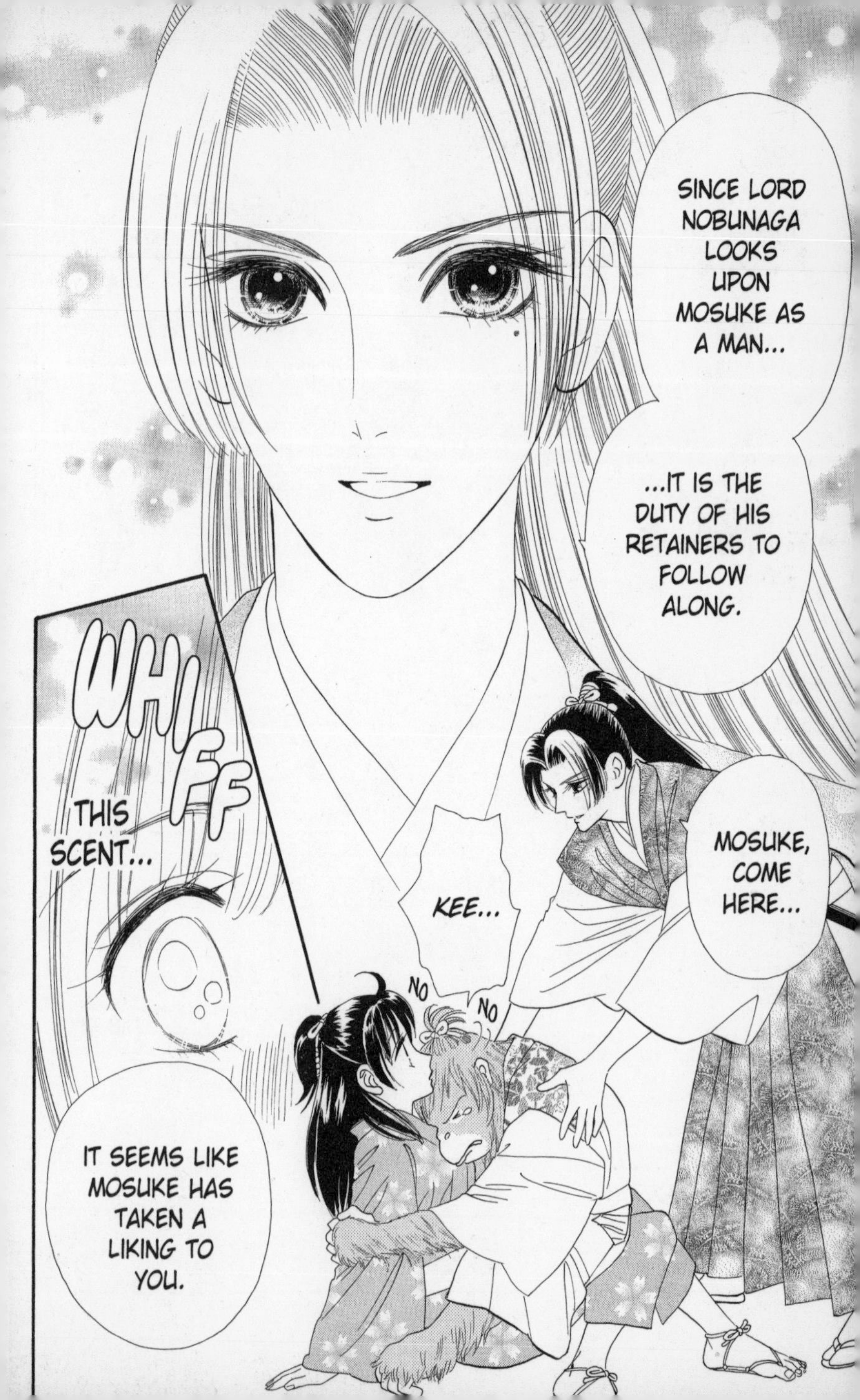
SINCE LORD NOBUNAGA LOOKS UPON MOSUKE AS A MAN...
...IT IS THE DUTY OF HIS RETAINERS TO FOLLOW ALONG.
MOSUKE, COME HERE...
KEE...
NO NO
WHIFF
THIS SCENT...
IT SEEMS LIKE MOSUKE HAS TAKEN A LIKING TO YOU.

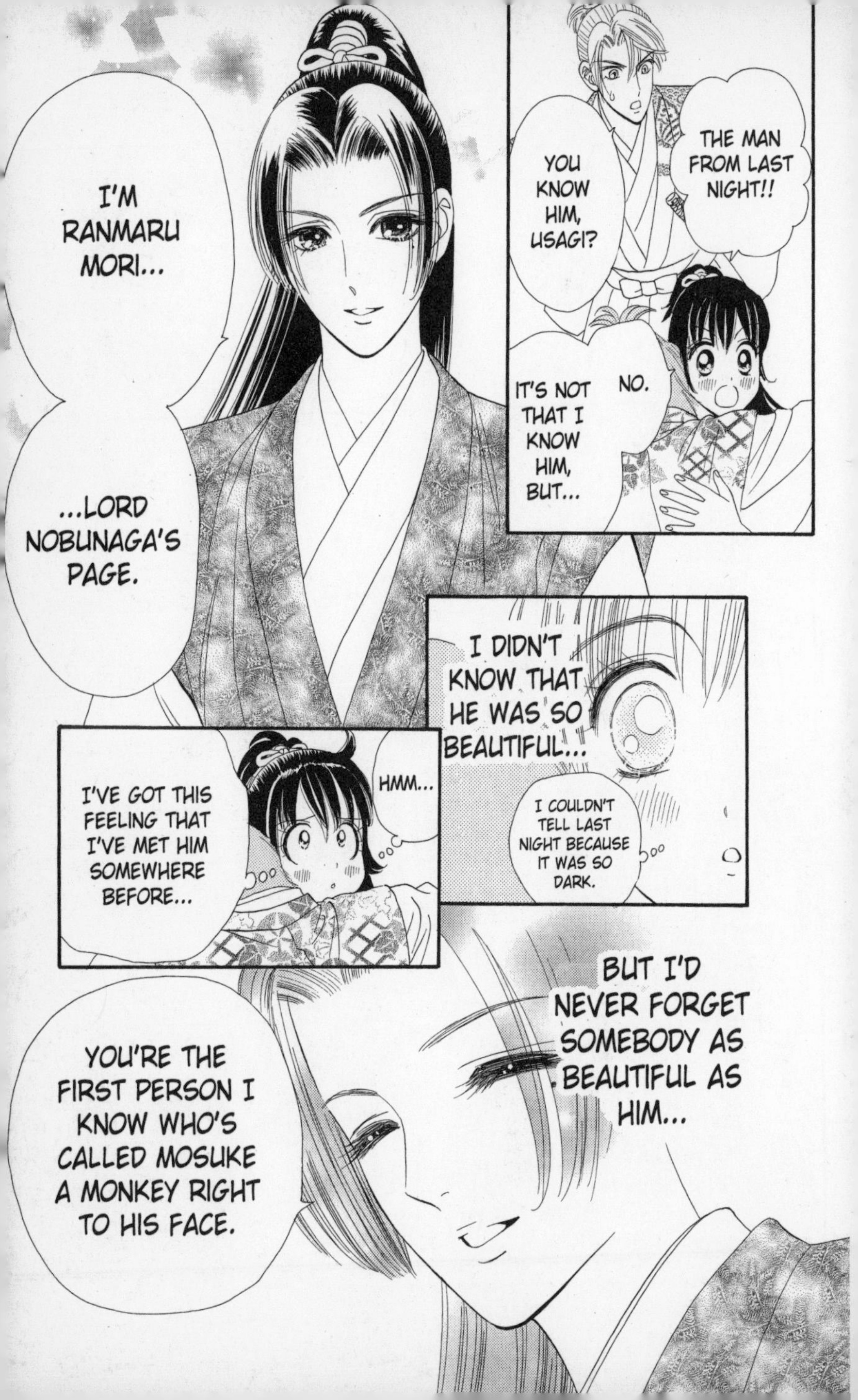
THE MAN FROM LAST NIGHT!!
YOU KNOW HIM, USAGI?
NO.
IT'S NOT THAT I KNOW HIM, BUT...
I'M RANMARU MORI...
...LORD NOBUNAGA'S PAGE.
I DIDN'T KNOW THAT HE WAS SO BEAUTIFUL...
I COULDN'T TELL LAST NIGHT BECAUSE IT WAS SO DARK.
HMM...
I'VE GOT THIS FEELING THAT I'VE MET HIM SOMEWHERE BEFORE...
BUT I'D NEVER FORGET SOMEBODY AS BEAUTIFUL AS HIM...
YOU'RE THE FIRST PERSON I KNOW WHO'S CALLED MOSUKE A MONKEY RIGHT TO HIS FACE.

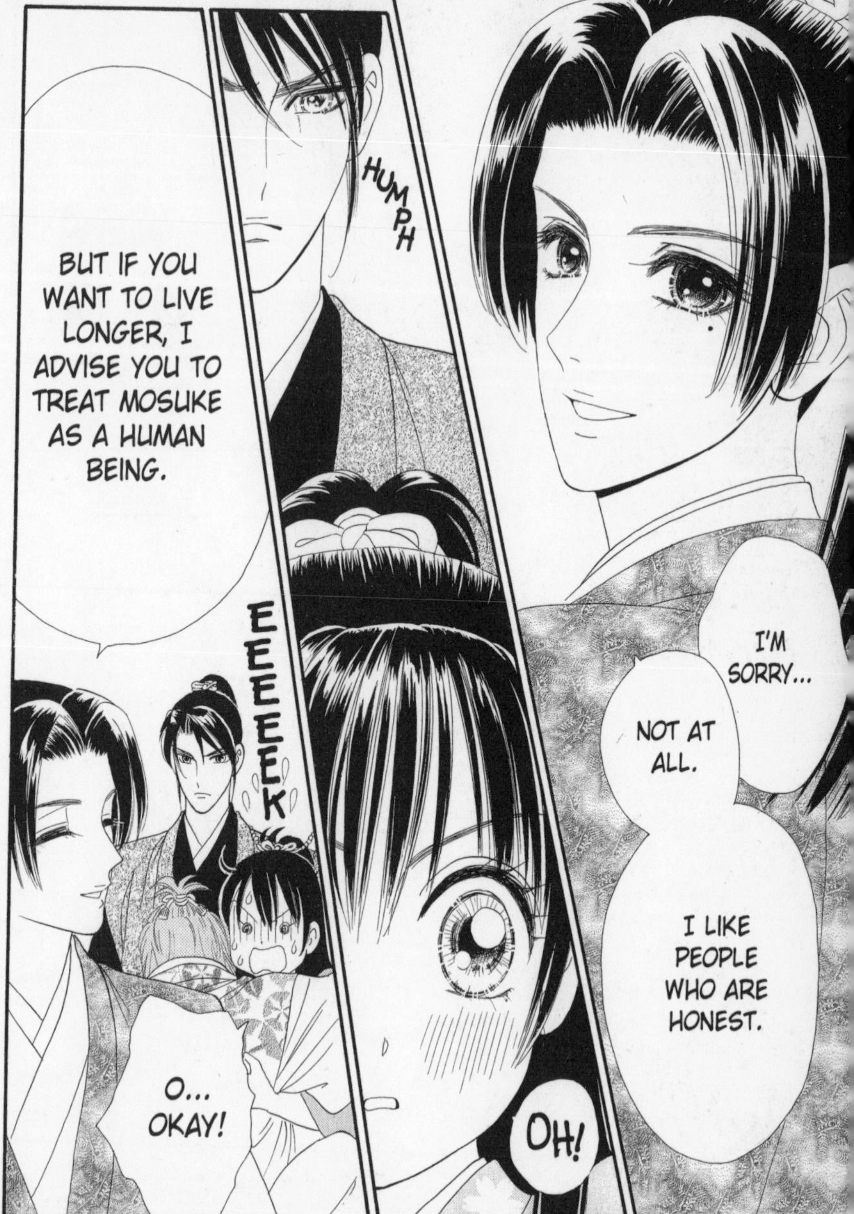
I'M SORRY...
NOT AT ALL.
I LIKE PEOPLE WHO ARE HONEST.
HUMPH
OH!
BUT IF YOU WANT TO LIVE LONGER, I ADVISE YOU TO TREAT MOSUKE AS A HUMAN BEING.
EEEEEEK
O... OKAY!

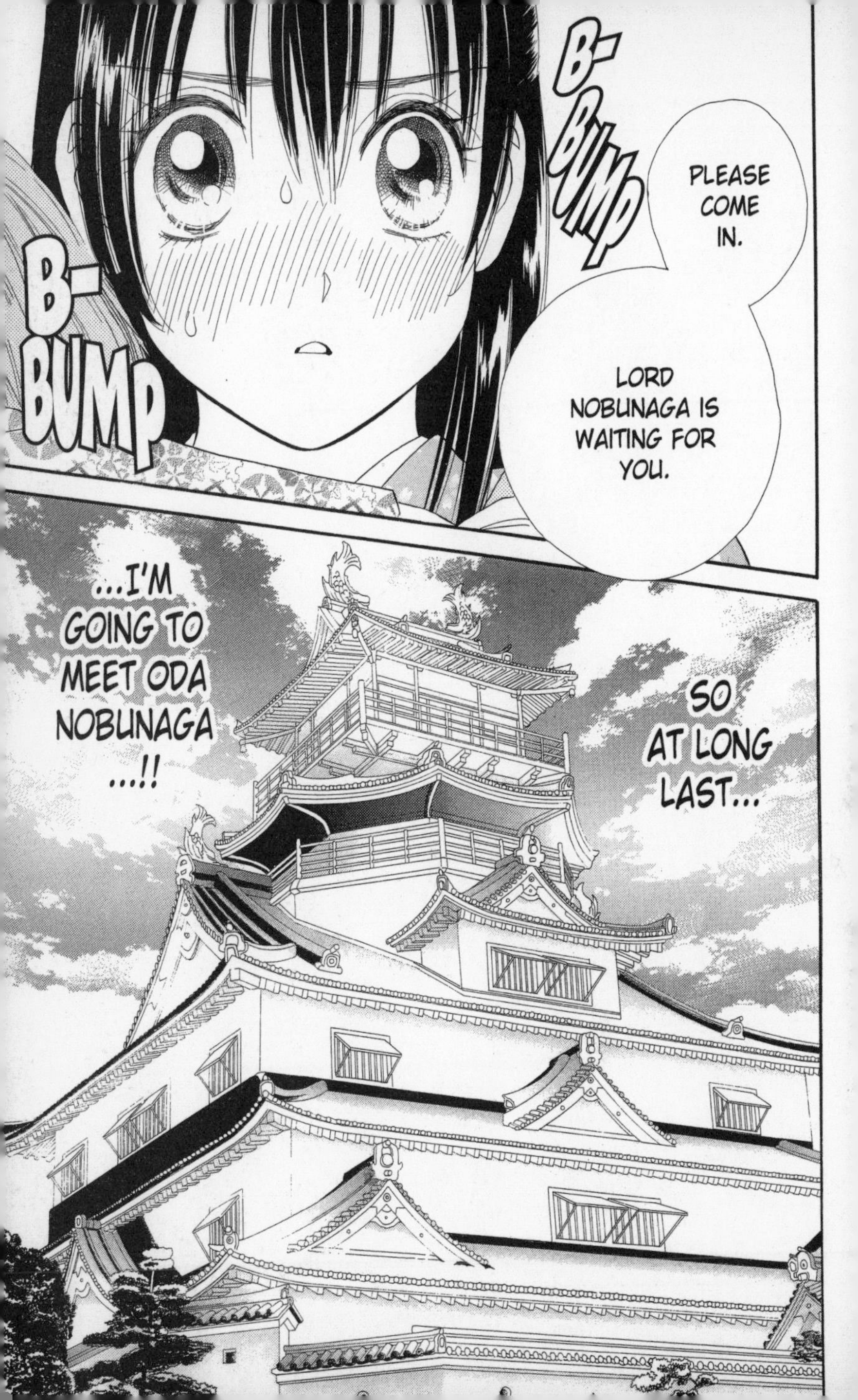
B-BUMP
PLEASE COME IN.
LORD NOBUNAGA IS WAITING FOR YOU.
B-BUMP
SO AT LONG LAST...
...I'M GOING TO MEET ODA NOBUNAGA ...!!

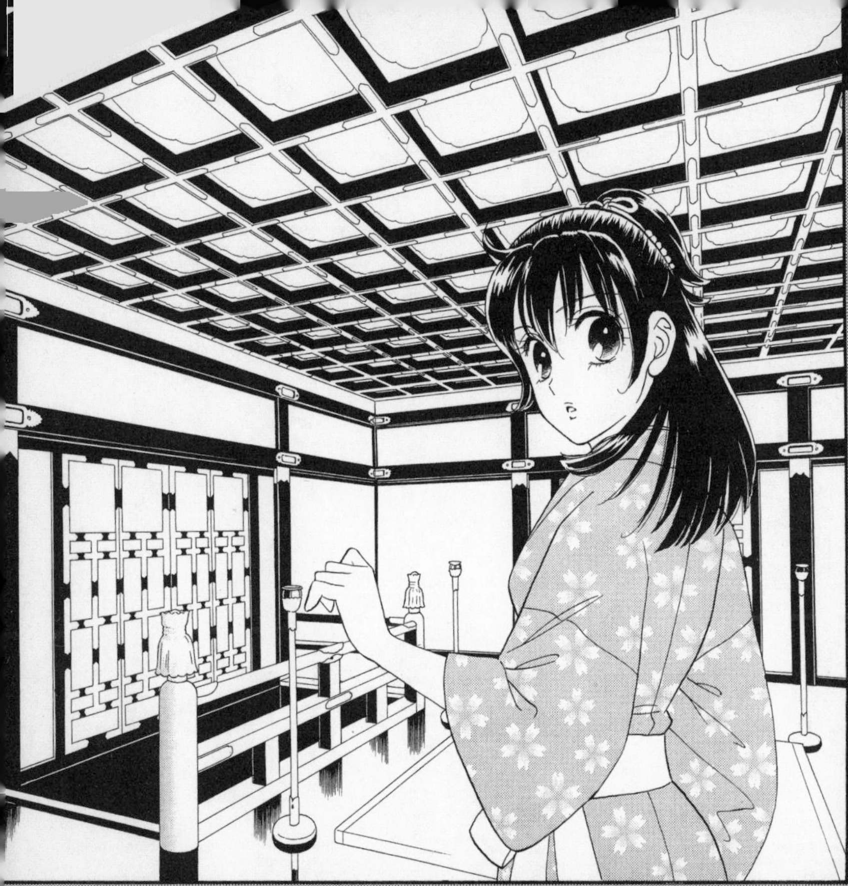

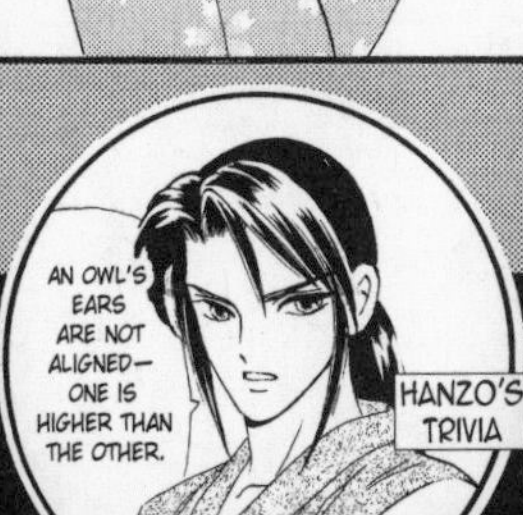
AN OWL'S EARS ARE NOT ALIGNED—ONE IS HIGHER THAN THE OTHER.
HANZO'S TRIVIA

Tail of the Moon

Chapter 49

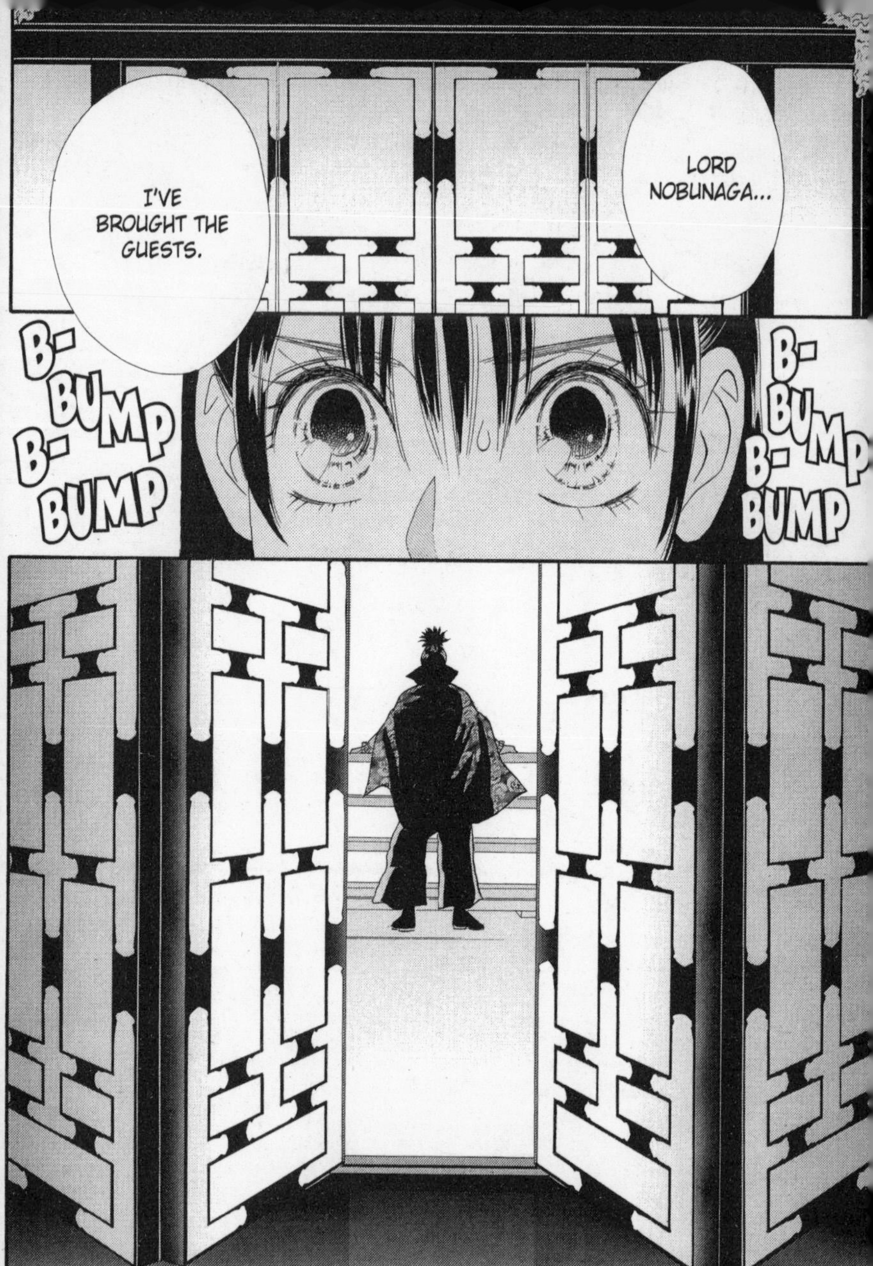
LORD NOBUNAGA...
I'VE BROUGHT THE GUESTS.
B-BUMP B-BUMP
B-BUMP B-BUMP

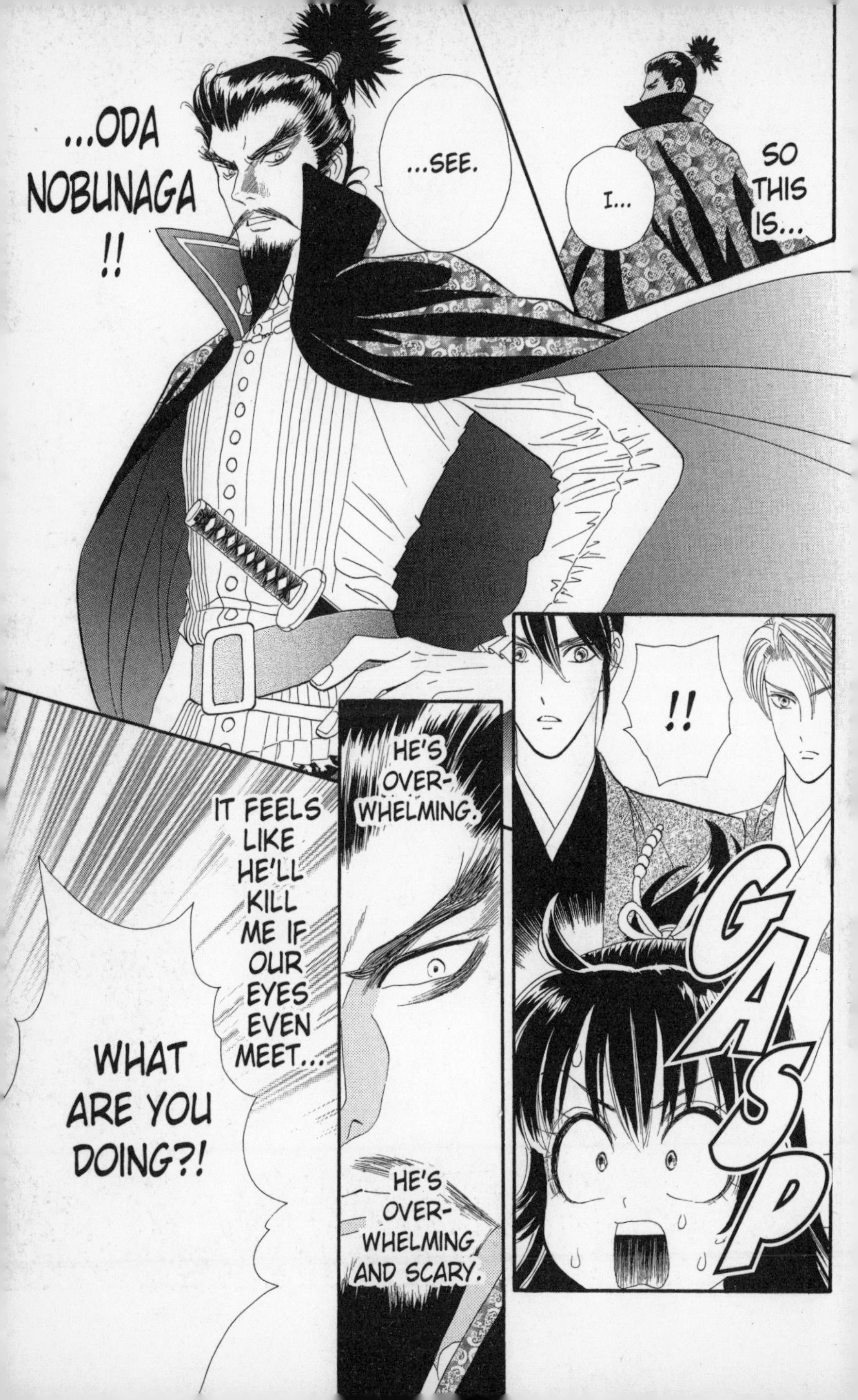
SO THIS IS...
I...
...SEE.
...ODA NOBUNAGA!!
!!
GASP
HE'S OVER-WHELMING.
HE'S OVER-WHELMING AND SCARY.
IT FEELS LIKE HE'LL KILL ME IF OUR EYES EVEN MEET...
WHAT ARE YOU DOING?!

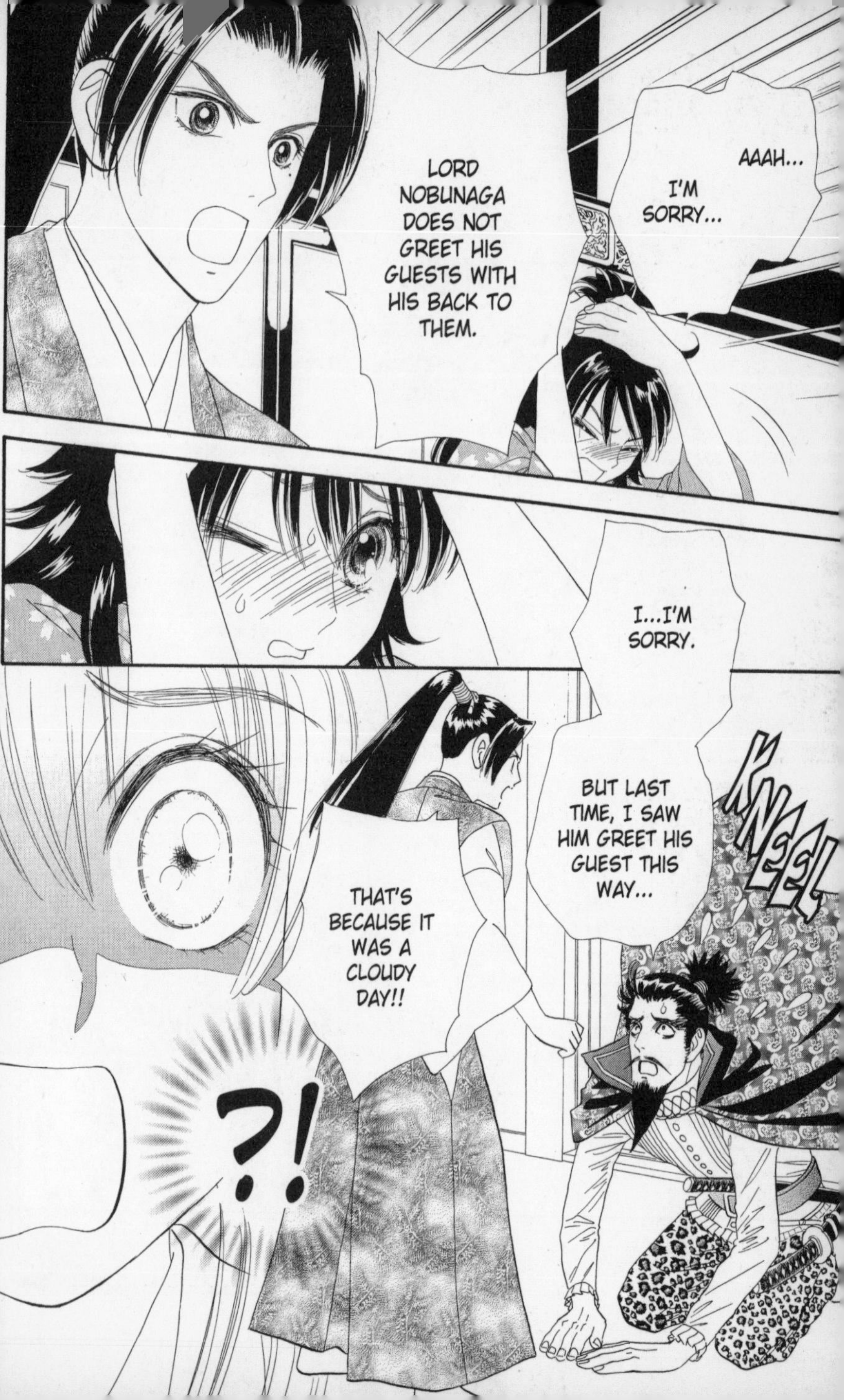
AAAH... I'M SORRY...
LORD NOBUNAGA DOES NOT GREET HIS GUESTS WITH HIS BACK TO THEM.
I...I'M SORRY.
BUT LAST TIME, I SAW HIM GREET HIS GUEST THIS WAY...
KNEEL
THAT'S BECAUSE IT WAS A CLOUDY DAY!!
?!

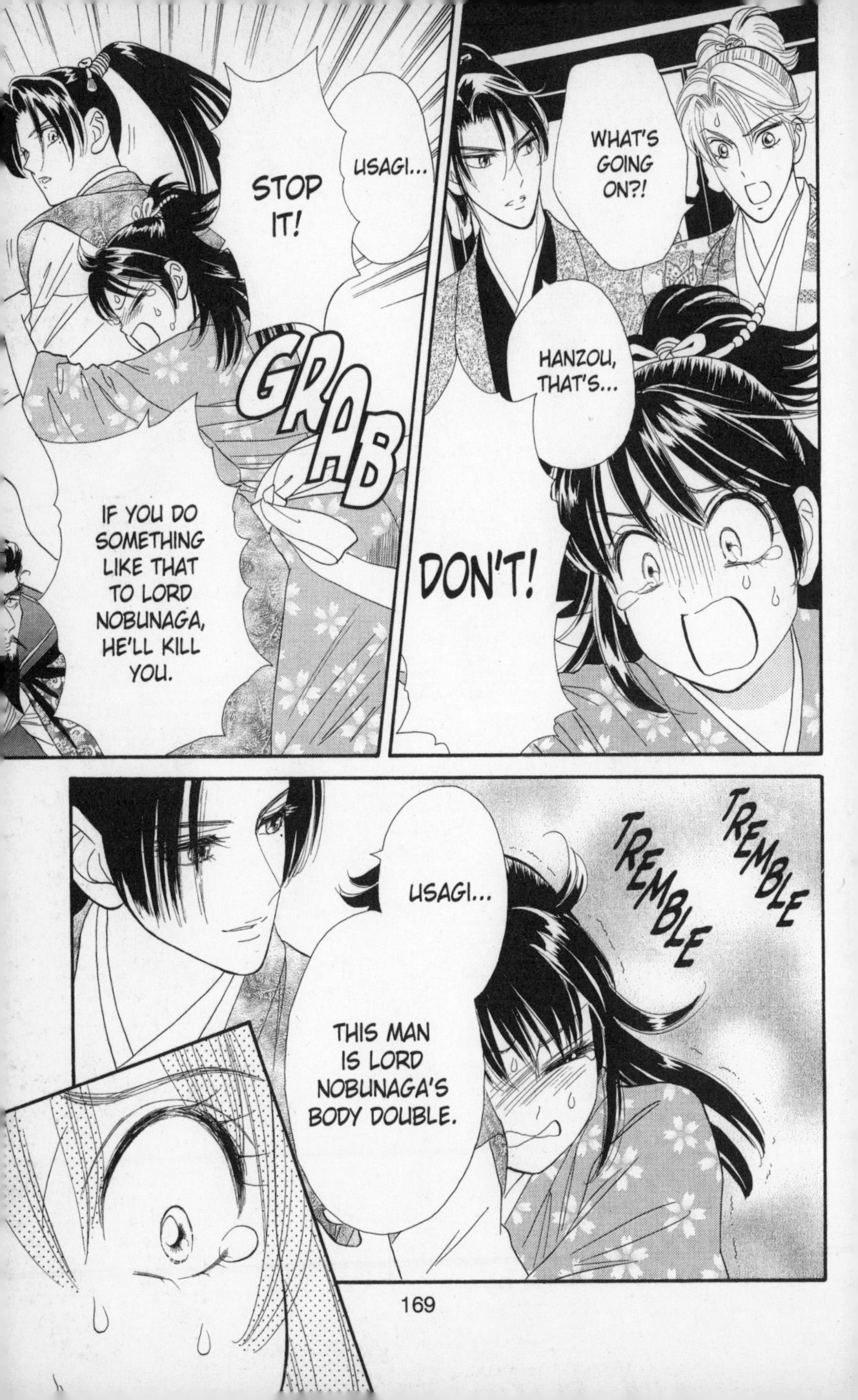
WHAT'S GOING ON?!
HANZOU, THAT'S...
DON'T!
USAGI...
STOP IT!
GRAB
IF YOU DO SOMETHING LIKE THAT TO LORD NOBUNAGA, HE'LL KILL YOU.
TREMBLE TREMBLE
USAGI...
THIS MAN IS LORD NOBUNAGA'S BODY DOUBLE.

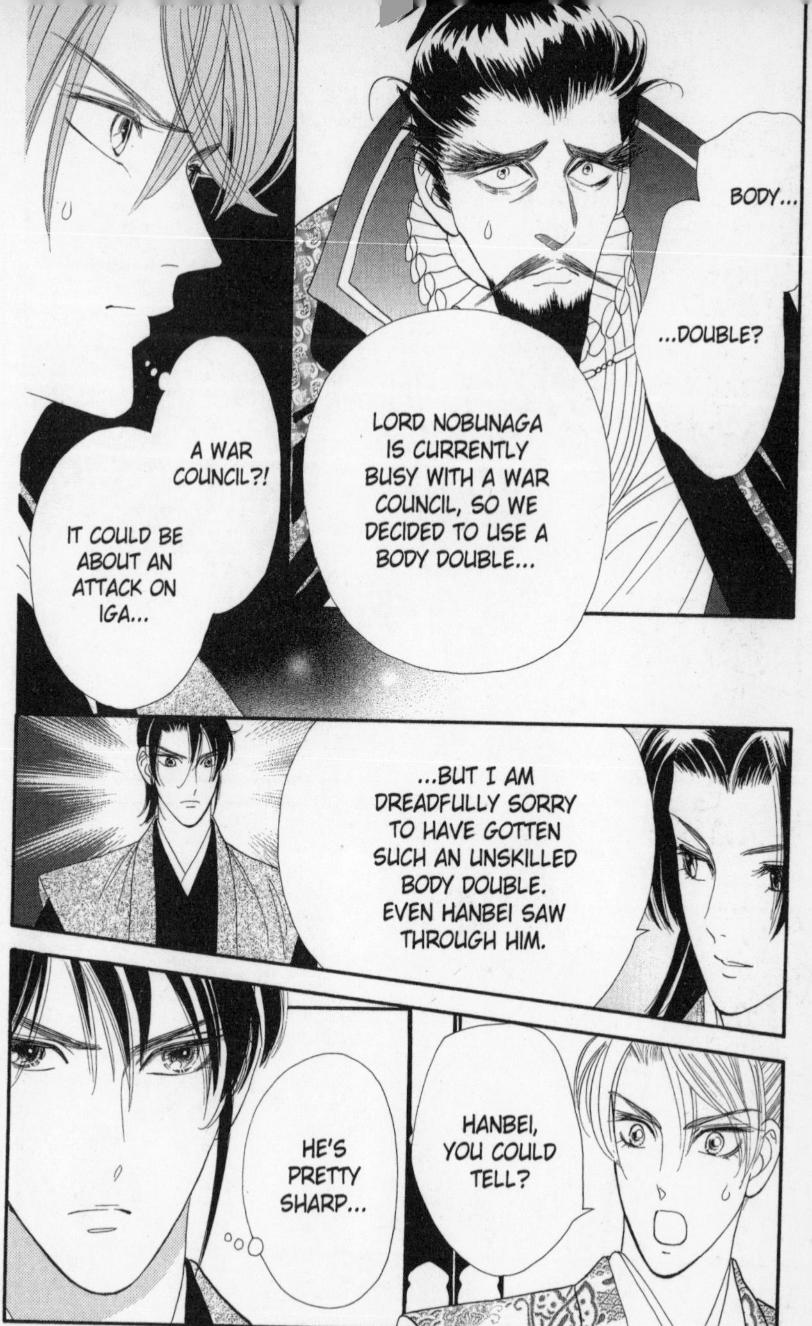
BODY...
...DOUBLE?
LORD NOBUNAGA IS CURRENTLY BUSY WITH A WAR COUNCIL, SO WE DECIDED TO USE A BODY DOUBLE...
A WAR COUNCIL?!
IT COULD BE ABOUT AN ATTACK ON IGA...
...BUT I AM DREADFULLY SORRY TO HAVE GOTTEN SUCH AN UNSKILLED BODY DOUBLE. EVEN HANBEI SAW THROUGH HIM.
HANBEI, YOU COULD TELL?
HE'S PRETTY SHARP...

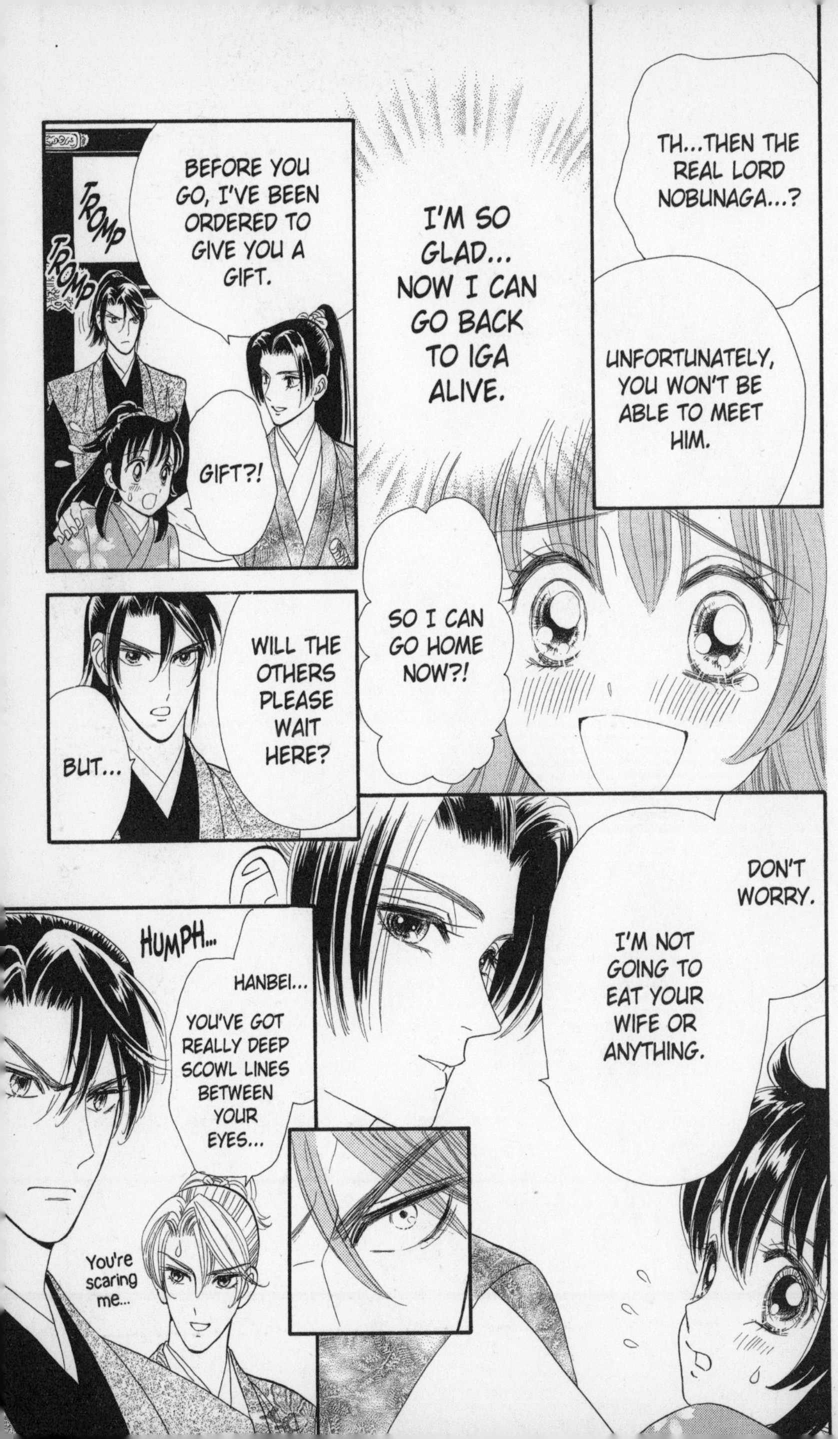
TH...THEN THE REAL LORD NOBUNAGA...?
UNFORTUNATELY, YOU WON'T BE ABLE TO MEET HIM.
I'M SO GLAD... NOW I CAN GO BACK TO IGA ALIVE.
SO I CAN GO HOME NOW?!
BEFORE YOU GO, I'VE BEEN ORDERED TO GIVE YOU A GIFT.
TROMP
TROMP
GIFT?!
WILL THE OTHERS PLEASE WAIT HERE?
BUT...
DON'T WORRY.
I'M NOT GOING TO EAT YOUR WIFE OR ANYTHING.
HUMPH...
HANBEI...
YOU'VE GOT REALLY DEEP SCOWL LINES BETWEEN YOUR EYES...
You're scaring me...

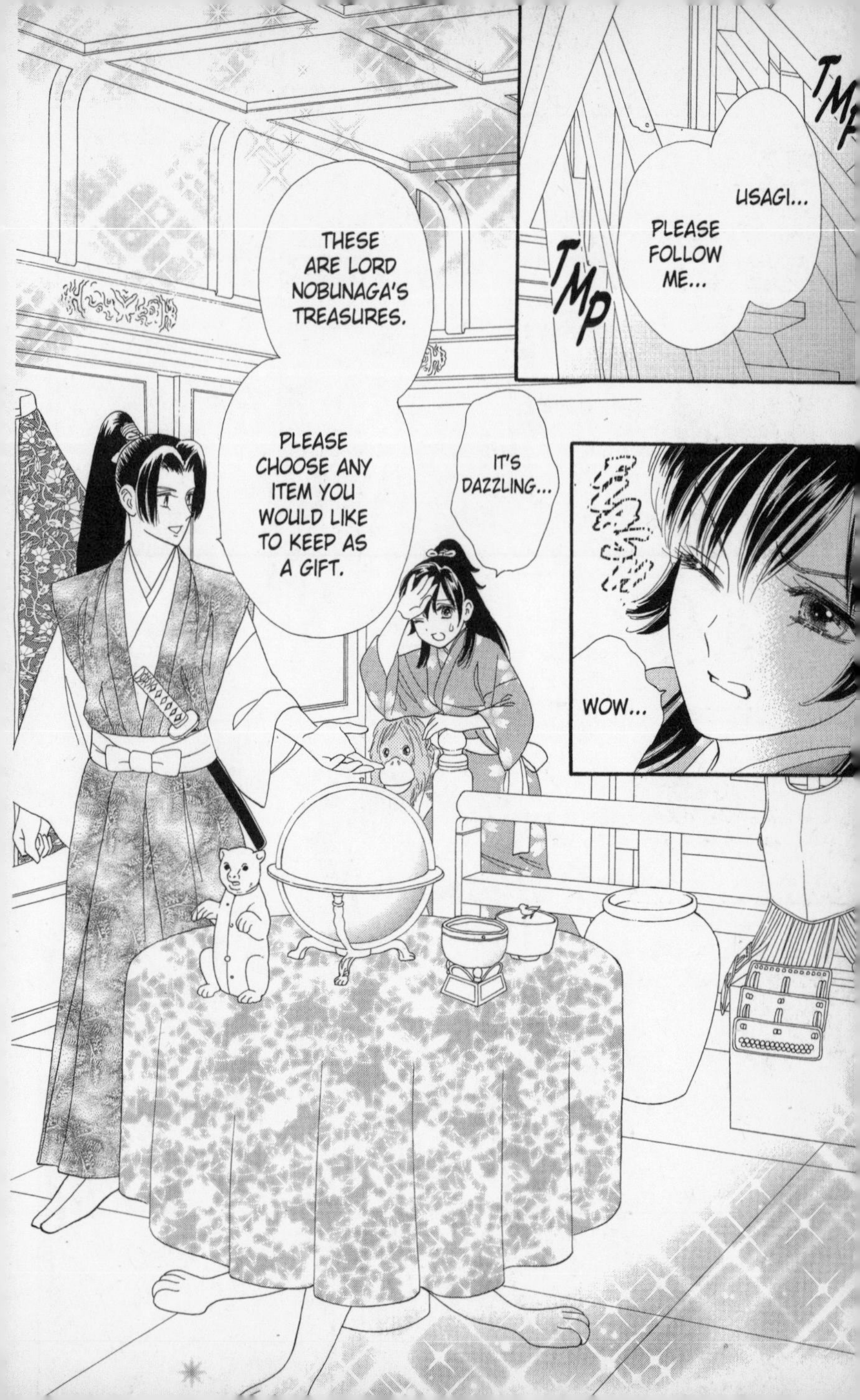
TMP
TMP
USAGI... PLEASE FOLLOW ME...
WOW...
THESE ARE LORD NOBUNAGA'S TREASURES.
PLEASE CHOOSE ANY ITEM YOU WOULD LIKE TO KEEP AS A GIFT.
IT'S DAZZLING...

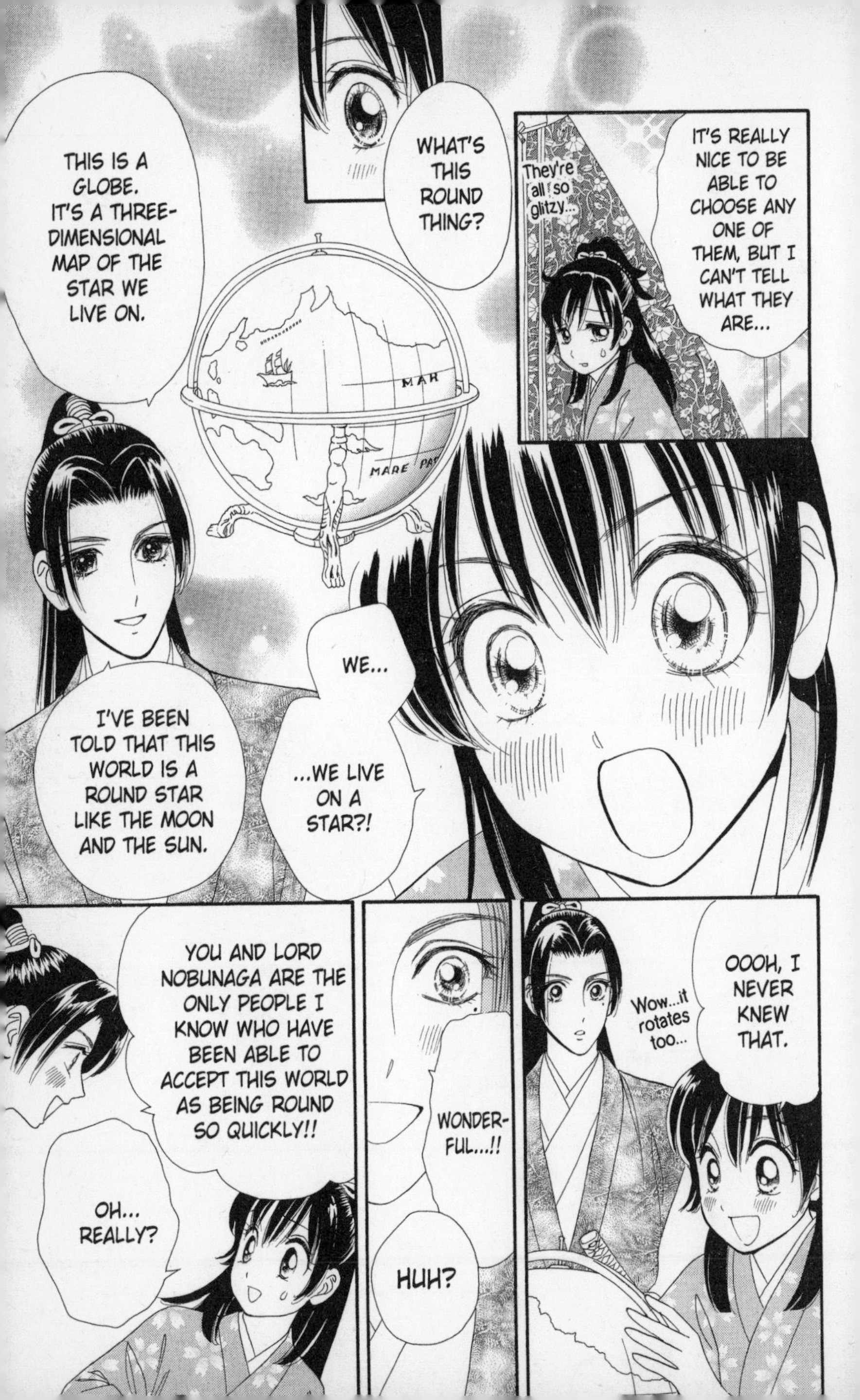

IT'S REALLY NICE TO BE ABLE TO CHOOSE ANY ONE OF THEM, BUT I CAN'T TELL WHAT THEY ARE...
They're all so glitzy...
WHAT'S THIS ROUND THING?
THIS IS A GLOBE. IT'S A THREE-DIMENSIONAL MAP OF THE STAR WE LIVE ON.
MAR
MARE PA
WE...
...WE LIVE ON A STAR?!
I'VE BEEN TOLD THAT THIS WORLD IS A ROUND STAR LIKE THE MOON AND THE SUN.
OOOH, I NEVER KNEW THAT.
Wow...it rotates too...
WONDER-FUL...!!
HUH?
YOU AND LORD NOBUNAGA ARE THE ONLY PEOPLE I KNOW WHO HAVE BEEN ABLE TO ACCEPT THIS WORLD AS BEING ROUND SO QUICKLY!!
OH... REALLY?

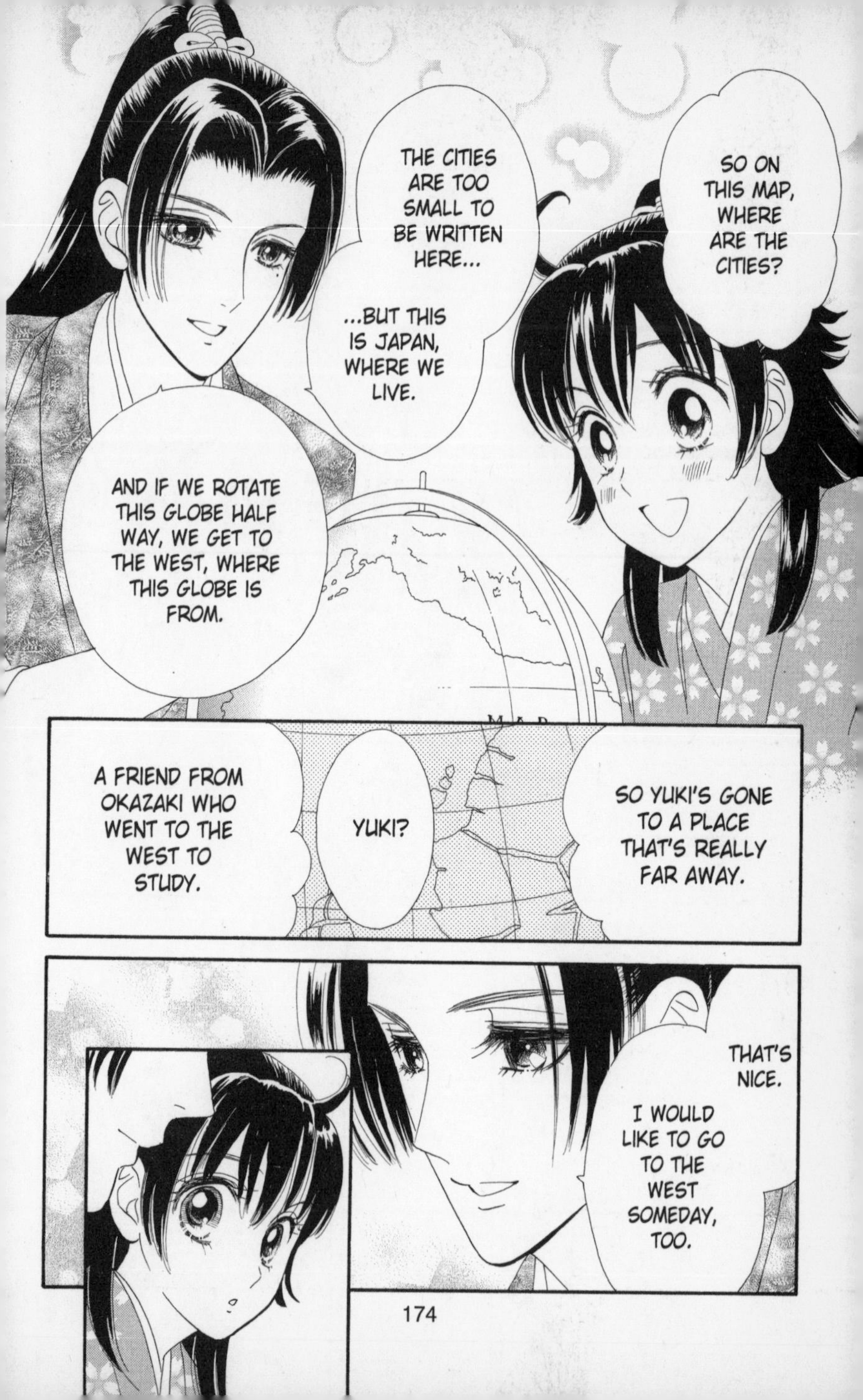
SO ON THIS MAP, WHERE ARE THE CITIES?
THE CITIES ARE TOO SMALL TO BE WRITTEN HERE...
...BUT THIS IS JAPAN, WHERE WE LIVE.
AND IF WE ROTATE THIS GLOBE HALF WAY, WE GET TO THE WEST, WHERE THIS GLOBE IS FROM.
SO YUKI'S GONE TO A PLACE THAT'S REALLY FAR AWAY.
YUKI?
A FRIEND FROM OKAZAKI WHO WENT TO THE WEST TO STUDY.
THAT'S NICE.
I WOULD LIKE TO GO TO THE WEST SOMEDAY, TOO.

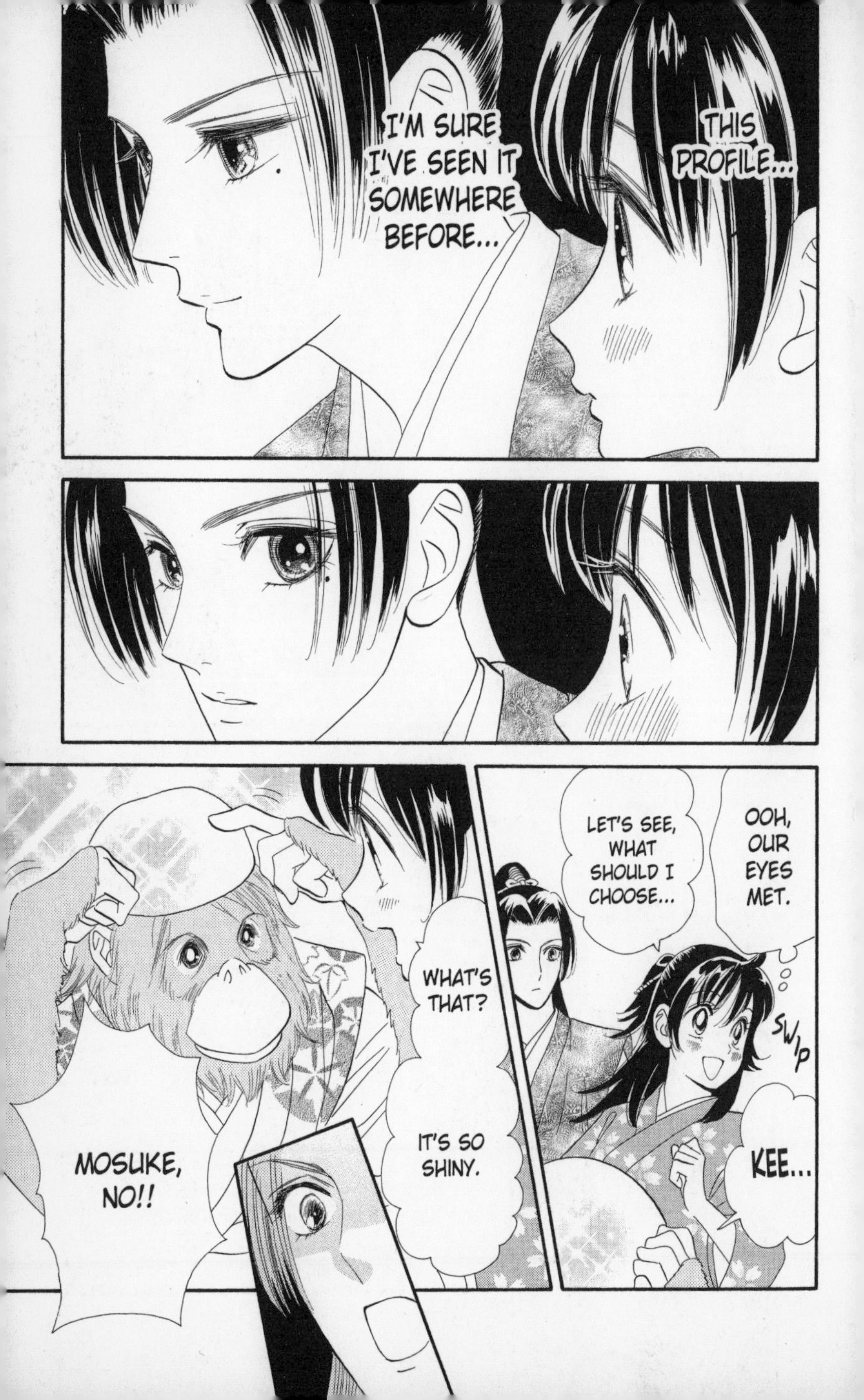
THIS PROFILE...
I'M SURE I'VE SEEN IT SOMEWHERE BEFORE...
OOH, OUR EYES MET.
LET'S SEE, WHAT SHOULD I CHOOSE...
SWIP
KEE...
WHAT'S THAT?
IT'S SO SHINY.
MOSUKE, NO!!

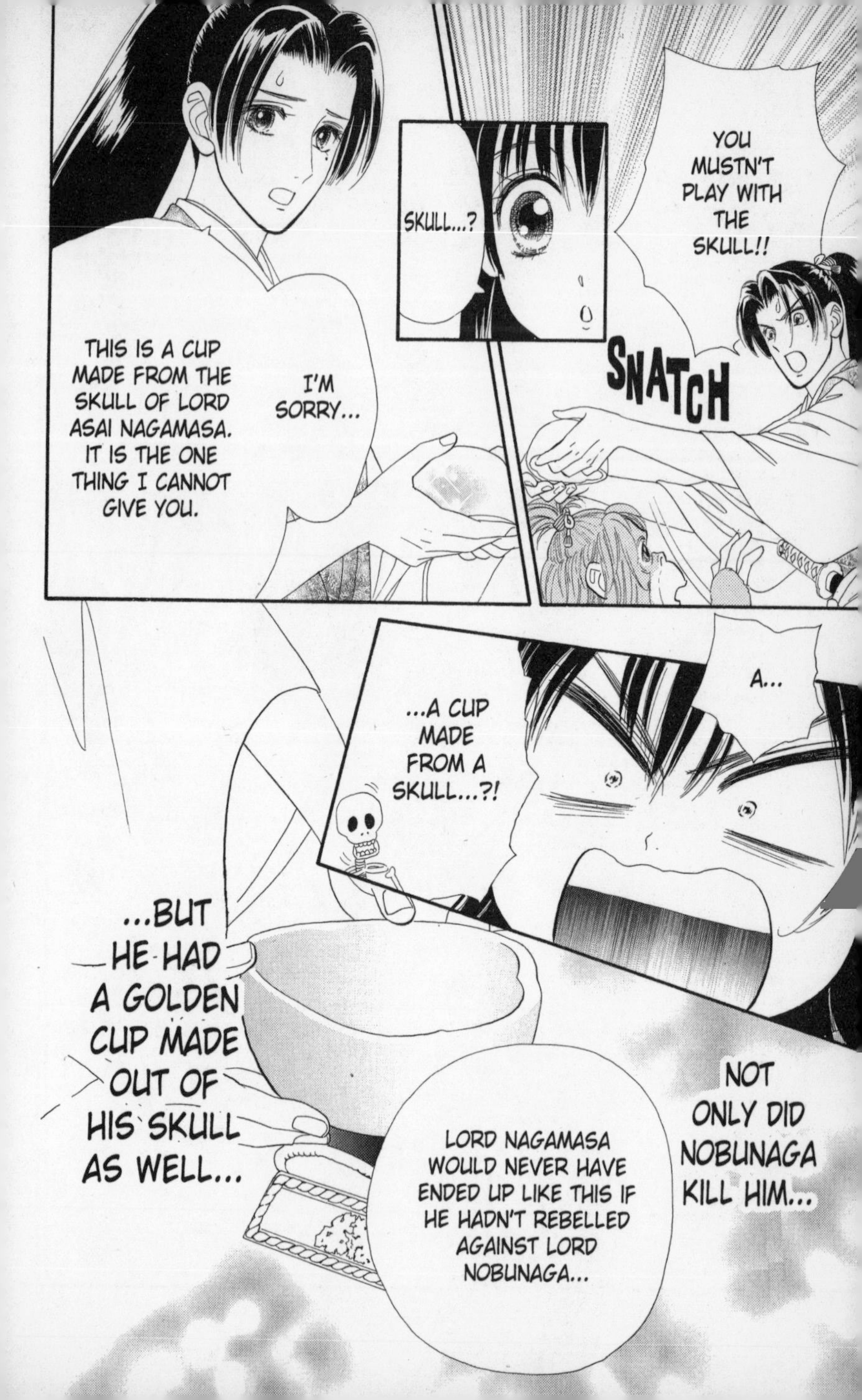
YOU MUSTN'T PLAY WITH THE SKULL!!
SNATCH
SKULL...?
THIS IS A CUP MADE FROM THE SKULL OF LORD ASAI NAGAMASA. IT IS THE ONE THING I CANNOT GIVE YOU.
I'M SORRY...
A...
...A CUP MADE FROM A SKULL...?!
NOT ONLY DID NOBUNAGA KILL HIM...
...BUT HE HAD A GOLDEN CUP MADE OUT OF HIS SKULL AS WELL...
LORD NAGAMASA WOULD NEVER HAVE ENDED UP LIKE THIS IF HE HADN'T REBELLED AGAINST LORD NOBUNAGA...

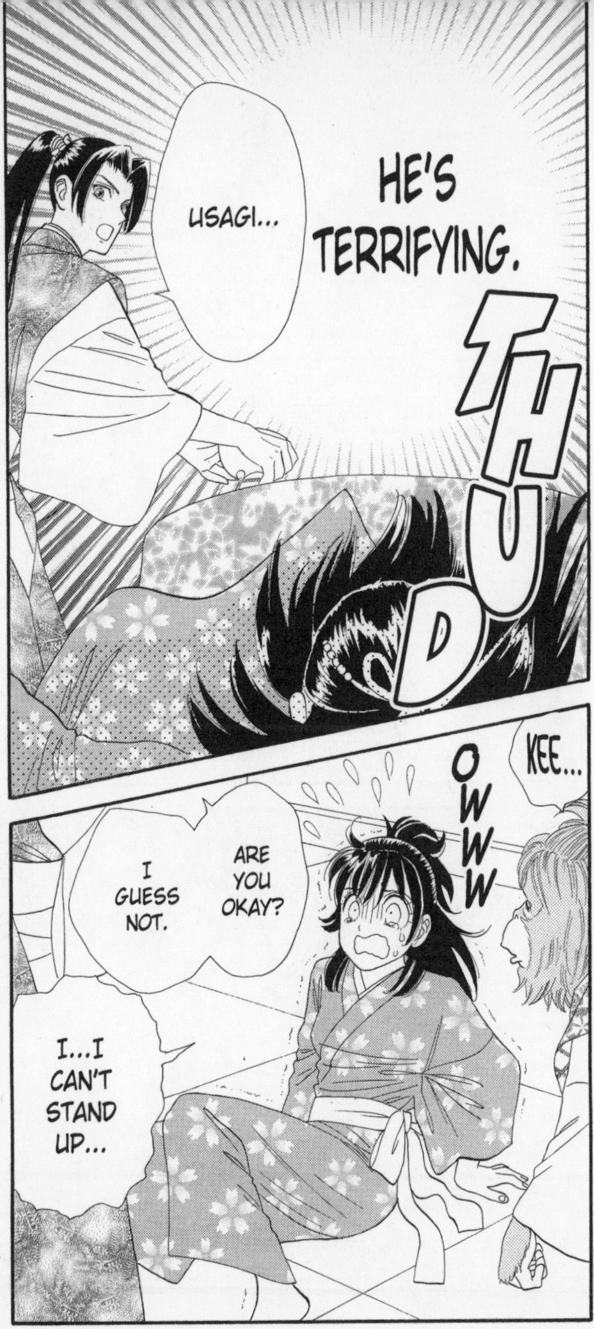
HE'S TERRIFYING.
USAGI...
THUD
KEE...
OWWW
ARE YOU OKAY?
I GUESS NOT.
I...I CAN'T STAND UP...

UE-RIN'S WAY OF THE MANGA ⑪

During the meeting, I brought along two 30-page manga pieces that I created during my summer vacation to prove to the editor that "this middle schooler's really trying hard." I had the editor look through my work and give me advice about it, but in the end, I was so nervous that I didn't remember anything I was told.

Argh...I should have taken notes...

I'm really sorry that my sentences are hard to read since I'm writing them down as I remember them off the top of my head. And since this is the last column in this volume, I'll write the rest in the next volume!

Send your messages and letters to the address below. We're looking forward to your requests for the Extra Missions as well!

Rinko Ueda
C/O Shojo Beat
Viz Media
P.O. Box 77010
San Francisco, CA
94107

Rinko Ueda

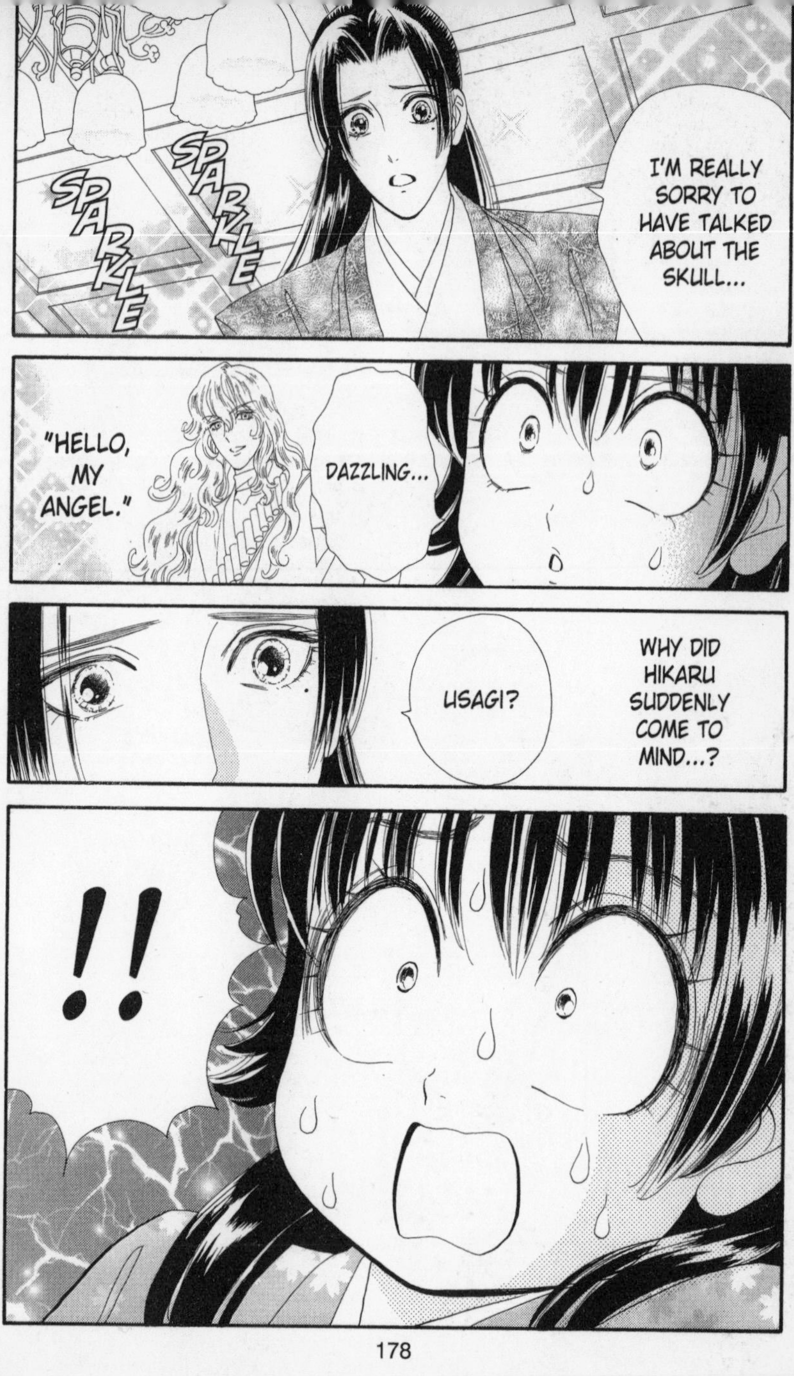
I'M REALLY SORRY TO HAVE TALKED ABOUT THE SKULL...
SPARKLE
SPARKLE
DAZZLING...
"HELLO, MY ANGEL."
WHY DID HIKARU SUDDENLY COME TO MIND...?
USAGI?
!!

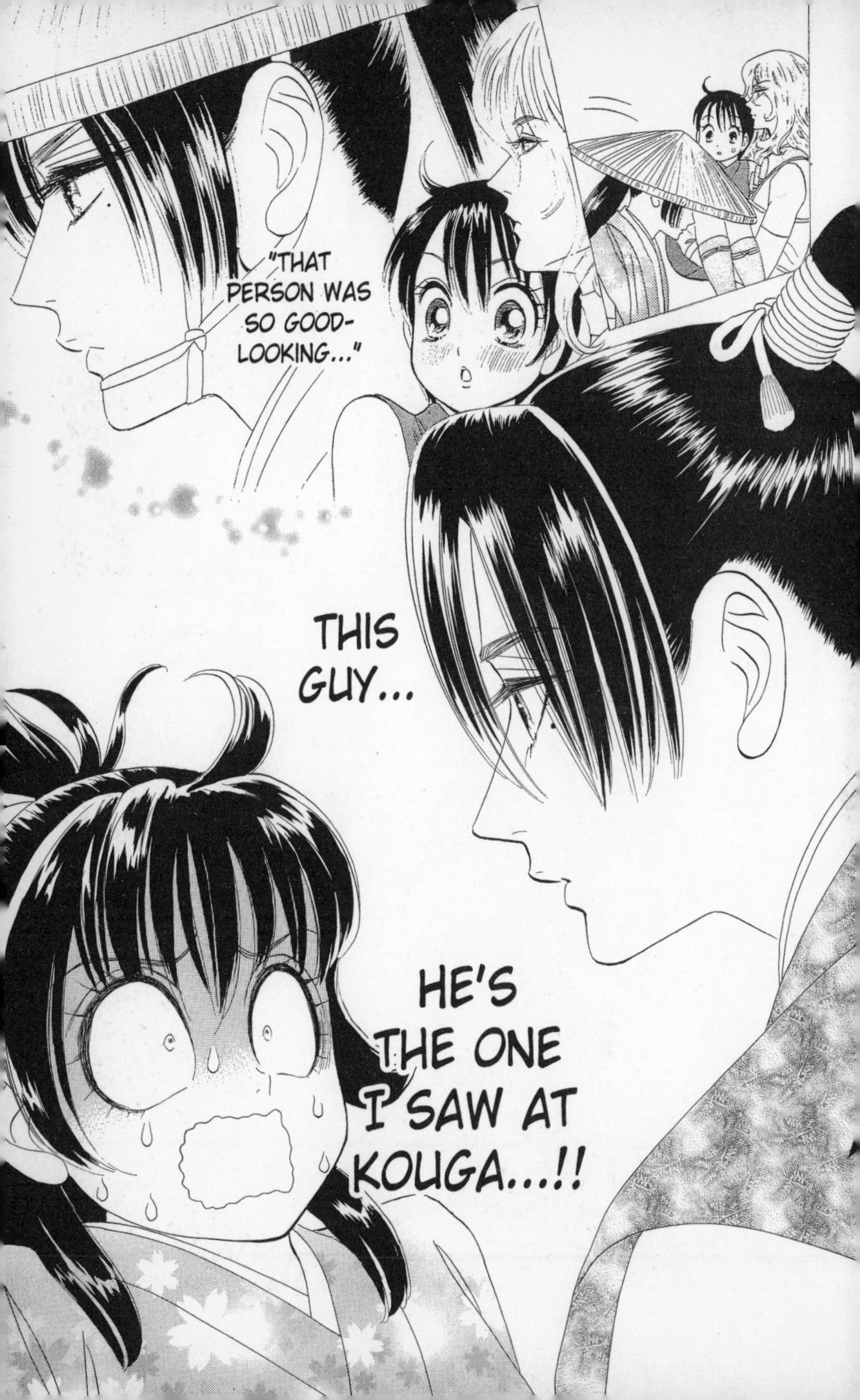
"THAT PERSON WAS SO GOOD-LOOKING..."
THIS GUY...
HE'S THE ONE I SAW AT KOUGA...!!

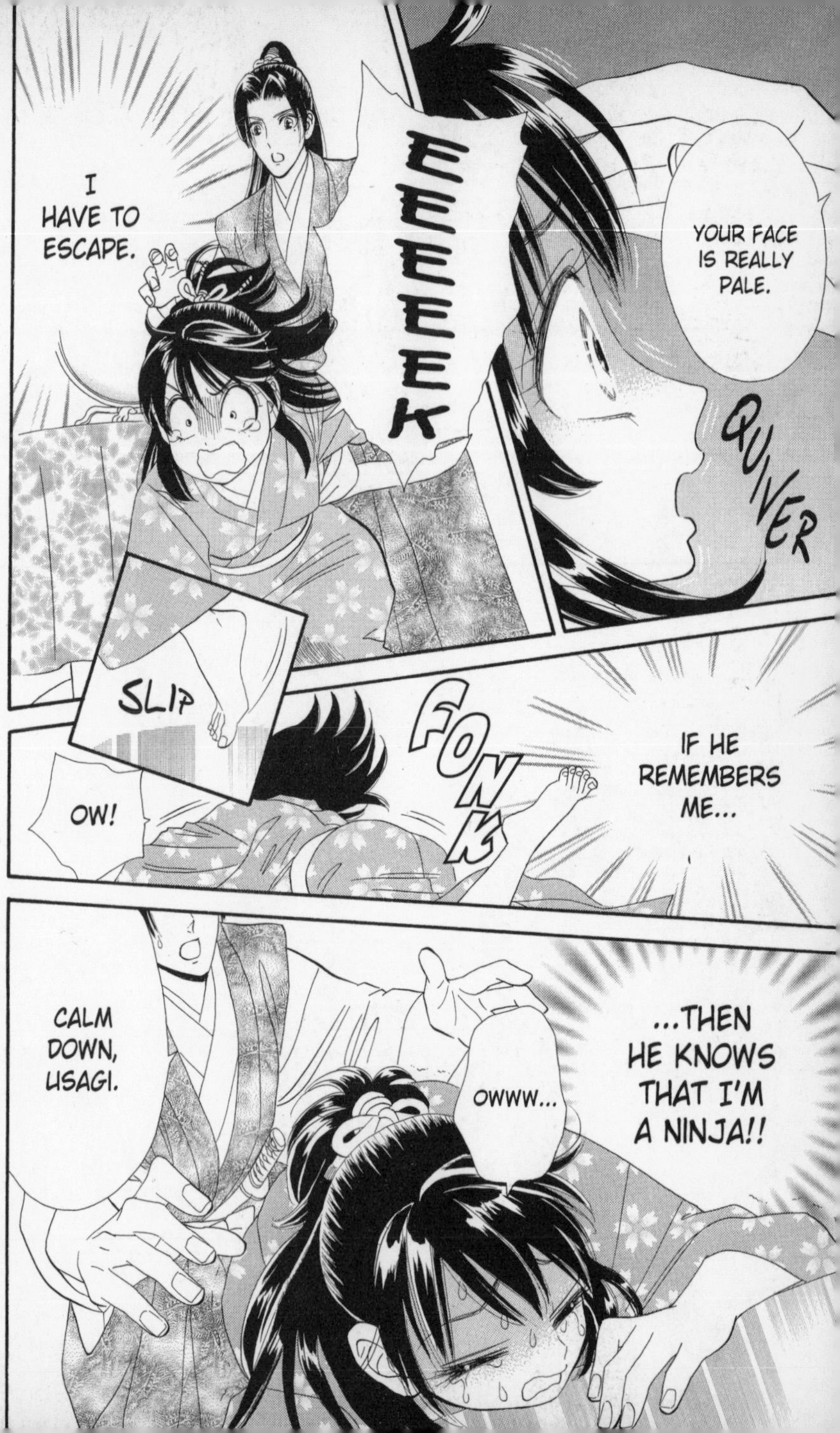
YOUR FACE IS REALLY PALE.
QUIVER
EEEEEEK
I HAVE TO ESCAPE.
SLIP
IF HE REMEMBERS ME...
FONK
OW!
...THEN HE KNOWS THAT I'M A NINJA!!
OWWW...
CALM DOWN, USAGI.

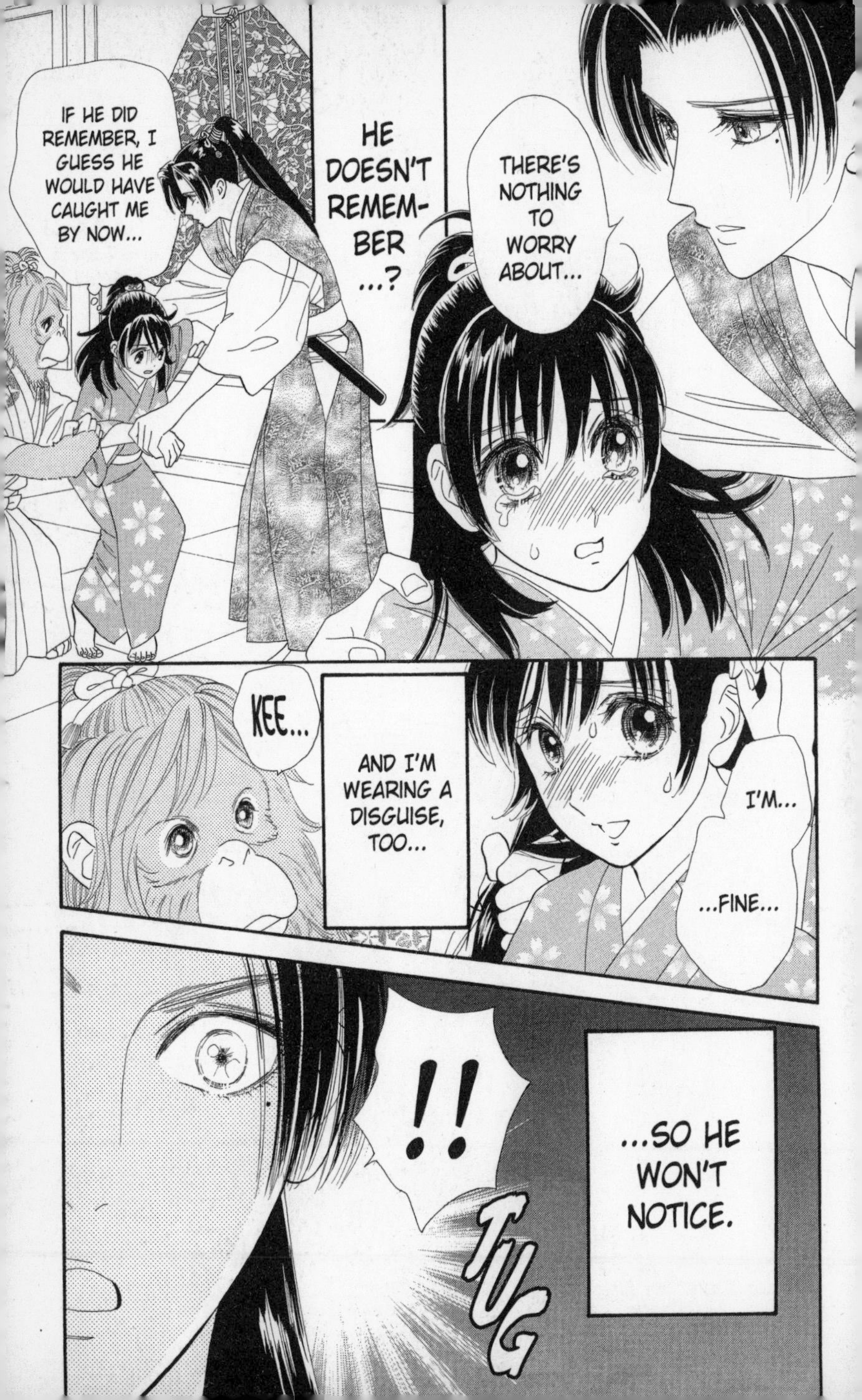
THERE'S NOTHING TO WORRY ABOUT...
HE DOESN'T REMEMBER...?
IF HE DID REMEMBER, I GUESS HE WOULD HAVE CAUGHT ME BY NOW...
I'M...
...FINE...
AND I'M WEARING A DISGUISE, TOO...
KEE...
...SO HE WON'T NOTICE.
!!
TUG

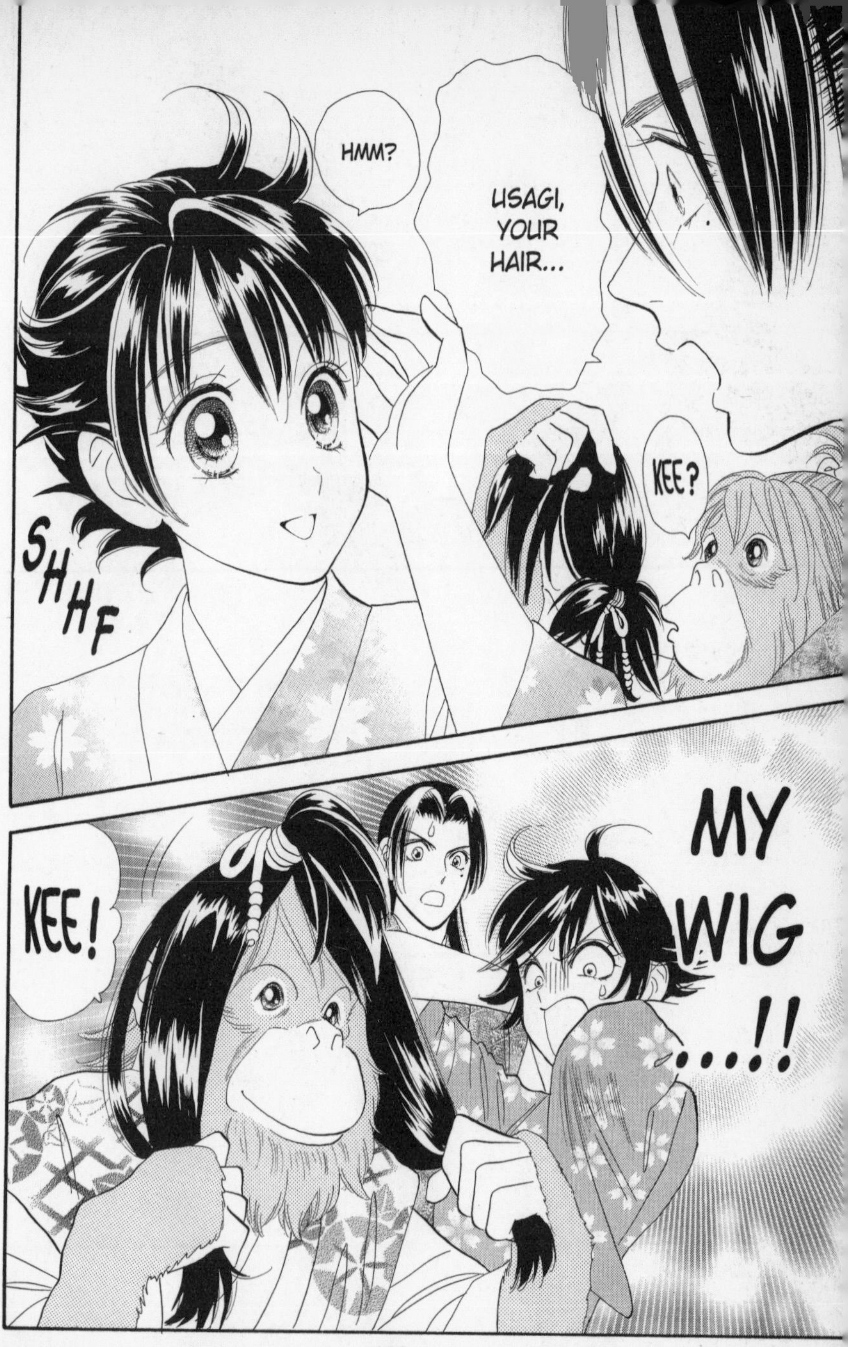
USAGI, YOUR HAIR...
HMM?
KEE?
SHHF
MY WIG...!!
KEE!

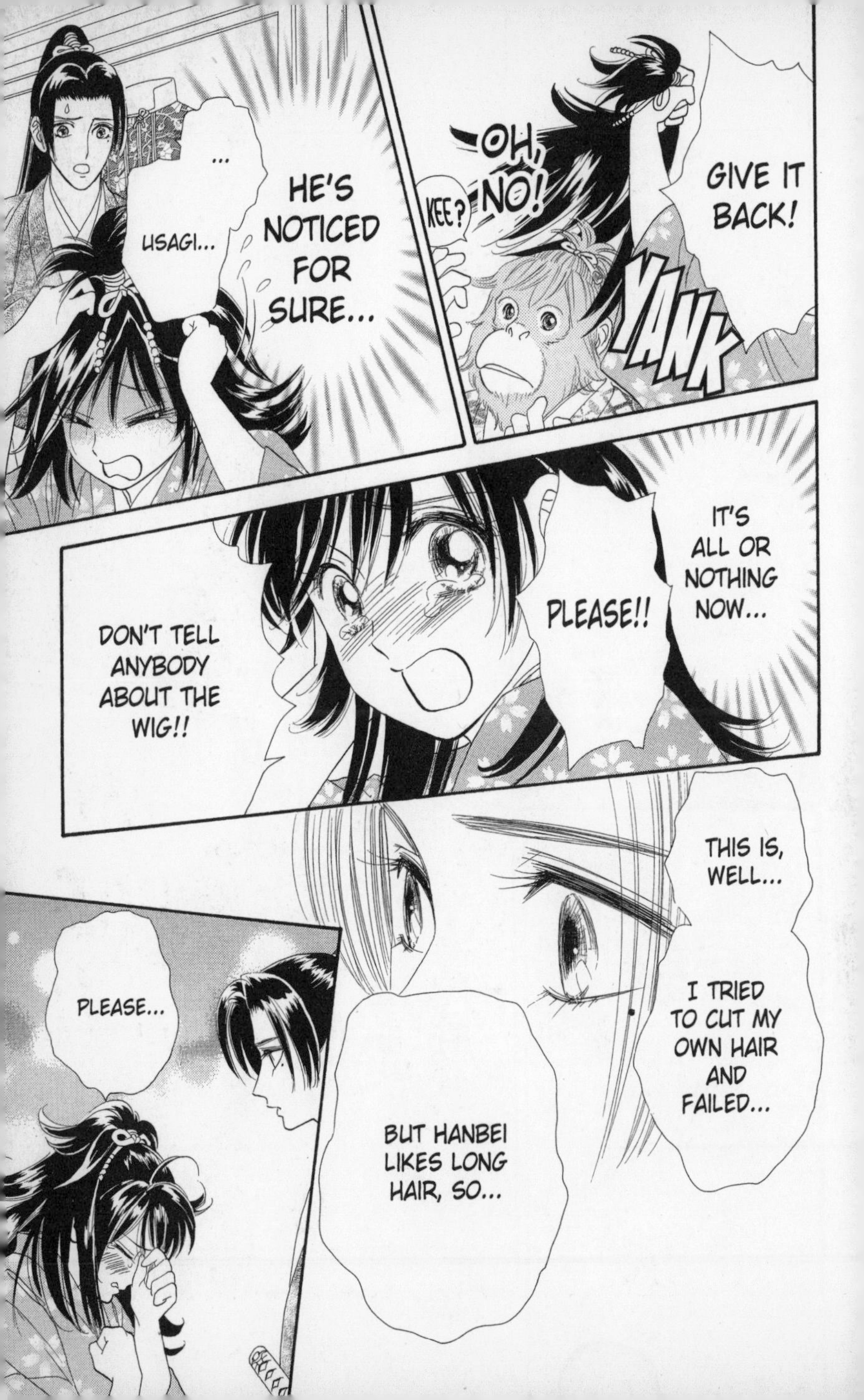
GIVE IT BACK!
OH, NO!
KEE?
YANK
HE'S NOTICED FOR SURE...
...
USAGI...
IT'S ALL OR NOTHING NOW...
PLEASE!!
DON'T TELL ANYBODY ABOUT THE WIG!!
THIS IS, WELL...
I TRIED TO CUT MY OWN HAIR AND FAILED...
BUT HANBEI LIKES LONG HAIR, SO...
PLEASE...

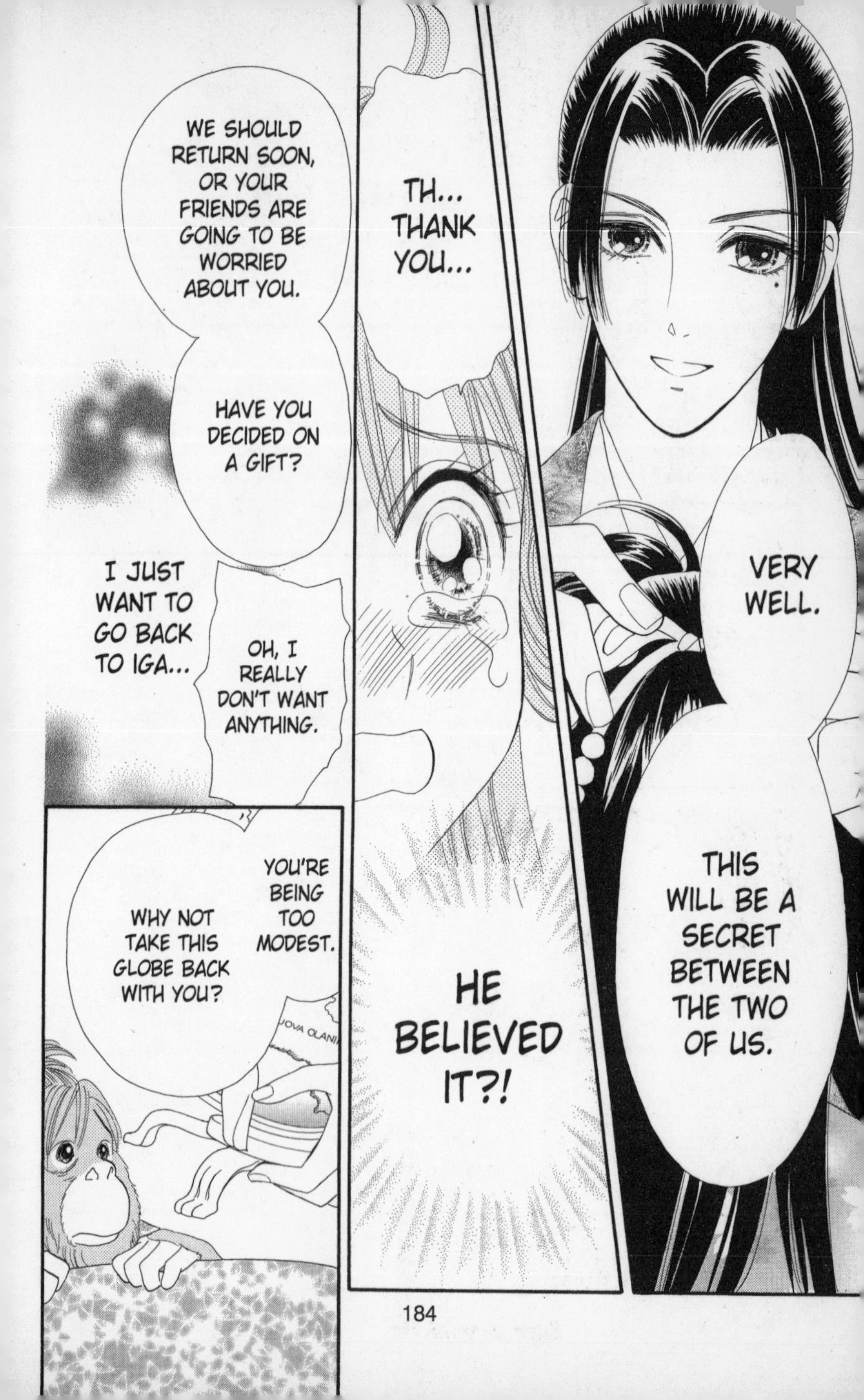
VERY WELL.
THIS WILL BE A SECRET BETWEEN THE TWO OF US.
TH... THANK YOU...
HE BELIEVED IT?!
WE SHOULD RETURN SOON, OR YOUR FRIENDS ARE GOING TO BE WORRIED ABOUT YOU.
HAVE YOU DECIDED ON A GIFT?
OH, I REALLY DON'T WANT ANYTHING.
I JUST WANT TO GO BACK TO IGA...
YOU'RE BEING TOO MODEST.
WHY NOT TAKE THIS GLOBE BACK WITH YOU?

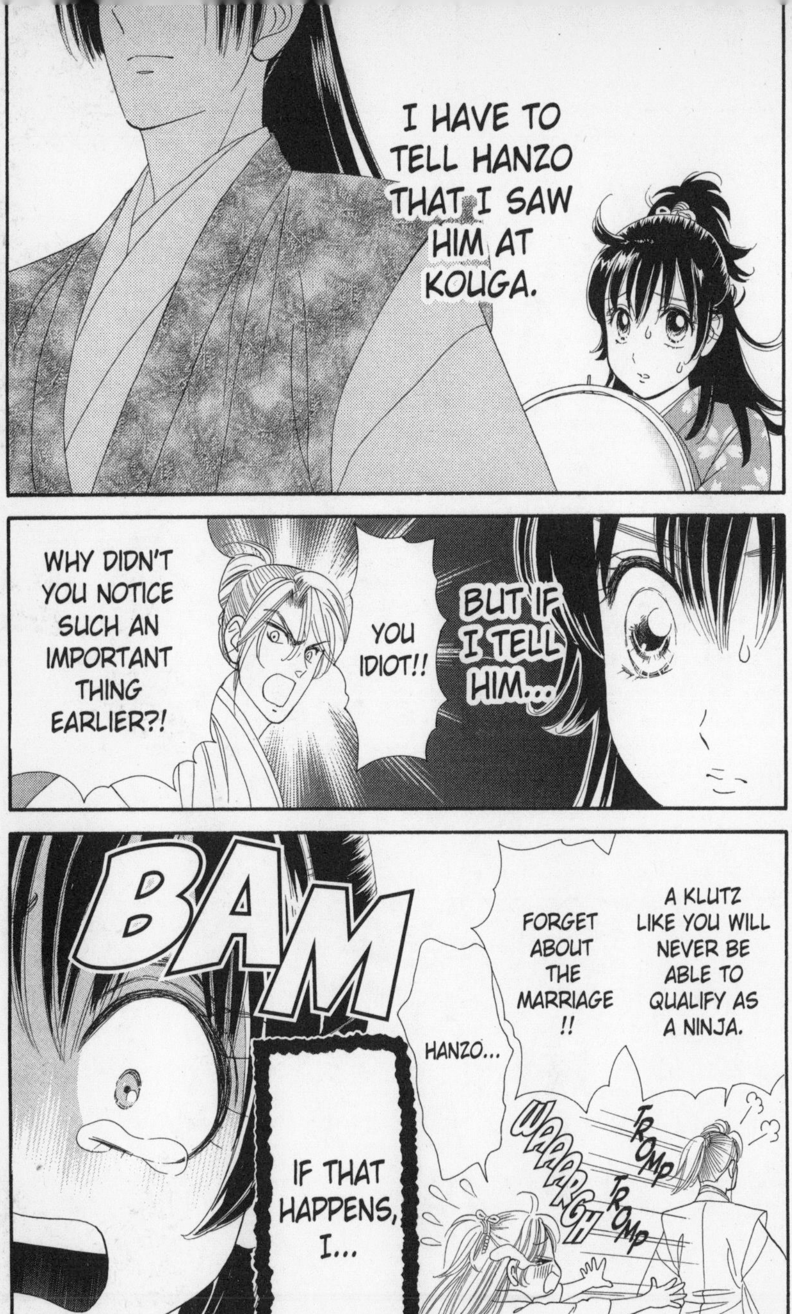
I HAVE TO TELL HANZO THAT I SAW HIM AT KOUGA.
BUT IF I TELL HIM...
YOU IDIOT!!
WHY DIDN'T YOU NOTICE SUCH AN IMPORTANT THING EARLIER?!
A KLUTZ LIKE YOU WILL NEVER BE ABLE TO QUALIFY AS A NINJA.
FORGET ABOUT THE MARRIAGE !!
BAM
HANZO...
TROMP TROMP
WAAARGH
IF THAT HAPPENS, I...

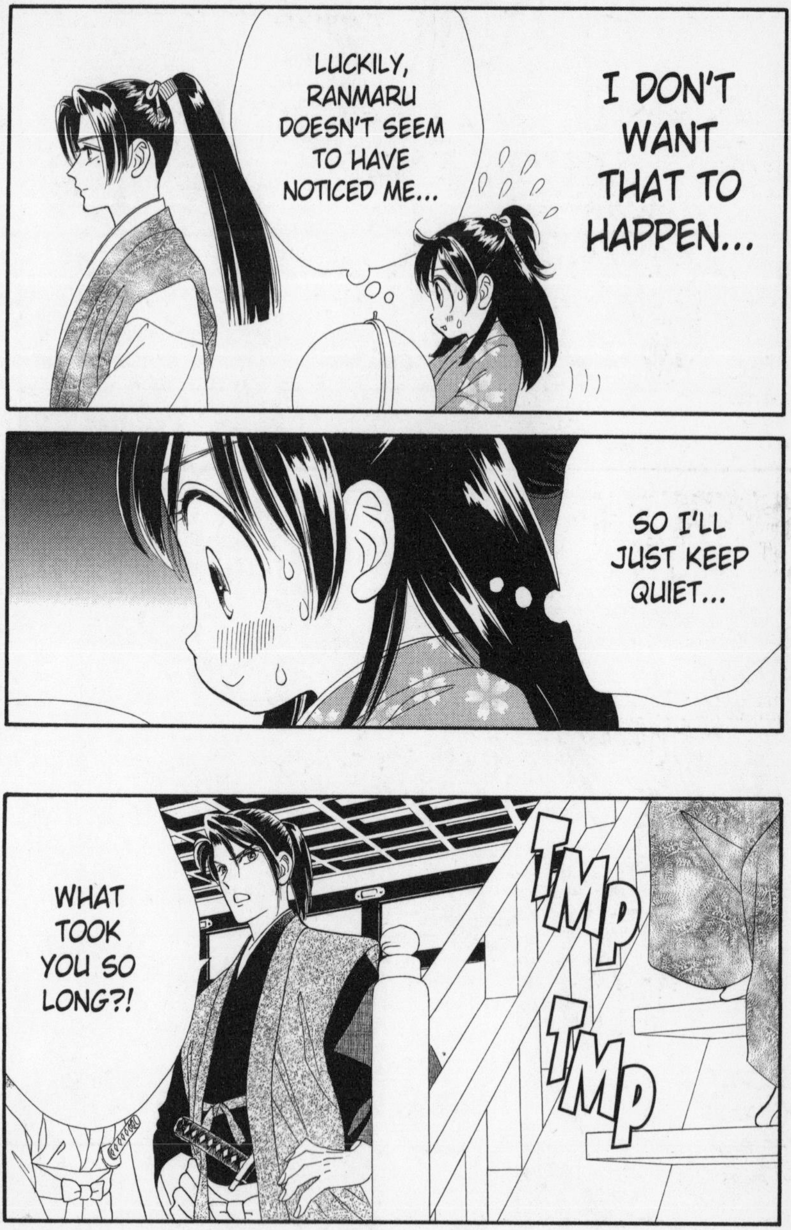
I DON'T WANT THAT TO HAPPEN...
LUCKILY, RANMARU DOESN'T SEEM TO HAVE NOTICED ME...
SO I'LL JUST KEEP QUIET...
TMP
TMP
WHAT TOOK YOU SO LONG?!

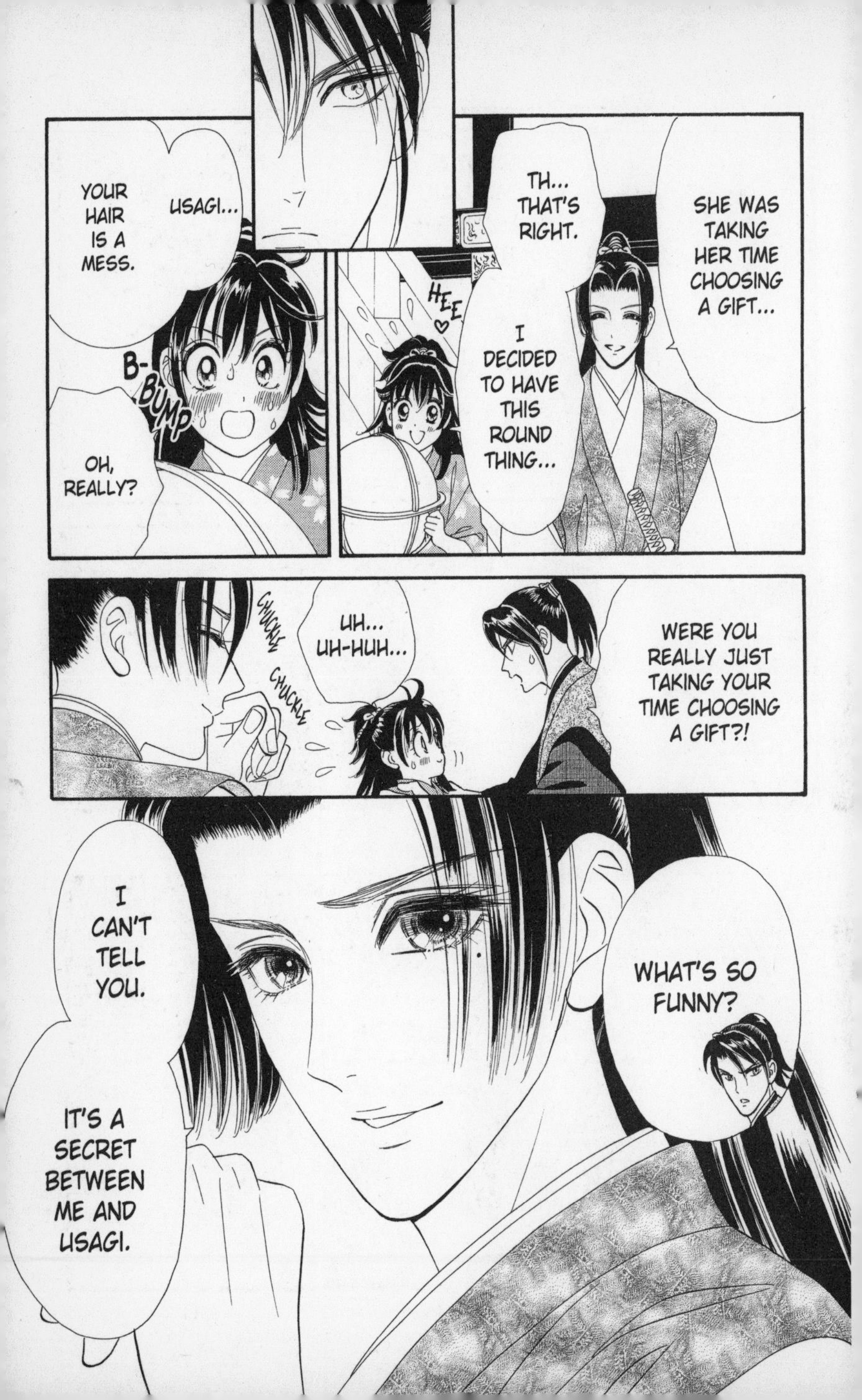
SHE WAS TAKING HER TIME CHOOSING A GIFT...
TH... THAT'S RIGHT.
HEE ♥
I DECIDED TO HAVE THIS ROUND THING...
USAGI...
YOUR HAIR IS A MESS.
B-BUMP
OH, REALLY?
WERE YOU REALLY JUST TAKING YOUR TIME CHOOSING A GIFT?!
UH... UH-HUH...
CHUCKLE
CHUCKLE
WHAT'S SO FUNNY?
I CAN'T TELL YOU.
IT'S A SECRET BETWEEN ME AND USAGI.

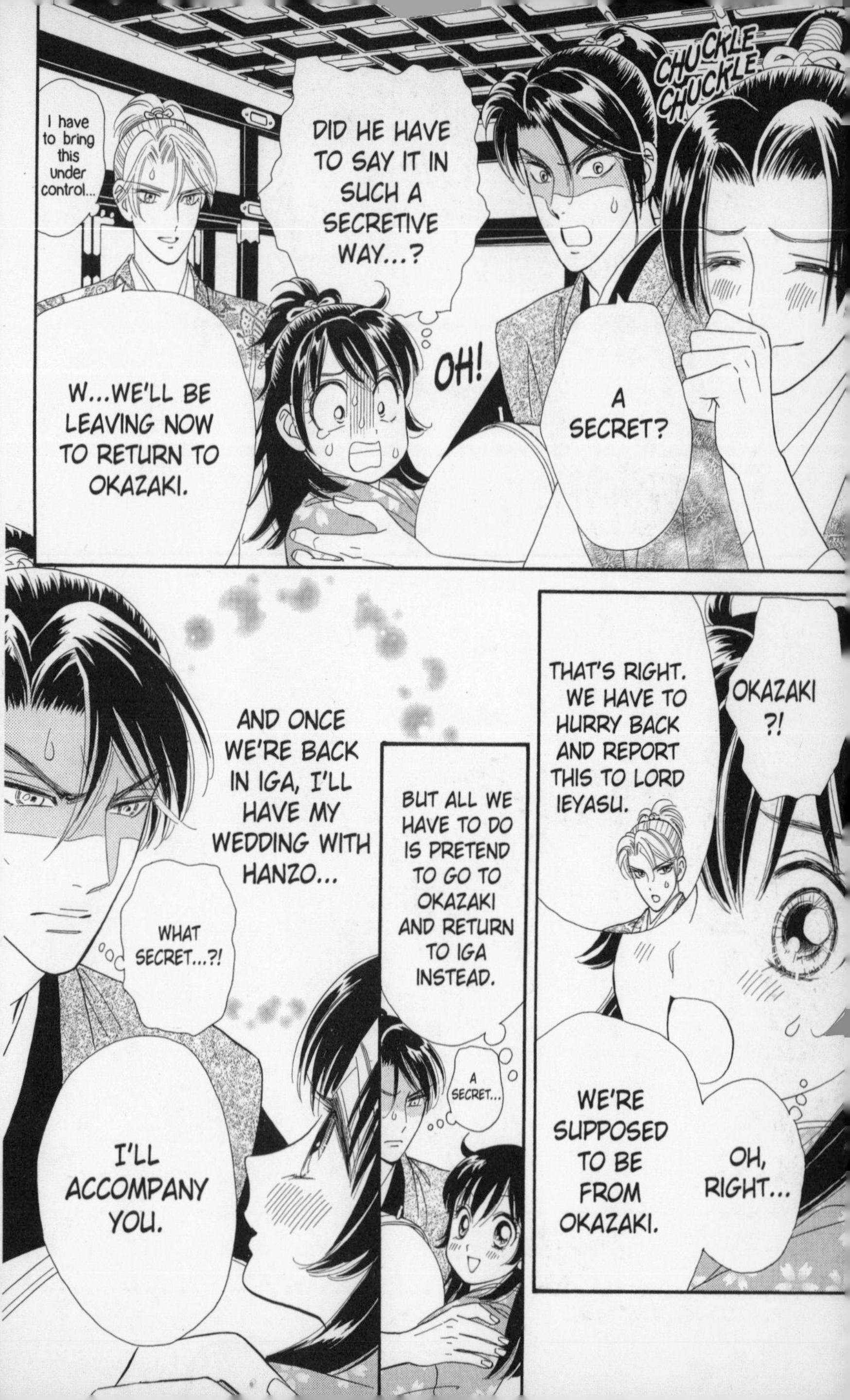
CHUCKLE CHUCKLE
A SECRET?
DID HE HAVE TO SAY IT IN SUCH A SECRETIVE WAY...?
OH!
I have to bring this under control...
W...WE'LL BE LEAVING NOW TO RETURN TO OKAZAKI.
OKAZAKI ?!
THAT'S RIGHT. WE HAVE TO HURRY BACK AND REPORT THIS TO LORD IEYASU.
OH, RIGHT...
WE'RE SUPPOSED TO BE FROM OKAZAKI.
BUT ALL WE HAVE TO DO IS PRETEND TO GO TO OKAZAKI AND RETURN TO IGA INSTEAD.
A SECRET...
AND ONCE WE'RE BACK IN IGA, I'LL HAVE MY WEDDING WITH HANZO...
WHAT SECRET...?!
I'LL ACCOMPANY YOU.

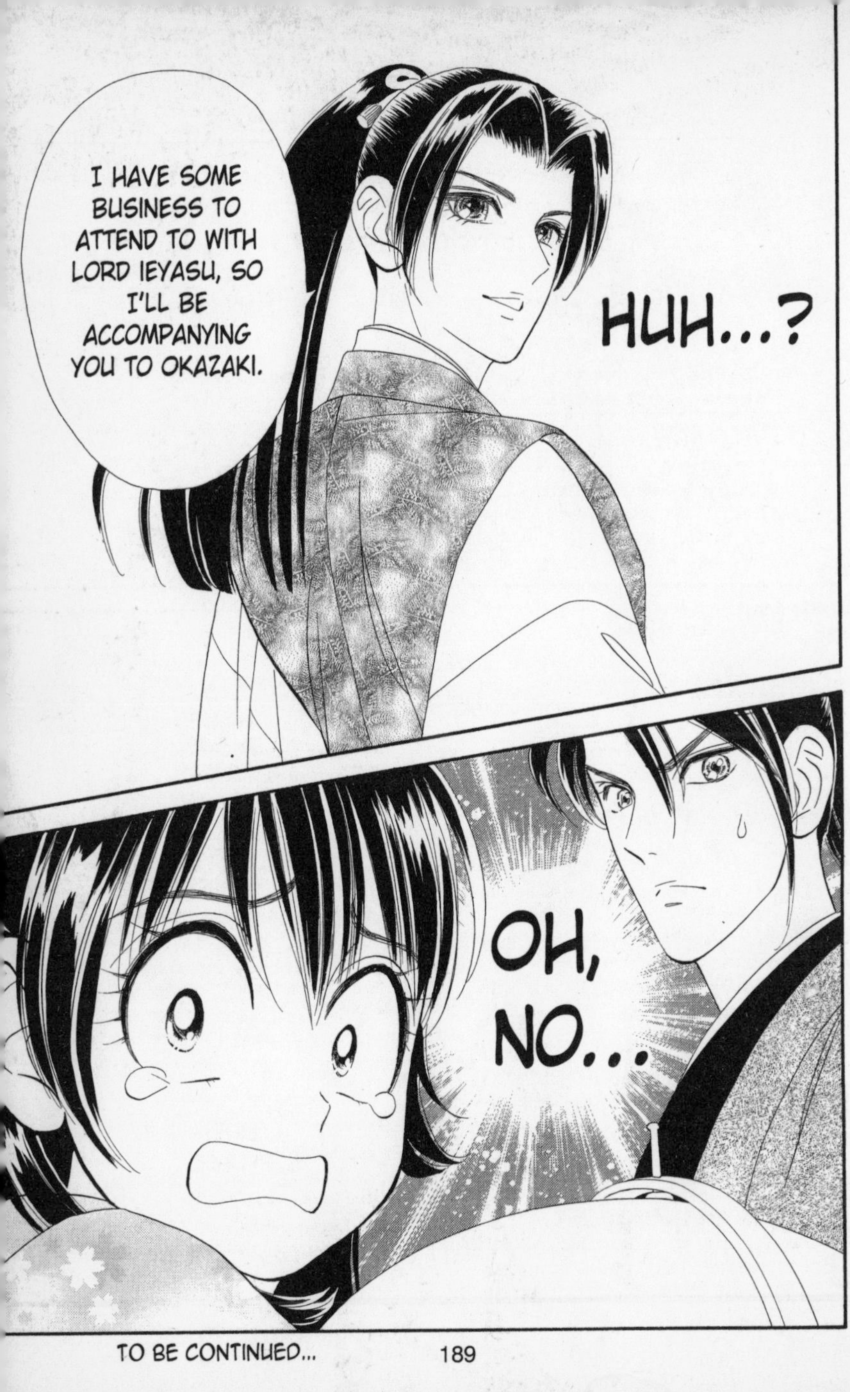
HUH...?
I HAVE SOME BUSINESS TO ATTEND TO WITH LORD IEYASU, SO I'LL BE ACCOMPANYING YOU TO OKAZAKI.
OH, NO...

The ways of the ninja are mysterious indeed, so here is a glossary of terms to help you navigate the intricacies of their world.

Page 32: Bae Yong Joon
Bae Yong Joon is the leading actor in *Winter Sonata*.

Page 35, panel 2: Nanmaida
Nanmaida is the shortened form of *Namu-amidabutsu*, which means "Hail Amida-buddha." It's a prayer from Pure Land Buddhism, and it's probably one of the most famous Buddhist prayers in Japan.

Page 49, panel 8: Princess
Sara is not a princess in the European sense of the word. The Japanese word *hime* means a young woman of noble birth.

Page 49, panel 8: Oda Nobunaga
Nobunaga lived from 1534 to 1582, and came close to unifying Japan. He is probably one of the most famous Japanese warlords. He was the first warlord to successfully incorporate the gun in battle, and is notorious for his ruthlessness. He completely razed Mt. Hiei, a major Japanese Buddhist site of the time, and spared no lives in the battle.

Page 50, panel 1: Azuchi
Azuchi is on Lake Biwa in Shiga Prefecture, where Nobunaga built his castle and the town that were the center of his operations.

Page 58: 108 Earthly Desires
Buddhists believe that humans have 108 earthly desires (though the number actually differs from sect to sect). That's why monks toll the bell 108 times on New Year's Eve to get rid of those desires.

Page 2: Shimo no Hanzo
Shimo no means "the Lower," and in this case refers to Hanzo's geographic location rather than social status.

Page 2: Ninjutsu
Ninjutsu means the skill or ability of a ninja.

Page 2: Iga
Iga is a region on the island of Honshu and also the name of the famous ninja clan that originated there. Another area famous for its ninja is Kouga, in the Shiga prefecture on Honshu. Many books claim that these two ninja clans were mortal enemies, but in reality inter-ninja relations were not as bad as stories might suggest.

Page 13, panel 3: Manga School
"Manga School" is a section in Japanese manga magazines for people who want to become manga artists. Participants who receive high scores for their sample manga submissions get an award along with a chance to make their debut in the magazine.

Page 32: Winter Sonata
Winter Sonata is a famous Korean TV drama series that was a big hit in Korea. It then became a huge hit in Japan, essentially starting the recent Korean drama/movie craze in Japan.

Page 127, panel 1: Dogu
Dogu are clay figurines that were made during the Jomon period of ancient Japan. Their purpose still remains unclear, but they were most likely used as effigies to which people could transfer illnesses and then destroy, clearing that person of that illness or misfortune.

Page 136, panel 4: Sen no Rikyu
Sen no Rikyu (1522-1591) is famous for having a huge influence on the Japanese tea ceremony, particularly in wabi-cha (a style that emphasizes simplicity). Rikyu became tea master for Oda Nobunaga when he was 58 years old.

Page 156, panel 3: Enryakuji
Enryakuji is a famous temple on Mt. Hiei and was a pretty significant symbol of Buddhism at the time. Because the Buddhists did not obey Nobunaga, he burned the temple to the ground in 1571, killing 20 to 30 thousand men, women, and children in the process.

Page 161, panel 2: Ranmaru Mori
Ranmaru Mori is one of Nobunaga's most famous vassals. He became Oda Nobunaga's attendant at a young age and was recognized for his talent and loyalty.

Page 176, panel 3: Asai Nagamasa
Asai Nagamasa (1545-1573) was the lord of Omi and also Oda Nobunaga's brother-in-law. He chose to join the Asakura family and the monks of Mt. Hiei against Nobunaga and was killed as a result.

Page 188, panel 2: Tokugawa Ieyasu
Tokugawa Ieyasu (1543-1616) was the first Shogun of the Tokugawa Shogunate. He made a small fishing village named Edo the center of his activities. Edo thrived and became a huge town, and was later renamed Tokyo, the present capital.

Page 59: Kanto vs. Kansai
The Kanto region is to the east of Honshu and is made up of seven prefectures: Gunma, Tochigi, Ibaraki, Saitama, Tokyo, Chiba, and Kanagawa. The Kansai region is to the west of Honshu and is made up of Nara, Wakayama, Mie, Kyoto, Osaka, Hyogo, and Shiga. The cultures of the two regions are often compared because of the differences in food, manners, accents, etc.

Page 71, panel 1: Uji
Uji is an area in Japan famous for its green tea.

Page 72, panel 7: Jizo
Jizo are considered the guardian deities of children. However, Jizo statues are also placed alongside travel paths throughout Japan, acting as guardians to those who travel on such paths.

Page 86: Kunoichi
A term often used for female ninja. The word is spelled くノー, and when combined, the letters form the kanji for woman, 女。

Page 112: Purikura
Purikura are photo stickers taken inside photo booth machines found in arcades and other places in Japan. Once the picture is taken, the subjects can customize and decorate the photo using a pen-sensitive touch-screen.

Page 117, panel 1: Okazaki
Okazaki is in Aichi prefecture on the main island of Honshu, about 22 miles from Nagoya.

This is the first volume in which Hanzo actually acts like a ninja. Even though *Tail of the Moon* is a ninja manga, you don't really see a lot of ninja action. These days, I'm trying to go against the "This is _____, so it must be like _____" rule since it only limits the freedom of my imagination. I hope to continue creating manga in a fun, carefree fashion.

–Rinko Ueda

Rinko Ueda is from Nara prefecture. She enjoys listening to the radio, drama CDs, and Rakugo comedy performances. Her works include *Ryo*, a series based on the legend of Gojo Bridge, *Home*, a story about love crossing national boundaries, and *Tail of the Moon (Tsuki no Shippo)*, a romantic ninja comedy.

TAIL OF THE MOON
Vol. 7
The Shojo Beat Manga Edition

STORY & ART BY
RINKO UEDA

Translation & Adaptation/Tetsuichiro Miyaki
Touch-up Art & Lettering/Mark McMurray
Design/Izumi Hirayama
Editor/Amy Yu

VP, Production/Alvin Lu
VP, Publishing Licensing/Rika Inouye
VP, Sales & Product Marketing/Gonzalo Ferreyra
VP, Creative/Linda Espinosa
Publisher/Hyoe Narita

Printed in Canada

Published by VIZ Media, LLC
P.O. Box 77064
San Francisco, CA 94107

Shojo Beat Manga Edition
10 9 8 7 6 5 4 3 2
First printing, October 2007
Second printing, February 2009

www.viz.com
store.viz.com

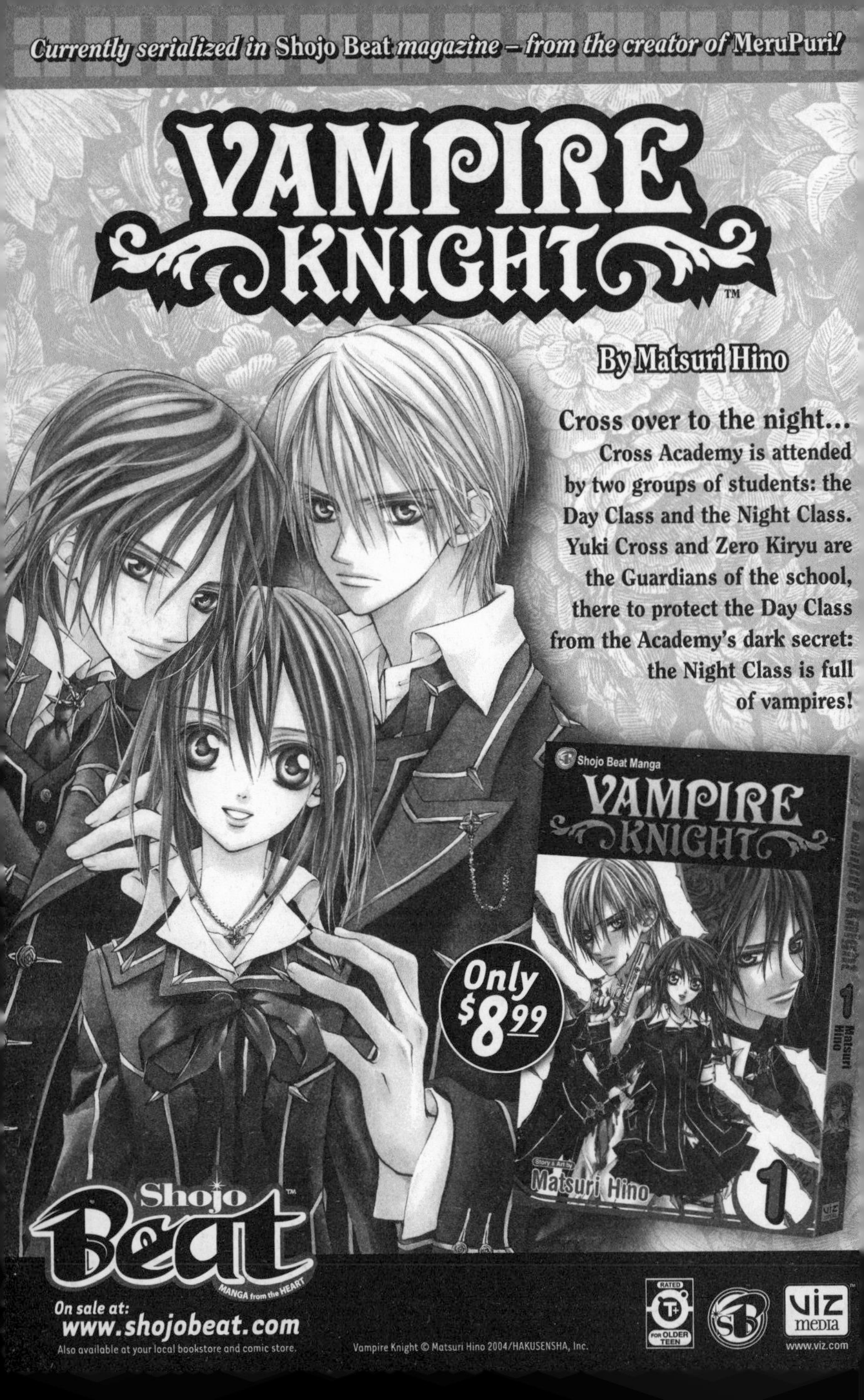
Currently serialized in Shojo Beat magazine – from the creator of MeruPuri!
VAMPIRE KNIGHT™
By Matsuri Hino
Cross over to the night...
Cross Academy is attended by two groups of students: the Day Class and the Night Class. Yuki Cross and Zero Kiryu are the Guardians of the school, there to protect the Day Class from the Academy's dark secret: the Night Class is full of vampires!
Shojo Beat Manga
VAMPIRE KNIGHT
Story & Art by
Matsuri Hino
1
Only $8.99
Shojo Beat™
MANGA from the HEART
On sale at:
www.shojobeat.com
Also available at your local bookstore and comic store.
Vampire Knight © Matsuri Hino 2004/HAKUSENSHA, Inc.
RATED T+ FOR OLDER TEEN
viz media
www.viz.com